Economics and the Enforcement of European Competition Law

For Samantha and Bridget

Economics and the Enforcement of European Competition Law

Christopher Decker

Regulatory Policy Institute and University of Oxford, UK

Edward Elgar

Cheltenham, UK • Northampton, MA, USA

Published by
Edward Elgar Publishing Limited
The Lypiatts
15 Lansdown Road
Cheltenham
Glos GL50 2JA
UK

Edward Elgar Publishing, Inc.
William Pratt House
9 Dewey Court
Northampton
Massachusetts 01060
USA

A catalogue record for this book
is available from the British Library

Library of Congress Control Number: 2009930877

ISBN 978 1 84844 307 5

Typeset by Cambrian Typesetters, Camberley, Surrey
Printed and bound in Great Britain by MPG Books Group, UK

Contents

Tables

Abbreviations

Article 81	Article 81 of the EC Treaty
Article 82	Article 82 of the EC Treaty
Bundeskartellamt	German Federal Cartel Office
CET	Chief Competition Economists Team of the Directorate General of the European Communities responsible for competition policy
CFI	Court of First Instance of the European Communities
Commission	Directorate of the European Commission responsible for competition policy
Courts	Courts of the European Communities (includes the Court of Justice and the Court of First Instance)
DG Comp.	Directorate of the European Commission responsible for competition policy
DG Economic & Financial Affairs	Directorate of the European Commission responsible for economic and monetary policy
DG Enterprise	Directorate of the European Commission responsible for policies which relate to the competitiveness of EU enterprises.
EC Treaty	Treaty of Rome establishing the European Economic Community as amended. Treaty Articles as renumbered by the Treaty of Amsterdam
ECHR	European Convention on Human Rights
ECJ	Court of Justice of the European Communities
ECMR	European Community Merger Regulation
ECSC Treaty	Treaty of Paris establishing the European Coal and Steel Community
FTC	United States Federal Trade Commission
ICN	International Competition Network
Merger Regulation	Council Regulation on the Control of Concentrations Between Undertakings
MMC	United Kingdom Monopolies and Mergers Commission (formerly the Monopolies Commission)

MTF	Merger Task Force of the Competition Directorate of the European Commission
OECD	Organisation for Economic Cooperation and Development
OFT	United Kingdom Office of Fair Trading
Shipping Regulation	Council Regulation (EC) 4056/86 Application of the competition rules to maritime transport
UNCTAD	United Nations Conference on Trade and Development
US Merger Guidelines	U.S. Department of Justice and the Federal Trade Commission 1992 Horizontal Merger Guidelines

Table of cases

EUROPEAN COURT DECISIONS

Court of Justice

Court of First Instance

EUROPEAN COMMISSION DECISIONS

Article 82 Decisions

Decisions under the European Community Merger Regulation

(a) Decisions referenced in the text

Fortis/ABN AMRO Assets (Case No COMP/M.4844) [2007] OJ C265 **74**

(b) Decisions not referenced in the text but included in the analysis of Chapter 4

Harrisons & Crosfield/AKZO (Case No IV/M.310) [1993] OJ C128/0.
SNECMA/ TI (Case No IV/M.368) [1993] OJ C042/0.
Akzo / Nobel Industrier (Case No IV/M.390) [1994] OJ C019/1.
Zeneca / Vanderhave (Case No IV/M.556) [1996] OJ C188/10.
Bertelsmann / CLT (Case No IV/M.779) [1996] OJ C364/3.
Baxter / Immuno (Case No IV/M.821) [1996] OJ C386/11.
Cardo / Thyssen (Case No IV/M.818) [1997] OJ C018/13.
P&O / Royal Nedlloyd (Case No IV/M.831) [1997] OJ C110/7.
DuPont/ICI (Case No IV/M.984) [1998] OJ C004/4.
Allianz/AGF (Case No IV/M.1082)) [1998] OJ C246/4.
Nestle/Dalgety (Case No IV/M.1127) [1998] OJ C143/28.
Seagram/Polygram (Case No IV/M.1219) [1998] OJ C309/8.
Pirelli/Siemens (Case No IV/M.1271) [1998] OJ C336/11.
American Home Products/Monsanto (Case No IV/M.1229) [1999] OJ C109/4.
Thomson/Lucas (Case No IV/M.1332) [1999] OJ C061/3.
Robert Bosch/Magnetti Marelli (Case No IV/M.1491) [1999] OJ C183/3.
SAIR Group/AOM (Case No IV/M.1494) [1999] OJ C245/29.
British Steel/Hoogovens (Case No IV/M.1595 and IV/ECSC.1310) [1999] OJ C277/5.
MAERSK/SEA-LAND (Case No IV/M.1651) [1999] OJ C313/6.
Castrol/Carless/JV (Case No IV/M.1597) [2000] OJ C016/5.
Monsanto/Pharmacia & Upjohn (Case No IV/M.1835) [2000] OJ C143/4.
France Telecom/Orange (Case No IV/M.2016) [2000] OJ C261/6.
Interbrew/Bass (Case No IV/M.2044) [2000] OJ C293/11.
Philips/Marconi Medical Systems (Case No IV/M.2537) [2001] OJ C321/12.
Pernod Ricard/Diageo/Seagram Spirits (Case No IV/M.2268) [2002] OJ C016/13.
BASF/Eurodiol/Pantochim (Case COMP/M.2314) [2002] OJ L132/45.
Norske Skog/Parenco/Walsum (Case No COMP/M.2499) [2002] OJ L233/38.
Cargill /Cerestar (Case No IV/M.2502) [2002] OJ C040/7.
Norsk Hydro/ VAW (Case No IV/M.2702) [2002] OJ C089/6.
Deloitte & Touche/Andersen UK (Case No IV/M.2810) [2002] OJ C200/8.
Ernst & Young France/Andersen France (Case No IV/M.2816) [2002] OJ C232/6.
Ernst & Young/Andersen Germany (Case No IV/M.2824) [2002] OJ C246/21.
Bunge /Cereol (Case No IV/M. 2886) [2002] OJ C250/3.

JCI / Bosch / VB Autobatterien JV (Case No IV/M.2939) [2002] OJ C284/4.
Pirelli/BICC (Case COMP/M.1882) [2003] OJ L070/35.
Newscorp/Telepiù (Case COMP/M.2876) [2004] OJ L110/73.
Arla Foods/Express Dairies (Case No IV/M.3130) [2003] OJ C297
Anglo American/Kumba Resources (Case No IV/M.3276) [2004] OJ C009
Outokumpu/Boliden (Case No IV/M.3284) [2004] OJ C025
Agco/Valtra (Case No IV/M.3287) [2004] OJ C011
Schneider Electric/MGE-UPS (Case No IV/M.3347) [2004] OJ C049
Toshiba/Samsung/JV (Case No IV/M.3349) [2006] OJ C25
Agfa-Geaert/Lastra (Case No IV/M.3439) [2004] OJ C304
Seiko Epson / Sanyo / Sanyo Epson Imaging Devices JV (Case No IV/M.3459) [2004] OJ C215
Kesko/Ica/JV (Case No IV/M.3464) [2005] OJ C8
Repsol YPF/Shell (Case No IV/M.3516) [2004] OJ C272
Siemens/V A Tech (Case No COMP/M.3653) [2006] OJ L353
Reuters/Telerate (Case No IV/M.3692) [2005] OJ C154
Pernod Ricard/Allied Domecq (Case No IV/M.3779) [2005] OJ C196
Maersk/Ponl (Case No IV/M.3829) [2005] OJ C207
Sea-Invest/EMO-EKOM (Case COMP/M.3848) [2007] OJ L282
Vattenfall/Elsam and E2 Assets (Case No IV/M.3867) [2006] OJ C184
Aster2/Flint Ink (Case No IV/M.3886) [2005] OJ C263
T-Mobile Austria/tele.ring (Case COMP/M.3916) [2007] OJ L88
OMV/Aral-CR (Case No IV/M.4002) [2006] OJ C25
Telenor/Vodafone Sverige (Case No IV/M.4034) [2006] OJ C71
Toepfer/Invivo/Soulès (Case No IV/M.4042) [2006] OJ C68
SKF/SNFA (Case No IV/M.4062) [2006] OJ C156
Apollo/Akzo Nobel IAR (Case No IV/M.4071) [2006] OJ C176
E.ON/Endesa (Case No IV/M.4110) [2006] OJ C114
Toshiba/Westinghouse (Case No IV/M.4153) [2007] OJ C10
Sonae Industria/Hornitex (Case No IV/M.4165) [2006] OJ C184
Gaz de France/Suez (Case COMP/M.4180) [2007] OJ L88
E.ON / Prazsk`Plynrenski (Case No IV/M.4238) [2006] OJ C242
Abertis/Autostrade (Case No IV/M.4249) [2006] OJ C268
Axa/Winterthur (Case COMP/M.4284) [2006] OJ C239
Nokia/Siemens (Case No IV/M.4297) [2007] OJ C0
Johnson & Johnson/Pfizer Consumer Healthcare (Case COMP/M.4314) [2007] OJ C39
Cinven/Warburg Pincus/Casema/Multikabel (Case No IV/M.4338) [2006] OJ C243
JT/Gallaher (Case No IV/M.4424) [2007] OJ C114
En+ / Glencore / Sual / Uc Rusal (Case No IV/M.4441) [2007] OJ C71
Mahle/Dana EPG (Case No IV/M.4456) [2007] OJ C94

UNITED STATES COURT DECISIONS

Table of treaties and regulations

TREATIES

EC Treaty (Treaty of Rome, as amended) [1957] 298 UNTS 11. Treaty Articles as renumbered by the Treaty of Amsterdam (EC Treaty) [1997] OJ C340/1

Convention for the protection of Human Rights and Fundamental Freedoms (European Convention on Human Rights, as amended) [1950] 213 UNTS 220

REGULATIONS

European Council

European Commission

NOTICES

European Commission

GREEN PAPERS, GUIDELINES AND WORKING DOCUMENTS

European Commission

Preface

> [W]hile industrial economics is highly developed as an academic discipline, application of economic theories and models in concrete cases remains an area fraught with difficulty and uncertainty[1]
>
> Justice Bo Vesterdorf, President of the European Court of First Instance (1998–2007)

Economics is on the ascendancy in European competition policy. In the past two decades economics has featured increasingly in policy discourse and in the official documents, notices and guidelines of both European Union institutions and Member States. Correspondingly, economic consultancies have flourished during this time, and new interdisciplinary academic centres and institutes have been established devoted to the study of competition law and economics. At the European Commission, a number of telling changes have occurred, including the appointment of a professor of economics as Commissioner of the European competition directorate, and the establishment of a Chief Competition Economist position. The rise of economics seems likely to continue as politicians and policymakers continue to call for the use of 'more economics' in European competition policy including the greater reception of economic concepts, theories and instruments in competition law enforcement.

There remain, however, a number of practical tensions and difficulties associated with translating these high-level policy ambitions into day-to-day enforcement practice; a point highlighted all too well by recent decisions of the European courts. In the words of Justice Vesterdorf above the application of economics in real-world cases remains 'fraught with difficulty'.

Against this background, it is the purpose of this book to take a step back from the general policy push for 'more economics', and to focus instead on exploring why it is that the relationship between economics and competition law enforcement can appear fraught. In doing so, it rejects the more simplistic explanations that decision-makers do not listen to economists and that, as a result, 'the economics' is systematically being incorrectly applied (as is sometimes said by economists), or that economics is simply too indeterminate

[1] B. Vesterdorf 'Standards of proof in merger cases: reflections in the light of recent case law of the Community Courts' (paper presented at the BIICL third annual merger control conference, 6 December 2004) 14.

to be applied in practice (as is sometimes heard from lawyers). Rather, it is argued that the use of economics in enforcement settings reflects a complex matrix of factors including the nature of economics, its multiple users in the enforcement process, and the characteristics and complexities of the enforcement setting in which it is sought to be applied.

This work has relatively humble origins. Its original scope was an examination of how, and in what ways, the mass of accumulated economic knowledge relating to tacit collusion was reflected in the enforcement decisions of the European competition authorities. It became immediately clear, however, that the process of transformation of economic ideas and knowledge into everyday enforcement practice was less straightforward – and more interesting – than I had initially (and perhaps naïvely) assumed. Accordingly the research broadened to an examination of two key empirical questions. First, the extent to which economics has *in fact* been influential in the enforcement of European competition law, and second, *in what way* precisely economics contributes to the enforcement process.

Although there is a significant body of normative economic literature on how economics should be used in competition law enforcement, and extensive legal commentary on specific cases, there is very little research in the European context that had sought to systematically examine how economics *is* used in practice by the different actors and institutions involved in European competition law enforcement.

This book seeks to fill this gap by providing much-needed empirical content to a number of specific questions regarding economics and enforcement such as: what precisely do we know about how economics contributes to the day-to-day enforcement activity of the European competition institutions? How are various contextual or institutional factors likely to impact on the ability for economics to have a more prominent role in the future enforcement of competition law in Europe? What is the role of sophisticated economic modelling vis-à-vis other economic evidence in the enforcement process? What standard do the courts apply when reviewing economic evidence? These issues are examined within the broader context of the relationship between expert knowledge and its practical application. In this respect, the book canvasses important questions regarding the manner in which economic knowledge, which is generated in one area, can be applied in another area with substantively different purposes and audiences. In considering all these questions, through a grounded examination of enforcement practice, it is the aim of this book to foster a more realistic and productive debate about the use, and potential use, of economics in competition law enforcement.

Chris Decker
Oxford
December 2008

1. Introduction

The enforcement of European competition law has the potential to affect all European businesses and consumers. Any European who drives a car; buys petrol, toilet paper, baby food, or bacon; catches a bus, train or aeroplane; uses a mobile phone; has an X-ray or ultrasound; listens to recorded music; or consumes any product that has been transported by a shipping line, along with any employee, manager or shareholder of such business has already been affected by the enforcement of the competition laws.[1] More broadly, the way that European competition law is enforced has a direct effect on the certainty and predictability of the business environment in terms of the incentives, or disincentives, it creates for business to invest, combine their activities through merger or to enter into co-operative technological and research and development projects.

Economics is widely considered to be increasingly influential in the enforcement of European competition law.[2] In the words of the current Chief Competition Economist of the European competition authority: 'the fact that economics has become more important in EU antitrust policy and practice ... is hardly controversial'.[3] The creation of the role of Chief Competition Economist at the competition authority is itself a relatively new development, the purpose of which was to provide an economic viewpoint to decision-makers, as well as on-going guidance to Commission investigative staff in the

---

[1] For consumers, these effects can relate to the price, availability, range and quality of products in a market. For management, enforcement activity can impact on a firm's activities and profitability and, correspondingly, influence decisions as to investment, workforce size and scale of production. The investment returns and decisions of shareholders can also be influenced by such effects.

[2] Compare L.H. Röller 'Using economic analysis to strengthen competition policy enforcement in Europe' (presentation at the ECN conference on Modelling European Mergers: theory, Competition Policy and Case Studies, 21 March 2005) 1; J. Vickers 'Merger policy in Europe: retrospect and prospect' (paper presented at the Charles River Associates conference, Washington, DC, 11 February 2004) 13–14; F. Jenny 'Competition law enforcement: is economic expertise necessary?' in B. Hawk (ed.) *International Antitrust Law and Policy: Fordham Corporate Law 1998* (Juris Publishing, New York, 1998) 186; Board of Editors 'Competition law and the turn of the century' (2001) 28 Legal Issues of Economic Integration 137.

[3] D. Neven 'Competition economics and antitrust in Europe' (2006) 21 Economic Policy 3.

enforcement process.[4] In addition, a substantial economic consulting sector has developed in Europe selling law firms and businesses economic expertise in relation to competition law matters. It is estimated that turnover of these firms increased by 25–30 per cent per annum in the decade from 1994 to 2004, increasing their revenues from £2.4 million to £24 million over that period.[5]

However, despite the widely held perception that economics is influential in the enforcement of the competition laws, two areas remain largely unexplored. First, the extent to which economics has *in fact* been influential in the enforcement of these laws at the case level. Second, *in what way* precisely economics is used in the enforcement process. The failure to examine in any detail the use of economics in the enforcement of European competition law is surprising as such use has always been controversial.[6] The European Courts have been particularly critical of the application of economics in a number of high profile decisions.[7] A recent President of the European Court of First Instance has noted that: '[W]hile industrial economics is highly developed as an academic discipline, application of economic theories and models in concrete cases remains an area fraught with difficulty and uncertainty'.[8]

---

4 Commission of the European Communities *Commission adopts comprehensive reform of EU merger control* press release IP/02/1856 (11 December 2002). Also L.H. Röller and P.A. Buigues 'The Office of the Chief Competition Economist at the European Commission' (Global Competition Review London 2005) 5.

5 Neven (n 3) 5.

6 The first judgment of the European Court of Justice in relation to oligopolies was critical of the Commission's use of economic evidence: Joined cases C-68/94 and C-30/95 *French Republic and Société commerciale des potasses et de l'azote (SCPA) and Entreprise minière et chimique (EMC) v Commission of the European Communities* [1998] ECR I-01375 paras [225]–[228]; equally the Court of First Instance was unconvinced by the Commission's economic assessment in an earlier case: Joined cases T-68/89, T-77/89 and T-78/89 *Società Italiana Vetro SpA, Fabbrica Pisana SpA and PPG Vernante Pennitalia SpA v Commission of the European Communities* [1992] ECR II-01403 para [336].

7 Case T464/04 *Independent Music Publishers and Labels Association (Impala, International Association) v Commission of the European Communities* [2006] ECR II-02289 para [526]–[528]; Case T-342/99 *Airtours plc v Commission of the European Communities* [2002] ECR II-02585 para [294]; Case T-77/02 *Schneider Electric SA v Commission of the European Communities* [2002] ECR II-04071 para [404]–[411]; Case T-80/02 *Tetra Laval BV v Commission of the European Communities* [2002] ECR II-04381 paras [141],[213],[337]; Compare D.J. Gerber 'Courts as economic experts in European merger law' in B. Hawk (ed.) *International Antitrust Law and Policy: Fordham Corporate Law 2004* (Juris Publishing, New York, 2004) 484, 493.

8 B. Vesterdorf 'Standard of proof in merger cases: reflections in the light of recent case law of the Community Courts' (paper presented at the BIICL third annual merger control conference, 6 December 2004) 14.

While there is an extensive literature on the substantive content and development of European competition law, and on the economic theory that relates to competition policy, a more limited number of studies have considered how economic expertise features in competition law enforcement. These studies have typically fallen into two categories.[9] One category of studies has adopted a normative approach, examining how economics *should* be used in competition law enforcement.[10] Two particular studies stand out in this category which, although presenting a thorough review of Commission enforcement practice in relation to the Merger Regulation and Article 81 of the EC Treaty, do so through a normative lens.[11] A second category of studies focus on applications of economics in specific decisions of the Commission and the Courts. These studies typically present binary assessments as to whether 'the economics' has been applied 'correctly' or 'incorrectly',[12] or

---

[9] Another set of studies have focused on enforcement practices, although not specifically on the use of economics in the enforcement process. These studies have attempted to 'model' and quantify enforcement decisions according to economic principles and techniques: M.A. Bergman, M. Jakobsson and C. Razo 'An econometric analysis of the European Commission's merger decisions' (Working Paper 6, Department of Economics, Uppsala University, 2003); J. Briones 'Oligopolistic dominance: is there a common approach in different jurisdictions? A review of decisions adopted by the Commission under the Merger Regulation' (1995) 16 European Competition Law Review 337; T. Nilssen 'On the consistency of merger policy' (1997) 45 Journal of Industrial Economics 89.

[10] Studies include: P. Florian and M. Walker 'The correct approach to the use of empirical analysis in competition policy' (2005) 26 European Competition Law Review 320; G. Niels 'Collective Dominance: more than just oligopolistic interdependence' (2001) 22 European Competition Law Review 168; M. Motta 'E.C merger policy and the Airtours case' (2000) 21 European Competition Law Review 199; E. Kloosterhuis 'Joint dominance and the interaction between firms' (2001) 22 European Competition Law Review 79; D.J. Neven '"Collusion" under Art 81 and the merger regulation' (paper presented at the 3rd Nordic Competition Policy Conference, Stockholm, 11 September 2000); Institut d'Économie Industrielle (IDEI) Toulouse 'The economics of tacit collusion' (2003) Final report prepared for DG Competition European Commission March 2003 1; Europe Economics 'Assessment criteria for distinguishing between competitive and dominant oligopolies in merger control' (Enterprise Papers No 6-2001 prepared for DG Enterprise European Commission, 2001).

[11] D. Neven, R. Nuttall and P. Seabright *Mergers in Daylight: The Economics and Politics of European Merger Control* (Centre for Economic Policy Research, London, 1993); D. Neven, P. Papandropoulos and P. Seabright *Trawling for Minnows: European Competition Policy and Agreements between Firms* (Centre for Economic Policy Research, London, 1998).

[12] Compare J. Ysewyn and C. Caffara 'Two's company, three's a crowd: the future of collective dominance after the Kali & Salz judgment' (1998) 19 European Competition Law Review 468; P. Christensen and V. Rabassa 'The Airtours decision: is there a new Commission approach to collective dominance?' (2001) 22 European Competition Law Review 227.

whether 'legal' or 'economic' considerations were more relevant in the specific case.[13]

There are three limitations of this existing work in explaining enforcement practice. First, the studies have typically adopted too narrow a conception of economics, assuming economic theory to be the sum of economic knowledge. Second, existing studies have focused on Commission and Court decisions, and have not examined in any detail how economics features in the wider enforcement process. Finally, existing studies have failed to account for the fact that economics is employed in the enforcement of competition law by a range of actors and institutions, all of whom have different perspectives and interests in using economic knowledge.

Studies on the use of expert knowledge in legal or regulatory settings tell us that the last of these points may be particularly relevant. These studies suggest that formal knowledge is selectively transformed in its application in practical settings on the basis of the purposive interests and perspectives of those who use it. Thus, for example, the use of expert knowledge by judges has been found to be influenced by multiple constituencies and concerns, such as the need to maintain the social standing of the institution assessing, and the anticipated social and political implications of their decision.[14] Lawyers, in using scientific knowledge, have been found to balance a trade-off between maintaining a perception of the institutional authority of scientific knowledge and using it as a tool in an adversarial process.[15] The interests of experts have been found to affect the narration given to knowledge in their area of exper-

---

[13] Compare J. Temple-Lang 'Oligopolies and joint dominance in community antitrust law' in B. Hawk (ed.) *International Antitrust Law and Policy: Fordham Corporate Law 2001* (Juris Publishing, New York, 2001) 269; K.S. Desai 'Limitations on the use of economic analysis in E.C. competition law proceedings – Part 1' (2002) 23 European Competition Law Review 524; B. Etter 'The assessment of mergers in the EC under the concept of collective dominance: an analysis of the recent decisions and judgments – by an economic approach' (2000) 23 Journal of World Competition 103; S. Stroux 'Is EC oligopoly control outgrowing its infancy?' (2000) 23 World Competition 3.

[14] G. Edmond 'Judging facts: managing expert knowledge in legal decision-making' in G. Edmond (ed.) *Expertise in Regulation and Law* (Ashgate, Aldershot, 2004) 159; S.M. Collins 'The use of social research in the courts' in W.M. Evan (ed.) *The Sociology of Law: A Social-structural Perspective* (Free Press, New York, 1980) 574. In the US, selections as to the importance and relevance of economic expertise in Antitrust cases has been argued to be influenced by the underlying 'social vision', or 'ideological conception of the relationship between the market and the state', of the court: J.E. Lopatka and W.H. Page 'Economic authority and the limits of expertise in antitrust cases' (2005) 90 Cornell Law Review 636, 638, 696.

[15] S. Jasanoff *Science at the Bar: Law, Science, and Technology in America* (Harvard University Press, Cambridge, MA, 1995) 53.

tise in legal and regulatory settings, along with their evidential interpretation of such knowledge.[16] Finally, the use of expert knowledge by regulatory agencies has been shown to be modulated by a complex dynamic of political and professional interests, which can change over time in ways that affect the way in which the knowledge is used.[17] These studies, which find theoretical support in the larger literature relating to sociology of knowledge, suggest that the use of expert knowledge in practical and enforcement settings will invariably be influenced by the specific perspectives and interests of those who engage with the knowledge[18] – including the way in which these actors balance a broader range of interests, expectations and obligations, some of which may be in tension – and of the institutional settings in which the knowledge is applied.[19] In a nutshell, this literature implies that the use of expert knowledge in a legal or regulatory context can be expected to be 'always situated, always purposive'.[20]

Against this background, this book has three specific aims. First, it seeks to understand the nature of the expertise that economics provides in a specific, but highly relevant, area of competition law enforcement (relating to oligopolistic markets). It does so by adopting a broad conception of economics, comprising economic theory, economic reasoning and approach, economic techniques and tools, and economic data. Second, it seeks to examine the influence of each of these strands in the entire enforcement process, from case selection to the design of remedies. This approach captures cases which are subject to the formal and full legal process, as well as 'non-cases' that have not yet arisen, are not selected for further investigation, or are abandoned during an investigation. Finally, it seeks to critically examine the conclusions about

---

16 S. Jasanoff 'Beyond epistemology: relativism and engagement in the politics of science' (1996) 26 Social Studies of Science 411–412; J. Abraham 'Scientific expertise and regulatory decision-making' in G. Edmond (ed.) *Expertise in Regulation and Law* (Ashgate, Aldershot, 2004) 53, 65.

17 M. Eisner 'Protecting the environment at the margin' in G. Edmond (ed.) *Expertise in Regulation and Law* (Ashgate, Aldershot, 2004) 83; M. Lynch and S. Jasanoff 'Contested identities: science, law and forensic practice' (1998) 28 Social Studies of Science 681–682.

18 The notion of perspectives and interests in this context does not capture merely a tendency to use the knowledge instrumentally but also the more deep-rooted and subconscious perspectives and interests of the actors which is a function of a variety of things including their different forms of reasoning, different standards of proof, and different audiences.

19 G. Edmond 'Expertise in regulation and law' in G. Edmond (ed.) *Expertise in Regulation and Law* (Ashgate, Aldershot, 2004) 2; G. Edmond 'Judicial representations of scientific evidence' (2000) 63 Modern Law Review 217; Jasanoff (n 16) 411–412; Jasanoff (n 15) 53.

20 Edmond (n 19) 2.

the use of economics in the enforcement of the relevant competition laws, having regard to the potential application of economic knowledge by actors and institutions with different perspectives and interests in the use of the knowledge.

There are a number of specific reasons why an investigation into the use of economics in competition law enforcement is important and timely. First, the legal provisions relating to mergers changed in 2004 to be more economic in focus and to broaden the enforcement powers of the Commission.[21] In addition, there are current proposals that economic evidence and reasoning feature more prominently in identifying and capturing past instances of anti-competitive behaviour.[22] Second, the European Commission is strongly encouraging the use of private litigation in relation to competition law, which, if it follows the experience of elsewhere, particularly the United States, will lead to economics becoming more prominent in legal proceedings.[23] Third, the number, and value, of merger investigations involving complex economics is very large and growing. For example, in addition to considering the unilateral effects of a merger, the Commission, in discharging its responsibilities, routinely has to take into account potential coordinated effects, non-coordinated effects, conglomerate effects, and more recently, so-called 'diagonal' effects. Fourth, the European Courts have increasingly taken a detailed interest in how the Commission uses economics in making assessments in competition matters. In at least four major decisions, the Court has been critical of the use of the Commission's use of economics and its approach to the economic evidence employed in the decision.[24]

---

21 Council Regulation (EC) No 139/2004 of 20 January 2004 on the control of concentrations between undertakings (the EC Merger Regulation) [2004] OJ L24/1 para [25]. Compare Commission of the European Communities *Commission adopts comprehensive reform of EU merger control* Press Release IP/02/1856 (11 December 2002); and J. Vickers 'Competition economics and policy' (paper presented at the occasion of the launch of the new social sciences building at Oxford University, 3 October 2002) 1.

22 Commission of the European Communities 'Guidance on the Commission's enforcement priorities in applying Article 82 EC Treaty to abusive exclusionary conduct by dominant undertakings' (COM) 2008 3 December 2008; Economic Advisory Group on Competition Policy Report 'An economic approach to Article 82' (paper prepared for the Chief Economist of the European Commission, July 2005) 2.

23 In the United States, for example, economists represent 11 per cent of all expert witnesses to appear before the Federal Court: Federal Judicial Center 'Expert testimony in Federal civil trials: a preliminary analysis' Report by the Federal Judicial Center (2000).

24 In *Impala v. Commission*, the CFI criticised the Commission's assessment of the effects of the merger on competition in the relevant market as 'succinct' 'superficial', 'purely formal'. In *Airtours v Commission* the court found the Commission's decision to be 'vitiated by a series of errors of assessment as to factors fundamental to

More generally it is evident that economics is on the ascendancy in European competition policy. Since the mid-1980s economics has featured increasingly in policy discourse and in the official documents, notices and guidelines of European Union institutions and Member States. This trend seems set to continue as politicians and policymakers across Europe call for the use of 'more economics' in competition policy, including the greater reception of economic concepts, theories and instruments in competition law enforcement.[25]

This book seeks to take a step back from this general policy push for 'more economics' and focus instead on the enforcement context in which economics is to have an increased role. In critically examining how economics is employed in the enforcement of European competition law this book does not seek to suggest that economics have no role in enforcement, or that it should be replaced with alternative approaches. The objective of the book is quite the opposite. Its purpose is to place economics on a more secure foundation in European policy discussions by highlighting the practical tensions that affect its use in practice, and then by suggesting ways in which these tensions might be addressed. In doing so, the book seeks to provide much-needed empirical content to a number of specific questions regarding economics and enforcement such as: what precisely do we know about how economics contributes to the day-to-day enforcement activity of the European competition institutions? How are various contextual or institutional factors likely to impact on the ability for economics to have a more prominent role in the future enforcement of competition law in Europe? What is the role of sophisticated economic modelling vis-à-vis other economic evidence in the enforcement process? What standard do the courts apply when reviewing economic evidence?

---

any assessment of whether a collective dominant position might be created'. In *Schneider Electric SA v Commission* the Court held that the Commission's errors of analysis and assessment were such as 'to deprive of probative value the economic assessment of the impact of the concentration': Case T-464/04 *Independent Music Publishers and Labels Association (Impala, International Association) v Commission of the European Communities* [2006] ECR II-02289; Case T-342/99 *Airtours plc v Commission of the European Communities* [2002] ECR II-02585; Case T-77/02 *Schneider Electric SA v Commission of the European Communities* [2002] ECR II-04071; Case T-80/02 *Tetra Laval BV v Commission of the European Communities* [2002] ECR II-04381.

25 For example see the roundtable discussion in 'Economics experts before authorities and courts roundtable' in B. Hawk (ed.) *International Antitrust Law & Policy: Fordham Corporate Law 2004* (Juris Publishing, New York, 2006) 621–622; N. Kroes 'Preliminary thoughts on policy review of Article 82' (speech at the Fordham Corporate Law Institute, New York, 23 September 2005); Commission of the European Communities 'Antitrust: consumer welfare at heart of Commission fight against abuses by dominant undertakings' Press Release IP/08/1877 (3 December 2008).

To fulfil its aims, this book adopts a case-study approach. Specifically, it examines the application of economics through a detailed empirical review of one area of enforcement activity, namely the competition laws relating to the potential for tacit coordination in oligopolistic markets. The role of economics in the enforcement of these laws – known as the 'collective dominance' laws, or more recently, 'the laws relating to coordinated effects' – has been selected for a number of reasons.

First, at a practical level, tight oligopolistic markets are one of the most common forms of industrial structure in Europe and exist in diverse areas, from petrol retailing to supermarkets to mobile phone service providers. Accordingly, advocates for 'more economics' in competition law will frequently be faced with the need to enforce provisions in relation to this form of market structure. As one economist has put it: 'oligopolies are the business of enforcement agencies, day in and day out'. In this respect it is important to note that the Commission is required under the European Merger Regulation guidelines to consider and assess the potential for collective dominance in *every* merger in tight oligopolistic markets.[26]

Second, although one of the most common forms of market structure in Europe, oligopolistic markets provide one of the most analytically challenging areas in which economics has to be applied. This is not because economists have ignored this area; quite the contrary. The economic examination of oligopolistic markets, and the potential for tacit collusion, is a well-established research area and one in which hundreds of new academic articles are published each year. In principle, then, economics has the potential to offer much in the enforcement of competition law in this area. Furthermore, the conclusions of a large body of this literature suggest that the incentives for firms to tacitly collude in tight oligopolistic markets can be substantial, and therefore the theoretical potential for the occurrence of this behavior is high.[27] Some economic studies have indicated that in 'oligopolistic markets a tendency toward the spontaneous co-ordination of business policies seems inevitable'.[28]

Third, the enforcement of the laws relating to coordinated effects has proven among the most controversial in European competition law, and one

[26] Commission guidelines on the assessment of horizontal mergers under the Council Regulation on the control of concentrations between undertakings [2004] OJ C31/5 paras [4] and [39].

[27] A. Jacquemin and M.E. Slade 'Cartels, collusion and horizontal merger' in R. Schmalensee and R.D. Willig (eds) *Handbook of Industrial Organization, Volume 1* (Elsevier Science Publishers, Amsterdam, 1989) 441.

[28] W. Fellner 'Collusion and its limits under oligopoly' (1950) 40 American Economic Review 58.

where the use of economics has been heavily criticised. Three of the most controversial merger decisions in recent years have involved issues of collective dominance and almost all of the decisions of the Commission in non-merger matters involving collective dominance have been appealed to the European Courts. The scope for these appeals has also arguably broadened in recent years as the Commission is now required to thoroughly justify the economic basis for its decision not only to prohibit, but also to *allow*, a merger on the basis of an examination of coordinated effects.[29]

Finally, the scope for the application of the concept of collective dominance is growing. In particular, the concept of coordinated effects has recently been included in guidelines for the Commission's assessment of non-horizontal mergers,[30] and has been incorporated into sector-specific European Directives.[31] In addition, National Competition Agencies in Member States such as Denmark, France, Italy and the United Kingdom have actively employed the concept of collective dominance (as developed in the European jurisdiction) under national competition laws.[32]

For all these reasons, the area chosen for the case study was considered to be analytically rich and of practical policy relevance. The area of collective dominance was also chosen as it is an enforcement activity amenable to exhaustive case review.[33]

---

[29] There is a so-called 'symmetrical standard of proof' for merger prohibitions and authorisations: Case C-413/06P *Bertelsmann AG and Sony Corporation of America v Independent Music Publishers and Labels Association (Impala)* [2008] ECR-00000 para [51]. Compare B. van Rompuy 'Implications for the standard of proof in EC merger proceedings: Bertelsmann and Sony Corporation of America *v.* Impala' (2008) 29 European Competition Law Review 608; K. Wright 'Perfect symmetry? Impala *v.* Commission and standard of proof in mergers' (2007) 32 European Law Review 408.

[30] Commission guidelines on the assessment of non-horizontal mergers under the Council Regulation on the control of concentrations between undertakings [2008] OJ C 265 paras [79]–[90].

[31] The European communications directive requires National Regulatory Agencies to assess whether markets are susceptible to joint dominance: Article 7 of the Directive 2002/21/EC of the European Parliament and of the Council of 7 March 2002 on a common regulatory framework for electronic communications networks and services (Framework Directive) OJ L 108/33.

[32] B. Hawk and G. Motta 'Oligopolies and collective dominance: a solution in search of a problem' (Treviso Conference on Antitrust Between EC Law and National Law, Fordham Law Legal Studies Research Paper number (1301693) 2008) 98. The Danish Competition Authority's first outright rejection of a merger was on the basis of coordinated effects: Decision of Konkurrencestyrelsen in *Lemvigh-Müllers overtagelse af Brdr. A & O Johansen*, 14 May 2008.

[33] In practical terms, cases dealing with collective dominance are readily identifiable, and the assessment of collective dominance invariably forms a discrete section of decisions.

However, it is argued that the conclusions of the case study are potentially generalisable to a broader area of enforcement activity. This is because collective dominance investigations are not a *peculiar* area of competition enforcement; the process used in collective dominance merger investigations is the same as in unilateral effects merger investigations, and the process used in collective dominance abuse cases is the same as in single dominance abuse cases. Complex economic assessments are frequently required in each of these investigations.

As an introduction to the case study, Chapter 2 of this book introduces the relevant enforcement context. It discusses how European law has responded to the potential economic 'mischief' that can arise in oligopolistic market structures, outlining the relevant legal provisions under the European Community Merger Regulation (EMCR) and Article 82 of the EC Treaty and the principal actors and institutions involved in enforcement matters. It also outlines the methodology adopted in the case study for examining how economics has featured in this specific enforcement setting.

Chapter 3 outlines the substantive law and economics underlying the empirical study. It describes the economic notion of tacit collusion and its key theories, concepts and methodological approaches, and details the predictions of economics as to the circumstances in which tacit collusion is more or less likely to occur (a fuller description of the theory of tacit collusion is presented in Appendix 1). The principal question explored in this chapter is: what is the relationship, if any, between the legal mechanisms for addressing the potential for tacit coordination in European law, and the predictions of the mass of models that comprise the economic theory of tacit collusion? The description in this chapter sets up a number of questions that are addressed in later chapters: what is the effect of the uncertainty associated with the multiplicity of economic models on their potential use? Are there inherent limitations in the application of economic models in factual settings? In combination, what potential do economic models of tacit collusion have as an applied tool in making legal determinations under Article 82 and the ECMR?

Chapters 4 and 5 detail the results of the empirical review. These chapters do not seek to assess or critique how economic expertise *should* be used in the enforcement of the collective dominance laws, or to comment on the merits or appropriateness of the reasoning or decisions of the Commission and Courts in specific cases. Rather, the purpose of these chapters is to *describe*, based on the published reasoning of the decision-makers and the experience of those involved in the wider enforcement process, how, in fact, economics influences the enforcement of the collective dominance laws. Accordingly, Chapter 4 presents the results of the review of how economics has featured in the enforcement of the relevant laws as indicated by the text of the reported decisions of the Commission and the Courts. Chapter 5 looks beyond these reported decisions to understand the influence of economics in the process surrounding, and leading up to, these final determinations, as revealed by those involved in these processes. Both chapters examine the use of economics through the multifaceted conception of economics described previously. These chapters explore a number of questions about past enforcement actions: What role did economic theory play in these actions? How did the economic theory applied relate to the underlying academic models? Was economic data systematically collected and analysed as part of the enforcement process? What kinds of economic techniques were employed in investigations? How influential was economic evidence relative to other evidence collected in an investigation? Did the use of economic expertise differ as between *ex post* assessments and *ex ante* assessments of collective dominance? Were expert economists systematically involved in enforcement actions? What were the relative roles, and interactions, of lawyers and economists in the enforcement process?

In brief, the evidence shows that while the overall predictions of particular theoretical models are frequently used to provide the basis for arguments in enforcement activity, the application of such models to the factual settings of individual cases is not typically, or systematically, associated with the collection or analyses of relevant data or evidence. In addition, there is variability in the use of different facets of economic expertise: descriptive techniques are employed far more frequently than quantitative techniques; factors derived from economic theory are employed variably across decisions; and aspects of economic reasoning and data are emphasised over others. A further insight to emerge is that the different perspectives and interests of those who use economics, and the specific characteristics of the enforcement setting, substantively impact on how economics has been applied.

Drawing on the findings of the case study, Chapter 6 outlines and examines the three principal functions identified for economics in collective dominance investigations. It concludes that the primary influence of economics in the enforcement process is located at a general level: it provides a broad theoretical framework, a conceptual approach and a descriptive expository technique. It is argued that this contribution is valuable, and, indeed, necessary to the enforcement of the laws, however areas of tension are also identified, especially in relation to the degree of flexibility of economic reasoning in the area under examination, and the changing nature of economic exposition – with its increased emphasis on hypothetical deduction from pure theory and decreased emphasis on supporting facts.

Chapter 7 examines the implications of the key conclusions of the book for the use of economics in European competition law enforcement and for the 'more economics' approach currently advocated in competition policy. At a general level, it is argued that it is likely to be inefficacious to advocate for 'more economics' at the policy level, without appreciating and considering a range of issues relating to the nature of economics and the enforcement context in which the economics will be applied. In this respect it is argued that a realistic and empirically grounded notion of 'economics' needs to be adopted in policy discourse which takes account of those parts of economic knowledge and expertise that are most capable of being usefully applied in enforcement settings. It is also argued that economics, as transformed by its application in specific enforcement settings, can exhibit a flexibility that can be inimical to the purposes of the enforcement process, and the law more generally, unless it is applied in a context in which there are appropriate institutional checks and balances. In this respect, there is scope for the consideration of institutional and procedural reforms. However, it is proposed that one of the most effective constraints on such flexibility is an enforcement process that provides a central role for the collection and considered weighing of economic facts and data

2. The enforcement context

2.1 INTRODUCTION

There are three principal contextual considerations relevant to an examination of the use of economics in the enforcement of European laws relating to oligopolies. First, the economic 'mischief' that has potential to exist in oligopolistic industries, which underlies the need for a regulatory response. Second, the specific regulatory response, in the form of the legal notion of collective dominance that has been developed to address this economic 'mischief'. Finally, the institutions and actors that are involved in the process of the enforcement of these laws. This chapter briefly introduces each of these contextual elements, and outlines the methodology adopted to examine how economics has featured in this specific enforcement setting.

2.2 THE ECONOMIC MISCHIEF

2.2.1 Oligopolistic Interdependence

Economics conceives of oligopolies as market or industry structures where there are a few sellers of a particular product, which can be distinguished from a market structure where there is only one seller of a product (monopoly) or a market structure where there are many sellers of a product (perfect competition). The key characteristic of an oligopolistic market structure is that there is a high degree of *interdependence* between firms. This means that the decisions of firms in the market as to production levels and prices substantively impact rivals who will be expected to respond in ways which will directly affect the profit capable of arising from those original decisions.[1] Again this can be

[1] To illustrate this interdependence consider a market with 3 identical firms (A, B, C) who produce the same product. Imagine a situation where firm A decides that it wishes to raise its individual profits by increasing the amount of product it offers for sale. Assuming that demand is downward sloping then this increase in supply by firm A will, other things equal, result in more of the product for sale, which may flood the market and consequently lower the market price. If firms B and C do not change their

distinguished from monopolistic markets (where there is only one seller who determines the price) and from perfectly competitive markets (where there are many sellers each of whom cannot directly influence price).

The important point to note – which is crucial for the discussion that follows – is that, in recognising this *interdependence*, each firm in an oligopoly must balance a trade-off between the profits it would earn if it aggressively competed with other firms, against the profits it would earn if all firms in the industry co-operated to maximise joint profits through collusion. Accordingly, at the extremes, firms in oligopolistic markets can behave in two possible ways. If they choose to compete aggressively with each other then the market will very closely resemble a perfectly *competitive* market structure. Alternatively, if the firms choose to collude in order to maximise joint profits the market structure will more closely approximate monopoly. In between these endpoints there is a spectrum of possible interactions which reflect the intensity of competition vis-à-vis collusion between firms in oligopolistic markets.[2]

In economics, two sets of assumptions are critical when considering whether firms are more likely to compete or collude in oligopolistic markets: assumptions about entry conditions into a market; and assumptions about the state of technological innovation in a market. Where an oligopolistic market is characterised by entry conditions that are restrictive or difficult, or by a static level of technological innovation, this is considered to make conditions more conducive for promoting, and sustaining, collusion. Conversely, where a market is characterised by relatively easy entry, or rapid technological innovation, these factors are viewed as having the potential to disturb any collusive arrangements between oligopolistic firms.

There are a number of other conditions under which economic theory predicts collusion will be more or less likely to be observed. These are examined in detail in the next chapter and in Appendix 1. The immediate point is

---

production levels, then as a result of A's actions, their individual profits will be reduced. This is because although they are offering the same amount of output as in the previous period they are forced to sell it at a lower market price in order to avoid customers switching to firm A. Firm A, on the other hand, would most likely earn a higher level of profits in the short term, as although the market price has fallen, it sells a larger quantity of its production on the market. However, in the longer term firms B and C can be expected to respond in ways which affect the profitability of firm A's initial decision to increase production.

2 Oligopolistic situations have thus been described as bargaining situations in the broad sense: W. Fellner 'Collusion and its limits under oligopoly' (1950) 40 American Economic Review 54.

that oligopolistic interdependence can present possibilities for both competitive and collusive behaviour.[3]

2.2.2 The Effects of Collusion

There is a large literature examining the costs and benefits of collusion. The basis of the literature which highlights the costs of collusion, focuses on the potential detrimental effects of oligopolistic market power in terms of efficiency and distribution.[4] Some of these studies have attempted to estimate the potential welfare losses associated with the restriction of competition associated with oligopoly power.[5] Other studies have highlighted the potential benefits of collusion in terms of dynamic efficiency,[6] and longer-term incentives for innovation,[7] and have concluded that in certain circumstances the benefits of collusion outweigh the costs of disallowing it.[8]

However, according to neoclassical economic theory, and as reflected in current European competition policy, the costs of collusion in terms of the distortions it creates to resource allocation, efficiency and distribution are

---

[3] This potential for collusion has long been recognised. Adam Smith noted that 'people of the same trade seldom meet together, even for merriment and diversion, but the conversation ends in a conspiracy against the public, or in some contrivance to raise prices': A. Smith *The Wealth of Nations* ed. by W. Letwin (Everyman's Library London 1975) 117. While John Stuart Mill noted: 'Where competitors are so few, they always end up agreeing not to compete': J.S. Mill *Principles of Political Economy: with Some of their Applications to Social Philosophy* (7th edn, Longman Green & Co, London, 1923) 143.

[4] Compare, for example, G.J. Stigler 'Monopoly and oligopoly by merger' (1950) 40 American Economic Review 32.

[5] A. Harberger 'Monopoly and resource allocation' (1954) 44 American Economic Review 77; K. Cowling and D.C. Mueller 'The social costs of monopoly power' (1978) 88 Economic Journal 727; G.K. Yarrow 'Welfare losses in oligopoly and monopolistic competition' (1985) 33 Journal of Industrial Economics 529.

[6] A. Jacquemin and M.E. Slade 'Cartels, collusion and horizontal merger' in R. Schmalensee and R.D. Willig (eds) *Handbook of Industrial Organization, Volume 1* (Elsevier Science Publishers, Amsterdam, 1989) 459.

[7] W.J. Baumol 'Horizontal collusion and innovation' (1992) 102 Economic Journal 129; C. Fershtman and A. Pakes 'A dynamic oligopoly with collusion and price wars' (2000) 31 RAND Journal of Economics 232,234; D. Dewey 'Information, entry and welfare: the case for collusion' (1979) 69 American Economic Review 587.

[8] Other studies have suggested that some form of co-operation between firms may be necessary in particular markets in order to obtain an equilibrium and consequently efficient exchange: L.G. Telser 'Cooperation, competition and efficiency' (1985) 28 Journal of Law and Economics 272, 294–5.

assumed to be greater than the benefits.[9] This is because the effects of oligopolistic collusion are generally seen as equivalent to the effects of monopoly in terms of impacts on competition, efficiency, innovation and consumers. That is, while the principal concern with monopoly is that a single firm has an ability to exercise market power, a similar concern exists when firms in an oligopoly coordinate their behaviour.[10] It is this potential for firms in oligopolistic markets to coordinate their behaviour with effects similar to a monopoly, known in the literature as the 'oligopoly problem', that is the economic 'mischief' that European competition policy is attempting to address.[11]

2.2.3 The Forms of Collusion

Collusive behaviour in oligopolistic markets can potentially take many forms but an important distinction can be made between *explicit* and *tacit* collusion. The principal feature of explicit collusion is that firms communicate explicitly to coordinate their behaviour, which typically takes the form of formal agreements between the firms. The most common form of explicit collusion is the cartel agreement which is typically a formal agreement between firms to segment markets or to fix prices, outputs or sometimes market shares at specific levels. Tacit collusion, on the other hand, refers to a situation where *no* explicit collusive agreement exists, but where firms 'agree to coordinate their actions in some way without explicit communication and discussion'.[12]

---

9 This has not always been the case, particularly in the early part of the 20th century. Contrast G.J. Stigler 'The economists and the problem of monopoly' (1982) 72 American Economic Review 39, in the US context; D.J. Gerber *Law and Competition in Twentieth Century Europe: Protecting Prometheus* (Oxford University Press, Oxford, 1998) 81–96, in the European context; J. Lever 'UK economic regulation: use and abuse of the law' (1992) 13 European Competition Law Review 57, in the British context.

10 G.J. Stigler and J.S. Bain 'Discussion' (1950) 40 American Economic Review 63.

11 In this respect it has been suggested that European competition policy should be more concerned with oligopolies than with monopolies: R. Whish and B. Surfin 'Oligopolistic markets and EC competition law' in A. Barav and D.A. Wyatt (eds) *Yearbook of European Law Volume 15* (Oxford University Press, Oxford, 1992) 59–60; D. Neven, P. Papandropoulos and P. Seabright *Trawling for Minnows: European Competition Policy and Agreements between Firms* (Centre for Economic Research, London, 1998) 51.

12 R. Rees 'Tacit collusion' (1993) 9 Oxford Review of Economic Policy 27; Friedman notes 'How they do this (tacitly collude) is not entirely clear, though one explanation is that their market moves are interpretable as messages. They converse in code, as it were. Another explanation is that the "tacit collusion" is spontaneous. Everyone is so aware of the shortsightedness of Cournot behaviour that they simply behave better': J.W. Friedman 'A non-cooperative equilibrium for supergames' (1971) 38 Review of Economics and Statistics 11.

The rationale for such behaviour is that each firm recognises, even in the absence of any explicit communication or agreement, that it is in their best interest to behave as if an agreement to coordinate their actions existed.[13]

The economic effects of explicit and tacit collusion are theoretically similar as they both involve behaviour with potentially negative effects on efficiency and resource allocation. This equivalence is well recognised by practitioners, enforcement officials and academics. However, unlike explicit collusion, which is more amenable to traditional legal means of identification, the ability to identify instances of tacit collusion poses non-trivial problems.[14] For this reason economics has featured more prominently in the enforcement of the laws relating to tacit collusion than in relation to cases of explicit collusion. Accordingly the specific focus of this book is tacit rather than explicit collusion.

2.3 THE LEGAL RESPONSE

European legal policy has responded to the potential for firms in oligopolistic industries to collude explicitly or tacitly through the use of three legal provisions: Articles 81 and 82 of the EC Treaty and the European Community Merger Regulation (ECMR).

Article 81(1) of the EC Treaty, which prohibits certain agreements or concerted practices between competing firms, captures instances of explicit collusion, and has, in the past, been considered to offer some scope for dealing with tacitly collusive behaviour as a form of concerted practice.[15] However, more recently this scope has been considered limited.[16]

As a result, the potential for tacit collusion is primarily addressed under two legal provisions: Article 82 of the EC Treaty and the ECMR. The ability of

---

13 E.H. Chamberlain *The Theory of Monopolistic Competition: A Re-orientation of the Theory of Value* (7th edn, Harvard University Press, Cambridge, MA, 1956) 47–48.

14 Compare L. McGregor 'The future for the control of oligopolies following *Compagnie Maritime Belge*' (2001) 22 European Competition Law Review 442.

15 In Case 48–69 *ICI v. Commission (Dyestuffs)* [1972] ECR 0619 para [64] the ECJ defined a concerted practice to be: 'co-ordination between undertakings which, without having reached the stage where an agreement, properly so called, has been concluded, knowingly substitutes practical co-operation between them for the risks of competition'.

16 The Courts have held that conduct resulting from oligopolistic interdependence, in the absence of further evidence suggestive of explicit collusion, cannot amount to evidence of concerted practice under Article 81(1): Joined cases C-89/85, C-104/85, C-114/85, C-116/85, C-117/85 and C-125/85 to C-129/85 *A. Ahlström Osakeyhtiö and others v Commission of the European Communities.* [1993] ECR I-01307 paras [71]–[72].

these provisions to deal with collusive behaviour relies on the judicially developed notion of collective dominance. Collective dominance is a controversial and complex legal notion and is discussed in more detail in Chapter 3. Put very simply, the ECMR can be used prospectively – by way of merger control – to prevent a number of undertakings from holding a collective dominant position on a market which would enable, or encourage them, to align or coordinate their behaviour.[17] Article 82 of the EC Treaty is used to capture the anti-competitive *effects* of past instances of collectively dominant undertakings coordinating their behaviour in a market. Thus, insofar as a merger raises concerns about coordinated behaviour, the ECMR can be used *ex ante* to prevent a merger creating, or strengthening, an environment where firms are more likely to tacitly collude than compete with one another. Article 82 of the EC Treaty is used *ex post* to capture past instances of tacit collusion in oligopolistic markets.[18] For simplicity, these legal provisions shall be referred to as the 'collective dominance laws' for the remainder of this book.

It is worth noting that there were a number of changes to the ECMR in 2004. In the Commission guidelines accompanying these changes reference was made to 'coordinated effects' as well as 'collective dominance'. This gave rise to some speculation that the notion of collective dominance had lost currency. It is clear, however, that this is not the case. The insertion of the term 'coordinated effects' was not intended to replace the notion of collective dominance, but to bring the terminology into line with that used more commonly in other jurisdictions such as the United States.[19] Moreover, the intention behind the change to the regulation itself was to address concerns that the ECMR, as it then stood, would not capture mergers that might result in what is known as

---

17 In addition, the ECMR is used to address unilateral effects and non-coordinated effects of a merger.

18 In the United States, a similar attempt in the late 1960s and early 1970s to extend Section 2 of the Sherman Act to address the oligopoly problem *ex post* through the notion of shared monopoly was seen as 'a largely academic suggestion' that was 'fundamentally unworkable': J.B. Baker 'Two Sherman Act section 1 dilemmas: parallel pricing, the oligopoly problem, and contemporary economic theory' (1993) 38 Antitrust Bulletin 207; S. Weaver *Decision to Prosecute: Organization and Public Policy in the Antitrust Division* (MIT Press, Cambridge, MA, 1977) 51–52, 128.

19 See for example M. Ivaldi, B. Jullien, P. Rey, P. Seabright and J. Tirole 'The economics of tacit collusion: Implications for merger control' (Institut d'Economie Industrielle (IDEI) Toulouse, 'Final report prepared for DG Competition European Commission, March 2003' <http://europa.eu.int/comm/competition/mergers/review/the_economics_of_tacit_collusion_en.pdf> (12 May 2004) 217. Similarly, Voigt and Schmidt note that 'the recent reforms modified the relevant wording: collective dominance is now called "coordinated effects".' S. Voigt and A. Schmidt *Making European Merger Policy More Predictable* (Springer, Dordrecht, 2005) 146.

'non-coordinated effects'.[20] The effect of the change was therefore not to replace the law relating to collective dominance or coordinated effects[21] but to *extend* its application to cover cases of non-coordinated effects.[22]

The Commission has conducted at least 66 merger investigations on the basis of concerns about collective dominance or future coordinated behaviour since the change to the ECMR. Moreover, the scope for collective dominance investigations has increased following the inclusion of the concept into sector-specific European Directives, such as the EC Communications Directive which requires National Regulatory Agencies to assess whether markets are susceptible to dominance prior to applying market remedies.[23]

There is a more detailed discussion about the notion of collective dominance in Chapters 3 and 5. The immediate point is the continuing relevance of the notion in EC competition investigations.

2.4 INSTITUTIONS AND ACTORS

The European Commission Directorate General for Competition is the principal institution responsible for the enforcement of the law in relation to

---

20 In very simple terms, this is where firms do not coordinate their behaviour (or tacitly collude), but, because of the highly concentrated structure of the market, adverse effects on competition nevertheless result from the merger. This can be distinguished from mergers which result in a market structure where it is likely that firms might have a greater ability and incentive to coordinate their behaviour (i.e.: tacitly collude); known as 'coordinated effects'.

21 The guidelines that accompanied the 2004 change to the ECMR explicitly recognised the link between coordinated effects and collective dominance, stating that:

> A merger in a concentrated market may significantly impede effective competition, through the creation or the strengthening of a collective dominant position, because it increases the likelihood that firms are able to coordinate their behaviour.

Commission guidelines on the assessment of horizontal mergers under the Council Regulation on the control of concentrations between undertakings [2004] OJ C31/5 para [39].

22 Council Regulation (EC) No 139/2004 of 20 January 2004 on the control of concentrations between undertakings (the EC Merger Regulation) OJ L24/1 para [25]. For commentary on this issue see: E. Elhauge and D. Geradin *Global Competition Law and Economics* (Hart Publishing, Oxford, 2007) 803–804.

23 Article 7 of the Directive 2002/21/EC of the European Parliament and of the Council of 7 March 2002 on a common regulatory framework for electronic communications networks and services (Framework Directive) OJ L 108/33. The specific reference in the Directive is to joint dominance, but these terms are conceptually synonymous.

oligopolies at the European level.[24] In enforcing the ECMR the Commission is responsible for: the collection and analysis of facts; making a determination; and accepting any appropriate undertakings proposed by the merging parties to address concerns raised by the Commission. In enforcing Article 82 the Commission has similar powers to initiate an investigation; collect and examine facts in relation to the alleged infringement; make determinations; and impose fines or other remedies.[25]

Commission decisions are subject to judicial review by the Community Courts ('the Courts'). The Courts are responsible for ensuring that the Commission has followed appropriate procedures, observed the law and kept within the powers of its administrative discretion. According to established standards a reviewing Court confers a certain discretion on the Commission in respect of assessments of an economic nature,[26] and will not substitute its own assessment for that of the Commission.[27] The Court of First Instance (CFI) is the principal body responsible for hearing actions of competition law cases in the first instance, except when a Member State is involved, in which case the European Court of Justice (ECJ) can perform judicial review in the first instance. A decision of the CFI can be appealed to the ECJ on a point of law only. The ECJ can also consider references from national courts on points of law in respect of the EC Treaty.[28]

Within, and surrounding, these institutions there are a broad range of actors that are involved in the enforcement of the collective dominance laws. These actors typically work for the Commission, the Courts or private parties.

---

[24] The potential for private enforcement, or enforcement by national courts or competition authorities, of Article 82 of the EC Treaty also exists. However, thus far this has been used relatively infrequently and is not considered in this book. Similarly, under Regulation 9 of the ECMR the possibility exists for mergers to be referred to national competition authorities.

[25] Council Regulation (EC) No 1/2003 of 16 December 2002 on the implementation of the rules of competition laid down in Articles 81 and 82 of the Treaty OJ L1/1 4.1.2003.

[26] Joined cases C-68/94 and C-30/95 *French Republic and Société commerciale des potasses et de l'azote (SCPA) and Entreprise minière et chimique (EMC) v Commission of the European Communities* [1998] ECR I-01375 paras [223]–[224].

[27] Case T-342/00 *Petrolessence and SG2r v. Commission* [2002] ECR II-1161 para [101]. In *Tetra Laval* the ECJ clarified the standard or review noting that: 'Not only must the Community Courts, *inter alia*, establish whether the evidence relied on is factually accurate, reliable and consistent but also whether that evidence contains all the information which must be taken into account in order to assess a complex situation and whether it is capable of substantiating the conclusions drawn from it' C-13/03P *Commission of the European Communities v Tetra Laval BV* [2005] ECR I-01113 para [39].

[28] Article 234 of the EC Treaty.

Professionally, these actors can be classed according to their area of expertise and vocation as either: economists (including consultant and academic economists), lawyers (including solicitors, barristers and judges) and general administrators. In short, there is a broad competition law community who interact frequently in a variety of forums and associations and help shape the enforcement process. The expert economists who work for private parties are typically employed by, or attached, to a small number of economic consulting firms. Unlike experts in many other areas of law, the economic consulting firms are typically multinational, well funded and resourced, and better equipped than the enforcement agencies.[29] These consulting firms are typically staffed by PhD trained economists and the management of the firms often maintain their academic credentials by retaining non-teaching posts at leading universities.

2.5 INVESTIGATING THE ENFORCEMENT SETTING

2.5.1 Methodological Approach

The methodological approach adopted to examine the enforcement setting described above involved an examination of the use of economics across the entire enforcement process. In this respect, the enforcement process was conceived of comprising a number of stages: case identification and selection or non-selection; case construction; substantive decision-making; and the development of remedies.

There are two data sets underlying the conclusions to this research. The first comprises the reported decisions of the Commission and the Courts in relation to collective dominance up to the year 2008. The second comprises the results of interviews with those involved in the various stages of the enforcement process. It is recognised that there is some overlap between the two data sets, as the interview data also refers to reported decisions.

The notion of 'economics' employed

Like other descriptions in social science such as 'law' or 'political science' the notion of 'economics' can be contentious and difficult to define precisely.

---

29 D. Neven 'Competition economics and antitrust in Europe' (2006) 21 Economic Policy 5. It is estimated that the top four economic consulting firms in the United States, all of whom also operate in Europe, had a combined revenue of 185 million dollars in the year 1997: M.J. Mandel 'Going for gold: economists as expert witnesses' (1999) 13 Journal of Economic Perspectives 115.

Working notions vary from economics as theory, statistics and history,[30] to it being a 'box of tools',[31] or simply 'what economists do'.[32]

For the purposes of the analysis in the study, 'economics' is conceived to include: (1) Economic theory, both 'pure'/axiomatic theory and generalised observational theory. It is important to note that the term 'economic theory' in this context does not refer to a single body of theory, but rather to a theoretical paradigm which includes a large collection of models and technical papers which share common characteristics and a common framework (such as assumptions regarding rationality, repeated game settings); (2) The economic approach, including economic reasoning and the economic methods of conceptualising problems and phenomena, often referred to as the 'economic way of thinking'; (3) Economic techniques, such as the economic 'tools' of analysis and exposition including quantitative techniques such as model building, statistical experiments and data interrogation and qualitative techniques such as the use of economic narratives based on stylised facts and anecdotal evidence; and (4) Economic data. The concept of economic data is difficult to define with precision, but is intended to capture information that is capable of being used in one of the techniques described above. For example, economic data might include price, sales or output data but would not include the terms of contracts or statements made by managers as to whether sales are 'high' or 'low'. The word 'economics' as used throughout this book is intended to capture the specialist application of economics as defined above.

2.5.2 The Reported Decisions

A review was conducted of 173 merger decisions (in 276 markets)[33] and seven Article 82 decisions published by the Commission, and of the judg-

---

30 J.A. Schumpeter *History of Economic Analysis* (Routledge, London, 1954) 12.

31 J. Robinson *The Economics of Imperfect Competition* (2nd edn, Macmillan, London, 1969) 1.

32 Attributed to Jacob Viner in: K.E. Boulding *Economic Analysis* (4th edn, Harper & Row, New York, 1941) 3.

33 A merger decision may include the assessment of the potential for collective dominance to occur in a number of relevant markets (i.e.: relevant product and geographic markets). For example, the *Exxon/Mobil* merger decision included an examination of the potential for collective dominance in seven separate relevant markets: the fuel retailing markets in the UK, the Netherlands, France, Luxembourg, Austria and Germany, as well as an assessment of the potential for collective dominance in the German long distance wholesale gas transmission market: *Exxon/Mobil* (Case No IV/M.1383) [2004] OJ L103 1.

ments of the European Courts in seven merger decisions and ten Article 82 decisions.[34] The merger decisions reviewed cover the period from 1991 to 2008, while the Article 82 decisions cover a period from 1973 to 2008.[35] The decisions are all the reported decisions of the Commission and the Courts published in English over these time periods in which collective dominance was addressed.

The purpose of the review was not to describe in detail the use of economics in any specific case but rather to present a picture – in aggregate – of the use of economics across all decisions.[36] This was considered appropriate for this research for two reasons. First, in relation to merger decisions at least, there are no insignificant decisions. The only mergers assessed at the European level are those which involve substantial economic undertakings, that is, whose combined global and European turnovers exceed 5000 million EUR and 250 million EUR respectively.[37] Second, a selection of cases on a more limited basis may have encouraged the consideration of predominantly controversial and high-profile cases in which there was likely to be a higher incidence of the use of economic expertise; that is, there was likely to be a selection bias.

The reported decisions are published in the *Official Journal of the European Union* and represent the official record of the decision used by lawyers and businessmen in understanding the law. In addition, as the official record of a decision, and its reasons, they represent the primary document upon which any appeal can be based. These decisions are typically quite detailed and according to a number of sources, including Commission

[34] In four of these decisions a national court of a Member State asked the Court for an opinion on the application of Article 82. The decisions were not preceded by an investigation by the Commission.

[35] These periods begin with the first reported decisions of the Commission relating to collective dominance under the ECMR and Article 82. The first decision under Article 82 which referred to the holding of a dominant position by more than one undertaking was *European Sugar Industry* (Case No.IV/26 918) [1973] OJ L140 17. The first decision under the ECMR which considered joint dominance was *Alcatel/AEG Kabel* (Case No IV/M.165) [1992] OJ C006 0.

[36] A similar approach is adopted in Neven, Nuttall and Seabright on the basis that 'a general tendency in the Commission's procedures cannot be revealed in single cases, and partly because (as will be seen) there has not always been consistency between the reasoning deployed in different cases': D. Neven, R. Nuttall and P. Seabright *Mergers in Daylight: The Economics and Politics of European Merger Control* (Centre for Economic Policy Research, London, 1993) 76.

[37] Article 1 (2) of Council Regulation (EC) No 139/2004 of 20 January 2004 on the control of concentrations between undertakings (the EC Merger Regulation) [2004] OJ L24/1.

officials, present a good and sufficiently rich basis upon which to draw conclusions as to the role of economics in the decision.[38]

In order to analyse decisions, a database was constructed of the Commission and Courts' reasoning in each of the cases under consideration. This involved the classification of the different elements of each decision according to the following: factors considered in assessments; indicators or processes examined in assessing each factor; and supporting evidence adduced in support of the conclusions regarding those factors. The completed database provided a comprehensive account of the different components of the Commission and Courts' published reasoning across all decisions under review.

In reviewing the reported decisions, the conception of economics described above was applied, and the analysis therefore sought to identify uses of economic theory, techniques and data and also for indications of an economic approach. In reviewing decisions for the use of economic theory, the focus was on assessing the following: (1) the extent of use of factors derived from economic theory; (2) the consistency of use of such factors with the underlying theory from which they are derived; (3) the consistency of use of factors across decisions; (4) the consistency of use of factors between the two types of decisions: *ex post* assessments of abuses of collective dominance under Article 82 and *ex-ante* assessments of the potential for collective dominance under the ECMR; and (5) the consistency of the use of factors between the two decision-making bodies: the Commission and the Courts. The process of reasoning in reaching a decision was also examined, with the aim of determining whether such reasoning could be categorised as indicative of an economic approach. An approach was considered economic where *economic indicators*, and *economic processes*, were used in the assessment of factors. In examining the type of economic techniques used to support analyses of economic factors in decisions, the focus was on identifying the extent to which 'low-tech' methods (such as simple calculations, or the postulating of hypotheses) were used to examine a particular factor or market as compared to more 'high tech' methods (such as statistical or econometric analyses). Finally, the source, and types, of economic data used in the assessment of factors were identified in order to

[38] The use of reported decisions as a basis for generalising about the Commission's practice can be seen in other studies: J. Briones 'Oligopolistic dominance: is there a common approach in different jurisdictions? A review of decisions adopted by the Commission under the Merger Regulation' (1995) 16 European Competition Law Review 334; Neven, Nuttall and Seabright (n 36); D. Neven, P. Papandropoulos and P. Seabright *Trawling for Minnows: European Competition Policy and Agreements between Firms* (Centre for Economic Policy Research, London, 1998).

examine the relative importance of economic data vis-à-vis other data; to assess the relative influence of different data sources; and to give an indication of the extent to which data was systematically collected as part of an assessment.

In conducting the analysis described above, differences in the powers and processes of the Commission and the Courts were recognised, in particular that the Court's role is limited to one of judicial review. However, it was also recognised that the depth and intensity with which the Courts perform their review function have at times been rigorous and included a detailed examination of the Commission's exercise of its discretion in respect of economic assessments.[39] In this respect, the Courts have, at times, examined both the appropriateness of the Commission's application of economic theory, and the merits of, and interpretation given to, the economic evidence upon which the Commission has based its assessments.[40]

Finally, it was recognised that economics invariably forms only one input into a complex set of factors at play in decisions, and that other non-economic factors influence the various approaches adopted and the balancing of evidence. While it was not considered possible to systematically identify and account for these other considerations within the confines of the text of reported decisions, this limitation is sought to be alleviated by the interview data reported in Chapter 5.

2.5.3 The Interviews

The review of reported decisions was supplemented by a range of detailed interviews with practitioners in this area. Interviewees were selected according to two criteria. The first criterion was to conduct interviews with people associated, in a direct and frequent way, in cases involving issues of collective dominance. The second criterion was to ensure that interviews were held with a representative sample of: the various actors in the process (lawyers, economists, Commission officials); the different stages in the process (solicitors, barristers, judges); the various parties typically involved in an action (the Commission, private parties and the judiciary).

---

[39] For example in Case T-464/04 *Independent Music Publishers and Labels Association (Impala, International Association) v Commission of the European Communities* [2006] ECR II-02289; Case T-342/99 *Airtours plc v Commission of the European Communities* [2002] ECR II-02585.

[40] Compare D.J. Gerber 'Courts as economic experts in European merger law' in B. Hawk (ed.) *International Antitrust Law & Policy: Fordham Corporate Law 2004* (Juris Publishing, New York, 2004) 476, 479, 484, 490–91.

The final sample of interviewees comprised Commission officials, officials of the Commission legal service, ex-Commission officials now in private practice; economic consultants in private practice; academic economists who also either provide consultancy advice or work for enforcement agencies; solicitors in private practice; barristers, and members of the judiciary.[41]

The interviews were semi-structured, with open-ended questions that focused on the cases that the interviewee had been involved in, specifically the point at which they became involved in the enforcement process, their interaction with other actors and institutions, and the work they typically undertook. Depending upon their role, interviewees were asked questions about the use of economics at the various stages of the enforcement process: in identifying activities or markets for initial investigation; in the selection or non-selection of entities for further investigation; in the construction of cases by both the Commission and relevant parties; in reaching a final decision and in developing remedies. Those interviewed were also asked about the extent to which they considered the text of reported decisions to adequately reflect the considerations of the decision-makers, and work undertaken, in the cases in which they were involved. Throughout the interview process contact was maintained with a small number of those interviewed on an informal basis which provided an opportunity to clarify any issues that arose, and to 'test' the accuracy or reasonableness of the information obtained during the interview process. In addition to the interviews, a number of less formal discussions were held with various key actors through participation at roundtable forums, and discussions with practitioners at conferences and seminars.

The purpose of the interviews and less formal discussions was to elicit factual material about the process in which economics is employed. Nevertheless, it is acknowledged that actors in collective dominance investigations take part in an adversarial process, and that their views and perceptions of the process may, at various points, be influenced by this fact. In synthesising and presenting data obtained from the interviews and discussions, every care was taken to ensure a fair representation of the information obtained.

41 The relevant population from which these people were drawn is relatively concentrated and only a small number of specialised lawyers, economists, members of Commission legal service and Commission officials tend to be repeatedly involved in these types of investigations. The final sample of interviewees therefore represented a high proportion of those actors regularly involved in such cases. The collective experience of those interviewed covered all of the significant collective dominance decisions, including: Nestlé/Perrier; Gencor/Lonrho; Airtours/FirstChoice; SONY/BMG; UPM-Kymmene/Haindl; Kali + Salz (France *v.* Commission); SCA/Metsä; Exxon/Mobil; PriceWaterhouseCoopers; TACA (Atlantic Container Line); Cewal; CMBT; French West Africa; and Irish Sugar.

This approach to the conduct of the interviews thus sits within the well-established methodological approach adopted in other studies of enforcement and administrative discretion, studies of the law's use of scientific expertise and experts, as well as studies that have examined the enforcement practices of competition enforcement agencies in other jurisdictions.[42]

2.6 CONCLUSION

European competition law has responded to the potential for tacit collusion to occur in oligopolistic markets in the form of the collective dominance laws. These laws involve the *ex ante* prohibition of mergers where it is assessed that, following the merger, firms in the market are more likely to tacitly coordinate than compete with one another, and the *ex post* use of Article 82 of the EC Treaty to capture past instances of tacit coordination in oligopolistic markets.

The relevant provisions are enforced by the Competition Directorate of the European Commission, and the enforcement process involves a range of actors including Commission officials, solicitors and barristers, consultant and academic economists and judges all of whom engage with economics at different points in the process. To survey the use of economics within this process a comprehensive review of reported decisions was undertaken, and interviews were conducted with those involved in the enforcement process, seeking to identify how the various elements of economics featured across the different stages of the enforcement process.

42 Compare, for example, the study of the Antitrust Division of the United States Department of Justice in S. Weaver (1977) *Decision to prosecute: Organization and Public Policy in the Antitrust Division*, Cambridge, Mass: MIT Press.

3. The law and economics of tacit coordination

3.1 INTRODUCTION

As we saw in Chapter 2, economic theory predicts that under certain circumstances firms operating in oligopolistic market structures may have incentives to collude rather than compete, which can result in detrimental welfare effects similar to those produced by a monopolist. As we have also seen, European law has responded to this prediction through a number of legal provisions. The purpose of this chapter is to provide an overview of the legal provisions relating to tacit collusion and to examine in detail the specific predictions of economic theory regarding when we might expect to observe firms colluding rather than competing which may be relevant in the enforcement of these provisions.

3.2 THE LAW OF COLLECTIVE DOMINANCE

3.2.1 Introduction

The potential for tacit collusion to occur in oligopolistic markets is known in the relevant literature as the 'oligopoly problem'. In Europe, and in other jurisdictions, the 'oligopoly problem' has not always been viewed as necessitating a legal response. In the United States, for example, the question of whether the 'oligopoly problem' should be of automatic concern to the law has been fiercely debated since the 1960s.[1] The debate about the 'oligopoly problem' in European legal policy has centred less on the need for the law to address the problem, which has generally been recognised,[2] but rather on the nature and scope of the

1 Compare D.F. Turner 'The definition of agreement under the Sherman Act: conscious parallelism and refusals to deal' (1962) 75 Harvard Law Review 661–681; R.A. Posner 'Oligopoly and the antitrust laws: a suggested approach' (1968–69) 21 Stanford Law Review 1592; 1571.

2 A. Jones and B. Sufrin *EC Competition Law* (Oxford University Press, Oxford, 2001) 663; P. Christensen and V. Rabassa 'The Airtours decision: is there a new Commission approach to collective dominance?' (2001) 22 European Competition Law Review 227.

appropriate legal response. In particular, there is ambiguity surrounding how the legal concept of collective dominance and the economic notion of oligopolistic interdependence relate to one another.[3] The problem stems from the fact that although firms in an oligopoly are interdependent, this does not necessarily mean those firms are tacitly colluding; they may in fact be competing with one another. However, because of the difficulty of distinguishing between collusive and non-collusive oligopolies the scope of the notion of collective dominance as developed under Article 82 and the ECMR has at times been unclear.[4] For example, at various points, the Commission has referred to collective dominance as if it was equivalent to oligopolistic interdependence.[5] Similarly, Court decisions have implied that factors relating to the oligopolistic structure of the market – which by its nature creates interdependence – alone may suffice as the connecting factor between firms necessary for a finding of collective dominance.[6]

---

3 The terms 'collective dominance', 'oligopolistic dominance' and 'joint dominance' are often used synonymously by the Courts and the Commission: Joined cases C-395/96 P and C-396/96 P *Compagnie maritime belge transports SA (C-395/96 P), Compagnie maritime belge SA (C-395/96 P) and Dafra-Lines A/S (C-396/96 P) v Commission of the European Communities* [2000] ECR I-01365 para [36] (*Compagnie maritime belge case*); *Airtours/FirstChoice* (Case IV/M.1524) [2000] OJ L093 1 paras [75]–[76]. However, in some decisions the Commission has appeared to give separate meanings to the different terms: *Price WaterhouseCoopers & Lybrand* (Case IV/M.1016)[1999] OJ L050 27 paras [94]; [106]; [113].

4 In economic terms this becomes a question of whether collective dominance is more closely related to models of oligopoly such as Cournot and Bertrand where firms maximise *individual* profits, or rather if it is related to dynamic models of strategic interaction where firms through their actions try to maximise *joint* profits. On this point: G. Robert and C. Hudson 'Past coordination and the Commission Notice on the appraisal of horizontal mergers' (2004) 25 European Competition Law Review 164; E. Kloosterhuis 'Joint dominance and the interaction between firms' (2001) 22 European Competition Law Review 86.

5 *Airtours/FirstChoice* (Case IV/M.1524) [2000] OJ L093 1 para [150]; *Gencor/Lonrho* (Case No IV/M.619) [1997] OJ L011 30 para [140]; Commission Notice on the application of the competition rules to access agreements in the telecommunications sector [1998] OJ C 265/02 para [79]; Commission Working Document On Proposed New Regulatory Framework for Electronic Communications Networks and Services – Draft Guidelines on market analysis and the calculation of significant market power under Article 14 of the proposed Directive on a common regulatory framework for electronic communications networks and services [2001] COM (2001) 175 para [85].

6 Case T-102/96 *Gencor Ltd v Commission of the European Communities* [1999] ECR II-00753 para [276]–[277] (*Gencor v Commission*); *Compagnie maritime belge case* (n 3) para [45]. Compare V. Korah 'Gencor *v* Commission: collective dominance' (1999) 20 European Competition Law Review 337; G. Niels 'Collective dominance: more than just oligopolistic interdependence' (2001) 22 European Competition Law Review 172; L. McGregor 'The future for the control of oligopolies following *Compagnie Maritime Belge*' (2001) 22 European Competition Law Review 437.

This controversy has, however, largely been resolved following the CFI's decision in *Airtours v. Commission*, where it was concluded that mere oligopolistic interdependence is insufficient for a finding of collective dominance.[7] The Court ruled that to show collective dominance: (1) the market structure must be conducive to tacit coordination, and (2) market participants must be both able, and likely to have incentives, to coordinate their behaviour which can be assumed to exist under three conditions which are derived from game theory. [8] These conditions, which are cumulative, are that:

- Each member of the dominant oligopoly has the ability to know how the other members are behaving in order to monitor whether or not they are adopting the common policy. That is, there must be sufficient market transparency for all members of the dominant oligopoly to be aware, sufficiently precisely and quickly, of the way in which the other members' market conduct is evolving;
- There are adequate deterrents to ensure there is a long-term incentive in not departing from the common policy; and
- The foreseeable reaction of current and future competitors, as well as consumers, does not jeopardise the results expected from the common policy.

The 2004 change to the substantive test under the revised ECMR has also clarified the position, as the merger regulation now unambiguously covers mergers in oligopolistic industries that are likely to result in the creation or strengthening of a collective dominant position as well as mergers where non-coordinated effects may arise.[9]

3.2.2 Collective Dominance in European Merger Law

The primary way that European law addresses the 'oligopoly problem' is through merger control. This control seeks to regulate changes to the structure of different industries, and thereby limit the *potential* for collective dominance to develop, by deciding whether undertakings should be able to

[7] Compare A. Overd 'After the Airtours appeal' (2002) 23 European Competition Law Review 375.

[8] Case T-342/99 *Airtours plc v Commission of the European Communities* [2002] ECR II-02585 para [62] (*Airtours v Commission*).

[9] Commission guidelines on the assessment of horizontal mergers under the Council Regulation on the control of concentrations between undertakings [2004] OJ C31/5 para [25].

combine their activities through merger.[10] Widely perceived difficulties in addressing the effects of coordinated behaviour *ex post* through the use of Article 82 has led to a greater emphasis on the *ex ante* use of merger control to prevent market structures developing which could facilitate such behaviour.[11] Consequently, it is in the *prospective* assessment of mergers under the ECMR that the concept of collective dominance has most frequently featured under European law.

Application of the ECMR

The ECMR applies to all concentrations[12] with a community dimension.[13] The substantive merger test upon which concentrations are appraised as compatible with the common market is contained within Article 2 of the ECMR.[14]

> Article 2
> 2. A concentration which would not significantly impede effective competition in the common market or in a substantial part of it, in particular as a result of the creation or strengthening of a dominant position, shall be declared compatible with the common market.
> 3. A concentration which would significantly impede effective competition, in the common market or in a substantial part of it, in particular as a result of the creation or strengthening of a dominant position, shall be declared incompatible with the common market.

---

[10] The merger regulation is based on the presumption that a dominant position would be abused if it is achieved: Compare D. Neven, R. Nuttall and P. Seabright *Mergers in Daylight: The Economics and Politics of European Merger Control* (Centre for Economic Policy Research, London, 1993) 6.

[11] The difficulty in enforcing Article 82 may reflect a general presumption of innocence that characterises legal systems and the fear of Type I errors (false positives): mistaking collusion for competition. Compare D.J. Neven '"Collusion" under Art 81 and the merger regulation' (paper presented at the 3rd Nordic Competition Policy Conference, Stockholm, 11 September 2000) 9; D. Neven, P. Papandropoulos and P. Seabright *Trawling for Minnows: European Competition Policy and Agreements between Firms* (Centre for Economic Policy Research, London, 1998) 52.

[12] A concentration may be a merger, an acquisition or full-function joint venture: Article 3 of Council Regulation (EC) No 139/2004 of 20 January 2004 on the control of concentrations between undertakings (the EC Merger Regulation) OJ L24/1.

[13] This is determined on the basis of worldwide and community turnover thresholds: Article 1(2)(3) of Council Regulation (EC) No 139/2004 of 20 January 2004 on the control of concentrations between undertakings (the EC Merger Regulation) OJ L24/1. Article 9 allows for referrals back to Member States.

[14] In the 1998 ECMR, which was applicable at the time at which some of the research for this book was conducted, these tests were based on whether the concentration created or strengthened a dominant position as a result of which effective competition would be significantly impeded in the common market or in a substantial part of it.

The current merger regulation was introduced in 2004 and amended the substantive test from a test based on 'the creation or strengthening of a dominant position' to a test based on whether a merger would 'significantly impede effective competition ... in particular as a result of the creation or strengthening of a dominant position'.[15] The change in the substantive test does not affect the status of the application of old case law based on the 'dominance' test, and despite the fact that it broadens the Commission's powers to block mergers in oligopolistic markets, enforcement officials and other practitioners do not consider this will result in a substantive change to how mergers are assessed in practice.[16]

The ECMR and collective dominance

Historically the question of whether the concept of dominance in the ECMR could be extended to apply to more than one undertaking was controversial.[17] Initially, it was argued that mergers which resulted in the creation or strengthening of a collective dominant position could not be prohibited under the ECMR.[18] However, recent Commission and Court decisions have interpreted the notion of dominance in the ECMR as including situations where a merger will create or strengthen a collective dominant position.[19]

---

15 Article 2 of Council Regulation (EC) No 139/2004 of 20 January 2004 on the control of concentrations between undertakings (the EC Merger Regulation) OJ L24/1. In addition, significant procedural changes were introduced. Somewhat curiously despite the revision to the ECMR, the language of Article 2 does not expressly provide for its application to cases of collective dominance. This is despite a number of Court decisions referring to collective dominance, and the express acknowledgment by the Commission in 1987 that 'it should be the aim of competition policy to prevent situations arising which form a hotbed for tacitly collusive behavior. This is one of the objectives of the proposal for the prior control of mergers at Community level': European Commission *XVIth Report on Competition Policy* (Luxembourg Office for Official Publications of the European Communities 1987) para [333].

16 Compare Commission of the European Communities 'Merger control: Merger review package in a nutshell' 1; U. Böge and E. Muller 'From the market dominance test to the SLC test: are there any reasons for a change' (2002) 23 European Competition Law Review 497; Freshfields Bruckhaus Deringer 'New EC merger regime: a director's overview' (client briefing April 2004) 1.

17 Compare D. Ridyard 'Joint dominance and the oligopoly blind spot under the EC Merger Regulation' (1992) 13 European Competition Law Review 164.

18 Most notably by Advocate General Tesauro in: Joined cases C-68/94 and C-30/95 *French Republic and Société commerciale des potasses et de l'azote (SCPA) and Entreprise minière et chimique (EMC) v Commission of the European Communities* Opinion of Mr Advocate General Tesauro delivered on 6 February 1997 [1998] ECR I-01375 para [78]; also A. Winckler and M. Hansen 'Collective dominance under the EC Merger Control Regulation' (1993) 30 Common Market Law Review 816, 828.

19 Joined cases C-68/94 and C-30/95 *French Republic and Société commerciale des potasses et de l'azote (SCPA) and Entreprise minière et chimique (EMC) v*

The Commission assesses a concentration on the basis of the effect on competition in the common market. In order to assess the potential for a collective dominant position to be created or strengthened through merger, the Commission is required to define a relevant market.[20] To prohibit a merger on the basis of collective dominance the Commission must then show that effective competition in that market will be significantly impeded through the creation or strengthening of a collective dominant position following the merger.

The Courts have stressed that, in assessing collective dominance, it is necessary to show that undertakings involved in the concentration, and one or more other undertakings, are together able to adopt a common policy on the market and act to a considerable extent independently of their competitors, their customers, and also of consumers.[21] In the one decision where the Court has upheld the Commission's assessment of collective dominance it noted that it was *not* necessary to show that any contractual or other structural links existed between the parties for a finding of collective dominance; mere oligopolistic interdependence was sufficient. [22] This decision broadened the concept of 'collective dominance' from the notion initially developed under Article 82,[23] allowing for a finding of collective dominance on the basis of the oligopolistic interdependence that exists in concentrated market structures, without the need to show any structural links.[24]

Although it is no longer necessary to demonstrate that structural links exist for a finding of collective dominance to be made, in order to prohibit a merger the Commission must adduce sufficient evidence to demonstrate that the *likelihood* that firms will tacitly coordinate their behaviour post-merger is high, or in the case of the decision to allow a merger, that the likelihood of tacit coordination post-merger is low.[25] In practice, this has proved a difficult burden for

---

Commission of the European Communities [1998] ECR I-01375 para [166] (*France v Commission*). It has been noted that this was to overcome the potential anomaly whereby a number of Member States have mechanisms for assessing oligopolies in mergers and yet at the European level no mechanism was available, and consequently 'large' mergers avoided such an assessment: J.Ysewyn and C. Caffara 'Two's company, three's a crowd: the future of collective dominance after the Kali & Salz judgment' (1998) 19 European Competition Law Review 469.

[20] *France v Commission* (n 19) para [143].

[21] *France v Commission* (n 19) para [221].

[22] *Gencor v Commission* (n 6) para [276].

[23] *Gencor v Commission* (n 6) para [273]–[277]. However, following the decision in *Compagnie maritime belge case* (n 3) the concepts are more in line.

[24] Compare Ysewyn and Caffara (n 19) 470.

[25] Compare P. Christensen and P. Owen 'Comment on the judgement of the Court of First Instance of 25 March 1999 in the merger case IV/M.619 – Gencor/Lonrho' (1999) Competition Directorate-General of the European Commission Competition Policy Newsletter, June 1999, page 19.

the Commission to discharge, and the Commission's approach to the assessment of the potential for tacit coordination to arise (or not arise) post-merger has been strongly criticised,[26] and rejected in three of the seven decisions relating to collective dominance that have been appealed to the Courts.[27]

3.2.3 Collective Dominance under Article 82 of the EC Treaty

A second way in which European law addresses the 'oligopoly problem' is by prohibiting certain conduct and behaviour by firms who collectively already hold a dominant position.

The substantive provision

Article 82 of the EC Treaty provides that (emphasis added):

> Any abuse by one *or more* undertakings of a dominant position within the common market or a substantial part of it shall be prohibited as incompatible with the common market insofar as it may affect trade between Member States.

The key elements of Article 82 for our purposes are as follows:

1. One or more undertakings
   The concept of an 'undertaking' has been widely construed by the European Courts to encompass 'every entity engaged in economic activity regardless of legal status of the entity'.[28] It is unclear if Article 82 was originally intended to apply to oligopolistic dominance or only to abuses of a single dominant position.[29] The initial interpretation given to the terms 'or more undertakings' by the Courts and the Commission was restricted to bodies that formed part of the same economic or corporate group.[30] Subsequently, however, the Court determined that there was 'no legal or economic reason' not to apply Article 82 to the conduct of two or

---

26 *Airtours v Commission* (n 8) para [294]; Case T-464/04 *Independent Music Publishers and Labels Association (Impala, International Association) v Commission of the European Communities* [2006] ECR II-02289 (*Impala v Commission*).

27 *Airtours v Commission* (n 8) paras [182]–[295]; *France v Commission* (n 19) paras [179]–[250]; *Impala v Commission* (n 26) paras [526]–[528].

28 Case C-41/90 *Höfner and Elser v. Macroton* [1991] ECR I-1979 para [21]

29 Most notably see the application of the United Kingdom acting as Intervener in: Joined cases T-68/89, T-77/89 and T-78/89 *Società Italiana Vetro SpA, Fabbrica Pisana SpA and PPG Vernante Pennitalia SpA v Commission of the European Communities* [1992] ECR II-01403 paras [340]–[345] (*Italian Flat Glass v Commission case*).

30 Case C-85/76 *Hoffman-La Roche & Co. AG v. Commission* [1979] ECR 461 para [39] (*Hoffman-La Roche case*).

more independent economic entities who are united by 'links' such that together they hold a collectively dominant position in a market.[31]

2. Dominant position

In their interpretation of dominance,[32] the Commission and the Courts have focused on the ability of an undertaking to: act independently of competitors, purchasers and suppliers;[33] prevent effective competition by virtue of its ability to act independently of its competitors and customers;[34] and to influence the conditions of competition in the relevant market.[35]

In order to assess dominance, a relevant market must first be defined.[36] Factors that have been considered in assessing both single and collective dominance in a relevant market have included: market shares;[37] levels of vertical integration; conduct; economies of scale; profits; access to important inputs; advertising and reputation; superior technology and efficiency; and overall size and strength. [38] In addition to the factors noted above, in assessing cases of collective dominance, the Courts have emphasised the

---

31 *Italian Flat Glass v Commission case* (n 29) para [357]–[358]; Case C-393/92 *Municipality of Almelo and others v NV Energiebedrijf Ijsselmij* [1994] ECR I-01477 para [42]–[43] (*Gemente Almelo case*).

32 It is noteworthy that the concept of 'dominance' has no technical meaning in economics. However, there is a close relationship between the legal concept of dominance and the economic concept of 'market power', and economics provides a number of 'tools' that allow market power to be measured. The economic concept of market power, therefore, provides a way of looking at the legal concept of dominance, including collective dominance: Compare J.P. Azevedo and M. Walker 'Dominance: meaning and measurement' (2002) 23 European Competition Law Review 367; W. Baxter 'Substantive review under merger regulation' in B. Hawk (ed.) *International Antitrust Law & Policy: Fordham Corporate Law 1990* (Juris Publishing, New, York 1990) 564; Christensen and Rabassa (n 2) 228, Ridyard (n 17) 161; Ysewyn & Caffara (n 19) 469.

33 *Re Continental Can Co Inc* (Case IV/26 811) [1972] JO L 7/25 part II B para 3; *Chiquita* (Case IV/26 699) [1976] OJ L095 1 para A2.

34 Case C-27/76 *United Brands Co and United Brands Continental BV v. Commission* [1978] ECR 207 para [65] (*United Brands case*).

35 *Hoffman-La Roche case* (n 30) paras [38]–[39].

36 Case C-6/72 *Europemballage Corp and Continental Can Co Inc v Commission* [1973] ECR 215 para [42] (*Continental Can case*).

37 The ECJ held that a market share above 50 per cent creates a presumption of dominance: *Hoffman-La Roche case* (n 30) para [41]; Case T-30/89 *Hilti AG v. Commission* [1991] ECR II 1439 paras [91]–[94](*Hilti case*); Case T-83/91 *Tetra Pak Rausing SA v. Commission* (Tetra Pak II) [1994] ECR II-755 paras [109]–[110] (*Tetra Pak II case*); Case C-62/86 *AKZO Chemie BV v. Commission* [1991] ECR I-3359 paras [59]–[60] (*AKZO case*).

38 These factors, and the relevant cases, are considered in detail in: A. Jones and B. Sufrin (n 2) 302–316; R. Whish *Competition Law* (4th edn Butterworths, London, 2001) 156–161.

need to examine any 'links'[39] or 'other connecting factors'[40] between undertakings which may be indicative of the adoption of a uniform or common conduct on the market. As discussed earlier, the Courts' view on whether mere oligopolistic interdependence is a sufficient link between undertakings has varied over time. In recent decisions under Article 82, the Courts have implied that oligopolistic interdependence, in certain market structures, can constitute a sufficient connecting factor between undertakings for a finding of collective dominance.[41] However, the question of exactly what 'structural conditions' might allow for a finding of collective dominance – in the absence of other links – under Article 82 remains unresolved.[42]

3. Abuse of a dominant position

Although the term 'abuse' is not defined within Article 82, the provision sets out a non-exhaustive list of possible examples of abusive conduct. These include: (1) imposing unfair purchase or selling prices; (2) limiting production, markets or technical development to the prejudice of consumers; (3) applying dissimilar conditions to equivalent transactions; and (4) making the conclusion of contracts subject to supplementary obligations which have no connection with the nature of the contract. In interpreting Article 82, the Courts have continually emphasised that an abuse is conduct that does not constitute 'normal competition'.[43] However, distinguishing between 'normal' and 'abusive' conduct by focusing on the effects on a market is both complex and controversial.[44]

The Courts have defined the notion of 'abuse' as an objective concept.[45] This has been interpreted to mean that it is not necessary to show that the dominant undertaking has used its dominant position,[46] and that the Court

---

39 Examples of such 'links' which might include agreements or licences, or a technological lead: *Italian Flat Glass v Commission case* (n 29) para [358].

40 *Compagnie maritime belge case* (n 3) para [45].

41 Ibid.; Compare C. Withers and M. Jephcott 'Where to now for E.C oligopoly control?' (2001) 8 European Competition Law Review 303.

42 Compare L. McGregor (n 6).

43 Case C-322/81 *Nederlandsche Banden-Industrie Michelin NV v. Commission* [1983] ECR 3461 para [701] (*Michelin case*); *Hoffman-La Roche case* (n 30) para [91].

44 Compare Weatherill and Beaumont who argue that the notion of abuse is: 'simultaneously unstructured and potentially unsophisticated. It leaves a considerable degree of discretion vested in the competition authorities to supervise dominant firms in accordance with their own perceptions of proper market development': S. Weatherill and P. Beaumont *EU Law* (3rd edn, Penguin, London, 1999) 848.

45 *Hoffman-La Roche case* (n 30) para [91].

46 Case T-51/89 *Tetra Pak Rausing SA v. Commission* [1991] ECR II-309 para [64].

will look at the effect of the conduct, rather than the reasons for it (i.e. intent). Broadly, the conduct of a dominant undertaking can be deemed abusive in two ways. [47] First, conduct that exploits the dominant position of an undertaking, such as charging unfair prices or limiting production has been adjudged abusive. Second, and more commonly, anti-competitive behaviour that weakens competition on a market and affects the competitive process, for example by excluding actual or potential competitors, has been found to be abusive.[48] In their judgments, the Courts have continually looked at the alleged abusive behaviour through the lens of the 'special responsibility' that dominant firms have towards the competitive process.[49] However, the Courts and Commission have accepted that dominant undertakings do have a right to engage in conduct to defend their commercial interests[50] – for example, to reflect cost savings – albeit on a reasonable and proportionate basis.[51]

There is some debate as to whether the notion of 'abuse' that applies to single-dominance is the same as the notion of 'abuse' that would apply in

---

[47] Examples of abuses of a single dominant and collective dominant position considered by the Courts include: excessive pricing (*United Brands case* (n 34) para [267]); low pricing (Case C-298/83 *CICCE v. Commission* [1985] ECR 1105 para [2]); predatory pricing (*AKZO case* (n 37) paras [66]–[74]; *Compagnie maritime belge case* (n 3) para [137]); price discrimination (*United Brands case* (n 34) paras [204]–[234]) including through discount and rebate schemes (*Italian Flat Glass v Commission case* (n 29) paras [197]–[202]; *Hoffman-La Roche case* (n 30) paras [89]–[90]; *Michelin case* (n 43) paras [73]–[86]); exclusive contracts (Case T-65/89 *BPB Industries PLC and British Gypsum Ltd v. Commission* [1993] ECR II-00389 para [94] (*British Gypsum case*); *Hilti case* (n 37) paras [115]–[119]); and refusal to supply (*Italian Flat Glass v Commission case)* (n 29) paras [23]–[29]; a dominant position and the abuse may occur in different markets (*Michelin case*) (n 43) paras [66]–[86]; *Tetra Pak II case* (n 37) paras [25]–[31]; a third potential type of abuse relates to conduct which is harmful to the single market: [Joined cases C-40–48,50,54–56,11,113,114/73 *Cooperatiëve Vereniging Suiker Unie UA v. Commission (European Sugar Cartel)* [1975] ECR 1663 para [33].

[48] *Continental Can case* (n 36) paras [19]–[27]; *Hoffman-La Roche case* (n 30) para [91]; *Michelin case* (n 43) para [70].

[49] *Michelin case* (n 43) para [57]; In the *Compagnie maritime belge case* (n 3) para [112]–[119] this 'special responsibility' not to engage in abusive behaviour was held to be particularly great where an undertaking is 'super dominant'.

[50] *British Gypsum case* (n 47) para [69].

[51] The notions of objective justification and proportionality are applied in assessing potential abuses to distinguish legitimate business conduct from illegitimate business conduct: Case C-311/84 *Centre Belge d'Etudes du Marché Télémarketing v CLT and Information Publicile Benelux SA* [1985] ECR 3261 para [26]; *Eurofix-Bauco v Hilti* (Case No. IV/30.787 and 31.488) [1988] OJ L65/19 paras [78]–[83]. However the accepted conduct is related to the strength of the dominant position: *Compagnie maritime belge case* (n 3) para [137].

collective dominance cases. That is, whether it is possible, and appropriate, to directly transpose the 'abuses' developed in the jurisprudence of single-firm dominance cases to collective dominance cases.[52] Arguably, a consideration of single dominance abuses is relevant insofar as the Court has, in one decision, held that a single undertaking, which holds a collective dominant position with other undertakings, is capable of engaging in abusive conduct.[53]

Powers of enforcement

The powers of the Commission to initiate and conduct formal proceedings, and impose remedies, in respect of Article 82 is detailed in Regulation 1/2003.[54] The remedies available to the Commission on establishing that a violation of Article 82 has occurred include: an order to cease and desist the abusive conduct,[55] and the imposition of fines on the undertaking up to 10 per cent of its turnover in the preceding year of business.[56]

Article 82 also has direct effect, meaning that it is possible for private actions to be instituted in, and awards of damages sought from, national courts in Member States.

3.2.4 Other Ways of Addressing the Oligopoly Problem

There are two other legal provisions that could potentially be used to address the oligopoly problem under European law. These are: the prohibition against concerted practices under Article 81(1) of the EC Treaty,[57] and the market

---

[52] A. Jones and B. Sufrin (n 2) 691–692.

[53] Case T-228/97 *Irish Sugar plc v Commission of the European Communities* [1999] ECR II-02969 para [66]. Compare J. Temple Lang 'Fundamental issues concerning abuse under Article 82 EC' (paper presented to the Oxford Competition Conference, 12 July 2005) 30.

[54] At the time to which some of the research in the following chapters relates the formal powers of the Commission to initiate and conduct formal proceedings, and impose remedies, in respect of Article 82 was detailed in Regulation 17/62. The main substantive change was to provide for a system of parallel competence between the Commission and Member States in the application of Article 81(3) of the Treaty.

[55] Article 7 of Council Regulation (EC) No 1/2003 of 16 December 2002 on the implementation of the rules of competition laid down in Articles 81 and 82 of the Treaty [2003] OJ L1/1.

[56] Article 23 Council Regulation (EC) No 1/2003 of 16 December 2002 on the implementation of the rules of competition laid down in Articles 81 and 82 of the Treaty [2003] OJ L1/1.

[57] A detailed discussion of concerted practices and can be found in Chapter 2 of Neven, Papandropoulos and Seabright (n 11) 57.

investigation powers of the Commission under Article 17 of Regulation 1/2003.[58] Both of these instruments have rarely been used in practice to address tacit coordination and they are not considered in the analysis presented in this research.[59]

3.2.5 Summary

The two principal legal vehicles for addressing the potential for tacit coordination and its effects in oligopolistic industries under European law are Article 82 of the EC Treaty and the ECMR.

The ECMR provides an *ex ante* method of using merger control to prevent market structures developing which could facilitate tacit coordination. Article 82 provides an *ex post* method for addressing the effects of coordinated behaviour by prohibiting collectively dominant undertakings from engaging in certain types of conduct. The scope of the legal concept of collective dominance under both Article 82 and the ECMR, and in particular how it relates to the economic notion of oligopolistic interdependence, has at times been unclear. In part, this stems from the fact that the concept of collective dominance is not directly derived from the wording of either Article 82 or the ECMR. Consequently, it has been left to the Courts and the Commission to extend, and interpret, these provisions to capture the potential for tacit coordination in oligopolistic markets.

---

[58] Formerly, Article 12 of Regulation 17/62. The European Commissioner for Competition indicated from the beginning of her appointment that she intended to use the sectoral investigation powers more frequently. Accordingly, sector investigations have recently been undertaken into the financial services, energy and pharmaceutical markets: N. Kroes 'Taking competition seriously – anti-trust reform in Europe' (paper presented at the International Bar Association/European Commission Conference 'Antitrust reform in Europe: a year in practice', 10 March 2005) 4.

[59] However, the sector inquiries have in some cases identified issues regarding possible collusion in markets. For example, the final report of the sector inquiry in the energy sector identified the possibility of collusion by incumbents to share markets. Similarly, the Commission inquiry into retail banking considered the possibility that product tying would constitute an abuse of a collective dominant position: Commission staff working document – Accompanying the Communication from the Commission – Sector Inquiry under Article 17 of Regulation (EC) No 1/2003 on retail banking (Final Report) COM(2007) (31 January 2007); Commission of the European Communities Commission 'Commission energy sector inquiry confirms serious competition problems' Press release IP/07/26 (10 January 2007).

3.3 THE ECONOMICS OF TACIT COLLUSION

3.3.1 Introduction

As we saw in Chapter 2, the economics of tacit collusion represents more of a theoretical paradigm than a unified 'theory' insofar as it comes in several forms – represented by a mass of models – but each form has a common set of features and assumptions. A unifying assumption of all of these models is that interdependence between firms in oligopolistic market structures can, under certain conditions, present possibilities for both competitive and collusive behaviour. Oligopoly theory presents explanations of how this tension between competition and cooperation can be expected to be resolved in different contexts and environments, and therefore presents a potential reference point for the assessments that need to be made under the collective dominance laws described above.

Given the complex trade-off oligopoly theory is attempting to explain, it is perhaps not surprising that there are many theories relating to oligopoly behaviour in economics, with no common or unified theory being universally accepted.[60] Nevertheless, it is possible to identify two broad methodological approaches to examining oligopolistic behaviour in economics. These approaches can be distinguished on the basis of whether they adopt a 'pure', or formal axiomatic, approach to examining oligopolistic interaction, or whether they are empirically developed theories on the basis of the collection and analysis of real-world data.

3.3.2 'Pure' Oligopoly Theories

Formal or 'pure' models of oligopoly behaviour have changed over time. Early 'static' models produced predictions about how we should expect oligopolistic firms to behave in a given period, and what equilibrium will prevail, but did not provide any explanation of *why* firms should be expected

---

60 Bork notes that 'there appear to be as many oligopoly theories as there are economists who have written on the subject': R.H. Bork *The Antitrust Paradox: A Policy at War with Itself* (Free Press, New York, 1993) 102. Similarly, Shapiro notes 'The various modern theories of oligopoly behavior are essentially a set of different games that have been analyzed; these games do not represent competing theories, but rather models relevant in different industries or circumstances': C. Shapiro 'Theories of oligopoly behavior' in R. Schmalensee and R.D. Willig (eds) *Handbook of Industrial Organization, Volume 1* (Elsevier Science Publishers, Amsterdam, 1989) 332.

to behave in this way.[61] In addition they suffered from the limitation that they modelled oligopoly behaviour in a *static* context (i.e. focused on one period).

'Dynamic' theories of oligopoly introduced game theoretic concepts to model oligopolistic behaviour.[62] Dynamic theories contemplate firms employing complex strategies in making decisions based upon what has occurred in previous periods, and in particular whether any competitors have breached a collusive agreement in a previous period.[63] These dynamic theories of oligopoly and tacit collusion model the repeated interaction of firms as a series of 'games'.[64] The general aim of modelling these 'games' is to predict how firms will behave, and what outcomes will prevail, in different contexts and under different behavioural assumptions. A common behavioural assumption underlying these models is that firms recognise their interdependence and that when they interact they do so with a tacit understanding to maximise joint profits. However, should a firm deviate from this tacit understanding to increase individual profits, for example by charging a lower price or increasing production, this will introduce a period of intensive *competition* to punish the deviating firm.

---

61 Put simply, the intuition behind these models is that each seller in an oligopoly attempts to maximise its individual profits subject to the fixed outputs (prices) of the other sellers. The earliest of these 'static' models, the Cournot model, examines a firm's decision as to its level of production in a specific period, which requires it to make an assessment of the production levels of its competitors. An alternative theory of oligopolistic interaction based on price rather than quantity, the Bertrand model, focuses on a firm's decision as to price based on its assessment of what price it believes its competitors will charge. The focus on price rather than quantity decisions results in very different predictions about oligopoly behaviour. Later models developed this framework to take account of firms that have limited capacity to produce in a given period (Edgeworth), or to allow for differences in timing between the output choices of the firms in a market (Stackelberg): A.A. Cournot *Researches into the Mathematical Principles of the Theory of Wealth* translated by N.T. Bacon (Macmillan, New York, 1897); J. Bertrand 'Théorie mathématique de la richesse sociale'(1883) 67 Journal des Savants 499; F. Edgeworth 'The pure theory of monopoly' in F. Edgeworth (ed.) *Papers Relating to Political Economy* (Macmillan, London, 1925) 111; H. von Stackelberg *Marktform und Gleichgewicht* (Springer, Vienna, 1934).

62 According to some economists, these dynamic theories also addressed some of the perceived inadequacies of static models: compare P.L. Joskow 'Firm decision-making processes and oligopoly theory' (1975) 65 American Economic Review 278; D. Fudenberg and J. Tirole 'Understanding rent dissipation: on the use of game theory in industrial organization' (1987) 77 American Economic Review 176.

63 Stigler is often attributed with the introduction of this dynamic approach: G.J. Stigler 'A theory of oligopoly' (1964) 72 Journal of Political Economy 44.

64 These are known as 'supergames' in the literature: J.W. Friedman 'A non-cooperative equilibrium for supergames' (1971) 38 Review of Economics and Statistics 1.

Dynamic theories of oligopoly therefore provide simple conditions under which we should expect to see tacit collusion sustained as equilibrium in a market by focusing on the temptation to cheat on tacitly collusive agreements. These models formalise the intuition that firms will tacitly collude if the sum of the profits that each firm derives under the tacitly collusive behaviour is *greater than* the profits a firm would derive from deviating from this behaviour in one period (and earning a high profit in that period) plus the profits that are derived by the firm during the punishment phase that follows. That is, we should expect to see tacit collusion in markets where the short-run gain from breaking the agreement is *less* than the long-run cost of the breakdown of the tacit agreement.[65] These models have become known in the literature as the folk theorem(s).[66]

A general result of these dynamic models of oligopoly is that where firms meet on an infinite number of occasions, and where there are no significant lags to reacting to a rival's behaviour, there may be *many* possible equilibrium

---

[65] Other relevant factors that influence whether the short-run gain from deviation is greater than the long term loss from the tacit agreement breaking down include: the rate of interest (as this is applied to discount future cash flows), how often the firms make decisions regarding price and output levels, the ability to detect and swiftly punish transgressors and the severity of the punishment payoff that is enforced in the event of deviation from the tacitly agreed equilibrium.

[66] Compare D.M. Kreps *Game Theory and Economic Modelling* (Clarendon Press, Oxford, 1990) 75–76. Friedman presents one version of the folk theorem where the future is discounted and the game is played infinitely. Aumann, Shapley and Rubinstein examine the folk theorem where there is no discounting, but where a hierarchy of punishments is used to coerce all parties to participate in the punishment phase. Fudenberg, Levine and Maskin extend the folk theorem to games of moral hazard, and specifically examine the case in which players can only observe public information about other players' actions. Finally, Fudenberg and Maskin examine the folk theorem in games of finite length and incomplete information about the possible actions of their opponents: Friedman (n 64) 1; R.J. Aumann and L.S. Shapley 'Long-term competition – a game theoretic analysis' (Economics Working Papers No 676, UCLA, September 23 1992) and A. Rubinstein 'Equilibrium in supergames with the overtaking criterion' (1979) 21 Journal of Economic Theory 1; D. Fudenberg, D.K. Levine and E. Maskin 'The folk theorem with imperfect public information' (1994) 62 Econometrica 997; D. Fudenberg and E. Maskin 'The folk theorem in repeated games with discounting or with incomplete information' (1986) 54 Econometrica 533. There are also a series of so-called 'Anti-folk theorem' papers which show that in certain settings, such as where firms have imperfect knowledge of each other's behaviour and cannot therefore coordinate a switch to a punishment phase where necessary, the folk theorem will not apply: M. Kaneko 'Some remarks on the folk-theorem in game theory' (1982) 3 Mathematical Social Sciences 281; J. Masso and R.W. Rosenthal 'More on the "anti-folk theorem"' (1989) 18 Journal of Mathematical Economics 281.

points which support tacit collusion.[67] In addition, any equilibrium point between monopoly and a competitive equilibrium could potentially be sustained by tacit collusion provided that the payoff to a firm from deviating from the agreement, and the resulting punishment, is less than the payoff for the firm in staying party to that tacit agreement. [68] Some economists consider that, for these reasons, tacit collusion may be a common occurrence in oligopolistic markets, and that tacit collusion can be sustained independent of the number of competitors or the demand conditions in the market, with the key condition being simply that firms can detect and respond to any cheating.[69] These economists argue that: 'the theoretical possibilities for tacit collusion are therefore large . . . It is hard to conceive of a real-world situation that is not characterised by one of these conditions'.[70] However other economists argue that the conditions necessary to sustain tacit collusion vary significantly across markets and that collusion may, in fact, be impossible for many firms.[71]

The methodology of game-theoretic oligopoly theory

It is useful to briefly consider the methodological approach underlying the construction, and consequent predictions, of game-theoretic models of tacit collusion. This is because, as we will see later, many of the predictions of models employing game theoretic approaches have been influential in the enforcement of the collective dominance laws. Stated simply, game theory uses formal models to *predict* outcomes where there is interdependence between different parties in a given situation. This focus on interdependence between parties suggests it is well suited to a study of oligopoly behaviour. Accordingly, the game theoretical approach is often seen as providing a useful taxonomy for economic contexts and situations (through the use of highly simplified games,

---

67 A full technical description is presented in: D. Fudenberg and J. Tirole 'Noncooperative game theory for industrial organization: an introduction and overview' in R. Schmalensee and R.D. Willig (eds) *Handbook of Industrial Organization, Volume 1* (Elsevier Science Publishers, Amsterdam, 1989) 278–288.

68 Friedman (n 64) 11 sees any equilibrium between the monopoly and Cournot–Nash equilibrium as sustainable; J. Tirole *The Theory of Industrial Organization* (MIT Press, Cambridge, MA, 1988) 246 extends the theory to any equilibrium between the monopoly and competitive price also being sustainable using the Bertrand equilibrium concept.

69 Shapiro (n 60) 364.

70 A. Jacquemin and M.E. Slade 'Cartels, collusion and horizontal merger' in R. Schmalensee and R.D. Willig (eds) *Handbook of Industrial Organization, Volume 1* (Elsevier Science Publishers, Amsterdam, 1989) 443.

71 Stigler (n 63) 44; OECD Directorate for Financial, Fiscal and Enterprise Affairs Committee on Competition Law and Policy 'Oligopoly' (Unclassified Document DAFFE/CLP(99) 25 October 1999) 34.

such as the often cited Prisoner's Dilemma game), to provide insights into the possible forms that future interaction between firms may take.[72]

The methodological approach of game theoretic oligopoly theory is both abstract and mathematical. It employs models of games to *deduce* what might be expected to happen in a specific context by building upon an 'intuitive insight in one context' and extending it to other more complex settings.[73] In particular, it is the Nash notion of equilibrium – a position at which it would not be in the self-interest of any of the parties to deviate – that is by far the most informative and useful for game theoreticians.[74] However, its usefulness is limited in many contexts by the possibility of more than one equilibrium solution, referred to in the literature as multiple equilibria.[75] To overcome the problem of multiple equilibria, stricter behavioural standards, known as refinements, are often employed which restrict the possible actions that a firm may take into the future to what seems to the author to be reasonable or rational.

There are two principal difficulties associated with game theoretic approaches to modelling tacit collusion. The first, as noted above, is the indeterminacy associated with the multiple equilibria which are predicted by many of these models, which has been called an 'embarrassment of riches' by some and 'theoretical chaos' by others.[76] A second, and related, issue is that when refinements are introduced to overcome such indeterminacy, these new assumptions are typically so abstract as to create a disjunction between the theory and real world oligopolistic markets.[77]

3.3.3 Empirical Oligopoly Theories

Early empirical models of collusion focused on applying specific structural and performance indicators to different industries in order to infer which industries were potentially colluding. This approach focused on testing various hypotheses about collusion using empirical models that incorporated

---

[72] Compare Kreps (n 66) 41.

[73] Kreps (n 66) 133.

[74] J.F. Nash 'Non-cooperative games' (1951) 54 Annals of Mathematics 286.

[75] That is, given the specification of the game theoretic model there may be a number of possible steady state outcomes from which each party will not have an incentive to deviate.

[76] Compare S. Peltzman 'The Handbook of Industrial Organization: A Review Article' (1991) 99 Journal of Political Economy 206; F.M. Fisher 'Games economists play: a noncooperative view' (1989) 20 RAND Journal of Economics 117–118; Shapiro (n 60) 379; Jacquemin and Slade (n 70) 441.

[77] Compare Peltzman (n 76) 207; Kreps (n 66) 185; Fudenberg and Tirole (n 62) 176.

structural indicators as proxies for the potential for collusion, for example the models discussed below which tested the concentration–profits hypothesis.[78] Two characteristics of these models, which limited their predictive power, was the lack of an underlying 'theoretical apparatus', and the inadequacy of the data that tended to be employed.[79] In relation to the first characteristic, some economists have argued that because these models were primarily based on 'verbal-theoretic writings' or an 'oral tradition', there was 'no hard analytic theory formalising the structure–conduct–performance paradigm'.[80] As regards data, the models primarily employed industry-wide census data and as such did not focus on differences between firms. In addition they neglected factors such as internal organisation, policies and strategy and how they affected performance.

A relatively small number of studies have attempted to empirically test the conclusions of game-theoretic oligopoly theory in real world situations. Such studies of tacit collusion have examined the breakfast cereals, automobile, retail petrol, NASDAQ, airline industry and spectrum auction markets.[81] A number of other studies have retrospectively applied the conditions for collusion identified in game-theoretic oligopoly theory to real world examples of *explicit* collusion or cartels.[82]

---

78 J.S. Bain 'Relation of profit rate to industry concentration: American manufacturing, 1936–1940' (1951) 65 Quarterly Journal of Economics 294.

79 P. Asch, A. Phillips and J.W. McKie 'Discussion' (1970) 60 American Economic Review 105–108; Joskow (n 62) 270.

80 Fisher (n 76) 113; Joskow (n 62) 273.

81 L.S. Karp and J.M. Perloff 'Dynamic oligopoly in the rice export market' (1989) 71 Review of Economics and Statistics 462; L.S. Karp and J.M. Perloff 'A dynamic model of oligopoly in the coffee export market' (1993) 75 American Journal of Agricultural Economics 448; T.F. Bresnahan 'Competition and collusion in the American automobile industry: the 1955 price war' (1987) 35 Journal of Industrial Economics 457; P. Cramton and J.A. Schwartz 'Collusive bidding in the FCC spectrum auctions' (2002) 1 Contributions to Economic Analysis and policy 1; J. McMillan 'Selling spectrum rights' (1994) 8 Journal of Economic Perspectives 153; W.G. Christie and P.H. Schultz 'Why do NASDAQ market makers avoid odd-eighth quotes?' (1994) XLIX Journal of Finance 1813; M.E. Slade 'Interfirm rivalry in a repeated game: an empirical test of tacit collusion' (1987) 35 Journal of Industrial Economics 499; P.M. Parker and L.H. Röller 'Collusive conduct in duopolies: multimarket contact and cross-ownership in the mobile telephone industry' (1997) 28 RAND Journal of Economics 320; W.N. Evans and I.N. Kessides 'Living by the "Golden Rule": multimarket contact in the US airline industry' (1994) Quarterly Journal of Economics 343.

82 A.R. Dick 'Identifying contracts, combinations and conspiracies in restraint of trade' (1996) 17 Managerial and Decision Economics 203; M.C. Levenstein and V.Y. Suslow 'What determines cartel success?' (Working Paper No. 02–001, University of Michigan Business School, 31 January 2002); Office of Fair Trading 'Predicting cartels' (Economic discussion paper 19, Prepared by P.A. Grout and S. Sonderegger, March 2005).

Compared to the volume of formal or 'pure' theoretical work examining tacit collusion, the number of *empirical* studies of tacit collusion has been limited. This is attributable, in part, to the difficulties inherent in applying the abstract and simplified game theoretic models to real world data.

A growing stream of research is, however, focused on testing game theoretical models using observable market characteristics to specify 'bounds' as to the set of potential equilibrium outcomes. [83] In addition, there are a small number of merger-simulation models and approaches being developed which combine game theoretic oligopoly theory with computational and empirical methods to present quantitative based 'predictions' of changes in prices and quantities post-merger.[84] While, in their current state, these models are recognised to have a number of practical problems and limitations, it is argued by some that they represent an innovative instrument which may provide an important complement to traditional approaches in the future.[85]

3.3.4 Predictions of Economic Theory

Introduction

The previous section examined the methodological approach and broad conclusions of general theories of oligopolistic interaction. This section focuses on the specific predictions of these models, and in particular, what they say about when, and under what conditions, tacit collusion is more or less likely to occur.[86]

As we have seen, the economics of tacit collusion represents a theoretical paradigm that predicts, using a common set of features and assumptions, that

---

[83] J. Sutton 'Market structure: the bounds approach' in M. Armstrong and R. Porter (eds) *The Handbook of Industrial Organization, Volume 3* (forthcoming); A. Shaked and J. Sutton 'Multiproduct firms and market structure' (1990) 21 RAND Journal of Economic 45; J. Sutton 'Explaining everything, explaining nothing' (1990) 34 European Economic Review 505.

[84] Compare P. Davis 'Coordinated effects merger simulation with linear demands' (Competition Commission Working Paper April 2006); P. Sabbatini 'How to simulate the coordinated effect of a merger' Autorità Garante della Concorrenza e del Mercato, Temi e Problemi (2006).

[85] O. Budzinski and I. Ruhmer 'Merger simulation in competition policy: a Survey' (2008) Joint Discussion paper in Economics, University of Marburg.

[86] The Commission's interpretation of these models can be seen in: Commission Notice on the appraisal of horizontal mergers under the Council Regulation on the control of concentrations between undertakings COM (2002) paras [40]–[74]. Also the Commission's contribution to the OECD Roundtable on oligopoly: OECD Directorate for Financial, Fiscal and Enterprise Affairs Committee on Competition Law and Policy 'Oligopoly' (Unclassified Document DAFFE/CLP(99) 25 October 1999) 216–221.

tacit collusion may be sustained as equilibrium under a range of conditions in different market contexts.

It is accepted that there is considerable variation in the focus and approach of the individual models that constitute the tacit collusion paradigm in economics and that, taken as a whole, they do not provide a precise and consistent 'blueprint' for the conditions under which tacit collusion is likely to be observed and sustained. However, it is argued here, consistent with other studies, that at least in the application of competition law, there is a degree of consensus among economists regarding a core set of factors that are likely to facilitate or hinder tacit collusion.[87] In determining the extent of this consensus, I have considered 16 major surveys of economic factors seen to influence collusive behaviour. These surveys have been produced by academic institutes and economic consultants (Table A1.1); Member State enforcement authorities (Table A1.2); international organisations (Table A1.3); and leading industrial economists (Tables A1.4–A1.5). Table 3.1 presents a summary of the positions adopted in the 16 surveys as to which factors facilitate or hinder tacit collusion.

Table 3.1 shows that substantial consensus exists across the surveys in respect of certain factors (for example, frequency of interaction, stable demand, number of competitors, symmetrical costs, multi-market contacts, entry barriers, market transparency, technology/innovation, buyer power and retaliation mechanism). However, in respect of other factors, the surveys differ both as to the factor's relevance to an examination of tacit collusion (for example, prices and margins have been considered relevant in only one of 16 surveys), and the direction of effect of the factor (for example, product homogeneity has been found to both facilitate and have no clear effect on tacit collusion).

While the surveys provide a good starting point for an examination of economic theory in this area, they do not provide a full and sufficient reflection of the corpus of economic theory relating to tacit collusion. This is because such surveys have typically been: commissioned by specific enforcement bodies; published by the enforcement agencies themselves; or substantively

[87] The International Competition Network note, for example, that 'There is a large degree of consensus regarding the factors that are likely to lead to coordinated interaction'. Similarly, Europe Economics in its report for the European Commission note that there is 'wide consensus in economic literature and in anti-trust experience about the factors that are most relevant to potentially facilitate collusion': International Competition Network 'Coordinated effects analysis under international merger regimes' (working paper presented at the International Competition Network Annual Conference, April 2004) 20; Europe Economics 'Assessment criteria for distinguishing between competitive and dominant oligopolies in merger control' (Enterprise Papers No 6–2001 prepared for DG Enterprise, European Commission, 2001) 27.

Table 3.1 Position of surveys of factors that facilitate or hinder collusion

Factor	Facilitates	Hinders	No clear prediction	Not considered in survey	Total	Consensus position*
Frequent interaction	13	0	0	3	16	Facilitates
Market share symmetry	6	0	1	9	16	Not clear
Stable demand	13	0	0	3	16	Facilitates
Small no. of competitors	13	0	0	3	16	Facilitates
Market growth	3	4	0	9	16	Not clear
Product homogeneity	8	0	7	1	16	Not clear
Demand elasticity	5	0	2	9	16	Not clear
Removal of 'maverick'	6	0	0	10	16	Facilitates
Business cycle effects	0	4	0	12	16	Hinders
High market concentration	12	0	0	4	16	Facilitates
Symmetrical costs	15	0	0	1	16	Facilitates
Multi-market contacts	9	0	0	7	16	Facilitates
Prices and margins	1	0	0	15	16	Facilitates
Entry barriers	15	0	0	1	16	Facilitates
Market transparency	16	0	0	0	16	Facilitates
Technology/innovation	0	10	0	6	16	Hinders
Symmetrical capacity constraints	4	0	2	10	16	Not clear
Excess capacity	4	0	5	7	16	Not clear
Bidding procedures	0	0	5	11	16	Not clear
Buyer power	0	14	0	2	16	Hinders
Structural links	7	0	0	9	16	Facilitates
Club and network effects	0	1	0	15	16	Hinders
Ability to retaliate	13	0	0	3	16	Facilitates
Post-capacity expansion & R&D	0	0	2	14	16	Not clear
Volatile market shares	0	1	0	15	16	Hinders
Size and financial strength	8	0	1	7	16	Not clear
Vertical integration	9	0	0	7	16	Facilitates

Note: * The consensus position is here defined as the unanimous position of surveys that considered a particular factor. Where a less than unanimous interpretation of a factor appears the consensus position has been taken as not clear. Other definitions are clearly possible, and the classification adopted is arguably too definitive in those cases in which only a small number of studies have considered the factor. The most obvious 'small numbers' cases are prices and margins, club and network effects and volatility of market shares.

distilled for the purposes of presenting a summary of the area in textbooks or articles. A number of important considerations follow from these facts. First, the surveys are typically pitched at a high level and do not always address contextual nuances or possible multidirectional effects resulting from the interaction of factors. Second, the surveys do not systematically canvass empirical work undertaken in respect of specific factors. Third, where a factor has not been considered in a survey, it is not clear from the survey whether it is because the factor is considered irrelevant to tacit collusion or because, for the purposes for which the survey was produced, it was not considered significant. Finally, the fact that the surveys have been prepared for particular purposes raises the possibility that they are comprised of selections from the theory to suit those specific purposes. For example, for the purposes of the development of guidelines (i.e. to add the development of enforcement agency checklists), to justify past decisions of the commissioning organization,[88] or to provide a general high-level summary of tacit collusion. For all of these reasons, it has been considered necessary to supplement the survey material with a review of a broader range of material in relation to factors that facilitate or hinder tacit collusion. The results of this review are presented in Appendix 1.

There are a large number of studies potentially relevant to a consideration of tacit collusion. Accordingly, in undertaking a broader literature review, judgement had to be exercised to determine the most significant of these studies. Two criteria were employed in making this selection. First, peer review insofar as a study was frequently cited as being of significance in respect of a particular factor. For example, Green and Porter's work on demand volatility is widely cited in papers examining this factor,[89] while the empirical studies of Asch and Seneca, Hay and Kelley, Levenstein and Suslow, and Dick are frequently referenced.[90] Second, a study was considered significant where it

---

[88] Two examples illustrate this point. The IDEI Toulouse study (for DG Competition) provides possible explanations as to why the Commission has adopted a particular position as to market growth in practice. Similarly, the Europe Economics study (for DG Enterprise) compares the approach of DG Competition to merger appraisal in key decisions with the underlying economic theory, and is, in some respects, highly critical of DG Competition's approach: Institut d'Économie Industrielle (IDEI) Toulouse 'The economics of tacit collusion' (2003) Final report prepared for DG Competition, European Commission, March 2003 28; Europe Economics (n 87) 71–90, 89.

[89] E.J. Green and R.H. Porter 'Noncooperative collusion under imperfect price information' (1984) 52 Econometrica 90.

[90] P. Asch and J.J. Seneca 'Characteristics of collusive firms' (1975) 23 Journal of Industrial Economics 230; G.A. Hay and D. Kelley 'An empirical survey of price fixing conspiracies' (1974) 17 Journal of Law and Economics 16; M.C. Levenstein and V.Y. Suslow (n 82); A.R. Dick 'When are cartels stable contracts?' (1996) 39 Journal of Law and Economics 241.

was seen to provide an important contextual nuance to a more generalised conclusion in respect of a factor, for example, the Compte, Jenny and Rey study on the different ways in which capacity can impact collusion.[91]

A comparison of the surveys and the broader literature provide generally consonant conclusions. However, tensions do exist in respect of the effect of certain factors on tacit collusion. These tensions generally arise in two circumstances. First, where the surveys are definite in their interpretation of a factor and the broader literature suggests that a particular factor will not always *necessarily* facilitate or hinder collusion. Second, a tension arises where the conclusions of empirical studies run contrary to the definite interpretation of a factor presented in a survey.

Specifically, in respect of five factors the broader literature tends to be less definite, or qualify, the position taken in the surveys. These factors are: number of competitors; high market concentration levels; demand stability; prices/margins and volatility of market shares. In respect of the first three factors (number of competitors, high market concentration and demand stability) some empirical studies conclude that these factors have not necessarily been observed in past cases of collusion. In respect of the fourth and fifth factors (prices/margins and volatility of market shares), each was considered relevant in only one survey, and some of the broader literature challenges the relevance of these factors to an assessment of tacit collusion.

Where such tensions exist it is difficult to determine the relative weight that should be given to: the surveys vis-à-vis the broader literature; potentially conflicting theoretical papers; and as between empirical and theoretical work. Again, judgement had to be exercised, and it was recognised that these judgements would necessarily impact upon the analysis in Chapter 4 where the predictions of economic theory are compared to the decisional practice of the Commission and the Courts. Ultimately, the alternative positions proposed in the broader literature in relation to all five factors were not considered sufficiently abundant or comprehensive in scope to depart from the majority position adopted in the surveys for the purposes of the analysis in Chapter 4. A summary of the position adopted in respect of the effect of each factor on tacit collusion is given in Table 3.2. This table presents for each factor the survey position; the position based upon the broader literature review; and the position adopted for the purposes of the analysis in Chapter 4.

A detailed discussion in respect of each of the factors listed in Table 3.2 is attached in Appendix 1. This discussion incorporates the conclusions of theoretical studies and, where available, empirical work in respect of each factor and its relevance to a consideration of tacit collusion.

---

91 O. Compte and F. Jenny and P. Rey 'Capacity constraints, mergers and collusion' (2002) 46 European Economic Review 1.

Table 3.2 Comparison of interpretation of factors in surveys, broader literature and the position adopted

Factor	Survey position	Broader review position	Position adopted in research
Frequent interaction	Facilitates	Facilitates	Facilitates
Market share symmetry	Not clear	Not clear	Not clear
Stable demand	Facilitates	Not clear	Facilitates
Small no. of competitors	Facilitates	Not clear	Facilitates
Market growth	Not clear	Not clear	Not clear
Product homogeneity	Not clear	Not clear	Not clear
Demand elasticity	Not clear	Not clear	Not clear
Removal of 'maverick'	Facilitates	Facilitates	Facilitates
Business cycle effects	Hinders	Hinders	Hinders
High market concentration	Facilitates	Not clear	Facilitates
Symmetrical costs	Facilitates	Facilitates	Facilitates
Multi-market contacts	Facilitates	Facilitates	Facilitates
Prices and margins	Facilitates	Not clear	Facilitates
Entry barriers	Facilitates	Facilitates	Facilitates
Market transparency	Facilitates	Facilitates	Facilitates
Technology/innovation	Hinders	Hinders	Hinders
Symmetrical capacity constraints	Not clear	Not clear	Not clear
Excess capacity	Not clear	Not clear	Not clear
Bidding procedures	Not clear	Not clear	Not clear
Buyer power	Hinders	Hinders	Hinders
Structural links	Facilitates	Facilitates	Facilitates
Club and network effects	Hinders	Hinders	Hinders
Ability to retaliate	Facilitates	Facilitates	Facilitates
Post-capacity expansion & R&D	Not clear	Not clear	Not clear
Volatile market shares	Hinders	Not clear	Hinders
Size and financial strength	Not clear	Not clear	Not clear
Vertical integration	Facilitates	Facilitates	Facilitates

3.4 CONCLUSION

Article 82 of the EC Treaty and the ECMR are the two primary legal mechanisms for addressing the 'oligopoly problem' in European law. The ECMR uses merger control to prevent market structures developing which could facilitate tacit coordination. Article 82 addresses the effects of tacit coordination by prohibiting collectively dominant undertakings from engaging in certain types of conduct. Both rely on the judicially developed notion of collective dominance which is both complex and controversial.

The substantially greater number of decisions under the ECMR than under Article 82 suggest that the 'oligopoly problem' is more commonly addressed through merger control than through Article 82 assessments. However, as will be examined further in Chapter 5, the reported decisions do not necessarily reflect the totality of enforcement activity undertaken in relation to Article 82.

The economic analysis of tacit collusion provides a possible reference point for assessments under the collective dominance laws. The potential contribution of such theories is in providing predictions of when, and under what conditions, tacit collusion, or tacit coordination, is more or less likely to occur. In particular, predictions exist as to how similarity between firms, market structure and other conditions relevant to the mechanics of tacit collusion, facilitate or hinder tacit collusion. Such predictions are most commonly derived from game theoretic oligopoly theory, which is both abstract and mathematical.[92] There have been relatively few empirical studies that test the robustness of these models in real-world market contexts.

Finally, it is clear that although the legal notion of collective dominance is not derived, or directly modelled, on the economic notion of tacit collusion the two notions are conceptually related.[93] It is a purpose of this research to understand more precisely the nature of this relationship by examining how, *in fact*, economic theory and other aspects of economics feature in the day to day enforcement of the collective dominance laws.

---

[92] It has been observed, for example, that this is important because it is the most significant application of game theory to public policy. P. Seabright 'The ups and downs of the doctrine of collective dominance: using game theory for merger policy' presentation to Japan Fair Trade Commission, 20 March 2007, page 2.

[93] Compare: Commission Green Paper on the Review of Council Regulation (EEC) No 4064/89 [2001] COM (2001) 745/6 paras [163]–[165]; Commission Notice on the appraisal of horizontal mergers under the Council Regulation on the control of concentrations between undertakings COM (2002) paras [40]–[74].

4. A review of collective dominance decisions

4.1 INTRODUCTION

The previous chapter outlined the legislative provisions that are used to address the potential for firms to tacitly align or coordinate their behaviour. It also outlined the economic theories relating to tacit collusion and the predictions from such theories that may be relevant to the enforcement of the legislative provisions.

In this chapter and the next, I examine how economics has, in fact, featured in the decisions of the Commission and the Courts in collective dominance cases and how it has featured in the enforcement process more broadly. In this chapter, the role of economics is assessed in each of these areas based on an examination of the reported decisions of the Commission and Courts. The next chapter looks beyond the text of the decisions, to the processes leading up to, and surrounding, these final determinations, including the identification and selection or non-selection of cases, case construction, the substantive decision-making process and the development of remedies.

Specifically, this chapter examines the use of economics in relation to three types of decisions:

1. Assessments of the potential for collective dominance in mergers assessed under the ECMR;
2. Assessments of alleged abuses of a collective dominant position under Article 82 of the EC Treaty; and
3. Reviews by the European courts of Commission decisions under the ECMR and Article 82.

As discussed in Chapter 2, economics is conceived, for the purposes of the review, as comprising economic theory, the economic approach, economic techniques and economic data. Accordingly, decisions have been analysed to identify uses of economic theory, techniques and data and also for indications of an economic approach.

There were a number of analytical dimensions to the assessment of the use of economics across the reported decisions. First, the examination of the use of economic theory involved an assessment of: the extent of use of factors derived from economic theory; whether the factors were used in such a way as to be consistent with the underlying theory from which they are derived; whether the same factors were employed consistently across decisions; the extent to which factors were employed consistently in *ex post* assessments of abuses of collective dominance under Article 82 and *ex ante* assessments of the potential for collective dominance under the ECMR; and, finally, whether the Commission and the Courts have interpreted factors in a consistent manner. Second, the reasoning employed in reaching a decision was examined with the aim of establishing whether such reasoning was indicative of an economic approach; that is, whether *economic indicators*, and *economic processes*, were systematically used in the assessment of factors. Third, the analysis involved an examination of the use of economic techniques to support analyses of economic factors in decisions. The focus was on identifying whether 'low-tech' methods (such as simple calculations, or the postulating of hypotheses) or more 'high tech' methods (such as statistical or econometric analyses) have been used to examine particular factors or markets. Finally, the analysis sought to identify the source, and types, of economic data used in the assessment of factors, with a view to an assessment of the relative importance and influence of economic data vis-à-vis other data in the enforcement process.

The purpose of this analysis was to garner empirical data as to how, and the extent to which, economics influences the decisional practice of the Commission and the Courts in collective dominance cases.

4.2 MERGER DECISIONS: THE COMMISSION

The assessment of a merger under the ECMR involves an *ex ante* assessment of the likelihood that a merger will significantly impede effective competition in the common market, including through the creation or strengthening of a collective dominant position. The Commission will therefore assess the likelihood that the undertaking will have an incentive and the ability to tacitly coordinate its behaviour with other undertakings after the merger. However, the Commission is not required to identify specific potential abuses of a collective dominant position *ex ante*.

The cases examined below cover the period both before and after the important decision of the Court in *Airtours v Commission* in 2002. At a general level it is clear from the reported decisions that the Commission's approach to prohibiting mergers on the basis of concerns relating to collective dominance has been more cautious following that decision. However, as discussed below, this does not necessarily mean that the various criteria established in the *Airtours v Commission* decision have been systematically employed to support assessments.

4.2.1 Economic Theory

In assessing the likelihood that undertakings will tacitly coordinate their behaviour post-merger the Commission has examined a range of factors derived from the predictions of economic theory outlined in Chapter 3. In addition, the Commission has, in some cases, considered factors not directly derived from a specific prediction of the economic theory relating to tacit collusion but which can be broadly classed as being derived more generally from oligopoly theory.

Consistency of factor interpretation with economic theory

Tables 4.1 and 4.2 compare the factors examined by the Commission in assessing the potential for firms to tacitly co-ordinate their behaviour post-merger with the predictions of the economic theory of tacit collusion. The tables are based on a review of 173 merger decisions, involving 276 markets, and incorporate assessments of 1561 factors.

Table 4.1 details the number of market assessments in which each factor has featured, and the Commission's interpretation of the factor in each assessment (i.e. the direction of the factor's effect on collusive behaviour). For the majority of the factors considered in Commission decisions it was possible to locate, or to reasonably infer from the text of the decision, the principle underlying the Commission's application of the factor (i.e. whether the factor facilitated or hindered coordinated behaviour). However, for some factors this was not possible and these factors have been marked in the 'Application of factor unclear' column.

The table reveals a number of points regarding the relationship between the Commission's decisional practice and the predictions of economic theory. First, the Commission has predominantly examined factors identified in the economic theory but has, in some cases, assessed a greater number of factors than considered in the economic theory. Second, in the majority of market assessments, the Commission's interpretation of factors has been consistent with economic theory. Of the remaining assessments, factors have been given a more, or less, definite interpretation than the theory suggests, or, in a very small number of assessments, interpreted inconsistently with economic theory.

As detailed in the table, 25 of the 28 factors employed by the Commission in assessments of collective dominance are identified in the economic theory as relevant to the potential for tacit collusion.[1] Of the factors employed that are derived from economic theory, 14 of these factors (56 per cent) have in all

---

[1] The three factors not specifically discussed in the economic theory are: existing competition, structural market change and efficiency effects. These factors can, however, be seen as being relevant in a more general way to economic theory insofar as they affect the surrounding competitive environment, and consequently, the stability of tacit collusion.

Table 4.1 Comparison of the interpretation of factors from economic theory and in the Commission's ECMR decisions

Factor	Position adopted from economic theory	Commission position	No. of markets	Facilitates	Not necessarily facilitates	Hinders	Application of factor unclear
High market concentration	Facilitates	Facilitates	**269**	269			
Entry barriers	Facilitates	Facilitates	**132**	115			17
Market transparency	Facilitates	Facilitates	**112**	105			7
Market share symmetry	Not clear	Facilitates	**103**	103			
Product homogeneity	Not clear	Facilitates	**98**	89			9
Buyer power	Hinders	Hinders	**91**			91	
Small no. of competitors	Facilitates	Facilitates	**80**	69			11
Structural links	Facilitates	Mixed	**72**	63	3		6
Market growth	Not clear	Hinders	**54**			48	6
Excess capacity	Not clear	Mixed	**52**	20		10	22
Symmetrical costs	Facilitates	Facilitates	**47**	47			
Technology/innovation	Hinders	Hinders	**42**			38	4
Inc./similar prices margins	Facilitates	Mixed	**39**	24	2		13
Ability to retaliate	Facilitates	Mixed	**36**	35	1		
Public bidding procedures	Not clear	Mixed	**33**	14		3	16
Removal of 'maverick'	Facilitates	Facilitates	**30**	25			5
Vertical integration	Facilitates	Facilitates	**25**	25			
Volatile market shares	Hinders	Hinders	**20**			10	10
Size and financial strength	Not clear	Facilitates	**19**	8			11
Demand elasticity	Not clear	Facilitates	**16**	15			1
Frequent interaction	Facilitates	Mixed	**16**	10		3	3
Symmetrical capacity constraints	Not clear	Mixed	**15**	10	2		3
Volatile demand/business cycle	Hinders	Mixed	**14**	1		13	
Multi-market contacts	Facilitates	Facilitates	**13**	13			
Post-capacity expansion & R&D	Not clear	Facilitates	**3**	3			

Table 4.2 Summary of the interpretation of factors from economic theory and in the Commission's ECMR decisions

	Facilitates	Hinders	Mixed	Total	Percentage where principle can be	Percentage of total factors
Consistent with theory	813	140	80	1033	**80.4**	66.18
More definite than theory	195	47	0	242	**18.8**	15.50
Less definite than theory	0	0	6	6	**0.5**	0.38
Inconsistent with theory	0	0	4	4	**0.3**	0.26
				1285	**100**	**82.32**
Factor application unclear				146		9.35
Factor not in theory	103	9	18	130		8.33
Total factor assessments				**1561**		**100**

assessments been interpreted consistently with economic theory. Of the remaining 11 factors (44 per cent) inconsistencies arise in interpretation in some market assessments. Specifically, in relation to these 11 factors, there have been 470 factor assessments. In 168 of these assessments the Commission's interpretation of factors has been consistent with economic theory, in the remaining factor assessments the Commission's interpretation has been either: more definite (243 assessments), less definite (6 assessments) or inconsistent (4 assessments) with what the theory suggests.

Table 4.2 presents a summary of the information in Table 4.1. The column of this table shows that where a principle of interpretation can be inferred in assessments of a specific factor (i.e. excluding the assessments in which the application of a factor was unclear, and the assessments of factors not identified in economic theory), the Commission has, across all of its decisions, interpreted factors consistently with the economic theory in 80 per cent of assessments; adopted a more definite position than the theory in 19 per cent of assessments; and adopted a less definite, or inconsistent, position than the theory in around 1 per cent of assessments.

While the summary statistics presented in these tables provide a general picture of how the Commission has applied economic theory across its decisions, it is useful to explore some specific examples of where the Commission's interpretation of a factor has been consistent with, or differed from, that suggested by economic theory.

There are many examples in individual decisions of where the Commission has adopted a position in respect of a factor that is consistent with the predictions of economic theory. In some of these decisions, the Commission has prefaced its interpretation of a particular factor by discussing the economic principles underlying its interpretation, most notably in its decision in *Exxon/Mobil*.[2] In other assessments, the Commission does not specifically reference relevant economic principles, but its conclusions about the effect of particular factors are nevertheless consistent with these principles.

In some assessments, the Commission appears to have interpreted factors more definitely than economic theory suggests. An example of this can be seen in respect of product homogeneity. The predictions of economic theory as to the impact of product homogeneity on collusion are unclear, and depend upon

2 *Exxon/Mobil* (Case No IV/M.1383) [2004] OJ L103 1 para [465]–[469] (*Exxon/Mobil case*). Other examples include: *Gencor/Lonrho* (Case No IV/M.619) [1997] OJ L011 30 para [140]–[142] (*Gencor/Lonrho case*); *Price Waterhouse/Coopers & Lybrand* (Case IV/M.1016) [1999] OJ L050/27 para [95]–[97]; *Linde/BOC* (Case No COMP/M.4141) [2006] OJ C181 para [181] (*Linde/BOC case*); *Amer/Salomon* (Case No IV/M.3765) [2005] OJ C318 para [151] (*Amer/Salomon case*).

the assumptions made about the ways in which products are similar. By comparison, the Commission has, in all assessments where this factor has been considered, adopted the position that product homogeneity facilitates the potential for coordinated behaviour.[3] Nevertheless, it appears that the definition of homogeneity has tightened over time, such that, across cases, only a small number of products (gas, petrol, helium and electricity) have been considered sufficiently homogenous to facilitate tacit coordination. A large number of products and services, such as mobile call termination, fine paper, baby food, milk, cement and in-flight catering have been judged to be insufficiently similar to facilitate coordination.

Another example where the Commission appears to have interpreted a factor more definitely than economic theory suggests is in relation to market growth. In Chapter 3 and Appendix 1, it was noted that the predictions of economic theory as to how market growth relates to tacit collusion are unclear. One argument, for example, is that growing markets, with a fixed number of participants, can facilitate tacit collusion insofar as firms face the prospect of earning greater joint profits in the future. In its decisions, however, the Commission has always adopted the position that market growth *hinders* coordinated behaviour on the basis that in growing markets there are 'higher incentives for existing players to compete for an increase in market share'.[4] Other examples of where economic theory is unclear as to the relationship between a particular factor and tacit collusion but the Commission has adopted a definite interpretation in all assessments can be seen in respect of the following factors: size and financial strength;[5] demand elasticity;[6] and market share symmetry.[7]

---

3 For example see: *Alcan/Alusuisse* (COMP/M.1663) [2002] OJ L090 1 paras [95]–[105] (*Alcan/Alusuisse case*); *Exxon/Mobil case* (n 2) para [467].

4 *Alcan/Alusuisse case* (n 3) para [96]; *Exxon/Mobil case* (n 2) para [475]; *Nestlé/Gerber* (Case COMP/M.4688) [2007] OJ C203 para [29] (*Nestlé/Gerber case*).

5 *Nestlé/Perrier* (Case No IV/M.190) [1992] OJ L356 1 paras [72]–[76] (*Nestlé/Perrier case*); *ABB/Daimler-Benz* (Case No IV/M.580) [1997] OJ L011 1 paras [64]–[67] (*ABB/Daimler-Benz case*) *Aster 2/Flint Ink* (Case COMP/M.3886) [2005] OJ C 263 para [27] (*Aster 2 Flint Ink case*); *EDF/AEM/Edison* (Case COMP/M.3729) [2005] OJ C222 para [100] (*EDF/AEM/Edison case*).

6 *Exxon/Mobil case* (n 2) paras [247],[479]; *Mannessman/Ilva/Vallourec* (Case No IV/M.315) [1994] OJ L102 15 para [55]; *Pilkington-Techint/SIV* (Case No IV/M.358) [1994] OJ L158 24 para [31] (*Pilkington-Techint/SIV case*)

7 *Agfa-Gevaert/Sterling* (Case No IV/M.1432) [1999] OJ L228 11 para [51]; *Rhodia Chemie/Albright & Wilson* (Case No IV/M.1517) [1999] OJ C248 10 para [73]; *MAN/Auwärter* (Case No COMP/M.2201) [2002] OJ L116 35 para [76]. *Amer/Saloman case* (n 2) para [152]; *Cargill/Degussa* (Case COMP/M.3975) [2006] OJ L316 para [24]; *Dow Chemical Company/Wolff Walsrode* (Case No IV/M.4550) [2007] OJ C157 para [36]; *Linde/BOC case* (n 2) para [141]–[142], [182]; *MAN/Scania* (Case No. COMP/M.4336) [2006] OJ C100 para [96] (*MAN/Scania case*).

In some assessments, the Commission has interpreted factors less definitely than the economic theory suggests. An example of this can be seen in relation to 'the ability to retaliate'. Economic theory considers a credible punishment mechanism necessary to sustain any tacitly collusive agreement. However, in its decision in *Airtours/FirstChoice*, a controversial case relating to the UK short-haul package holiday market and the first prohibition of a four-to-three merger, the Commission stated that it did not see a retaliation mechanism as 'a necessary condition for collective dominance'.[8] Other examples where the Commission has taken the position that a particular factor is not relevant, or necessarily indicative, for a finding of collective dominance can be seen in respect of high/increasing prices and profits, [9] and structural links.[10]

In the assessment of two factors (in four decisions), the Commission has interpreted a factor inconsistently with economic theory. The first is in relation to frequent interaction. Economic theory predicts that frequent interaction between firms facilitates tacit collusion. By contrast, in three of nine assessments of this factor the Commission has adopted an alternative position. For example, in *Outokumpu/Norzink*, the Commission concluded that 'short-term contracts prevent the oligopolists to sustain any co-ordinated outcome over time as the premium part can be implicitly renegotiated'.[11]

The second example of where the Commission has interpreted a factor inconsistently with the theory is in relation to volatile demand. The prediction of economic theory is that demand volatility hinders tacit collusion. In its decision in *Airtours/FirstChoice*, however, the Commission adopted the position that 'volatility of demand makes the market more conducive to oligopolistic dominance'.[12]

It is difficult, based on the text of the reported decisions, to propose why the interpretation of some factors in some cases differs from economic theory.

---

8 *Airtours/FirstChoice* (Case IV/M.1524) [2000] OJ L093 1 para [55].

9 *Candover/Cinven/Bertelsmann-Springer* (Case No IV/M.3197) [2003] OJ C207 25 para [47]; *Pilkington-Techint/SIV* (n 6) para [35].

10 *Danish Crown/Vestjyske Slagterier* (Case IV/M.1313) [2000] OJ L020 1 para [177] *(Danish Crown/Vestjyske Slagterier case)*; *Grupo Villar Mir/EnBW/Hidroeléctrica del Cantábrico* (Case COMP/M.2434) [2001] OJ L048 para [71] (*Grupo Villar case*).

11 *Outokumpu/Norzink* (Case No IV/M.2348) [2001] OJ C175 12 para [20] *(Outokumpu/Norzink case)*. In another case the Commission adopted the position that anti-competitive parallel behaviour was not likely to arise, in part, because contractual prices were re-negotiated regularly: *CVC/Danone/Gerresheimer* (Case No IV/M.1539) [1999] OJ C214/7 paras [32]–[33] *(CVC/Danone/Gerresheimer case)*. Similarly, in a recent decision it was noted monthly contractual negotiations made it difficult for suppliers to stick to a common pattern: *Ineos/Kerling* (Case COMP/M.4734) [2008] OJ C219 para [184].

12 *Airtours/FirstChoice case* (n 8) para [97].

The purpose of this review is not to assess the appropriateness of individual Commission decisions, but the influence of economics more broadly. It is also acknowledged that alongside the simplistic argument that the Commission 'got the economics wrong' there are a range of other influences with explanatory potential, including the impact of specific market-contextual considerations on assessments, and, as is discussed in greater detail in Chapter 5, the impact of specific features of the enforcement process on decisions.

Consistency of relative emphasis of factors

While the Commission's interpretation of the effect of individual factors on tacit coordination is predominantly consistent with the economic theory of tacit collusion, a separate issue for consideration is the relative emphasis given to different factors in assessments and how this relates to economic theory. While it is not possible to rank precisely the factors identified in economic theory in terms of their relative importance, there is, as we saw in Chapter 3, a degree of consensus regarding those factors which are key to any consideration of tacit collusion. These include: frequency of interaction, stable demand, market concentration and number of competitors, symmetrical costs, multi-market contacts, entry barriers, market transparency, technology/innovation, buyer power and the existence of a credible retaliation mechanism.

Table 4.3 indicates that the importance the Commission places on selected factors, implied by frequency of use, differs from that of the economic theory. It shows that some factors considered important in the theory such as market concentration (considered in 97 per cent of assessments), entry barriers (48 per cent) and market transparency (41 per cent) do feature prominently in the Commission's decisions. However, other key factors are examined relatively infrequently. These include: buyer power (33 per cent); the degree of symmetry in costs (17 per cent); the rate of technological innovation (15 per cent); the ability to retaliate (13 per cent); frequency of interaction (6 per cent); multi-market contact (5 per cent) and the stability of demand (5 per cent).

Again, based on the text of the reported decisions, it is difficult to account for the Commission's selection and focus on specific factors. An obvious explanation is practical considerations, in that, the factors that are most frequently considered are either those which are simplest to assess (i.e. market concentration measures) or for which information is more readily available (i.e. can be based on submissions received from competitors and customers). Choices may also reflect considerations regarding relevance in a specific factual context.[13] This issue, and issues such as who prepares and undertakes

---

[13] Case T-282/06 *Sun Chemical Group BV v. Commission of the European Communities* [2007] ECR II -02149 para [56]–[61].

Table 4.3 Economic factors examined under the ECMR by the Commission

	No. of markets	Percentage of markets examined
High market concentration	269	97
Entry barriers	132	48
Market transparency	112	41
Existing competition	103	37
Market share symmetry	103	37
Product homogeneity	98	36
Buyer power	91	33
Small no. of competitors	80	29
Structural links	72	26
Market growth	54	20
Excess capacity	52	19
Symmetrical costs	47	17
Technology/innovation	42	15
Increasing/similar price margins	39	14
Ability to retaliate	36	13
Public bidding procedures	33	12
Removal of 'maverick'	30	11
Vertical integration	25	9
Structural market change	24	9
Volatile market shares	20	7
Size and financial strength	19	7
Demand elasticity	16	6
Frequent interaction	16	6
Symmetrical capacity constraints	15	5
Volatile demand/Bus. cycle	14	5
Multi-market contacts	13	5
Efficiency effects	3	1
Post-capacity expansion & R&D	3	1

the economic analysis in merger cases, is considered in more detail in the discussion relating to Commission enforcement practice in Chapter 5.

Internal consistency of factor interpretations

Of the 28 factors examined by the Commission, the majority, 20 of these factors, have been interpreted consistently across decisions. The remaining eight factors have been given alternative – but not always opposing – interpretations in different market assessments.[14]

[14] These factors include: frequency of interaction; prices and margin movements; volatile demand; symmetrical capacity constraints; excess capacity; bidding procedures; structural links; and ability to retaliate.

As noted in Chapter 3, the economic theory is unclear in relation to the effect of some factors on tacit collusion and can depend heavily on contextual considerations. This underlying ambiguity appears to be reflected in certain Commission decisions, resulting in opposing interpretations of the same factor in different assessments. An example is the interpretation of the effect of excess capacity in a market. In *Usinor/Arbed/Aceralia*, a case relating to a merger that would create an industry structure with three suppliers holding roughly equal shares of the Western European steel for beverage packaging market, the existence of excess capacity in the relevant market was viewed as working *against* parallel behaviour.[15] In another market assessment, where post-merger two firms would supply 77 per cent of the German mainline train market, the existence of excess capacity was seen as *promoting* non-competitive behaviour.[16] Another example of opposing interpretations of the same factor in different assessments is the interpretation of the effect of public bidding procedures. In assessing a merger that would create Europe's second largest producer of medical wounds closure products, and where, post merger, four firms would supply the entire market, the Commission's position was that public tendering acts to *prevent* collective dominance developing in a market.[17] Conversely, in *MAN/Auwärter*, where, post merger, two firms would control 98 per cent of the supply of German city buses, the Commission adopted the broader position that public tendering *does not necessarily prevent* coordinated behaviour.[18]

The relevance of price and margin movements is another example. In *Exxon/Mobil*, which involved the largest industrial merger ever at that time, and followed a wave of mergers in the international oil industry, the Commission took the position that high price levels and movements *can* be taken as a strong indication of a deficit in competition in the market and of a tendency toward coordinated behaviour in that market.[19] By comparison, in

---

15 *Usinor/Arbed/Aceralia* (Case COMP/ECSC.1351) [2003] OJ L088 1 para [181]; *Agco/Valtra* (Case No IV/M.3287) [2003] OJ C011 para [49]; *Umicore/Zinifex/Neptune* (Case No IV/M.4450) [2007] OJ C65 para [84].

16 *ABB/Daimler-Benz case* (n 5) para [93].

17 *TYCO International/US Surgical International Corp.* (Case No IV/M.1223) [1998] OJ C282 5 para [11] (*TYCO International/US Surgical International Corp. case*).

18 *MAN/Auwärter* (Case No COMP/M.2201) [2002] OJ L116 35 para [35] (*MAN/Auwärter case*). However, in the subsequent *MAN/Scania* decision the existence of public tendering was seen to act against tacit collusion: *MAN/Scania case* (n 7) para [159]

19 *Exxon/Mobil case* (n 2) para [634]; [667]–[669]. Conversely, in other decisions the presumption has been that decreasing prices are an indicator of competition in a market: *Schneider Electric/MGE-UPS* (Case No IV/M.3347) [2004] OJ C049 para [42] (*Schneider Electric/MGE-UPS case*); *Toshiba/Samsung/JV* (Case No IV/M.3349) [2004] OJ C25 para [16].

Candover/Cinven/Bertelsmann-Springer, despite price increases of up to 20 per cent in the market for academic publishing, the Commission's position was that price increases and high margins are characteristics that *do not allow* for a determination to be made on the potential for future collective dominance.[20] Differing interpretations across decisions can also be seen in respect of the following factors: frequency of interaction;[21] volatile demand;[22] structural links;[23] and ability to retaliate.[24]

Standards applied in factor assessments

In addition to questions of factor selection and interpretation, assessments require a judgement as to whether the effect of a factor is sufficient to aid or hinder coordination. A difficulty faced by the Commission in making assessments is that economic theory in general reveals little about the standard to apply in making this judgement. Accordingly, the Commission is afforded substantial discretion in this respect. The reported decisions indicate that the Commission appears to apply broadly consistent standards across decisions. However, in a minority of assessments, the standards adopted in respect of particular factors demonstrate some notable variation. For example, when determining what constitutes a 'growing' market in *P&O Stena*, the Commission assessed that a growth rate of 5 per cent in cross-channel ferry traffic provided 'sufficient incentive to compete for new demand',[25] while, in prohibiting the *Gencor/Lonrho* merger, a growth rate of 3 per cent in the worldwide platinum market was seen as an *insufficient* basis 'to provide a high incentive for competition'.[26] Another example of varying standards can be seen in relation to assessments as to the impact of the removal of a competi-

[20] *Candover/Cinven /Bertelsmann-Springer* (Case No IV/M.3197) [2003] OJ C207 25 para [47].

[21] Compare *Outokumpu/Norzink case* (n 11) para [20] and *CVC/Danone/Gerresheimer case* (n 11) paras [32]–[33] with *ALCOA/British Aluminium* (Case No IV/M.2111) [2000] OJ C348/14 para [14] and *Agfa-Gevaert/Sterling* (Case No IV/M.1432) [1999] OJ L228 11 paras [27]–[28] (*Agfa-Gevaert/Sterling case*) para [27].

[22] Compare *Airtours/FirstChoice case* (n 8) para [97] with *Mannessman/Ilva/Vallourec* (Case No IV/M.315) [1994] OJ L102 15 para [55].

[23] Compare *CVC/Danone/Gerresheimer* (n 11) para [34] and *Danish Crown/Vestjyske Slagterier case* (n 10) para [177].

[24] Compare *Rexam (PLM)/American National Can* (Case No IV/M.1939) [2001] OJ C325 11 para [24] (*Rexam (PLM)/American National Can case*) and *Shell/DEA* (Case COMP/M.2389) [2003] OJ L015 35 para [121] with *Airtours/FirstChoice case* (n 8) para [55].

[25] *P&O Stena Line (Holding) Limited* (Case No IV/M.2838) [2002] OJ C206 5 para [25] (*P&O Stena Line (Holding) Limited case*).

[26] *Gencor/Lonrho case* (n 2) para [151].

tor. In *SCA/Metsä Tissue*, the Commission prohibited a merger between two suppliers of kitchen and toilet tissue in Finland principally on the basis that the merger resulted in the removal of a competitor, in circumstances where that competitor had only a *5* per cent market share.[27] This can be contrasted with the standard adopted in *Alcatel/AEG Kabel*, where the impact of the removal of a competitor with a *13* per cent market share, and which would reduce the number of suppliers in the German power cable market from four to three, was assessed as an insufficient basis to conclude that competition would *cease* to exist on that market.[28] Finally, the standard by which the Commission assesses what constitutes a sufficient level of technological innovation to affect coordination has, at times, been opaque. For example, in *Danish Crown/Vestjyske Slagterier*, where the Commission found a duopolistic dominant position would be created by a merger between a number of Europe's pig slaughterhouses, the rate of innovation in the pig slaughtering market was compared to the rate of innovation in high-tech industries such as computers. [29]

Different standards have also been applied in assessing post-merger market shares,[30] and the degree of symmetry of market shares.[31] Again, it is

---

27 *SCA/Metsä Tissue* (Case COMP/M.2097) [2002] OJ L057 1 para [147] (*SCA/Metsä Tissue case*). Similarly, in another decision the removal of a firm with a less than 5 per cent market share was considered as the removal of a maverick which would increase the risk of coordination: *Linde/BOC case* (n 2) para [192].

28 *Alcatel/AEG Kabel* (Case No IV/M.165) [1992] OJ C006 0 paras [19]–[24] (*Alcatel/AEG Kabel case*).

29 *Danish Crown/Vestjyske Slagterier case* (n 10) para [176].

30 Compare two decisions where the merger was approved despite two undertakings holding a 100 per cent market share post-merger, with other decisions where mergers were challenged and where two undertakings had a 75–80 per cent post-merger market share, or three undertakings would have had up to 85 per cent market share post merger: *Akzo Nobel/Hoechst Roussel Vet* (Case No IV/M.1681) [2000] OJ C011 5 para [38] (*Akzo Nobel/Hoechst Roussel Vet case*); *Rhodia Chemie/Albright & Wilson* (Case No IV/M.1517) 1999] OJ C248 10 paras [70]–[72] (*Rhodia Chemie/Albright & Wilson case*). Contrast: *New Holland/CASE* (Case No IV/M.1571) [2000] OJ C130/11 para [73] (*New Holland/CASE case*); *Airtours/FirstChoice case* (n 8) paras [72]–[73].

31 In one decision a 5 per cent to 10 per cent difference in market shares was sufficiently asymmetrical; in another decision a distribution of 10 per cent to 15 per cent was evidence of 'strong market share asymmetries'; while a variation of 10 per cent was assessed as 'almost symmetrical' in another decision: *Glaverbel/PPG* (Case No IV/M.1230) [1998] OJ C282 2 para [21] *(Glaverbel/PPG case)*; *New Holland/CASE case* (n 30) para [48]. Contrast *Alcan/Alusuisse case* (n 3) paras [92]–[94]. More recently, in one decision a difference in market shares of at least 10 per cent was taken to be asymmetrical, whereas in another decision a similar difference of at least 10 per cent was taken to suggest a prima facie symmetrical duopoly. *Vinnolit/Ineos CV's Specialty PVC Business* (Case No COMP/M.4572) [2007] OJ C160 para [27]; *Superior Essex/Invex* (Case No COMP/M. 4706) [2007] OJ C217 para [39].

acknowledged that market-contextual considerations may provide explanations for these variations. However, the texts of the reported decisions are not sufficiently detailed to easily yield this information.

4.2.2 Economic Approach

In Chapter 2 the economic approach was described as the economic methods of conceptualising problems or phenomena. At the case level, this approach translates to whether *economic indicators* are used, and *economic processes* examined, in the assessment of factors. Three assessment approaches of this kind can be identified in Commission decisions.

The first, and most common, approach employed by the Commission is to identify whether a specific economic indicator for an economic factor exists. For example, to assess buyer power the Commission has considered whether customers multi-source their supply from more than one supplier;[32] in assessing bidding markets it has looked for the existence of public tenders [33] or published price lists;[34] to assess excess capacity it has examined the level of capacity, or capacity utilisation in an industry.[35] Other examples of this approach can be seen in the Commission's assessment of: cost similarity;[36]

---

[32] *BP Amoco/Castrol* (Case No IV/M.1891) [2000] OJ C301 23 para [36]; *DUPONT/Hoechst/Herberts* (Case No IV/M.1363) [1999] C064 2 para [27],[32]; *UPM-Kymmene/Haindl* (Case No COMP/M.2498) [2002] OJ L233 38 para [100]; *Outokumpu/Norzink case* (n 11) para [27]; *Rexam (PLM)/American National Can case* (n 24) para [26]; *State Street Corporation/Deutsche Bank Global Securities* (Case No IV/M.3027) [2003] OJ C048 14 para [18]; *Solvay/Montedison-Ausimont* (Case No IV/M.2690) [2002] OJ C153 11 para [125] *(Solvay/Montedison-Ausimont case)*; *Anglo American/Kumba Resources* (Case COMP/M.3276) [2004] C 009 para [21]; *MAN/Scania* (n 7) para [137]

[33] *Kodak/Imation* (Case No IV/M.1298) [1999] OJ C017 2 paras [37]–[42]; *Agfa-Gevaert/Sterling case* (n 21) paras [27]–[28]; *TYCO International/US Surgical Corp. case* (n 17) para [11]; *MAN/Scania case* (n 7) para [163].

[34] *LITE-ON/PBDS* (Case No IV/M.4502) [2007] OJ C72 para [36]; *SKF/SNFA* (Case COMP/M.4062) [2006] OJ C156 para [60]; *Heidelbergcement/Hanson* (Case COMP/M.4719) [2007] OJ C221 para [87].

[35] *UCB / Solutia* (Case No IV/M.3060) [2003] OJ C078/6. paras [37]–[38]; *VA Stahl/Thyssen Schienen Technik* (Case COMP/ECSC.1357) [2001] OJ C236/12 para [21]; *Rohm and Haas/Morton* (Case No IV/M.1467) [1999] OJ C157/7 para [32]; *Akzo Nobel/Monsanto* (Case No IV/M.523) [1995] OJ C037/3 para [47]; *Krupp/Thyssen /Riva/Falck/Tadfin/AST* (Case No IV/M.484) [1995] OJ L251/18. paras [62],[68]; *Aster 2 Flint Ink case* (n 5) para [27]; *LSG Lufthansa Service Holding/Gate Gourmet Switzerland* (Case COMP/M.4170) [2007] OJ C11 para [42] (*LSG Lufthansa Service Holding/Gate Gourmet Switzerland case*).

[36] Indicators examined include: source of raw material; the level of transportation, labour and distribution costs; sales focus of the company; relative percentage of fixed to variable costs.

product homogeneity;[37] similarity in size and strength;[38] removal of competitor;[39] and market transparency.[40]

A second approach of the Commission is to focus on examining an economic process – such as the buying or selling process – as part of its assessment. For example, in assessing tendering and bidding procedures the Commission has on a number of occasions examined the specific mechanics of the tendering process.[41] A detailed examination of the mechanics of the tendering process featured prominently in the assessment of the worldwide market for global telecommunications services in *MCI Worldcom/Sprint*, where the Commission proposed and examined two potential bidding methods by which the merged entity and another competitor may coordinate their behaviour.[42] Similarly, in assessing buyer power, the Commission has examined discount policies, and the processes by which they are applied, for different buyers. For example, in *Gencor/Lonrho* where post-merger two suppliers would control over 90 per cent of the world-wide reserves of platinum grade metals, the Commission's examination of the level of discounts and restrictive contractual terms provided to buyers, was a strong contributing factor in its decision to prohibit the merger.[43] Finally, in assessing market transparency the Commission's approach has in some decisions focused on the procurement procedures used to award contracts and whether, for example, wholesalers are used[44] or prices are individually negotiated.[45]

---

37 Indicators examined include: the number of products produced; the different varieties of the product on the market; whether similar/different customer specifications or requirements exist (including packaging and finishing); specific properties of different products (such as concrete setting times).

38 Indicators examined include: the existence of global operations and divisions; differences of strength in 'home' regions; and the relative size of their overall production facilities and portfolios.

39 Indicators examined include: the size and historical development of the firm being 'removed' or acquired and the number of independent suppliers.

40 Indicators examined include: the number of sellers on the market; whether public procurement procedures are used to award contracts; whether rebates are offered; whether price lists are employed and the extent to which private/individual negotiations between the parties occur.

41 *UPM-Kymmene/Haindl case* (n 32); *MAN/Auwärter case* (n 18) paras [44]–[46]; *ABB/Daimler-Benz case* (n 5) paras [74]–[85];[114]–[119]; *LSG Lufthansa Service Holding/Gate Gourmet Switzerland case* (n 35) para [47].

42 *MCI WorldCom/Sprint* (Case COMP/M.1741) [2003] OJ L300 1 paras [78]–[83], [272]–[278] (*MCI WorldCom/Sprint case*).

43 *Gencor/Lonrho case* (n 2) paras [150]; [162]–[164].

44 *Rhodia Chemie/Albright & Wilson case* (n 30) paras [70]–[71].

45 *State Street Corporation/Deutsche Bank Global Securities* (Case No IV/M.3027) [2003] OJ C048 14 para [18] (*State Street Corporation/Deutsche Bank Global Securities case*); *Degussa/DOW (superabsorbent polymers)* (Case COMP/M.4154) [2006] OJ C177 para [29]; *Cargill/Degussa case* (n 7) para [24].

A third approach of the Commission is to undertake a 'global' economic assessment of a market, and then use this as a basis for inferring potential behaviour in a specific relevant market. For example, it may conduct a high level economic assessment of the general characteristics of an industry and how the features of this type of industry might facilitate or frustrate coordinated behaviour. This approach was adopted in *Kali+Salz/MDK/Treuhand*, a case subsequently appealed to the ECJ, where the Commission's assessment of the entire European Community market (apart from Germany) for potash based agricultural products was used to infer the potential for collective dominance in a national market.[46] This approach was also adopted in *Exxon/Mobil*, where the Commission presented a detailed general assessment of structural characteristics of the market for motor fuel retailing prior to its assessment of the individual national markets.[47] More recently this type of approach can be seen in the *Amer/Salomon* and *MAN/Scania* decisions.[48] In other decisions, the Commission has used the assessment of a factor in one market (such as buyer power) as the basis for the conclusion in another market (i.e. a different geographic market).[49]

Finally, it is interesting to consider the extent to which the Court decision in *Airtours v Commission* – and the criteria established for tacit coordination in that decision – has impacted on the approach of the Commission in its assessments. A review of the decisions assessed after the publication of the *Airtours v Commission* decision indicates that such criteria have not been systematically presented by the Commission in every decision, and that only a small number of decisions have explicitly framed the analysis in terms of the three criteria.[50] For example, the requirement to show credible retaliation possibilities has been referred to in only 23 markets (out of at least 115 market assessments) since the publication of the CFI's *Airtours v Commission* decision. In addition, the depth of analysis of the potential retaliation mechanisms has varied across decisions from detailed examinations of how possible retaliation mechanisms might operate,[51] to one line summaries such as the following:

---

[46] *Kali + Salz/MDK/Treuhand* (Case No IV/M.308) [1998] OJ C275 3 paras [51]–[68].

[47] *Exxon/Mobil case* (n 2) paras [465]–[489].

[48] *Amer/Salomon case* (n 2); *MAN/Scania case* (n 7).

[49] *SCA/Metsä Tissue case* (n 27) paras [159]–[176].

[50] These include: *Amer/Salomon case* (n 2); *TUI/FirstChoice* (Case COMP/M.4600) [2007] OJ C137 (*TUI/FirstChoice case*); *KarstadtQuelle/MyTravel* (Case COMP/M.4601) OJ C113 (*KarstadtQuelle/MyTravel case*); *KORSNē/ ASSIDOMĎ CARTONBOARD* (Case No IV/M.4057) [2006] OJ C209 (*KORSNē/ ASSIDOMĎCARTONBOARD case*); *EDF/AEM/Edison* (Case COMP/M.3729) [2005] OJ C222; *Antalis/MAP* (Case COMP/M.4753)[2007] OJ C289.

[51] *KarstadtQuelle/MyTravel case* (n 50) paras [109]–[113]; *Travelport/ Worldspan* (Case COMP/M.4523) [2007] OJ L314 paras [66]–[72].

The larger number of vendors also reduces the transparency in the market and would make retaliatory actions more difficult.[52]

4.2.3 Economic Techniques

As outlined in Chapter 2, economic techniques are defined as the economic methods of analysis and exposition. These include 'low-tech' methods – such as simple calculations, or the postulating of hypotheses – which are used to examine a particular factor or market. They also include 'high-tech' methods which might involve the development of models using econometrics, or other statistical methods which attempt to estimate the relationship between, or quantify the value of, a specific factor examined and the potential for coordinated behaviour.

The review of the reported decisions shows that there is no common economic technique used by the Commission in assessing factors, and that the Commission employs a range of techniques when assessing the same factor in different markets. For example, the Commission has used at least ten different methods of calculation for market share indices.[53] In addition, the time period over which market shares are calculated has ranged considerably. [54] In the prohibited *Airtours/FirstChoice* merger, the Commission examined market share indices for UK short-haul package holidays over one season,[55] while in *Exxon/Mobil*, market share indices for the Austrian motorway fuel retailing market was examined over four years;[56] and, in its assessment of the French market for trams and light rail vehicles in *Bombardier/ADtranz*, the time period was five years.[57]

The Commission has also adopted a range of techniques to assess buyer power. In different assessments it has based its analysis on: the views of the largest customer;[58] the absence of customer concerns about a merger;[59] the

---

52 *Oracle/PeopleSoft* (Case No COMP/M.3216) [2005] OJ L218 para [40].

53 Market shares have been calculated on the basis of: volume; value; volume and value; the flow of new orders or tenders won; new registrations; working production capacity; installed production capacity; total revenue as reported in industry reports; average market volume, including attribution of participation in consortia bids; imports; production less captive production.

54 Time periods considered include: a specific year, two years, three years, four years, five years, two non-consecutive years, three non-consecutive years, 'latest available data', data for one semester, five months, nine months, or one specific summer season.

55 *Airtours/FirstChoice case* (n 8) para [72].

56 *Exxon/Mobil case* (n 2) para [503].

57 *Bombardier/Adtranz* (Case COMP/M.2139) [2002] OJ L069 50 para [40].

58 *ABB/Daimler-Benz case* (n 5) paras [74],[84]–[85].

59 *Johnson Professional Holdings/Diverseylever* (Case No IV/M.2665) [2002] OJ C079 11 para [34].

presence of large customers[60] or the degree of sophistication of customers;[61] and quantitative techniques such as the examination of the percentage of sales to the largest customers.[62] Other examples where a variety of techniques have been adopted to assess the same factor in different markets can be seen in the Commission's assessment of: potential competition,[63] and tendering and bidding procedures.[64]

It is, again, difficult to determine from the text of decisions how the Commission makes choices as to which technique to apply in different market assessments. Obvious considerations might include the availability of data; the suitability of any data or information for use in particular quantitative or other techniques; time and resource constraints; and specific market context considerations. It is acknowledged that these are not insignificant practical considerations, which are more fully explored in subsequent chapters.

'Low tech' methods

In general, the economic techniques used by the Commission are low-level quantitative or descriptive. Three techniques of this type can be identified.

The most common technique is for the Commission to refer to an economic

---

60 *Amer/Salomon case* (n 2) para [157].

61 *Seiko/Epson/Sanyo/Sanyo Epson Imaging Devices JV* (Case No IV/M.3459) [2004] para [15].

62 *BP/E.on* (Case No COMP/M.2533) [2002] OJ L276 31 para [80] (*BP/E.on case*) and *Shell/DEA* (Case COMP/M.2389) [2003] OJ L015 35 para [80] *(Shell/DEA case)*; *Danish Crown/Vestjyske Slagterier case* (n 10) para [143],[147],[183]; *Nestlé/Perrier case* (n 5) paras [77]–[78]; *Solvay/Montedison-Ausimont case* (n 32) para [62]; *Alcatel/AEG Kabel case* (n 28) para [25]; *Knorr-Bremse/Allied Signal* (Case No IV/M.337) [1993] OJ C298 0 para [39]; *Rexam (PLM)/American National Can case* (n 24) para [26]; *VALEO/ITT Industries* (Case No IV/M.1245) [1998] OJ C288 5.

63 Two decisions in the market for newsprint provide a good illustration of the varying types of analysis. In *Enso/Stora* the Commission's assessment of potential competition was limited to proposing a hypothesis and offering the following as support: 'apparently there is some potential competition, notably from Canada'. In *UPM-Kymmene/Haindl* the Commission employs more sophisticated economic techniques and evidence such as a detailed analysis of the percentage of fixed costs of total costs on a machine basis and how profitability relates to its level of capacity utilisation: *Enso/Stora* (Case No IV/M.1225) [1999] OJ L254 9 para [68]; *UPM-Kymmene/Haindl case* (n 32) paras [108]–[111].

64 Compare two decisions in the medical sector. In *Agfa-Gevaert/Sterling* the Commission undertakes a detailed analysis of the past consortia and composition of bids in 93 invitations to tender, while in *TYCO International/US Surgical International Corp* the Commission presents the unsupported hypothesis that: 'the widespread use of public tendering for medical suppliers means that prices and shares are not transparent': *Agfa-Gevaert/Sterling case* (n 21) paras [27]–[28]; *TYCO International/US Surgical International Corp. case* (n 17) para [11].

factor and use this as a basis to postulate a theory of competitive harm or make inferences, or predictions about how this factor might impact the incentives for co-ordinated behaviour. For example, in *State Street Corporation/Deutsche Bank Global Securities*, the Commission assessed the future ability of four firms to raise prices in the European global custody, fund administration and securities lending markets by referring to potential competition and postulating the following hypothetical: 'there are several global competitors … which could readily benefit from any theoretical attempt of price increase by the four largest players'.[65] This technique also features frequently in Commission assessments of post-merger incentives of market participants.[66] For example, in assessing the potential for coordination in the Western European market for hot and cold stainless steel tubes in *Mannessman/Ilva/Vallourec*, the Commission referred to a 70 per cent post-merger market share of two firms, and, on this basis developed the hypothesis that there was 'prima facie a strong incentive for these producers to act together to sell the same volumes at higher prices, rather than to compete with each other on price in order to obtain higher market shares'.[67] Some other examples of the use of this technique in the Commission's assessment of different factors:

> [G]iven the market shares symmetry, JCB and the merged entity would appear to have … similar competitive incentives.[68]

> [T]he possibility of oligopolistic dominance does not appear realistic after the merger. The new entity and Viking would have different cost structures and different competition incentives.[69]

> [A]s to the possibility of joint dominance, it is worth noting that such a risk is even more unlikely given the complexity of the products in question.[70]

> [T]he presence of other rather important competitors …, there is no margin for the functioning of collective dominance.[71]

---

65 *State Street Corporation/Deutsche Bank Global Securities case* (n 45) para [18].

66 *Rhodia Chemie/Albright & Wilson case* (n 30) para [64]; *Solvay/Montedison-Ausimont case* (n 32) para [58]; *Akzo Nobel/Hoechst Roussel Vet case* (n 30) para [38]; *MAN/Auwärter case* (n 18) para [76]; *BAT/Rothmans* (Case No IV/M.1415) [1999] OJ C120 21 para [23] (*BAT/Rothmans case*).

67 *Mannessman/Ilva/Vallourec* (Case No IV/M.315) [1994] OJ L102 15 para [55].

68 *New Holland/CASE case* (n 30) para [73].

69 *Staples/Guilbert* (Case No IV/M.2965) [2002] OJ C262 17 para [20].

70 *Agfa-Gevaert/Sterling case* (n 21) para [40].

71 *BAT/Rothmans case* (n 66) para [23].

> [I]mports from East Europe and China are limited but might go up should the suppliers … try to increase prices.[72]

> The market is a new and technology-driven market, which expands rapidly and where technologies and products change constantly, and which therefore provides few incentives for collusion or for conscious parallel conduct.[73]

> The fact that prices for these services are not observable as they result from private negotiations is sufficient to discard any scenario of a creation of a collective dominance.[74]

> Parallel conduct … might also be encouraged by the openness of public procurement in rail technology markets.[75]

> [C]ustomers procure through open tender procedures … so that this market is not sufficiently transparent and, therefore, any tacit collusion between suppliers appears unlikely.[76]

A notable aspect of each of the examples provided is that analysis was not provided in the decision in support of the inference or prediction. This type of approach has recently been subject to criticism by the CFI, most notably in *Impala v. Commission*, on the basis of insufficient reasoning. Specifically, the Court described the Commission's economic assessment in that case as 'succinct', 'superficial', 'unsubstantiated' and 'purely formal' and, in respect of the Commission's assessment of the effect of factors on the relevant market, stated:

> [V]ague assertions, which fail to provide the slightest detail of, in particular, the nature of campaign discounts, the circumstances in which such discounts might be applied, their degree of opacity, their size or their impact on price transparency, cannot support to the requisite legal standard the finding that the market is not sufficiently transparent to allow a collective dominant position.[77]

---

72 *Rhodia Chemie/Albright & Wilson case* (n 30) para [55].

73 *Lucent Technologies/Ascend Communications* (Case No IV/M.1440) [1999] OJ C139 4 para [18].

74 *State Street Corporation/Deutsche Bank Global Securities case* (n 45) para [18].

75 *ABB/Daimler-Benz case* (n 5) para [89].

76 *GEC Alsthom/Cegelec* (Case No IV/M.1164) [1998] OJ C181 3 para [22].

77 Case T-464/04 *Independent Music Publishers and Labels Association (Impala, International Association) v Commission of the European Communities* [2006] ECR II-02289 para [289] *(Impala v Commission)*.The CFI goes on to note at paragraph 320 that: 'It follows that the few assertions relating to campaign discounts contained in the section of the Decision dealing with the examination of the coordination of prices in the large countries, in so far as they are imprecise, unsupported, and

A second, and related, 'low-tech' method employed by the Commission in assessing factors is the presentation of a hypothesis along with some non-quantitative support for its inferences. For example, in three prohibited mergers, the Commission advanced the hypothesis that the removal of a competitor would facilitate tacit coordination. In these decisions, the Commission developed a detailed profile, based on documentary evidence, of the firm being removed, and used this profile to infer the potential effects of the firm's removal on the market's structure.[78] Examples of this technique can be seen in other cases, where the Commission refers, as support for its hypotheses, to: customers' views regarding the level of innovation in a market;[79] the views of the largest customer;[80] discussions with industry executives; [81] and documents submitted to the Board of Directors.[82]

A third 'low-tech' method used by the Commission in assessing factors is the presentation of simple quantitative analysis in support of its conclusions. Examples of the type of analyses used are shown in Table 4.4, and include: calculations of demand and supply side concentration indices, estimation of market and demand growth, and the use of a variety of methods to measure the degree of symmetry between undertakings. While some forms of simple quantitative analysis, such as the calculation of concentration indices, are common to a number of assessments, the other forms appear only relatively infrequently in the reported decisions.

'High tech' methods

In a relatively small number of decisions the Commission has used 'high-tech' economic methods in its assessment. The techniques used by the Commission have typically involved the consideration, or development, of a model, or some form of statistical estimation and analysis. Table 4.5 presents a list of

---

indeed contradicted by other observations in the Decision, cannot demonstrate the opacity of the market or even of campaign discounts. Those assertions are confined, moreover, to indicating that campaign discounts are less transparent than file discounts, but do not explain how they would be relevant for the transparency of the market and do not make it possible to understand how they in themselves might compensate for all the other factors of transparency of the market identified in the Decision and thus eliminate the transparency necessary for the existence of a collective dominant position'.

78 *Gencor/Lonrho case* (n 2) paras [186]–[192]; *Airtours/FirstChoice case* (n 8) paras [140]–[141]; *SCA/Metsä Tissue case* (n 27) para [145]–[150].

79 In relation to the level of innovation in the market: *Solvay/Montedison-Ausimont case* (n 32) para [50].

80 In relation to buyer power: *ABB/Daimler-Benz case* (n 5) paras [74],[84]–[85].

81 In relation to demand elasticity: *Pilkington-Techint/SIV case* (n 6) para [31].

82 In relation to the ability to retaliate: *Gencor/Lonrho case* (n 2) para [158].

Table 4.4 'Low-tech' methods used in factor assessments by the Commission under the ECMR

Examples of analysis
Calculation of concentration indices
Calculation of post-merger market shares of main competitors
Calculation of capacity utilisation ratios,[a] and the distribution of available capacity
Comparison of relative input costs and turnover levels of main companies[b]
Comparison of installed capacity[c]
Examining past participation in consortia for tenders[d]
Comparison of the historical variation in market shares[e]
Estimation of the rate of market growth[f]
Calculation of the Hirschmann-Herfindahl indices for cross-shareholdings to measure links[g]
Comparing relative market share movements of main competitors[h]
Examining past distribution of market growth[i]
Examining relative price movements[j]
Comparison of transport costs
Comparison of profit margins in the industry
Comparison of relative research and development spending[k]
Calculating demand-side concentration and percentage of sales to biggest customers[l]
Calculation of the level of discounts to different customers[m]

Notes:

a. *Alcan/Alusuisse case* (n 3) para [55].
b. *Danish Crown/Vestjyske Slagterier case* (n 10) para [101], [114]–[120], [31]–[134]; *Fortis/ABN AMRO assets* (Case COMP/M.4844) [2007] OJ C194 para [162]; [196].
c. *UPM-Kymmene/Haindl case* (n 32) paras [41]–[42], [69]; *KORSNē/ASSIDOMĎ CARTON-BOARD case* (n 50) para [68]; *LSG Lufthansa Service Holding/Gate Gourmet Switzerland case* (n 35) para [42].
d. *ABB/Daimler-Benz case* (n 5) para [74]–[79], [114].
e. *Nestlé/Perrier case* (n 5) para [46].
f. *Gencor/Lonrho case* (n 2) paras [161], [200]–[203]; *KarstadtQuelle/MyTravel case* (n 50) para [94]; *TUI/Firstchoice case* (n 50) para [102].
g. *Exxon/Mobil case* (n 2) para [256].
h. *Akzo Nobel/Hoechst Roussel Vet case* (n 30) para [34]–[39]; *Glaverbel/PPG case* (n 31) para [21].
i. *Nestlé/Perrier case* (n 5) para [67]–[70].
j. *Nestlé/Perrier case* (n 5) para [121]–[124]; *Sony/BMG* (Case COMP/M.3333) [2007] OJ C94 paras [18]–[23] (*Sony/BMG 2007 case*).
k. *Solvay/Montedison-Ausimont case* (n 32) para [57].
l. *BP/E.on case* (n 62) para [138]; *Shell/DEA case* (n 62) para [138]; *Knorr-Bremse/Allied Signal* (Case No IV/M.337) [1993] OJ C298 0 para [39].
m. *Gencor/Lonrho case* (n 2) paras [150], [162]–[164].

Table 4.5 *'High-tech' methods used in factor assessments by the Commission under the ECMR*

Examples of analysis
Use of external study which estimates the economies of scale[a]
Studies of price data and product substitutability[b]
Analysis of price movements and alignment[c]
Undertaking event studies or natural experiment analysis[d]
Analysis of installed capacity and long-run price movements[e]
Estimation of price elasticity estimates[f]
Analysis of structural and competitive advantages of independent competitors[g]
Analysis of how profitability relates to capacity utilisation[h]
Detailed examination of the mechanics of tendering and bidding procedures[i]
Analysis of potential impact of entry on prices in a related financial market[j]
Consideration of an empirical analysis of stock market movements and merger announcement[k]
Analysis of how potential retaliation mechanisms might operate[l]
Detailed examination of how the adequacy of interconnection capacity could affect prices[m]
Analysis of potential for coordination on capacity expansions or capacity downtime[n]
Detailed analysis of potential ways in which a market could be shared between competitors[o]

Notes:

a. *Danish Crown/Vestjyske Slagterier case* (n 10) para [177].
b. *Airtours/FirstChoice case* (n 8) para [88]–[91], [98].
c. *Sony/BMG 2004 case* (n 83) para [15]; *Sony/BMG 2007 case* (n 182) paras [20]–[21].
d. *UPM-Kymmene/Haindl case* (n 32) para [68],[73]; *Grupo Villar case* (n 10) para [43]–[48].
e. *UPM-Kymmene/Haindl case* (n 32) para [69].
f. *UPM-Kymmene/Haindl case* (n 32) para [88].
g. *Nestlé/Perrier case* (n 5) paras [72]–[76].
h. *UPM-Kymmene/Haindl case* (n 32) para [66]–[69].
i. *UPM-Kymmene/Haindl case* (n 32) paras [59]–[65]; *MAN/Auwärter case* (n 18) para [44]–[49]; *MCI WorldCom/Sprint case* (n 42) paras [78]–[83], [272]–[278]; *Toepfer/InVivo/Soulès* (Case COMP/M.4042) [2005] OJ C300 paras [45]–[48].
j. *EDF/AEM/Edison case* (n 5) paras [106]–[110].
k. *Airtours/FirstChoice case* (n 8) paras [154]–[157].
l. *Airtours/FirstChoice case* (n 8) paras [150]–[153]; *BP/E.on case* (n 62) para [116]–[125]; *Shell/DEA case* (n 62) paras [116]–[125]; *Outokumpu/Norzink case* (n 11) paras [24]–[25]; *EDF/AEM/Edison case* (n 5) para [103]–[104]; *KarstadtQuelle/MyTravel case* (n 50) paras [108]–[113]; *TUI/Firstchoice case* (n 50) paras [116]–[121]; *Linde/BOC case* (n 2) paras [146]; [188]; [202].
m. *Grupo Villar case* (n 10) paras [110]–[127].
n. *UPM-Kymmene/Haindl case* (n 32) para [128]–[139].
o. *MAN/Auwärter case* (n 18) paras [38]–[49]; *KORSNē/ASSIDOMĎ CARTONBOARD case* (n 50) paras [70]–[71]; *Linde/BOC case* (n 2) para [141]–[143]; *Grupo Vilar* case (n 10) para [116]–[120].

examples where detailed analysis has been undertaken or considered by the Commission in its assessment of different factors.

An important point to note in relation to the 'high-tech' economic methods detailed in Table 4.5 is that the majority of such analysis was undertaken in a small number of merger decisions.[83] Among these, the *UPM-Kymmene/Haindl* decision, which involved a merger in the highly concentrated markets for newsprint and magazine paper, where sophisticated economic analysis featured prominently, and the parties and the Commission both recruited a number of academic economists. In a number of the examples shown in Table 4.5 the analysis was undertaken by the parties, or their economic consultants, and submitted to the Commission who then reviewed the merits of the analysis.[84]

4.2.4 Economic Data

Economic data is conceived here as information that is capable of being quantified or statistically analysed. For example, economic data would include sales or output figures but would not include the terms of contracts or statements made by managers as to whether sales are 'high' or 'low'.

An understanding of the source, and types, of economic data used in the assessment of factors by the Commission under the ECMR is important for three reasons. First, an understanding of the types of information and data used in Commission assessments is important when examining the relative importance given to economic data vis-à-vis other types of information, such as documentary evidence. Second, identifying the providers, or sources, of data gives an indication of the relative influence of different data providers, such as the parties or their economic consultants, competitors and customers. Third, the Commission has at times been criticised by the Courts for its practices regarding data collection and analysis. For example, in its decision to overturn the prohibition of the *Airtours/FirstChoice* merger, the CFI was critical of the Commission's reliance on a market study which, upon investigation by the Court, turned out to be a one-page extract from that study.[85] The CFI was also critical of the Commission's failure to produce an econometric

---

[83] Notably *UPM-Kymmene/Haindl case* (n 32); *Sony/BMG* (Case No COMP/M.3333) [2004] OJ L062 *(Sony/BMG 2004 case)*; *Airtours/FirstChoice case* (n 8); *MAN/Auwärter case* (n 18).

[84] *Danish Crown/Vestjyske Slagterier case* (n 10) para [177]; *Airtours/FirstChoice case* (n 8) para [91], [155].

[85] Case T-342/99 *Airtours plc v Commission of the European Communities* [2002] ECR II-02585 para [128].

study upon which it alleged it had relied in its decision. [86] Likewise, in the *Impala v. Commission* decision, the CFI was highly critical of how the Commission had interpreted various statements received by retailers. The Court concluded that the Commission had misrepresented the number received and that further the statements did not support the conclusion the Commission drew from them.[87]

Sources of economic data

In over half of the factors assessed by the Commission no data source has been referenced. This may reflect the fact that the Commission has collected data but omitted the source in its decisions, or that data was not collected. Table 4.6 indicates that where data is referenced the most frequent sources are the market investigation (10 per cent), the parties (9 per cent); customers and competitors combined (7 per cent), or customers (4 per cent).

In assessing specific factors the Commission typically relies on data provided by particular sources. These sources are shown in Table 4.7. This table shows that data is frequently sourced from those with a purposive interest in its

Table 4.6 Frequency of use of different sources of data in Commission decisions under the ECMR

	Weighted overall rank* (%)
No source	56
Market investigation	10
Parties	9
More than one source (i.e. customers and competitors)	7
Customers	4
Other (includes confidential sources)	4
Trade association/third party data	3
External competition authorities	3
Competitors	2
External economists/studies/reports	2

Note: * The rank has been weighted by the overall frequency with which the factor has been considered multiplied by the various sources cited in the assessment of each individual factor

86 *Airtours plc v Commission of the European Communities* (n 85) para [132].
87 *Impala v Commission* (n 77) paras [385]–[387].

Table 4.7 Sources of data for specific factors in Commission decisions under the ECMR

	No. of markets	No source (%)	Parties (%)	Customers (%)	Competitors (%)	Trade assoc/3rd party (%)	External authorities (%)	External studies (%)	Market investigation (%)	Multiple sources(%)	Other (%)
Concentration levels	**266**	56	21	0	1	6	2	0	6	6	2
Potential competition	**130**	43	5	7	6	0	4	2	12	1	21
Existing competition	**103**	50	13	7	7	0	8	1	7	9	0
Buyer power	**91**	55	5	10	0	0	1	0	9	18	2
Market growth	**72**	61	8	1	3	0	0	1	4	11	10
Links	**53**	68	15	0	0	8	0	0	2	8	0
Symmetrical costs	**47**	51	19	0	0	4	13	6	2	0	4
Prices and margin movements	**39**	33	8	23	0	0	18	0	13	3	3
Ability to retaliate	**36**	50	17	6	3	0	3	0	8	11	3
Removal of competitor	**30**	47	7	13	10	0	13	0	7	3	0
Size and financial strength	**19**	47	5	0	0	5	0	0	5	37	0

presentation. For example, the parties are the most common source of the data on concentration levels, symmetrical costs and the ability to retaliate. Customers are the most frequently cited source of data for past price and margin movements and the potential impact of the removal of a competitor. The Commission frequently uses data from competitors in its assessment of existing, and potential, competition. Finally, the Commission has tended to use data from multiple sources in its assessment of possible coordination mechanisms, the relative size and financial strength of the companies and buyer power.

Who supplies the data, and the form in which it is supplied, is an important issue and one that was significant in *Impala v. Commission*. In that decision the CFI queried the reliability of evidence submitted by the parties to the Commission, and the Commission's acceptance of this evidence (where the evidence was found to have a large number of errors).[88]

Types of data examined

Although it is difficult to classify precisely the type of data examined by the Commission, it is possible to distinguish between those factors where the Commission has predominantly referred to documentary information and those where it has referred to economic data.

The Commission has used raw economic data, or data in the form of external economic studies or reports, in its assessment of at least nine factors. This type of economic data is used most commonly in the assessment of factors such as: the price elasticity of demand,[89] past prices and margin movements,[90] the level of similarity in costs,[91] and existing,[92] and

---

88 *Impala v Commission* (n 77) paras [415]; [422]–[425].

89 *Airtours/FirstChoice case* (n 8) para [98]; *Gencor/Lonrho case* (n 2) para [42]; *UPM-Kymmene/Haindl case* (n 32) para [88]; *Pilkington-Techint/SIV case* (n 6) para [31]; *SCA/Metsä Tissue case* (n 27) para [148].

90 *Gencor/Lonrho case* (n 2) para [165]–[166]; *UPM-Kymmene/Haindl case* (n 32) paras [69]–[70],[136]–[137]; *Pilkington-Techint/SIV case* (n 6) paras [33]–[34]; *Exxon/Mobil case* (n 2) para [604]; *TotalFina/Elf* (Case No COMP/M.1628) [2001] OJ L143 1 paras [211]–[212]; *Vattenfall/Elsam and E2 Assets* (Case COMP/ M.3867) [2005] OJ C184 paras [52]–[53];[67].

91 *Nestlé/Perrier case* (n 5) para [63]; *Mitsui/CVRD/Caemi* (Case COMP/M.2420) [2004] OJ L092 50 para [178]; *Danish Crown/Vestjyske Slagterier case* (n 10) para [177]; *Airtours/FirstChoice case* (n 8) para [99]; *Exxon/Mobil case* (n 2) paras [536],[660]–[661]; *Statoil/Hydro* (Case COMP/M.4545) [2007] OJ C130 para [108] (*Statoil/Hydro case*).

92 *Airtours/FirstChoice case* (n 8) para [84]; *Gencor/Lonrho case* (n 2) para [138]; *Wallenius Lines AB/Wilhelmsen ASA/Hyundai Merchant Marine* (Case No IV/M.2879) [2003] OJ L030 31 paras [18]–[19]; *Statoil/Hydro case* (n 91) para [107].

potential, competition.[93] In addition, the Commission has referenced economic reports of external agencies in at least 11 markets, including reports by: the European Commission Directorate of Transport and Energy; the UK Office of Fair Trading; the Spanish National Energy Commission; the Monopolies & Mergers Commission in the UK; the Bundeskartellamt; the U.S. Federal Trade Commission; the OECD and the Government of the Netherlands. These reports have been used to assess factors such as: symmetrical costs,[94] existing competition,[95] potential competition,[96] and possible post-merger incentives.[97]

The Commission has mainly used documentary information – such as the minutes of meetings, boardroom statements or the content of agreements – in its assessment of factors such as: potential for multi-market retaliation,[98] potential coordination mechanisms,[99] intention of parties to remove a competitor,[100] and links between the parties.[101]

In assessing some factors the Commission has used a combination of economic data and documentary information. For example, in *P&O Stena*, when assessing the amount of excess capacity in the cross-Channel freight transport market, the Commission referred to press announcements about capacity levels as well as conducting its own survey of the level of capacity in the market.[102] Other examples of where the Commission has combined economic data with documentary evidence can be seen in assessments of factors such as: size and financial strength,[103] and product homogeneity.[104]

---

93 *Danish Crown/Vestjyske Slagterier case* (n 10) para [160]; *Nestlé/Perrier case* (n 5) para [101],[106]; *Schneider Electric/MGE-UPS case* (n 19) para [38]–[40].

94 *Exxon/Mobil case* (n 2) para [661]–[662]; *UPM-Kymmene/Haindl case* (n 32) para [89]; *Air Liquide/BOC* (COMP/M.1630) [2004] OJ L092 1 para [276].

95 *Airtours/FirstChoice case* (n 8) para [76]; *Otto Versand/Freemans* (Case No IV/M.1527) [1999] OJ C211 15 paras [17],[31]; *Thorn EMI/Virgin Music* (Case No IV/M.202) [1992] OJ C120 0 para [39].

96 *Airtours/FirstChoice case* (n 8) para [114]; *Exxon/Mobil case* (n 2) para [736].

97 *Exxon/Mobil case* (n 2) para [754]; *Pilkington-Techint/SIV case* (n 6) para [32].

98 *Gencor/Lonrho case* (n 2) para [158].

99 *UPM-Kymmene/Haindl case* (n 32) para [72].

100 *Solvay/Montedison-Ausimont case* (n 32) para [41]; *Gencor/Lonrho case* (n 2) para [187]; *Procter & Gamble/Wella* (Case No IV/M.3149) [2003] OJ C195 6 para [44].

101 *Alcan/Alusuisse case* (n 3) para [97]; *BP/E.on case* (n 62) paras [63]–[71]; *Shell/DEA case* (n 62) paras [63]–[71].

102 *P&O Stena Line (Holding) Limited case* (n 25) para [24].

103 *UPM-Kymmene/Haindl case* (n 32) paras [48]–[52].

104 *Airtours/FirstChoice case* (n 8) paras [88]–[90].

4.2.5 Summary

Economic theory plays an important role in the decisions of the Commission in assessments of the potential for collective dominance under the ECMR. In particular, the Commission considers a range of factors, derived primarily from economic theory, in their assessment of the potential for coordinated behaviour post-merger. In the majority of these assessments the Commission has interpreted factors in a manner consistent with economic theory. In some assessments, the Commission has adopted a more, or less, definite position than suggested by the theory. Only rarely has a factor been interpreted inconsistently with theory. Commission practice does, however, differ substantively from economic theory in the relative emphasis given to different factors in assessments. While some factors considered important in the economic theory are considered frequently by the Commission, others are considered in only a relatively small number of assessments: a fact which may reflect practical considerations,[105] or other influences in the enforcement process as discussed in Chapter 5.

The Commission's approach to the assessment of factors can be broadly described as economic in the sense that the Commission examines economic indicators and processes. In this respect, three approaches can be seen: (1) identifying if a specific economic indicator for an economic factor exists; (2) examining an economic process; or (3) undertaking a global economic assessment to infer behaviour in a specific market.

The decisions indicate that the economic techniques employed by the Commission in assessing factors are primarily low-level quantitative or descriptive. In only a small number of decisions are 'high-tech' economic methods evident. The principal economic technique used by the Commission in assessing factors involves advancing a hypothesis, with varying levels of support, about how a factor may or may not promote coordination. In making its assessments, the Commission uses economic data to varying degrees. Where referenced, the main sources of economic data used by the Commission are the parties or the parties' customers. However, in a large number of decisions the Commission provides no source for the data that underlies its assessment. In assessing particular factors the Commission tends to rely on data from specific sources. The types of economic data used by the Commission include raw economic data, economic studies, and the reports of foreign competition authorities. In some cases, factor assessments are based on a combination of economic data and documentary information.

---

105 Compare D. Neven, R. Nuttall and P. Seabright *Mergers in Daylight: The Economics and Politics of European Merger Control* (Centre for Economic Policy Research, London, 1993) xiii.

4.3 ARTICLE 82 DECISIONS: THE COMMISSION

An assessment under Article 82 of the EC Treaty involves an *ex post* examination of whether an abuse of a collective dominant position has occurred. There are three limbs that need to be considered in an Article 82 assessment:

1. That the undertakings are capable of being collectively assessed;
2. That the collective undertakings hold a dominant position; and
3. That the undertakings have abused that dominant position

This section examines the use of economics – economic theory, approach, techniques and data – in Commission assessments under these limbs.

It is worth noting at the outset that there have only been seven Commission decisions involving collective dominance under Article 82. Accordingly, the data set underlying the discussion in this section, although exhaustive, is not large. The small number of decisions under this provision is however, in itself, of potential interest for the examination in this book, and Chapter 5 offers some insights as to whether the complexities of economics in this area are related to the infrequency of investigations under this provision.

4.3.1 Economic theory

The Commission has examined a range of factors derived from the predictions of economic theory in its assessments under Article 82. However, as in the assessment of mergers, some of the factors considered are not directly derived from a specific prediction of economic theory but rather reflect more general predictions of economic theory.

Consistency of factor interpretation with economic theory

Tables 4.8 and 4.9 compare the Commission's interpretation of factors in assessing whether undertakings hold a collective dominant position – the second limb of an assessment under Article 82 – and the predictions of economic theory in relation to tacit collusion. The tables reveal a high level of consistency between Commission interpretation and economic theory. However some differences do exist, and are discussed below in more detail.

Tables 4.8 and 4.9 show that in its assessment of factors where a principle of interpretation can be inferred, the Commission has in 19 assessments (83 per cent) been consistent with economic theory. In the remaining four assessments (17 per cent) the Commission has in all cases adopted a more definite interpretation than the theory suggests. In *Italian Flat Glass*, for example, the Commission adopted the position that the slow growth of the flat glass market would enhance the dominance, and the ability to engage in coordinated behav-

Table 4.8 Comparison of the interpretation of factors from economic theory and in the Commission's Article 82 decisions

Factor	Prediction from economic theory	Commission position	No. of markets	Facilitates	Hinders	Application of factor unclear
High market concentration	Facilitates	Enhances dominance	**6**	6		
Structural links	Facilitates	Enhances dominance	**6**	6		
Weak existing competition	Not considered	Enhances dominance	**4**	4		
High entry barriers	Facilitates	Enhances dominance	**3**	3		
Size and financial strength	Not clear	Enhances dominance	**3**	3		
Buyer power	Hinders	Hinders coordination	**1**		1	
Market growth	Not clear	Hinders dominance	**1**		1	
Increasing/similar price margins	Facilitates	Enhances dominance	**1**	1		
Volatile market shares	Hinders	Hinders dominance	**1**		1	
Vertical integration	Facilitates	Enhances dominance	**1**	1		
Ability to price discriminate	Not considered	Enhances dominance	**1**	1		

Table 4.9 Summary of the interpretation of factors from economic theory and in the Commission's Article 82 decisions

	Facilitates	Hinders	Mixed	Total	Percentage where a principle can be inferred	Percentage of total factors
Consistent with theory	17	2	0	19	**83**	68
More definite than theory	3	1	0	4	**17**	14
Less definite than theory	0	0	0	0	**0**	0
Inconsistent with theory	0	0	0	0	**0**	0
				23	**100**	**82**
Factor application unclear	0	0	0	0		0
Factor not in theory	5	0	0	5		18
Total factor assessments				**28**		**100**

iour, of the existing flat glass producers.[106] This is a more definite position than economic theory which is unclear as to how coordinated behaviour relates to market growth.

These tables also show that the majority of factors (82 per cent) considered by the Commission in its assessment of collective dominance under Article 82 are related to specific predictions of the theories of tacit collusion. However, two of the 11 factors considered by the Commission – the ability to price discriminate and the effect of existing competition – are not directly related to theories of tacit collusion. In *TACA*, for example, the Commission's 'presumption of the dominance' of the TACA conference was 'confirmed, inter alia, by the fact that the TACA parties have succeeded in maintaining a discriminatory price structure'.[107] Price discrimination is not considered relevant to an assessment of tacit collusion in the economic literature, and in addition, there is a general scepticism within that literature that it is possible to test for price discrimination within liner shipping conferences.[108]

Table 4.8 also shows the relative importance the Commission places on selected factors as implied by frequency of use. It shows that the Commission has examined market concentration in all but one of its assessments (86 per cent). However, other key factors identified in the economic theory are examined relatively infrequently, or not examined at all. For example, entry barriers were examined in only three of seven assessments (43 per cent), while buyer power was examined in only one market assessment (14 per cent). The other key factors identified in economic theory that do not feature in the Commission's assessments under Article 82, include: market transparency, the degree of symmetry in costs, the level of technological innovation, the ability to retaliate, the frequency of interaction, the extent of multi-market contact and the stability of demand. Once again, it is difficult, based on the text of the reported decisions, to account for the Commission's focus on particular factors in making assessments under Article 82. However, the small number of formal decisions under this provision, and the concentration of these decisions in specific sectors (i.e. shipping conferences) with particular characteristics (such as some form of agreement between the parties) may provide some insight into this.

Consistency between Article 82 and ECMR assessments

Tables 4.10 and 4.11 compare the factors considered in an *ex post* assessment

---

106 *Flat Glass* (Case No IV/31. 906) [1989] OJ L033 44 para [79] (*Italian flat glass case*).

107 *Trans-Atlantic Conference Agreement* (Case No IV/35.134) [1999] OJ L095 1 para [534] (*TACA case*).

108 Compare W. Sjostrom 'Price discrimination by shipping conferences' (1992) 28 Logistics and Transportation Review 213.

of collective dominance under Article 82 with factors that are employed in an *ex ante* assessment of collective dominance under the ECMR. Such a comparison reveals similarities and differences in both the factors considered and the frequency in which the factors are used. At a conceptual level such a comparison is interesting in so far as it reveals insights as to the degree of correspondence in the use of factors in *ex ante* assessments of the future potential for tacit coordination under the ECMR, and *ex post* assessments of past instances of tacit coordination under Article 82.

Table 4.10 compares the Commission's interpretation of factors under Article 82 and under the ECMR with the predictions of economic theory. This shows that fewer factors have been assessed under Article 82 than under the ECMR – 11 factors as compared to 28 factors.[109] Where a common set of factors are examined, the Commission is consistent in its interpretation of those factors under the two legal provisions in all but two cases. In respect of these two factors – similar price movements and structural links – the Commission's interpretation appears to differ in an *ex ante* assessment of the potential for collective dominance under the ECMR from an *ex post* assessment of collective dominance under Article 82. However, in the case of prices and margin movements it is difficult to generalise as there has only been one assessment of this factor under Article 82.[110] In respect of structural links the difference appears to reflect varying perceptions of the necessity under the two provisions to identify structural links in order to show collective dominance.

Table 4.11 compares the frequency by which factors are examined under both legal provisions. This table shows that while factors such as the degree of market concentration and the extent of existing competition are commonly examined under both provisions, the frequency with which other factors are examined differs. For example, buyer power is assessed in 33 per cent of markets under the ECMR and in only 14 per cent of markets under Article 82. Similarly, the Commission has examined the extent of structural links between the parties in 86 per cent of assessments under Article 82, while this factor has featured in only 26 per cent of assessments under the ECMR. In addition,

---

109 This may not simply reflect the fact that there has been a smaller number of Article 82 decisions than merger decisions. Rather, Article 82 investigations have involved less comprehensive assessments of economic factors than have occurred in certain merger investigations. For example, the Commission examined an average of 14 factors in the merger decisions where it concluded that collective dominance will be created or strengthened as a result of the merger (prior to commitments), and examined 20 factors in its outright prohibition decisions in *Airtours/FirstChoice* and *Gencor/Lonrho*.

110 *TACA case* (n 107) para [543].

Table 4.10 Comparison of the interpretation of factors from economic theory and in the Commission's decisions under Article 82 and the ECMR

Factor	Prediction from theory	Position under Art. 82	Position under ECMR
Buyer power	Hinders tacit collusion	Hinders coordination	Hinders coordination
High market concentration	Facilitates tacit collusion	Enhances dominance	Facilitates coordination
Market growth	Not clear	Hinders dominance	Hinders coordination
High entry barriers	Facilitates tacit collusion	Enhances dominance	Facilitates coordination
Inc./similar prices margins	Facilitates tacit collusion	Enhances dominance	Mixed positions
Structural links	Facilitates tacit collusion	Enhances dominance	Mixed positions
Size and financial strength	No clear prediction	Enhances dominance	Facilitates coordination
Volatile market shares	Hinders tacit collusion	Hinders dominance	Hinders coordination
Vertical integration	Facilitates tacit collusion	Enhances dominance	Facilitates coordination
Weak existing competition	Not considered	Enhances dominance	Facilitates coordination

Table 4.11 Comparison of frequency of examination of economic factors under Article 82 and the ECMR by the Commission

	Percentage of markets under Article 82	Percentage of markets under ECMR
High market concentration	86	97
Structural links	86	26
Weak existing competition	57	37
High entry barriers	43	48
Size and financial strength	43	7
Buyer power	14	33
Market growth	14	20
Increasing/high and similar prices and margins	14	14
Volatility of market shares	14	7
Vertical integration	14	9
Ability to price discriminate	14	0

some factors that are increasingly seen as important to an assessment under the ECMR, such as the identification of a retaliation mechanism and the level of market transparency, have not been considered at all under Article 82.

Finally, a comparison of the actions or practices identified under the third limb of Article 82 as 'abuses' of a collective dominant position with the potential coordination mechanisms identified by the Commission under the ECMR reveals some differences. The potential coordination mechanisms investigated under the ECMR typically relate to the ability of the collectively dominant undertakings to either: restrict capacity;[111] co-ordinate capacity expansions or investments;[112] split markets, either geographically or according to products;[113] or coordinate on auction outcomes as a means of market splitting.[114] While some of these coordination mechanisms, such as market segmentation and alterations to the structure of a bidding market, do appear as *ex post* abuses under Article 82, differences exist in relation to coordination on prices. Put simply, while the potential coordination mechanisms identified under the ECMR focus principally on coordination of capacity decisions or allocations,

111 *Airtours/FirstChoice case* (n 8) paras [147],[153].
112 *UPM-Kymmene/Haindl case* (n 32) paras [128]–[129].
113 *MAN/Auwärter case* (n 18) paras [38]–[49].
114 *MCI WorldCom/Sprint case* (n 42) paras [272]–[278].

the abuses identified *ex post* under Article 82 are more focused on coordinated decisions relating to prices, such as coordination on discounts,[115] identical pricing[116] or the terms of pricing agreements.[117] Although it is difficult to fully account for this difference in emphasis in *ex ante* and *ex post* assessments of coordination, one possible explanation is that, in practical terms, evidence of *ex post* instances of cocoordinated pricing abuses may be easier to collect and interrogate, whereas *ex post* evidence of coordination on capacity decisions, or of market splitting, may be both less readily available and more difficult to analyse and assess.

4.3.2 Assessment Approach

As discussed in relation to merger decisions, the economic approach translates at the case level to whether economic *indicators* are used, and economic *processes* examined, in the assessment of factors.

The Commission's broad approach to the assessment of factors under Article 82 can be described as a combination of legal and economic insofar as it involves a consideration of both economic indicators, and economic processes, and a range of documentary evidence. It is important to note in this respect that the majority of undertakings assessed under Article 82 have previously been investigated under Article 81 of the EC Treaty.[118] Consequently, the Commission already has in its possession evidence submitted by the parties in either applying for an Article 81(3) exemption, or as part of the Commission's investigation as to whether an agreement was prohibited by

---

115 *Italian flat glass case* (n 106) paras [20]–[21],[80]; *Irish Sugar plc* (Case No. IV/34.621, 35.059/F-3) [1997] OJ L258 1 paras [128]–[129] (*Irish Sugar case*); *Cewal, Cowac and Ukwal* (Case No. IV/32.448 and IV/32.450) [1993] OJ L034 20 para [84] (*Cewal case*).

116 *Italian flat glass case* (n 106) paras [18]–[19],[80].

117 *Irish Sugar case* (n 115) para [123],[136]; *European sugar industry* (Case No.IV/26 918) [1973] OJ L140 17 paras [E1]–[E2] (*European sugar case*).

118 Article 81(1) of the EC Treaty prohibits certain agreements or concerted practices between competing firms. An exemption may be sought by undertakings in respect of the applicability of this provision under Article 81(3). The types of information submitted as part of an Article 81(3) procedure are discussed in D. Neven, P. Papandropoulos and P. Seabright *Trawling for Minnows: European Competition Policy and Agreements between Firms* (Centre for Economic Policy Research, London, 1998) 114. Article 82 cases where the undertakings were investigated under Article 81(1) or sought an exemption under Article 81(3) are: *Cewal case* (n 115); *Italian flat glass case* (n 106); *European sugar case* (n 117); *TACA case* (n 107); *French-West African shipowners' committees* (Case No.IV/32.450) [1992] OJ L134 1; *P&I Clubs, IGA* (Case No. IV/D-1/30.373) and *P&I Clubs, Pooling Agreement* (Case No IV/D-1/37.143) [1999] OJ L125 12 (P&I Clubs case).

Article 81(1).[119] Bearing this in mind, three particular assessment approaches of the Commission in Article 82 cases can be identified.

One approach is for the Commission to rely on an analysis of economic indicators and processes undertaken as part of an Article 81 assessment. The Commission adopted this approach in assessing market growth in the flat glass market in *Italian Flat Glass*.[120] Similarly, in *TACA*, the Commission assessed the potential for entry into the trans-Atlantic liner shipping market, based on its Article 81 assessment of the costs associated with increasing capacity, and the incentives for the market to be contestable.[121]

A second assessment approach, as with merger assessments, is for the Commission to identify whether an economic indicator for an economic factor exists. For example, in *French West Africa*, which related to abuses in the markets for shipping liner services between France and 11 West African nations, the Commission relied on indicators such as network coverage and relative capacity levels as indicators of the size and strength of the undertakings.[122] Similarly, the Commission has assessed potential competition by examining demand levels and forecasts, and estimated levels of investment costs.[123]

A final assessment approach in Article 82 cases is more legal than economic in nature, and focuses on agreements between undertakings. Where this assessment approach has been adopted, the Commission has not referred to any economic indicators or processes in determining the effect of a factor, relying instead on an analysis of the content, and indicative meaning, of documents. Examples of this approach can be seen in *Cewal*, a case involving liner shipping between Northern Europe and Zaire, and in respect of some factors in *TACA*. In both of these cases, the Commission focused on key documents and on the respective conference agreements to substantiate its findings that the shipping lines had held, and abused, a collective dominant position.[124]

---

119 As to the legality of this approach see: Joined cases T-68/89, T-77/89 and T-78/89 *Società Italiana Vetro SpA, Fabbrica Pisana SpA and PPG Vernante Pennitalia SpA v Commission of the European Communities* [1992] ECR II-01403 para [360]; Joined cases T-191/98, T-212/98 to T-214/98 *Atlantic Container Line AB and Others v Commission of the European Communities* [2003] ECR II-03275 paras [184]–[187], [1275]–[1277].

120 *Italian flat glass case* (n 106) paras [12],[79].

121 *TACA case* (n 107) paras [545]–[546].

122 *French-West African shipowners' committees* (Case No.IV/32.450) [1992] OJ L134 1 para [65] (*French-West African case*).

123 *Italian flat glass case* (n 106) para [79].

124 *TACA case* (n 107) paras [551], [555], [563]–[564]; *Cewal case* (n 115) para [32], [64], [73].

4.3.3 Economic Techniques

As is the case with merger assessments, the Commission generally uses 'low-tech' economic methods in assessing factors under Article 82. Once again, three 'low-tech' methods can be identified. First, the postulating of an unsupported hypothesis.[125] Second, the presentation of a hypothesis with non-quantitative support, such as documentary or other written evidence.[126] Third, presentation of an hypothesis supported by basic quantitative analysis, such as simple calculations and estimations of indicators relating to market concentration, costs, market growth and relative price movements. An example of this third method can be seen in *Italian Flat Glass*, where the Commission supported its conclusions relating to abusive behaviour by the three firms in operating an unfair discount policy, segmenting the market, and pricing identically, with simple quantitative analysis, using 'natural experiment' data, of these factors.[127] Other examples of analyses employed using this technique are shown in Table 4.12.

In two decisions, the Commission has employed 'high-tech' economic methods in Article 82 assessments. Specifically, in *TACA* and *French West Africa* the Commission assessed some factors using econometric or statistical studies (see Table 4.13).

Where the Commission has relied on 'high-tech' economic analysis, this analysis has always been externally sourced. For example, in *TACA*, the Commission relied, in its assessment of buyer power, on a report commissioned by the European Commission Directorate of Transport and Energy, which showed a limited ability of shipping customers to switch to alternative suppliers.[128] Similarly, in *French West Africa*, in assessing the level of existing competition in liner shipping routes between French ports and 11 West

---

[125] In the *Italian flat glass case*, the Commission postulated, without referencing support, that the three flat glass producers were protected from competition because they displayed similar levels of vertical integration. *Italian flat glass case* (n 106) para [79].

[126] For example, when presenting the hypothesis that the level of internal competition was limited within a shipping conference in various shipping decisions, the Commission has relied on previous Court decisions (*TACA case* (n 107) para [522]–[525]) and on European sector-specific regulations (*French-West African case* (n 122) para [51]). Similarly, in *Irish sugar*, in hypothesising that the common ownership of the sole producer of sugar beet and the sole distributor of sugar in Ireland created incentives for coordinated behaviour, the Commission referred for support to documents relating to ownership structure, as well as board minutes: *Irish sugar case* (n 115) para [114], [123]–[125].

[127] *Italian flat glass case* (n 106) paras [18],[20],[23]. This was combined with documents such as internal memorandum and notes.

[128] *TACA case* (n 107) fn [43]

Table 4.12 *'Low-tech' methods used in Article 82 assessments by the Commission*

Examples of analysis
Calculation of concentration indices
Examination of the historical increase in market shares[a]
Examination of the number of products, frequency of service and network coverage[b]
Calculation of estimates of the costs of new investments[c]
Calculation of estimates of rate of market growth[d]
Examination of past price increases and profitability[e]
Comparison of historical relative price movements of undertakings[f]

Notes:
a. *Italian Flat glass case* (n 106) para [11].
b. *P&I Clubs, IGA* (Case No. IV/D-1/30.373) and *P&I Clubs, Pooling Agreement* (Case No IV/D- 1/37.143) [1999] OJ L125 12 para [57] (*P&I Clubs case*); *French-West African case* (n 122) para [65]; *Cewal case* (n 115) para [59].
c. *Italian flat glass case* (n 106) para [12]; *TACA case* (n 107) para [545].
d. *Italian flat glass case* (n 106) para [12].
e. *TACA case* (n 107) para [543].
f. *TACA case* (n 107) para [308].

Table 4.13 *'High-tech' methods used in Article 82 assessments by the Commission*

Examples of analysis
Analysis of customer switching behaviour[a]
Analysis of various external studies showing degree of substitutability between various seaports in Europe and Africa, and also considering the rate of deflections of trade between these seaports[b]
Consideration of studies that present an analysis of relative maritime to inland transport costs in Europe and Africa[c]

Notes:
a. *TACA case* (n 107) para [540], [122].
b. *French-West African case* (n 122) para [61].
c. *French-West African case* (n 122) para [60].

African countries, the Commission relied on a number of external studies that examined substitutability and relative costs. [129]

[129] *French-West African case* (n 122) fn [26] fn [28].

4.3.4 Economic Data

Source of data

Table 4.14 reveals that in just over two-thirds of Article 82 decisions the Commission presents a source for the data underlying its assessment. The most frequently cited source of data is the parties; such data commonly comprising materials submitted by the parties in applying for an Article 81(3) exemption.[130] In assessing a small number of factors, the Commission has relied on economic data from external sources such as trade associations, or from economic studies or reports produced by external consultants, foreign competition agencies or international bodies, such as the OECD.

In assessing specific factors under the different limbs of Article 82, the Commission typically relies on data from particular sources. These sources are shown in Table 4.15. As is the case in merger assessments, data is often sourced from those with a purposive interest in its presentation. For example, data is frequently sourced from the parties in assessments of: buyer power, existing level of competition, and past price and margin movements.

Table 4.14 Frequency of use of different sources of data by the Commission in Article 82 decisions

	Weighted overall rank* (%)
No source	31
Agreement between parties	16
Parties' documentary evidence submitted	16
Article 81 application	10
Previous decision	9
Parties' data	9
External economists/studies/reports	3
Trade association	3
Regulation 4056/86	2
External references – foreign competition authority, OECD	1
Other	1

Note: * The rank has been weighted by the overall frequency with which the factor has been considered multiplied by the various sources cited in the assessment of each individual factor.

130 *TACA case* (n 107) para [533], [546], [551], [563]; *P&I Clubs case* (n 118) paras [128]–[129].

Table 4.15 Sources of data for specific factors in Commission decisions under Article 82

	No. of markets	No source (%)	Parties' data (%)	Parties' documents (%)	Previous decision (%)	Art. 85/Art. 81 Application (%)	Agreement between parties (%)	External studies (%)	Trade association (%)	Other (%)
Concentration levels	**6**	71	29							
Structural links	**6**	17		17		17	50			
Existing competition	**4**	50	19		19	6		6		
Size and financial strength	**3**	83			17					
Potential competition	**3**	17				33	17		17	17
Volatile market shares	**1**	100								
Market growth	**1**								100	
Ability to price discriminate	**1**		50					50		
Vertical integration	**1**	100								
Buyer power	**1**		33	33				33		
Prices and margin movements	**1**	33	33					33		

Types of data collected

In assessing factors under Article 82, the Commission has most commonly relied on documents such as the minutes of meetings, boardroom statements or the content of agreements. However, economic studies have been used in some assessments, including in the assessments of factors such as: the existence of economic links;[131] existing competition;[132] buyer power;[133] and prices and margin movements.[134] The Commission also references economic reports from external agencies in its assessment of two alleged abuses of collective dominance in one decision,[135] and the raw economic data of a trade association in assessing two factors in another decision.[136]

4.3.5 Summary

The Commission uses factors derived from economic theory in its assessment of alleged abuses of a collective dominant position under Article 82. Where employed, there is a high level of consistency between the Commission's interpretation of these factors and the predictions of economic theory. However, the Commission has considered some factors that are not directly derived from the theory of tacit collusion, and its interpretation of a small number of factors has sometimes been more definite than the theory suggests. The reported decisions indicate that the economic factors examined, and the frequency with which such factors are examined, differs in an *ex post* assessment of collective dominance under Article 82 from an *ex ante* assessment of the potential for collective dominance under the ECMR, implying that economic theory is used in different ways in enforcing the two legal provisions. The Commission's approach to the assessment of factors under Article 82 can be considered both legal and economic insofar as it considers economic indicators, and economic processes, as well as documentary or other non-economic evidence. This approach reflects, in part, the fact that the majority of decisions under Article 82 involve undertakings that have previously applied for an Article 81(3) exemption in respect of which they have been required to provide detailed documentary information to the Commission. As with merger assessments, the economic techniques employed by the Commission in assessing factors under Article 82 are primarily 'low-tech'. This typically involves the Commission postulating a

131 *TACA case* (n 107) paras [531], [197].
132 *French-West African case* (n 122) paras [60]–[61].
133 *TACA case* (n 107) para [540].
134 *TACA case* (n 107) para [543].
135 *Cewal case* (n 115) paras [67], [69], [77].
136 *Italian flat glass case* (n 106) paras [79], [22].

hypothesis relating to an abuse under Article 82, with varying levels of support. High-tech economic methods feature relatively infrequently. In assessing the majority of factors the Commission has relied on documents or other non-economic information to support its conclusions. However, the Commission has referenced economic data in assessments of some factors, including economic studies and the findings of foreign competition authorities. The main sources for such data have been: the parties; external competition agencies; and trade associations.

4.4 MERGER DECISIONS AND ARTICLE 82 DECISIONS: THE COURTS

All decisions of the Commission are subject to review by the Community Courts. The Court of First Instance (CFI) is the principal body responsible for hearing competition law cases in the first instance, except when a Member State is involved where the European Court of Justice (ECJ) can perform judicial review in the first instance. A decision of the CFI can subsequently be appealed to the ECJ on a point of law only. The ECJ can also consider references from national courts on points of law in respect of the EC Treaty.

This section considers how economic theory, approach and data have featured in the reported decisions of the Courts in collective dominance cases.[137] The examination is based on a review of all CFI and ECJ decisions under the ECMR and Article 82 involving collective dominance.[138]

---

137 As the Courts do not specifically refer to economic techniques in their review, this strand of economics is not considered.

138 In four decisions a national court of a Member State has asked the Court for an opinion on the application of Article 82. The decisions were not preceded by an investigation by the Commission and did not involve the Court specifically assessing whether an abuse of a collective dominant position had occurred: Joined cases C-140/94, C-141/94 and C-142/94 *DIP SpA v Comune di Bassano del Grappa, LIDL Italia Srl v Comune di Chioggia and Lingral Srl v Comune di Chiogga* [1995] ECR I-03257 (*DIP SpA case*); Case C-393/92 *Municipality of Almelo and others v NV Energiebedrijf Ijsselmij* [1994] ECR I-01477 (*Gemente Almelo case*); Case C-309/99 *J.C.J. Wouters, J.W. Savelbergh and Price Waterhouse Belastingadviseurs BV v Algemene Raad van de Nederlandse Orde van Advocaten* [2002] ECR I-01577 (*Wouters case*); Joined cases C-215/96 and C-216/96 *Carlo Bagnasco and Others v Banca Popolare di Novara soc. coop. arl. (BNP) (C-215/96) and Cassa di Risparmio di Genova e Imperia SpA (Carige) (C-216/96)* [1999] ECR I-00135 (*Bagnasco case*).

4.4.1 Economic Theory

Mergers

The economic factors that can be considered by the Courts are limited to those that are contested and feature in the pleas of the parties. Table 4.16 details the 13 factors considered by the Courts in their review of decisions under the ECMR. It shows that 11 of these factors have been interpreted in a manner consistent with the predictions of economic theory.[139]

Of significant interest is how the Courts' interpretation of factors compares to the Commission's interpretation of those same factors in merger assessments. A comparison of Table 4.16 and Table 4.1, shows that the Courts' interpretation of certain factors has been *more* consistent with economic theory than the Commission's interpretation of the same factors.[140] For example, in *Airtours/FirstChoice* the Commission concluded that a retaliation mechanism was not a necessary condition for collective dominance, whereas on appeal the CFI held, consistent with economic theory, that such a mechanism is necessary to establish coordination.

The Courts have also been internally consistent in the direction of their interpretation of economic factors – whether a factor aids or hinders collusion – in the decisions it has reviewed. However, the relative importance of different factors to an assessment of collective dominance has at times varied. For example, the Courts have made varying statements as to how 'links' should be assessed. In *France v Commission* the ECJ concluded that the legal standard required that the Commission not only identify links, but also present an

---

[139] In one decision, the Court appears to have adopted a stronger, but not necessarily inconsistent, position on the relevance of a particular factor than that suggested by theory. In *Sun Chemical v Commission* the CFI's interpretation of the relevance of excess capacity/capacity constraints is by reference to their omission in relation to coordinated effects from the merger guidelines, and on this basis it concludes that the 'existence of capacity constraints plays a significant role only in the examination of non-coordinated effects' (paras [123]–[124]). Similarly, in that same decision, the CFI notes – again by reference to the merger guidelines – that the absence of homogeneity of products sold hindered coordination (paras [117]–[118]). Case T-282/06 *Sun Chemical Group BV v Commission of the European Communities* [2007] ECR II-02149 (*Sun Chemical v Commission case*).

[140] This is an interesting observation, given the different specialist skills and access to economic expertise of the two bodies. One explanation may lie in the differing strategies of the two institutions. While the Commission may be well served by employing wide-ranging arguments, relying on a number of economic factors and interpretations of those factors, the Court is limited to reviewing the economic arguments that feature in the contested parts of the case. In addition, any elements of theory that are contested at the Court stage have typically been supported by extensive economic support and references.

Table 4.16 Comparison of the interpretation of factors from economic theory and in the Courts' ECMR decisions

Factor	Prediction from theory	Courts' position
Volatile demand/ bus. cycle	Hinders tacit collusion	Hinders coordination
Small no. of competitors	Facilitates tacit collusion	Can facilitate coordination
Ability to retaliate	Facilitates tacit collusion	Can facilitate coordination
Symmetrical costs	Facilitates tacit collusion	Facilitates coordination
Structural links	Facilitates tacit collusion	Facilitates coordination
Declining market	Hinders tacit collusion	Hinders coordination
Market transparency	Facilitates tacit collusion	Facilitates coordination
Excess capacity	Not clear	Relevant only to non-coordinated effects
Product homogeneity	Not clear	Can facilitate coordination
High market concentration	Facilitates tacit collusion	Market shares important but not determinative
Entry barriers	Facilitates tacit collusion	Facilitates coordination
Volatile market shares	Hinders tacit collusion	Hinders coordination
Buyer power	Hinders tacit collusion	Hinders coordination

analysis of how they impact upon competitive behaviour.[141] By contrast, in *Gencor v. Commission*, the CFI concluded that it was sufficient for the Commission to show that links exist between the parties in its assessment of collective dominance.[142]

Article 82

As with mergers, the factors considered by the Courts in Article 82 decisions are determined by the pleas that are presented by the parties. Accordingly, the Courts have examined different factors in reviewing Article 82 decisions than reviewing decisions under the ECMR.

The Courts' examination of factors in Article 82 cases has typically focused not on the causal relationship between the factor and collective dominance, but rather on whether the factor should be considered relevant to an assessment of collective dominance based on the previous decisional practice of the Commission and the Courts. For example, as shown in Table 4.17, in relation to

[141] Joined cases C-68/94 and C-30/95 *French Republic and Société commerciale des potasses et de l'azote (SCPA) and Entreprise minière et chimique (EMC) v Commission of the European Communities* [1998] ECR I-01375 para [166] (*France v Commission*).

[142] Case T 102/96 *Gencor Ltd v Commission of the European Communities* [1999] ECR II 00753 para [273]–[277] (*Gencor v Commission*).

Table 4.17 Comparison of the interpretation of factors from economic theory and the Courts' decisions under Article 82 and the ECMR

Factor	Prediction from theory	Courts' position under Art. 82	Courts' position under ECMR
Structural links	Facilitates collusion	Enhances dominance	Facilitates coordination
Market concentration	Facilitates collusion	Strong indication of dominance	Important, not determinative
Entry barriers	Facilitates collusion	Enhances dominance	Facilitates coordination
Increasing/similar price margins	Facilitates collusion	Relevant to assessment	Not considered
Buyer power	Hinders collusion	Relevant to assessment	Hinders coordination
Homogenous product	No clear prediction	Relevant to assessment	Can facilitate coordination
Volatile market shares	Hinders collusion	Relevant to assessment	Hinders coordination

four factors – price and margins, buyer power, homogenous product and volatility of market shares – the Courts have concluded that these factors are relevant to the assessment of collective dominance, but have not stated how these factors should be interpreted. In addition, the ECJ has stated that the three cumulative criteria for collective dominance established in *Airtours v. Commission* apply in relation to Article 82 matters (although it does not then examine these).[143]

Table 4.17 above compares the Courts' interpretation of economic factors under Article 82 and under the ECMR with the predictions of economic theory. It reveals that the Courts' interpretation of factors under Article 82 has been generally consistent with the predictions of economic theory, and with the Courts' interpretation of the same factors under the ECMR. However, the Courts' assessment of the significance of structural links in supporting a finding of collective dominance has varied under the two legal instruments. While the Courts have adopted the position in their review of merger decisions that structural links are *not* a necessary condition for a finding of collective dominance,[144] in their decisions under Article 82 they have adopted varying positions. For example, in *Gemente Almelo*, where the Court was asked to consider whether Article 82 precluded the application by a Dutch regional electricity distributor of an exclusive purchasing clause that prohibited a local distributor from importing electricity, the ECJ ruled that undertakings *must* be linked in a way that they adopt a common conduct for a finding of collective dominance.[145] A similar position was adopted by the Court in *Wouters* where the 'absence of sufficient structural links' between members of the Dutch Bar implied that they could not be regarded as occupying a collective dominant position.[146] However, in hearing the appeal of the Commission's *Cewal* decision in *Compagnie Maritime Belge*, the ECJ ruled that links were not 'indispensable' to a finding of collective dominance.

4.4.2 Economic Approach

Mergers

As discussed above, the Court is limited to reviewing the pleas raised in respect of a contested decision, and this may involve the Court considering

[143] Case T 193/02 *Laurent Piau v Commission of the European Communities* [2005] ECR II-00209 para [111] (*Piau v Commission*).

[144] *Gencor v Commission* (n 142) para [273]–[277]; Case T 342/99 *Airtours plc v Commission of the European Communities* [2002] ECR II 02585 para [60] (*Airtours v Commission*).

[145] *Gemente Almelo case* (n 138) para [42].

[146] *Wouters case* (n 138) para [114].

the Commission's assessment of various economic factors. Two approaches of the Court to this review process are evident. First, in some reviews, the Courts' approach has been confined to a textual analysis of the contested decision. In such cases, the Court has limited its analysis to identifying whether a factor features in the contested decision,[147] or is consistent with the published guidelines of the Commission.[148] This approach was frequently evident in *Gencor v Commission* where the Court's review of various factors was focused on establishing whether the Commission took 'due account' of the factor and gave proper reasons for its decision.[149] Accordingly, the Court in that case would not, for example, enter into a substantive discussion in relation to Gencor's claim that the Commission, in assessing price movements, had ignored evidence prepared by their economic consultants showing that prices in platinum grade metals had declined in real terms over the last decade. Instead, identification by the Court of paragraphs relating to price movements in the contested decision satisfied it that the Commission had taken due account of this factor.[150] Likewise, in *Sun Chemicals Group v Commission*, the Court largely limited its review to whether or not the various criteria employed by the Commission in its decision featured in the relevant sections of its merger guidelines.[151]

However, in reviewing some factors, the Courts have extended their review to examining the economic indicators upon which the Commission relied, and have also considered the submissions made by the parties, and their economic consultants, as to how various indicators should be interpreted in the specific context.[152] This approach featured prominently in *Airtours v Commission* where the Court considered in some detail the Commission's assessment of factors such as: market volatility, market growth, market transparency, existing competition, potential competition, vertical integration, buyer power, and the existence of a retaliation mechanism.[153] The approach was also evident in *Impala v*

---

147 Gerber refers to this approach as being consistent with the normal fact-finding role of the Court: D.J. Gerber 'Courts as economic experts in European merger law' in B. Hawk (ed.) *International Antitrust Law and Policy: Fordham Corporate Law 2004* (Juris Publishing, New York, 2004) 480. Examples can be seen in: *France v Commission* (n 141) para [226], [219], [249]; and *Gencor v Commission* (n 142) paras [231]–[237].

148 *Sun Chemical v Commission* (n 139) paras [114]–[129]; [133]–[140].

149 *Gencor v Commission* (n 142) paras [228], [241]–[242], [261], [295].

150 *Gencor v Commission* (n 142) paras [293]–[295].

151 *Sun Chemical v Commission* (n 139) para [114]–[122].

152 Examples of this approach can be seen in: *Gencor v Commission* (n 142) paras [231]–[237]; *Airtours v Commission* (n 144) para [212].

153 *Airtours v Commission* (n 144) paras [85]–[92], [101]–[108], [127]–[133], [139]–[143], [159]–[180], [191]–207], [208]–[241], [274]–[276]; *Gencor v Commission* (n 142) para [218]; *France v Commission* (n 141) paras [228]–[232], [245]–[248]; Gerber (n 147) 482.

Commission where the CFI considered in depth the economic evidence and analysis relied on by the Commission in relation to: market transparency, the existence of a retaliation mechanism and past price movements.[154]

Article 82

In reviewing the Commission's assessments under Article 82 the Courts have typically focused on procedural issues, or on whether factors have been interpreted consistently with previous decisions, and with European sector-specific regulations.[155] For example, in *Compagnie Maritime Belge* the Court examined whether the Commission adopted the correct procedures in assessing abuses in accordance with EC regulations.[156] Similarly, in *Piau* the ECJ examined whether the Commission was remiss in not considering whether a dominant position was held on a relevant market.[157] This approach was also used in the Courts' assessment of factors such as structural links,[158] market concentration,[159] and existing competition[160] in other decisions. Where this approach has been adopted the Courts have *not* typically examined the economic indicators and evidence upon which the Commission has relied in its assessment of factors. However, in the CFI's decision in *Atlantic Container Line*, an appeal from the Commission decision in *TACA*, the Court examined the underlying economic evidence relied upon by the Commission in its assessment of certain factors. For example, in reviewing the level of existing competition in the market for containerised liner shipping between Northern Europe and the United States, the Court examined data relating to: Canadian port movements; the rate of growth of cargo transported by each carrier; and customer switching behaviour.[161] The Court also reviewed the underlying economic evidence

---

154 *Impala v Commission* (n 77) paras [77]–[459]; [460]–[462]; [463]–[474].

155 In particular see Joined cases C-395/96 P and C-396/96 P *Compagnie maritime belge transports SA (C-395/96 P), Compagnie maritime belge SA (C-395/96 P) and Dafra-Lines A/S (C-396/96 P) v Commission of the European Communities* [2000] ECR I-01365 para [28]–[31], [61]–[88], [99], [129], [142]–[146] (*Compagnie maritime belge case*).

156 *Compagnie maritime belge case* (n 155) para [116], [130].

157 *Piau v Commission* (n 143) paras [107]–[120]

158 Case T-228/97 *Irish Sugar plc v Commission of the European Communities* [1999] ECR II-02969 paras [41]–[46], [49]; Cases T-24/93, T-25/93, T-26/93 and T-28/93 *Compagnie maritime belge transports SA and Compagnie maritime belge SA, Dafra-Lines A/S, Deutsche Afrika-Linien GmbH & Co. and Nedlloyd Lijnen BV v Commission of the European Communities* [1996] ECR II-01201 para [62]–[64] (*CMBT case*); *Compagnie maritime belge case* (n 155) para [48]; *Gemente Almelo case* (n 138) para [40].

159 *CMBT case* (n 158) para [76]–[79].

160 *DIP SpA case* (n 138) paras [14]–[28].

161 Joined cases T-191/98, T-212/98 to T-214/98 *Atlantic Container Line AB and*

for the Commission's assessments in relation to: market concentration; potential competition and price and margin movements.[162]

The preparedness of the CFI in recent ECMR and Article 82 decisions to review the underlying economic evidence, and the Commission's appraisal of such evidence, may follow from concerns about how the Commission's exercise of its wide discretion in complex economic assessments interacts with the protection of fundamental rights, such as arise under the European Convention on Human Rights. This issue is taken up further in Chapter 5.

4.4.3 Economic Data

Mergers

Table 4.18 reveals that the most frequent source of data referenced by the Courts in its review of Commission assessments has been either the contested decision itself, submissions made to the Court as part of the review, or primary data or information submitted as part of the Commission's initial assessment.[163]

The Courts have specifically referenced economic studies or reports in reviewing six factors, most commonly in assessments of market transparency, price and margin movements, and volatility of market shares.[164] In *Airtours v. Commission*, for example, in assessing a number of factors, the CFI relied on a study of the UK package holiday market undertaken by the Monopolies and Mergers Commission in the United Kingdom.[165] In addition, in reviewing demand volatility, buyer power, and market growth the CFI has relied on studies and data used in the Commission's assessments of these factors.[166] In *Impala v Commission*, the CFI referred at a number of points to economic evidence submitted by the economic advisors to the parties, although it questioned its reliability.[167]

Others v Commission of the European Communities [2003] ECR II-03275 paras [985]–[996]; [957]–[969]; [782]–[817] (*Atlantic Container Line case*).

[162] *Atlantic Container Line case* (n 161) paras [910]–[922], [1013]–[1021], [1031]–[1035], [1078]–[1085].

[163] However, in reviewing the Commission's assessment of market growth and the state of existing competition in *France v Commission* the ECJ referred to data from French customs submitted by the French Government, who were not an original party to the merger: *France v Commission* (n 141) para [187].

[164] *Airtours v Commission* (n 144) paras [117]–[120], [161]–[164]; *Gencor v Commission* (n 142) para [225]–[229], [235], [293]–[296]; *Impala v Commission* (n 77) para [415]–[434].

[165] *Airtours v Commission* (n 144) paras [96]–[98], [101]–[107].

[166] *Airtours v Commission* (n 144) paras [140], [276], [128]–[131]; Compare also *Gencor v Commission* (n 142) para [241]–[245].

[167] *Impala v Commission* (n 77) paras [345]; [415].

Table 4.18 Use of different sources of data by the Courts under the ECMR

	Weighted rank (%)
Contested decision	31
Contested decision – primary data/information	14
Previous interpretations of Court	12
No source	12
Commission guidelines	9
External economists/studies/reports	8
Market shares	6
Other	4
Parties	4

In some decisions the Courts have referred to both economic data and documentary evidence in support of their conclusions. For example, when assessing the level of discounts offered by the parties in *Impala v Commission* the CFI refers to the results of a market questionnaire as well as economic data on past pricing and discounts.[168] In *Airtours v Commission*, the CFI relied on an economic report prepared by a professor of economics as well as documentary evidence to assess potential competition.[169] In *Gencor v Commission* the CFI relied on a report by economic consultants as well as documentary evidence in reviewing existing competition, and, on appeal, the CFI appeared to favour the documentary evidence over the economic report.[170]

Article 82

The Courts have limited their review to data or information that featured in the Commission's initial assessment of factors under Article 82. In two decisions the Courts have specifically relied on economic data and evidence that was submitted as part of the original proceedings. For example, in *Atlantic*

[168] *Impala v Commission* (n 77) para [384–[387]; [415]–[434].

[169] *Airtours v Commission* (n 144) paras [224], [226]. The documentary evidence included statements by the presidents of two competing companies.

[170] *Gencor v Commission* (n 142) paras [182]–[193]. In this case, documentary evidence including a circular to shareholders, and a statement by the former chairman of one of the merging companies as to the ability for existing competitors to expand, was seen as more probative than the analysis contained in a report prepared by the economic consultants.

Container Line the CFI re-examined the economic studies and surveys that were submitted as part of the Commission's assessment of potential competition, as well as a survey of prices and margin movements.[171] In reviewing the remaining factors the Court predominantly referred to documents submitted as part of the original proceedings.[172]

4.4.4 Summary

The Courts have examined factors derived from economic theory in their review of cases under the ECMR and Article 82. In interpreting these economic factors the Courts have been consistent with economic theory and generally consistent across decisions. In merger cases, the Courts' approach has, on occasion, involved the review of the Commission's assessment of economic indicators. However, this has not been the case in reviews of decisions under Article 82, where the Courts' approach has predominantly been to focus on procedural issues and consistency with previous decisions and other regulations. The data considered by the Courts in reviewing decisions under the ECMR has included economic studies and reports submitted as part of the original proceedings. However, in Article 82 decisions the Courts primarily refer to documentary data such as agreements, board minutes or written statements in support of their conclusions, and have on only limited occasions referred to economic data.

4.5 CONCLUSION

Both the Commission and the Courts employ economic theory, as represented by economic factors, in their assessments of the existence of, or potential for, collective dominance under Article 82 and the ECMR. The interpretation of such factors is, in the majority of cases, consistent with the underlying theory, although some exceptions do exist. The relative frequency with which specific factors are examined vary across decisions, and suggest some departure from the factors considered most important in the economic theory of tacit collusion. Certain factors considered important in economic theory are examined with a high degree of frequency in assessments, however, other key factors are assessed with relative infrequency. In addition, the factors considered relevant

171 *Atlantic Container Line case* (n 161) para [1015]–[1017], [1080]–[1081].

172 *Atlantic Container Line case* (n 161) para [1274]–[1376]; Compare also *CMBT case* (n 158) paras [105], [147].

to an *ex ante* assessment of collective dominance under the ECMR are not the same set of factors used in an *ex post* assessment of collective dominance under Article 82, and differ in some important respects (i.e. relevance of market transparency and retaliation mechanisms). The text of the decisions does not easily yield information to account for these variations in factor selection; it may be that market-contextual and practical considerations are significant in choices.

In assessing factors, the Commission, and at times the Courts, have adopted an economic approach, particularly in merger cases, insofar as economic indicators and processes are examined. The most frequent economic technique employed in assessments by the Commission is the presentation of a hypothesis, with varying degrees of supporting analysis, about a factor, and how it may promote or hinder coordination. In a large number of assessments where this technique is employed, no supporting analysis is presented in the text of the decisions and, in these circumstances, it is difficult to determine what analysis underlies the assessment. Where supporting analysis is presented, it is most commonly descriptive or low-level quantitative. The use of high-tech methods such as modelling or statistical estimation is relatively infrequent. This is particularly the case in relation to assessments under Article 82 where documentary and legal analysis feature prominently.

In general, the Commission and the Courts refer to a combination of economic data and documentary evidence in support of their conclusions. Where economic data is referenced, such data has a number of sources including the parties, competitors, customers and external agencies. However, in some assessments, particularly assessments made by the Commission under the ECMR, no reference to data underlying conclusions is presented. This may reflect the fact that data was not available or not collected, or only that the decisions have failed to reference the data. It is difficult to assess the relative weight of economic data vis-à-vis other data on the outcome of decisions; however, particularly in relation to Article 82 assessments, where documentary evidence exists, it features more prominently than economic data in support of conclusions.

In sum, the use of economics in assessments of collective dominance principally involves the use of some of the predictions of economic theory, the adoption of a broadly economic approach and the application of 'low-tech' economic methods. Within this use, a degree of variation can be observed across decisions. In particular, variations exist in respect of: which factors feature in assessments; the frequency of use of different factors; the standard by which factors are assessed; the extent to which an economic approach is adopted and economic techniques are employed; and the data collected and analysed to support assessments.

It is difficult to account for these variations on the basis of the text of the reported decisions alone. Market-contextual and practical considerations may have some explanatory potential. Chapter 5 of this book examines these considerations in more detail and canvasses other explanations in the context of the wider enforcement process.

5. Economics in the enforcement process

5.1 INTRODUCTION

In Chapter 4 we examined the extent to which economics features in the reported decisions of the Commission and Courts in collective dominance cases. This chapter looks beyond the reported decisions to understand the role and influence of economics in the *process* of enforcement surrounding and leading up to these final determinations. Specifically, it considers where economics is used in the selection of cases for investigation, the construction of those cases by the Commission and the parties under investigation, in reaching a final decision, and in developing remedies. The role of economics in appeals before the European Courts is also examined. The methodology for the research in this chapter is described in Chapter 2.

Although focused on the use of economics in the enforcement of the collective dominance laws, this examination has potential relevance to other areas of competition law enforcement where economics is used. This is because the enforcement process and procedures under the ECMR and Article 82 in collective dominance investigations is similar to other areas of competition law enforcement such as unilateral effects merger investigations and single abuse of dominance cases under Article 82.

5.2 MERGER ENFORCEMENT PROCESS: THE COMMISSION

Parties to proposed concentrations which satisfy certain requirements must notify an intention to merge to the European Commission.[1] Upon notification, the Commission has 25 working days to undertake a 'Phase I' investigation of

[1] Article 1 of Council Regulation (EC) No 139/2004 of 20 January 2004 on the control of concentrations between undertakings [2004] OJ L24/1('the ECMR') requires that concentrations have a community dimension and sets out various thresholds that must be satisfied; Article 4 of the ECMR sets out the specific time limits. Parties must submit a 'Form CO' to the Commission, which requires substantial information about their activities, the industry and the activities of their competitors.

the concentration. At the end of this time, if the Commission assesses the concentration as being compatible with the common market it can allow the concentration.[2] If, however, the Commission has 'serious doubts' as to the concentration's compatibility with the common market it can initiate a 'Phase II' investigation.[3] A Phase II investigation is ordinarily required to be completed within 90 days. During this period the Commission must provide the parties with a written statement of its objections to the merger, and the merger parties have a right to reply to the objections, access the Commission files, and be heard orally. There is also an opportunity for commitments to be submitted, which may alleviate the Commission's concerns about the merger, and for third parties to comment on such commitments. At the end of a Phase II investigation the Commission must again conclude on the compatibility of the concentration with the common market.[4]

In practice, much work is done informally by the merger parties and Commission before official notification. This front-loading of cases prior to 'official' notification to the Commission is widely perceived as necessary because of the time constraints imposed by the formal process. In practical terms this means that the pre-notification stage and the Phase I investigation effectively represent the same stage in the process. In a typical case, pre-notification discussions and exchanges of information will have elicited a picture of the Commission's view of the proposed concentration and of any concerns that will need to be addressed.[5] This informal exchange may continue for a number of months and will involve the Commission assembling a case team and opening an unofficial file. It is usually only once the Commission is satisfied that it has sufficient information to assess the concentration that it will encourage formal notification and 'start the clock'.

5.2.1 Economics in Case Identification and Selection

Concentrations that are subject to the above procedure are, in effect, self-selected for investigation. However, the Commission has discretion in relation

---

[2] Article 6(1)(b) of the ECMR; Article 6(2) of the ECMR allows for a concentration to be compatible with the common market following modifications made by the parties.

[3] Article 6(1)(c) of the ECMR.

[4] Article 8(2) of the ECMR if the merger is compatible; Article 8(3) of the ECMR if the merger is incompatible.

[5] The importance of the 'pre-notification' procedure in merger investigations is discussed in detail in: D. Neven, R. Nuttall and P. Seabright *Mergers in Daylight: The Economics and Politics of European Merger Control* (Centre for Economic Policy Research, London, 1993) 142, 151.

to the amount of evidence it will collect and analyse in the pre-notification stage and in a Phase I investigation of each proposed concentration.

Involvement of economists

The case team assembled at the Commission early in the pre-notification process and for a Phase I investigation will be multidisciplinary and, because of a shortage of economists – particularly industrial economists[6] – will not necessarily include a dedicated economist.[7] Accordingly, the case team will comprise people with different levels of knowledge of economics.[8]

The merger parties themselves may employ economists in the preliminary stages of a merger investigation. The appointment of economists in these preliminary stages typically depends on the complexity and sensitivity of the issues raised by the merger. In highly sensitive cases, economists may be involved from the very start in planning the transaction to address any potential competition law issues as they arise.[9] However, an economist is not necessarily appointed for every merger case at this early stage. The appointment of an economist depends in part on how 'delicate' a merger case is perceived to be.[10]

The work performed by economists for merger parties at this early stage may not be known to the Commission. This is because of a perception that the introduction of economists or economic analysis at an early stage may unnecessarily 'raise the suspicions' of the Commission.[11]

---

6 As the former Chief Competition Economist at the Commission has noted the Commission has mainly macroeconomists: L.H. Röller 'Recent economic developments in EU competition policy' (presentation at the Charles River Associates conference on the Role of Economics in Competition Law, Brussels, 26 May 2004); and L.H. Röller 'Using economic analysis to strengthen competition policy enforcement in Europe' (presentation at the ECN conference on Modelling European Mergers: Theory, Competition Policy and Case Studies, 21 March 2005) 4.

7 The Commission has acknowledged that it has a relatively low percentage of economists dedicated to merger analysis: International Competition Network 'The role of economists and economic evidence in merger analysis' (working paper, International Competition Network First Annual Conference, September 2002) 2.

8 Only case teams investigating concentrations with 'special' or 'complex' issues are automatically assigned an economist: L.H. Röller (n 6) 3.

9 This is consistent with the more general conclusion that the bulk of the experts' work in legal proceedings lies in 'behind the scenes' work at the pre-trial stage: C.A.G. Jones *Expert Witnesses* (Clarendon Press, Oxford, 1994) 128,158.

10 Perhaps not surprisingly, the failure to appoint, or the late appointment, of economists was seen by many economists as putting the merging parties at a significant disadvantage in cases where collective dominance is an issue. For example, one economist noted the appointment of economists only in Phase II in *Airtours/First Choice* caused 'problems that could have been avoided'.

11 Compare N. Yoerg 'The use of an economist in a contested merger' (1987) 56 Antitrust Law Journal 794.

> The economist is not necessarily on display as you want to create the impression that there are no economic issues … you don't tend to present any economic analysis until the end of Phase I. (Lawyer)

> [T]he strategy at this stage is typically to keep the economists at home. Because the perception is that if you bring your economists it means you know you have a problem. (Economist)

The economist 'kept at home' may perform a range of functions for the merger parties. This may include advising the parties on how to best present information so as to 'turn' a case to appear less vulnerable to the suspicions of the Commission. An economist may also be involved in 'coaching' executives or other business or operational staff who might be informally questioned by the Commission,[12] or in trying to 'bury' or 'discount' statements made by bankers early in the merger process regarding the benefits of the transaction.

Use of economic theory and approach

In some jurisdictions, legislation provides economic 'triggers', based on economic theory, to identify mergers where coordination might be an issue.[13] In others, enforcement authorities have adopted informal working rules, based on 'widely shared economic beliefs', to identify mergers where coordinated effects may be an issue.

In Europe, there are no legislative triggers for investigation of mergers, nor are there any systematic working rules applied in the selection of cases for further investigation.[14] Historically, there was a 'checklist' of factors, derived from some of the predictions of economic theory discussed in Chapter 3, that were examined in investigating mergers in tight oligopolistic markets.[15] However, this checklist approach was abandoned because it was viewed by

---

[12] According to one lawyer, this involves ensuring that operational staff do not contradict the statements made by the lawyers or economists concerning, for example, how prices are set in the market, or the extent of observation of competitors' actions.

[13] These are largely based on the presumption that collusion is more likely in concentrated markets. Such provisions exist in Germany, Brazil, Japan, Australia and Canada: International Competition Network 'Coordinated effects analysis under International Merger Regimes' (working paper, International Competition Network Annual Conference, April 2004) 6.

[14] Commission of the European Communities Competition Directorate-General 'Merger review and horizontal merger guidelines: the economic framework for assessing mergers' (paper presented at the MTF House meeting on horizontal merger guidelines, 15 January 2003) 11.

[15] Kühn suggests the checklist was 'largely a restatement of factors facilitating collusion in the classic textbook by Scherer and Ross (1990)': K.U. Kühn 'Closing Pandora's Box? Joint dominance after the "Airtours" judgment' (Research Paper No. 02-013, Michigan Law and Economics, 2002) 18.

Commission economists as inappropriate for identifying the potential for collective dominance post-merger.[16]

The abandonment of the checklist means the Commission's approach at the preliminary stages of investigations is no longer systematised. The Commission's general approach is to encourage the parties to undertake any relevant economic analysis in the pre-notification stage and present it to the Commission for review.[17] The Commission uses 'signals' or 'hints' to highlight areas of concern. These are typically based on distilled economic theory, intuitive understandings or rules of thumb. As one Commission official describes it:

> Seventy per cent of the staff of DG Competition are lawyers, and over the years lawyers have developed easy rules of thumb, and now we are seeing the same tendency with economics.

The 'signals' and 'hints' made by the Commission at this stage can, however, be fairly general and might involve statements such as: 'you know it doesn't look good'. In short, there is typically no detailed negotiation on substantive economic issues at this stage.

Use of economic techniques and data

Economic techniques were classified in Chapter 2 as 'high-tech' or 'low-tech'. In the early stage of merger investigations, 'high-tech' methods rarely feature. It is common, however for some 'low-tech' techniques, including low-level quantitative analysis (such as the consideration of the number of competitors, and calculation of market shares) to be employed by the Commission in making a decision as to whether to investigate a merger more closely. These analytical exercises are based on a general presumption that firms in more concentrated industries are more likely to engage in coordinated behaviour (because of lower transaction costs where there are fewer people to form agreement with).[18] Commission officials indicate that a 'red light' will arise

---

[16] Neven, Nuttall and Seabright (n 5) 156–160 suggest that the 'checklist' may have had the positive effect of signalling the Commission's 'toughness', allowing it to develop its credibility and show its unwillingness to be manipulated in view of the 'bargaining' nature of merger proceedings (i.e. to limit the perception of firms that they can 'bargain their way out').

[17] This differs from other jurisdictions, such as the United States, where economic analysis is undertaken by the enforcement agencies as an 'initial screen' of the effects of a merger.

[18] Not all economists accept the correctness of this presumption. Some economists are sceptical of the usefulness of concentration indices in assessing the potential for collective dominance. They stress that much will depend on who is merging, and

where a merger will reduce numbers from three to two (or in some cases from four to three).

The Commission's decision to investigate a merger more closely can also be influenced by non-economic factors. If previous mergers in an industry have involved concerns about collective dominance this will act as an almost automatic trigger for a detailed investigation.[19] The number, and nature, of objections the Commission receives in relation to a merger can be influential in the Commission's decision to launch a more in-depth investigation.[20] In addition, where a merger is hostile, one of the merging parties may actively support the Commission in its decision to undertake a detailed investigation of the proposed merger.[21]

A detailed investigation of a merger might also occur because the Commission has concerns about the structure of a particular industry,[22] or is seeking to test or develop an aspect of the legislation.[23] Finally, there is an extensive lobbying 'industry' in Brussels which is seen by some as playing a role in early decisions in relation to an investigation and the direction in which it is developed.[24]

In light of these considerations, the data and information that is collected and assessed in the preliminary stage of a merger investigation varies, and can involve a range of economic and non-economic evidence, including the content of the parties' submissions, responses that may have been received from customers and competitors, and publicly available information.[25]

---

what assets are being combined. Compare H. Vasconcelos 'Tacit collusion, cost asymmetries and mergers' (2005) 36 RAND Journal of Economics 39.

19 For example, a number of reported decisions examined in Chapter 4 were concentrated in certain industries such as: newspaper and newsprint, music publishing, flat glass production, aluminium, paints, petrol retailing and liner shipping.

20 For example, the decision to investigate the *Sony/BMG* merger in detail was, in part, attributed to remarks made by customers in response to initial Commission enquiries. A large number of retailers told the Commission that the 'majors' were making a mistake in their discount levels – a collective mistake.

21 In *Gencor/Lonrho*, for example, there was active lobbying of the Commission by one merger party.

22 Long-running concerns about the potential for collective dominance in the music publishing industry was influential in the decision to investigate the *Sony/BMG* merger.

23 One influence on the original decision to investigate the *Airtours/FirstChoice* merger in detail was a desire to test whether the dominance provisions of the ECMR would extend to cover mergers involving non-coordinated effects.

24 One lawyer explains that 'Basically that is why all the law firms have offices in Brussels, to be close to the Commission'. Compare Neven, Nuttall and Seabright (n 5) 142, 215, 218, 219.

25 DG Competition Best Practices on the conduct of EC merger proceedings [2002] points 14–19.

Summary
The involvement of economists in the early stage of investigations, both at the Commission and as appointees of the merger parties, is variable, as is the nature of the work done by economists who become involved at this stage. There is, in addition, not a direct relationship between the involvement of economists and the use of economics in preliminary investigations. This is because Commission lawyers or administrators, or the lawyers of the merger parties, may 'do the economics'. Where economics does feature at this preliminary stage, it typically takes the form of low-level quantitative analysis, such as the calculation of concentration indices. Typically, the parties perform such analysis and the Commission responds to, and critiques, the analysis presented to them. Distilled economic understandings may also influence the course of the early stage of investigations through the use of rules of thumb or intuitive understandings of economic predictions. However, a range of other factors can play a part in the decision to allow the merger or move to a Phase II investigation. Among these: political and historical matters, a desire to test or develop aspects of the law, general concerns about the structure of an industry, and the number and nature of objections to the merger.

5.2.2 Economics in Case Construction

If, at the end of a Phase I investigation, the Commission has serious doubts as to a proposed concentration's compatibility with the common market, it can initiate a 'Phase II' investigation.

Involvement of economists in Phase II
As discussed above, the composition of the case team assembled at the Commission to assess merger cases is typically multidisciplinary and may not include an economist. It is common, however, in a Phase II investigation for an economist to have some input into the construction of the case. In addition, although the Chief Economist's Team (CET) has in the past tended to operate separately from the rest of the economists in DG Competition, and only tended to get involved in important cases that may have an impact on policy, it is increasingly becoming involved in Phase II merger investigations.[26]

There are two other avenues in the institutional process through which economists can potentially become involved in merger investigations. First, a sectoral 'sister' unit within the Commission follows each case, and can comment on any draft decision. Second, a central coordination unit will be

---

[26] A member of the CET notes, for example, that a CET economist was involved in all Phase II investigations conducted in 2008.

given information on the progress of the case at crucial stages of the investigation. In addition, other units and Directorates within the European Commission such as the Legal Service, DG Economic & Financial Affairs and DG Enterprise can be called upon to provide technical, economic and industrial expertise throughout the procedure, and can be called upon to comment on preliminary opinions.[27]

As is the case in preliminary investigations, the Commission's general approach to conducting a case in Phase II is to voice its concerns, based on distilled economic understandings, about the potential adverse effects of the merger and to encourage the merging parties to undertake or submit any economic analysis or evidence to alleviate these concerns.[28] Again, therefore, the principal task of the Commission case team is to critique any economic analysis and evidence presented by the parties rather than to actively assemble economic evidence and perform economic analysis to support its own case.

> We try to encourage the merging parties to undertake more analysis where necessary, to keep the onus on them to disprove certain claims. Typically if the data comes in the form of a report we ask to see the original data so as to manipulate for ourselves the model and data used ... but it's our job at the MTF to be naturally sceptical, to probe the picture. (Commission official)

The ability to 'probe the picture' presented by the parties in depth will, of course, depend on the extent of economic expertise within the Commission.[29] Some practitioners express doubts about this expertise because case handlers are typically not economists but lawyers or general administrators.

In only one merger case where collective dominance had been a concern, has the Commission appointed an external economist to present an alternative analysis and evidence to that presented by the parties.[30] However, the Commission has, in some other mergers, enlisted the economic expertise (and analysis) of competitors or customers to use in its investigation.

---

[27] Commission Green Paper on the Review of Council Regulation (EEC) No 4064/89 [2001] COM (2001) 745/6 para [247].

[28] It has been argued that keeping the onus on the parties to provide analysis and information may be a deliberate attempt to overcome information asymmetries between the parties and the Commission and may encourage parties to reveal more information: Neven, Nuttall and Seabright (n 5) 206.

[29] The former Chief Competition Economist of the Commission has acknowledged that the 'interdisciplinary' composition of case teams 'may not facilitate high-quality economic analysis': L.H. Röller (n 6) 5.

[30] *UPM-Kymmene/Haindl* (COMP/M.2498) [2002] OJ L233 38. Experts have also been appointed relatively infrequently in unilateral effects cases, most notably in *Volvo/Scania* (COMP/M.1672) [2002] OJ L143 para [72].

It follows from the above discussion that it is economists acting on behalf of the merger parties, or complainants, who principally undertake any economic analysis that features in Phase II investigations. Economists who become involved at this stage are typically appointed either by lawyers acting on behalf of the merging parties or for a complainant, and operate through the instruction of the lawyers.

In selecting economists, flexibility, a lack of potential conflicts of interest, and an understanding of legal process, are seen as important qualities.[31]

> Economists are chosen on the basis of their flexibility. Often they can be too arrogant, or can produce theories not useful to the basic argument. I had one case where we appointed an academic economist. I won't do that again! He came up with disappointing arguments, and once he saw something of interest to him in the case he produced a paper that excited him but was unusable. ... This was an example of where the economist doesn't understand what we are trying to do. (Lawyer)

> You select them as best you can. First of all you have to be sure that they don't have a conflict of interest. Secondly, there aren't all that many in Europe – so your choice isn't all that great, and you try to use the ones that you know are good. (Lawyer)

Appointing academic economists is seen as a 'double-edged sword'. On the one hand, it is accepted that if the economist is a 'world expert' or is 'high flying' he or she can lend credibility to a case through their reputation and their previous work.[32] However, it is recognised that accompanying this reputation there is often a risk that the economist may be 'too wild' or might misunderstand the process.[33]

The economist's ability to be clear and persuasive as an expert witness in oral hearings before the Commission is highly valued.[34] However it is also recognised that economists need to be subtly, rather than overtly, persuasive because they need to sound like impartial experts rather than advocates.

In some cases, multiple economists might be involved in the construction of the same case either because they are acting for different parties to a merger, or because a second opinion is sought where the first opinion is perceived as weak or unhelpful to the case.

---

[31] In the United States four factors are seen to control the selection process: philosophical bias, time, personality and cost: S.E. Nagin 'Selection, use and pay of an economist in an antitrust case' (1981) 35 University of Miami Law Review 261.

[32] Compare J. Greenfield 'The use of experts from the plaintiff's perspective' (1992) 60 Antitrust Law Journal 343.

[33] More generally on this issue of the use of experts in legal processes, compare Jones (n 9) 140–42.

[34] Compare Jones (n 9) 139.

The functions of economists vary according to the basis upon which they have been employed. In some cases, economists have detailed involvement in the process of case construction and are included in a constant interaction with the lawyers and the client, participating in brainstorming sessions and assisting in the development of a list of relevant questions and issues about the Commission's case.[35]

In these cases, the economist's function is to provide economic 'substance' to the legal arguments developed by the lawyers and the merger parties. In other cases, the economist's involvement is more specific and may be limited to producing a report for the lawyers, which may or may not ultimately be used in the presentation of the case. In these cases, the economists are asked to address specific issues and typically the information flows are channelled, and access to clients controlled, by the lawyers.[36] The primary function of the economist in these cases is to produce a useful and persuasive document which 'hits the point' for the client's case. Where the economist's report is to be submitted to the Commission, an iterative process typically occurs between the lawyers and the economist until the lawyers are happy with the content of the report.[37]

> We see the economic report as a pleading document. It can be redrafted as many times as needed, and in some cases the report is not necessarily submitted if it is not needed or considered useful. Again, in some cases if we submit the report it may create the impression of the need for a real investigation. (Lawyer)

> I want to see a draft of any statement or report before it's submitted. In some cases a high level of filtering can go on before the statement is submitted. … I want them to use clear language, and often I need to say to them to make the language simpler. Sometimes I ask them to strengthen some bits, or to run with one theory if a couple are presented. (Lawyer)

---

35 Similarly, in the United States it is widely accepted that the economist can play an important role in shaping the prosecution or defence strategy, and in shaping the 'theory' of the complaint or answer: I.M. Stelzer 'Experts – use and abuse (Part I): the expert's view' (1992) 60 Antitrust Law Journal 356; Nagin (n 31) 259.

36 More generally, compare Jones (n 9) 143.

37 When taken to the extreme this practice has been criticised in other jurisdictions. For example, in one US case involving collusion, the economic expert, a Nobel Prize winning economist, was criticised by the Court on the basis that: 'His expert's report was redrafted by Class Plaintiffs' counsel in its entirety and included what counsel wanted. In Dr. Lucas' own words: "I don't think there's a single sentence in this affidavit that's intact from the first draft that I proposed …"': *In re Brand Name Prescription Drugs Antitrust Litigation* (1999) No. 94 C 897, MDL 997, WL 33889 para [11] (*Brand Name Prescription Drugs*).

Rather than being perceived as an impartial expert, the economist's role in the construction of a case is perceived by some lawyers as that of an advocate, and very similar to that performed by the lawyer.[38]

> The function of the economist is to advocate for their party or client who is paying them – they are not interpreters of theory. They now play a central part in the process of mergers, and in mergers they are advocates and not interpreters. (Commission lawyer)

> The team is like the orchestra, all sharing bits of the argument, and the economists are solo performers required to provide a moving solo performance that will bring tears to the eyes of the audience. ... This can be difficult in some cases because whereas a lawyer knows that they are a hired gun an economist can be more difficult to handle if they firmly believe in something. They can behave like a primadonna. (Lawyer)

The use of economic theory and approach in ECMR

Although most of those involved in the enforcement process take the view that economic theory influences merger investigations involving collective dominance, the manner of use of such theory differs between the Commission and private practitioners.

Commission officials emphasise the role of theory in providing an analytical frame for an investigation, but say it has little practical relevance in the specifics of an investigation. In the words of one Commission official: '[T]heory gives you something to frame the analysis. ...Theory is useful for focusing, and for rooting out silly arguments, but is hard to model in practice'. Economic theory is also considered to be useful insofar as it allows for the case investigation to be connected to a larger body of knowledge.

The Commission has, however, on occasion, speculated, based on new or novel interpretations of economic theory, about the potential for coordination in specific cases. In *Airtours/FirstChoice*, the theoretical predictions relating to the requirement that a retaliation mechanism must exist to sustain collusion

---

[38] In US cases involving collusion the economic expert has at times been criticised by the Court on this basis. For example in *Brand Name Prescription Drugs* the expert was found to have: 'abdicated entirely the concept of the independence of expert witnesses and simply became the sponsor for the Class Plaintiffs' theory of the case': *Brand Name Prescription Drugs* (n 37) para [11]. In other cases, the Court has described the expert as 'clearly a hired gun' for whom 'any semblance of objectivity is lacking': *Lantec, Inc. v Novell, Inc.* 146 F.Supp.2d 1140 (2001) para [9], or simply as 'an expert for hire': *In re Aluminum Phosphide Antitrust Litigation* 893 F.Supp.1497 (1995) para [4]. Compare Nagin (n 31) 264. In Australia, the Federal Court has published strict guidelines which state clearly that the expert is not to act as an advocate for a party: Section 1.2 Federal Court of Australia *Guidelines for Expert Witnesses in Proceedings in the Federal Court of Australia* (version 3) 19 March 2004.

were a major point of contention between the Commission and the merging parties. As one Commission official accepts: 'The Commission invented a theory in *Airtours*. It's a well established theory in economics that the Commission tried to change'. Similarly, in *UPM-Kymmene/Haindl*, the Commission presented a new theory relating to the future coordination of capacity decisions. The theory was that coordination would take place not in output or prices but in capacity installation decisions between the four or five big players.

In contrast to the Commission's occasional use of novel economic theory, the merger parties typically place a heavy emphasis on the use of broadly accepted theory, where it exists, in the construction of their cases. A lawyer describes the assessment process:

> You have to use as strong an economic theory as you can possibly find that fits your facts. ... The more widely accepted the theory is, the better, the more obvious it is the better, the less controversial it is the better, the more often its been accepted by other competition authorities the better, if it's been accepted in America but not in Europe that's good and so on. (Lawyer)

Judicial acceptance of particular interpretations of economic theory is typically more important to the Commission than the parties. For example, the CFI's decision in *Airtours v. Commission* is now seen to constrain the Commission's ability to apply novel interpretations of economic theory in cases of collective dominance. By comparison, economists working for the merger parties, although mindful of judicial interpretations, feel less constrained by precedent in employing economic theory. An economist describes this approach:

> We leave the Court stuff behind in conducting our analysis ... I don't feel constrained by the case law, we are governed by data not the case law. (Consultant economist)

The available evidence shows that while there is no general, or systematic, approach to the construction of cases, a broadly economic approach is adopted, in terms of the overall 'thinking' of merger parties and enforcement officials, and the indicators and evidence that are considered in an investigation. The general approach adopted both by the Commission and the merger parties is typically based on examining indicators that are derived from 'economic intuition' and 'economic understandings'. This reflects a presumption on the part of Commission officials, and economists acting for the merger parties, that they intuitively understand what is important to consider in a particular case.

The Commission's approach is in part determined by published guidelines, which reflect economic thinking. However, these guidelines are expressed at a high level of generality and are not binding on the approach to be adopted in any specific case.[39] As one Commission official describes it:

> There is no formal manual. The analysis proceeds more on the accumulated knowledge of the office. We use internal papers that have been published – speeches or new draft guidelines for example etc. But I would not call them an internal guide or manual … there is no formal manual or practice notes used, there is however, a manual of procedure. But economists know what this area is about, and they know what is important to look at in a coordinated effects case.

The Commission's pragmatic approach to the economic indicators it examines is illustrated by the different ways it has assessed the degree of similarity of firms in different decisions. As discussed in Chapter 3, a strong implication of economic theory is that similar firms are more likely to coordinate their behaviour. The Commission has, however, acknowledged difficulties in translating this implication in practice. As one Commission official accepts:

> Theoretically the asymmetry literature makes some sense, but … empirically it is very difficult to show asymmetries ... it should have less emphasis in an investigation.

In the view of one former Commission official this flexible and pragmatic approach to case construction is part of the Commission's strategy to remain adaptive,[40] and to not limit itself to areas of analysis that are non-persuasive:

> [T]he Commission isn't disorganised, it adapts its thinking to whatever the features are of the particular market and concentrates on whatever issues seem to be crucial in light of its preliminary views. And it refines those views, or changes them if appropriate, in the course of the couple of months that it has to think about all this.

Not surprisingly, economists who act for merger parties are critical of the substantial discretion this adaptive approach allows the Commission. According to some of these practitioners, such broad discretion allows the Commission's approach to be ad hoc as well as inconsistent with its own guidelines. The non-systematic approach of the Commission is also seen by some to allow for any bias of the case team to remain within the process.[41]

---

39 Compare S. Bishop and D. Ridyard 'Prometheus unbound: Increasing the scope for intervention in EC merger control' (2003) 24 European Competition Law Review 361.

40 This is similar to the approach adopted by competition agencies in the United States as described in: S. Weaver *Decision to Prosecute: Organization and Public Policy in the Antitrust Division* (MIT Press, Cambridge, MA, 1977) 76.

41 D. Neven 'Competition economics and antitrust in Europe' (2006) 21 Economic Policy 30.

The use of economic techniques

Contrary to the picture promoted by some economists, the construction of cases by the merger parties and the Commission typically does not involve much quantitative or 'hard' analysis such as formal merger simulation modelling or econometrics. This is because, despite the relatively large body of economic theory that examines tacit collusion, some of which is discussed in Chapter 3 and Appendix 1, the majority of such papers employ abstract and formal models to analyse particular markets. As a result, there are few accepted empirical methods or models, or econometric techniques, which can usefully and practically be applied to the empirical question of whether a merger will increase the potential for coordinated behaviour.[42]

> We don't use hardly any econometric analysis in mergers with coordinated effects, because it is simply too hard to use econometrics to show that collusion could happen in the future. … Economics does not give predictions that will show how the fundamental behaviour of the company will change after the merger. (Commission official)

> You can't do coordinated effects with econometric analysis. … it's not usual to do any simulation analysis in a merger. You can only do price analysis or variation in pricing analysis, they are the only techniques that are available. (Consultant economist)

> What you are trying to predict is whether a particular merger will pull the trigger, or the switch, between competitive and coordinated conduct. It is incredibly difficult – you can not predict that economically through any form of modeling. You cannot do it. (Consultant economist)

> We tried to use empirical regression to underpin our theoretical work but didn't have adequate data. In the end we didn't do any regression analysis or experiments because they would have been misleading as there were a number of key unknown facts, such as promotion campaigns and advertising and consumer tastes. (Commission official)

The use of merger simulation models and econometric analysis to predict the potential for coordinated behaviour is also perceived as having limited persuasiveness for decision-makers, and to make a case vulnerable to attack.

---

42 A review of some of the more innovative and emerging merger simulation models is presented in Budzinski and Ruhmer. They note that although there is potential for the greater use of such models in the future, there are a number of important practical limitations associated with the models and that, to be useful, they must be combined with more traditional instruments of competition policy. O. Budzinski and I. Ruhmer 'Merger simulation in competition policy: a survey' (Joint Discussion paper in Economics, University of Marburg, May 2008) 32.

As a result of the difficulties economists face in undertaking 'high-tech' analysis, or developing models, of the potential for coordination, the primary economic techniques adopted by economists in collective dominance investigations are low-level quantitative or descriptive in nature. A major type of expository technique used by economists acting for the merger parties is the development of intuitive and persuasive 'stories' or 'pictures' of what might potentially occur after the merger.

> You need to present analysis such that the competition authority or the Court believe this reflects reality, you need to present a pretty clear story of what will happen after the merger. (Consultant economist)

The Commission also uses the descriptive expository technique of presenting intuitive stories or pictures. Indeed, the ability of the Commission to cast the anti-competitive consequences of a merger in terms of a simple, persuasive story can be decisive in outcomes. For example the Commission's decision to allow the merger in *UPM-Kymmene/Haindl* was, on the Commission's own account, principally based on its failure to construct and present a sufficiently persuasive story to support its objections. A Commission official recalls: 'In the end the MTF dropped the case as it was too complicated, it was a story we could not run with.' Similarly, in the initial *Sony/BMG* merger investigation, the Commission, recognising that a story that the merger would *create* collective dominance would not be compelling (given long-running concerns about collective dominance in that industry) had to adapt its story to focus on how the merger would *strengthen* collective dominance.

It follows from the above that Commission economists focus on presenting low-tech quantitative economic analysis and evidence which complements the story or the picture being developed, rather than using complicated or sophisticated models.

> We have very good economists working for us, but when it comes to what we actually use we rely on relatively basic or elementary analysis. (Commission official)

> The modelling is literally low tech in this area. It is simply considered too difficult to do anything but low tech analysis. (Consultant economist)

Thus, in *Sony/BMG*, the Commission relied simply on a chart showing price movements over time as evidence of price parallelism. Similarly, the Commission's analysis of the 'punishment mechanism' in *Airtours/FirstChoice* was based solely on information obtained from interviews about capacity decisions and the amount of available capacity.

Although merger parties are sometimes critical of the Commission constructing a case on the basis of such low-tech techniques, economists acting for the merger parties typically employ similarly low-level quantitative techniques to complement the picture or story they wish to present. This may involve undertaking historical analysis of the behaviour of firms in an industry, such as looking at switching between various competitors or changes in relative market shares and prices.

High-tech analytical techniques and methods developed by academic economists to test for collective dominance – such as critical discount factor analysis – are viewed by both sides as being unhelpful (too indeterminate and unreliable) and impracticable within the time constraints of a merger investigation.

Low-tech quantitative analysis that complements an 'intuitive story' is also seen by merger parties to be more useful for their case because of a perception that the Commission will simply disregard any analysis that is too complex, or sophisticated, or that it does not understand.

> If you have a way of putting together some evidence that is fairly intuitive and doesn't require excessive sophistication that's always preferred ... you know it will be better received if it is approachable. (Consultant economist)

> The analysis needs to have an intuitive basis, so that a non-expert can understand the intuition behind it. You need to present an intuitive story. ... If they can't appraise the technical evidence they will go for an intuitive result. (Consultant economist)

Commission economists indicate this perception is accurate:

> It is incumbent on economists wanting to have an impact on competition law that they are able to explain their reasoning clearly to a non-expert in economic modelling. (Commission official)

> There's no point in getting sophisticated, complex models and analysis because ultimately you must convince the decision-makers and judges. (Commission official)

Despite this general conclusion, on some rare occasions, 'high-tech' quantitative analysis of the potential for collective dominance has been employed in merger investigations. In *UPM-Kymmene/Haindl*, for example, both the Commission and the merger parties presented sophisticated economic models of capacity expansion.

The use of economic data

The availability, character and sources of data collected and analysed by the Commission and the economists acting for the merger parties is of obvious relevance to the depth and quality of any analysis that is undertaken. The Commission has a formal right to request a broad range of data, including non-economic data, and has increasingly used this right to make large information requests of merging parties. This right includes open access to data such as boardroom discussions and statements, reports prepared for the board, and data from third parties on a mandatory basis. As a result, the Commission will, as part of a Phase II investigation, typically write to large numbers of customers and competitors requesting information.

> They will write to hundreds of people in a Phase II. The merger parties have to provide a list of all that competitors and customers, they write to all of them with different information requests. On the basis of what comes back, and with information on their own file, they will attempt to construct some arguments. (Consultant economist)

Despite the fact that much of the economic analysis used in merger investigations is undertaken by economists acting for the merger parties, access to data for these economists is less comprehensive than for the Commission, and is highly dependent on the merging parties', and their lawyers', willingness and ability to share specific data. As two economists observe:

> Data retrieval is an inexact science. We send out a typical list of questions. … You try to get transaction data, you ask questions about the transaction; look for prices with lists; discounts; capacity etc., you get all this data from the client. Usually your client has this type of data for its competitors – if not, you know collusion is not a problem.

> In a lot of cases, you end up having a lot less information than you think you would want. You have to make do with what you have got. You might ask the client and he'll give you ten data points for the past ten years. You have to really struggle to get usable stuff.

External data series, such as data collected by AC Nielsen or industry bodies, are only rarely sourced in investigations in part because it is unclear how data on past events can be used to make inferences about the potential for future coordinated behaviour. Similarly, international data – which could be used as the basis of comparison of the relative performance and characteristics of the industry being investigated with that of the same industry in other countries – was only infrequently collected.

> If it was proven that collusion had existed in another country then this could be seen as useful to the case. But otherwise it's too difficult and time consuming to undertake any detailed econometric analysis of overseas experience – so it's not undertaken at that level. However international experience can potentially be useful as anecdotal evidence or for comparing shock analysis. (Commission Official)

The collection and analysis of documents, such as statements by the merging companies, opinions of the merger by the companies' competitors, or external reports, upon which the potential rivalry between competitors can be inferred, is commonly an important component in the construction of the Commission's case. This type of documentary material is, however, most useful when it is consistent with the underlying economic analysis:

> If you have evidence of intention, one way or another … you obviously use it. But statements are often made for marketing or stock exchange reasons, or megalomania of the managing director. They are not always good evidence – the underlying economics, whatever that is, is much more important and I think that would be true in almost all cases. In Airtours, the statements that had been made tended to confirm the underlying economics, most of them. (Commission official)

> If you have documentary evidence that progresses your case and moves in the same direction as the economic evidence then good. … The argument in part is a theory of understanding what might happen and press statements are better than nothing to show intention. (Commission official)

Summary

The involvement of Commission economists in Phase II investigations is more common than in Phase I investigations but not invariable. The extent to which merger parties appoint economists to assist in the construction of their case varies, but a tendency for the Commission to place the onus on the merger parties to undertake any economic analysis of the potential effect of the merger increases the incidence of merger parties employing economists. Economists selected by merger parties will often be chosen on the basis of 'soft' skills such as persuasiveness as a witness, flexibility and adaptiveness to legal advocacy in addition to their technical capability.[43]

It is widely accepted that there are practical limitations on the ability to model economic theory or undertake econometric analysis in collective dominance investigations. However economic theory plays an important role in these investigations as an 'analytical frame', and as the basis for prognostications as to the potential for collective dominance to develop post merger. An economic approach also informs the overall thinking adopted, and the factors and indicators considered, by the Commission and merger parties in constructing their cases within the context of the investigation. The primary economic technique adopted by economists in merger investigations is descriptive expository, and involves the presentation of intuitive 'stories' or 'pictures' of what might potentially occur after the merger. Documentary or low-level quantitative analysis, rather than 'high-tech' quantitative analysis, is typically

---

43 More generally, compare Jones (n 9) 133–4.

used to complement the picture being presented. The extent of economic data used by the Commission and the parties varies according to quality and availability. Typically, non-economic data such as statements of intention, boardroom documents or views of customers and competitors also feature prominently in the construction of the case on both sides.

5.2.3 Economics in Final Decisions and Remedies

Following an investigation by a case team the formal decision-making procedure for Phase II merger investigations involves the consideration of the Advisory Committee on Concentrations, and the formal approval of the College of Commissioners. [44]

Before this formal procedure is invoked, and a draft decision sent to the Advisory Committee, an internal review panel is typically assembled within the Merger Task Force of the Commission. The internal review panel is charged with preparing an 'attack' on the Commission's case. The internal review panel historically operated fairly informally and did not necessarily include an economist. However, as part of recent reforms of the merger procedure, the setting up of 'devil's advocate' panels to scrutinise decisions is now becoming more formalised.[45]

Economic evidence in the final decision

Perceptions as to the degree of influence economic evidence plays in the final decision of the Commission vary greatly among practitioners. For some, economic evidence is the key piece of evidence. They point to instances where the Commission has been prepared to block a merger primarily on the basis of economic analysis showing the potential for collective dominance.[46] However, other practitioners suggest the use of economic evidence can be largely cosmetic, presented only when useful to the Commission's position,[47] or, in the case of the parties, as a defence tactic to bridge gaps in the facts.

---

[44] Following recent procedural changes, the Chief Competition Economist can submit final advice to the College of Commissioners: L.H. Röller and P.A. Buigues 'The office of the Chief Competition Economist' (2005) Global Competition Review, June, 3.

[45] P. Lowe 'Review of the EC merger regulation – forging a way ahead' (paper presented at the European Merger Control Conference, Brussels, 8 November 2002) 12; L.H. Röller (n 6) 5.

[46] One lawyer, for example, observes that, in his view, the sole basis for a negative decision in *Airtours/FirstChoice* was the economic analysis, and in particular the fact that the evidence was '100 per cent economic'.

[47] Compare F. Jenny 'Competition law enforcement: is economic expertise necessary?' in B. Hawk *International Antitrust Law & Policy: Fordham Corporate Law 1998* (Juris Publishing, New York, 1998) 198–9.

This research indicates that economic evidence is, in itself, usually insufficient to be determinative in decisions. In particular, there are indications that documentary evidence – a 'smoking gun' – is needed to support any economic analysis in order for the Commission to block a merger on the basis of concerns about collective dominance. In the view of one lawyer:

> The theory on which the cases proceed is necessarily speculation by the Commission. If the Commission has something real, non-economic, then that changes the picture.

In *Gencor/Lonrho*, for example, documentary evidence relating to the intention of the parties is widely perceived as having been the most important factor underlying the Commission's decision to block the merger in that case.

Economics in the development of remedies

Rather than being a distinct stage in the enforcement process, the development of remedies occurs throughout the process of a case investigation.[48] Discussions can start as early as the pre-notification stage. The extent of involvement of economists acting for the merger parties in the remedies process is variable and depends greatly on the case, and on the lawyers who manage the case.

In general, the main responsibility for remedies rests with the lawyers, and economists are typically called upon only if there is a specific economic issue. In part, this reflects perceptions that the remedy process is an exercise in commercial negotiation, to which lawyers are better suited.

> At the end of the day, remedies are often about finding something that solves the problem in face to face discussions with the Commission. ... The lawyers are very well versed in commercial negotiation. (Consultant economist)

> The lawyer will sense what is needed in order to get the deal through. An economist would not normally be involved unless there is an economic issue to which the economist can provide a solution. (Lawyer)

As with other parts of the enforcement process, the influence of economics in the design of remedies varies greatly depending upon the case. The Commission's general approach to the development of remedies is informal and involves encouraging the parties to develop appropriate remedies and to present any supporting analysis.

---

[48] Compare DG Competition Best Practices on the conduct of EC merger proceedings [2002] para 36.

Potential remedies submitted to the Commission by the parties are 'market-tested' with competitors and customers to assess their views. In some cases the economists or lawyers for the merger parties may have already market-tested the potential remedies with competitors prior to submission. Beyond 'market testing', the extent of economic analysis of the effects of potential remedies is very limited. In the view of some economists this is particularly concerning given that an 'inappropriate remedy may paralyse a market'.[49]

More generally, the process of remedy design is widely perceived to be a bargaining game between the Commission and the lawyers acting for the merger parties, where little or no substantive analysis of the effects of different remedies is presented. [50]

Some practitioners suggest that the lack of analysis of different remedies, and the informal way in which the process occurs, is part of a strategy of the Commission to maintain bargaining power. Specifically, the threat of implementing particular remedies can be used by the Commission as a bargaining tool throughout the entire investigation.[51]

> In order for them [the Commission] to issue a positive press statement they want to squeeze out commitments from companies, so they can be seen as doing something for the small man, the consumer … it's going to cost you to get the deal approved. (Lawyer)

An alternative view is that the extent of bargaining within the remedy process reflects resource asymmetries between the Commission and parties which, in some cases, compel the Commission to seek compromise solutions.

In any event, lawyers and economists acting for the merger parties are typically aware of the bargaining process surrounding remedies and adopt their own bargaining strategies to reach a desired outcome.[52]

> The remedies game is a great big horse trading exercise. It's a great game of poker. It's not really often done on a hugely rational basis and the point is that the Commission wants something – you want to give them as little as you can and you have to come to a compromise. But that compromise is a horse trading exercise. … There are some trade-offs, often it's the case that the lawyer must come up with clever wording that in fact doesn't mean anything but the Commission is willing for

---

[49] Compare O. Compte, F. Jenny and P. Rey 'Capacity constraints, mergers and collusion' (2002) 46 European Economic Review 1.

[50] Compare Neven, Nuttall and Seabright (n 5) 78, 117, 224.

[51] For example, the former CEO of GE, Jack Welch, has described his discussions with the Commission 'as although the Commission were merely seeking to extract a toll – pay enough and they would let the deal through': NERA 'Fixing remedies in European merger control' Competition Policy Insights July/August 2002 5.

[52] Compare Neven, Nuttall and Seabright (n 5) 130.

a variety of reasons to accept that as a remedy because it saves their face. … The point is that you make it look as if it's really hard – to show the Commission that you've given up something – but maybe you wanted to divest of it anyway.

Summary

The Commission's formal decision process will not necessarily include the detailed input of an economist. Increasingly, however, an internal review panel that includes an economist, is assembled to prepare an attack on the Commission's case prior to the final determination. Perceptions as to the importance of economic evidence to the final decision vary from it being the key piece of evidence, to it being largely cosmetic. In general, however, documentary evidence that complements the economic evidence is widely perceived as necessary to block a merger on concerns about collective dominance.

The development of remedies is not a distinct step in the enforcement process but is under consideration throughout the entire investigation, and the involvement of economists in remedy design tends to correlate with the extent to which they are involved in the investigation more generally. However, in many cases economists are not substantively involved in the remedy process because it is perceived as an exercise in commercial negotiation. Despite the potential for poorly designed remedies to have adverse effects on a market, economic analysis of the effects of potential remedies is very limited. This issue is an increasingly important one because the use of remedial measures to address concerns about collective dominance has increased in recent years, particularly following the CFI's decision in *Airtours v. Commission*. Of particular note is the focus on parties divesting of specific units or assets to create a viable third-party competitor. [53] Although this remedy is aimed at disturbing the potential for future coordinated behaviour, some economic research suggests that remedies which establish a viable symmetrical competitor may, in fact, increase the potential for tacit collusion.[54] However, as discussed above, economic analysis of the effect of potential remedies is currently very limited in the enforcement process.

---

[53] For example, see, *Antalis/MAP* (Case COMP/M.4753)[2007] OJ C289 paras [83]–[94]; *Linde/BOC* (Case No COMP/M.4141) [2006] OJ C181 paras [252]–[254].

[54] M. Fonseca and H.T. Norman 'Merger, asymmetries and collusion: experimental evidence' (2008) 118 Economic Journal 387; Compte, Jenny and Rey (n 49) 1.

5.3 ARTICLE 82 ENFORCEMENT PROCESS: THE COMMISSION

5.3.1 Introduction

The Commission's powers and responsibilities in initiating and conducting an investigation under Article 82 of the EC Treaty are conferred on it from a number of sources, including legislation and decisions of the European Courts. The Commission's discretion in handling complaints received is governed by Commission Regulations and Notices,[55] Court decisions,[56] and the EC Treaty.[57]

The formal powers of the Commission to initiate and conduct proceedings in respect of Article 82 are contained in Regulation 1/2003.[58] This Regulation provides that the Commission can undertake an investigation either on its own initiative, or on application of Member States or other undertakings with a legitimate interest.[59] It sets out the Commission's general investigative powers;[60] powers in respect of obtaining information;[61] allows for the hearing of the parties;[62] and confers on the Commission an ability to impose fines in respect of infringements of Article 82.[63]

---

55 Commission Regulation (EC) No 773/2004 of 7 April 2004 relating to the conduct of proceedings by the Commission pursuant to Articles 81 and 82 of the EC Treaty [2004] OJ L123/18; Commission Notice on the handling of complaints by the Commission under Articles 81 and 82 of the EC Treaty [2004] OJ C 101/65.

56 The Commission is required to maintain a 'duty of vigilance': C-210/81 *Demo-Studio Schmidt v Commission* [1983] ECR 3045 para [22].

57 Article 232 of the EC Treaty allows for complainants to bring actions for the Commission's 'failure to act'.

58 Council Regulation (EC) No 1/2003 of 16 December 2002 on the implementation of the rules of competition laid down in Articles 81 and 82 of the Treaty [2003] OJ L1/1 ('Regulation 1/2003'). At the time some of the research for this chapter was conducted, and when the cases discussed were investigated, the powers of the Commission were detailed in Regulation 17/62: Council Regulation (EEC) 17/62 First regulation implementing Articles 85 and 86 [now Articles 81 and 82] of the Treaty [1962] OJ Spec Ed 87 as amended [1999] OJ C148/5 ('Regulation 17/62').

59 Article 7 of Regulation 1/2003. Rules as to the handling and form in which complaints must be submitted to the Commission are detailed in Commission Regulation (EC) No 773/2004 of 7 April 2004 relating to the conduct of proceedings by the Commission pursuant to Articles 81 and 82 of the EC Treaty [2004] OJ L123/18; Commission Notice on the handling of complaints by the Commission under Articles 81 and 82 of the EC Treaty [2004] OJ C 101/65.

60 Article 18 of Regulation 1/2003.

61 Article 18–21 of Regulation 1/2003.

62 Article 27 of Regulation 1/2003.

63 Article 23 of Regulation 1/2003.

An Article 82 investigation typically commences with a Statement of Objections being served on the undertakings concerned. This contains all the matters in which the Commission intends to take action against the parties, along with details of any proposed remedy. The parties must respond to this statement within prescribed time limits and will be offered access to Commission files and an oral hearing. Following an investigation, the Commission – as represented by the College of Commissioners – takes a final decision as regards the alleged infringement.[64]

This formal procedure does not, however, occur in all cases and the Commission can, at various points in the process, adopt informal measures which result in the closure or termination of a case. These informal measures can occur either before or after the Statement of Objections has been issued, and can involve the administrative closure of a file, or be the result of an informal settlement between the Commission and the undertakings.[65]

5.3.2 Economics in Case Identification and Selection

The Commission has two principal areas of discretion in selecting cases for further investigation under Article 82. First, the Commission has discretion in determining which of the complaints it receives it will investigate further, along with the amount of resource and effort it will devote to such investigation. Second, once the Commission initiates an investigation, it has discretion as to whether the case will be handled in a formal manner, or attempts made to resolve the matter through informal measures. This section examines the use of economists and economics in informing the Commission's exercise of these two areas of discretion.

Involvement of economists

The Commission rarely initiates a collective dominance investigation under Article 82 *ex officio*. Complainants effectively 'sponsor' the Commission's decision to investigate and may present an economic basis for launching an investigation.[66]

---

64 Prior to this the Commission consults the Advisory Committee on Restrictive Trade Practices and Monopolies.

65 Informal settlements are often publicised through press releases or details are published in the Commission's Annual Reports of Competition Policy.

66 Complainants are also important in other competition law proceedings under the EC Treaty: D. Neven, P. Papandropoulos and P. Seabright *Trawling for Minnows: European Competition Policy and Agreements between Firms* (Centre for Economic Policy Research, London, 1998) 130. Complainants are also important in US Antitrust law: R.A. Katzmann *Regulatory Bureaucracy: The Federal Trade Commission and Antitrust Policy* (MIT Press, Cambridge, MA, 1980) 18–19; Weaver (n 40) 60–61.

The limited amount of *ex officio* activity under Article 82 means that the Commission has not typically looked to its own economists to identify cases of suspected abuse of collective dominance.[67] There is, for example, currently no monitoring or analysis of specific concentrated markets for suspicious behaviour, for which resource constraints, and the practical difficulties of the task, are often cited as reasons.[68]

The heavy reliance on complainants to sponsor the initiation of an investigation under Article 82 means that the main involvement of economists is as appointees of a complainant or an accused party. The role, and level of involvement, of these economists varies widely. In some cases, economists are used 'pre-emptively' and undertake discussions with parties who are concerned about their potential exposure to Article 82 actions prior to any investigation. More typically, economists working for the accused become involved only after a company has been named in a Statement of Objections issued by the Commission.

An economist working for a complainant can play a significant role in the development of the substantive arguments that are presented to convince the Commission to initiate an investigation. However, economists working for the complainants do not necessarily continue to work alongside the Commission once an investigation is initiated; the Commission may complete the investigation without further input from the complainants and their economic advisors.

Use of economic theory and approach in Article 82 investigations

There have been only a small number of formal investigations of abuse of a collective dominant position under Article 82. This reflects, in part, a perception that the theory underlying the legal notion of abuse of collective dominance is unclear. In particular, uncertainty exists as to how the concept of an

---

[67] The former Chief Competition Economist at the Commission acknowledged a need to undertake more *ex ante* analysis of markets on the basis that 'whenever an agency relies exclusively on complaints, firms' incentives may be negatively effected': L.H. Röller (n 6) 10.

[68] Formerly, Commission economists did perform some general analysis and monitoring of different markets which had some influence on the Commission's decision to initiate proceedings under Article 82. More recently, as discussed in Chapter 3, sector enquiries have been used in some cases to examine the potential for collusion in markets. For example, in the energy sector and retail banking inquiries: Commission of the European Communities *Commission energy sector inquiry confirms serious competition problems* Press Release IP/07/26 (10 January 2007); Commission staff working document – Accompanying the Communication from the Commission – Sector Inquiry under Article 17 of Regulation (EC) No 1/2003 on retail banking (Final Report) COM(2007) (31 January 2007).

'abuse' of collective dominance under Article 82 relates to the economic theory of tacit collusion.

> Article 82 is a bit weird. … If collective dominance is tacit collusion then are you saying you're abusing your tacitly collusive position. It's a very complicated construct. (Consultant economist)

> Collective dominance doesn't exist under Article 82, the Commission just haven't found the agreement yet. (Consultant economist)

The limited role that economic theory plays in the selection of these cases also reflects a historical reluctance by the Commission to employ economic theory more generally under Article 82 (i.e. in single dominance cases).[69]

> In Article 82 cases of abuse of a dominant position, the Commission has not really taken on board very much economic thinking at all at any stage. This is where its thinking has got left behind, as it were, by its thinking in other areas. (Commission official)

The limited usefulness of economic theory as a screen for *ex officio* action has meant that the Commission's decision to initiate an investigation into suspected abuses of a collective dominant position under Article 82 relies heavily on information and analysis that it receives from complainants. Typically, the complainant must satisfy a particular burden of proof before the Commission will act on a complaint. However, even where the Commission finds the complainant's argument convincing, its discretion to investigate may be influenced by the complexity of the case being presented, and the nature of the complainant.[70] In very technical cases the Commission likes to have serious, professionally well-informed and committed complainants because as

---

[69] Compare J. Vickers 'Abuse of market power' (paper presented at the 31st conference of the European Association for Research in Industrial Economics, Berlin 3 September 2004) 2. However, the recent publication of the enforcement guidelines for Article 82 is intended to introduce a more 'economic and effects-based approach' to enforcement: European Commission 'Guidance on the Commission's Enforcement Priorities in Applying Article 82 EC Treaty to Abusive Exclusionary Conduct by Dominant Undertakings' (COM) 2008 3 December 2008. See also: Commission of the European Communities 'Antitrust: consumer welfare at heart of Commission fight against abuses by dominant undertakings' Press Release IP/08/1877 (3 December 2008).

[70] Compare Katzmann who, in his study of US Antitrust activity, concludes that 'the determinants of antitrust activity are not necessarily or primarily economic. In deciding whether to bring a case, antitrust agencies are in many situations more concerned with the probability of success than with ultimate economic effects'; Katzmann (n 66) 7; also Weaver (n 40) 53–4.

one former Commission official put it 'it needs to have allies'. As with decisions to undertake merger investigations, Commission officials acknowledge the role of 'intuitions' or 'hunches', often based on distilled economic theory and understandings, in the Commission's decision to act.[71]

Use of economic techniques and data

As is the case in merger investigations, there are no particular economic techniques systematically employed by the Commission to identify and 'screen' potential cases. In some instances, economic analysis that has been undertaken by external bodies and foreign competition agencies has been influential in the selection of cases. For example, in the 'shipping cases' initiated under Article 82, the initial suspicions of the case team were to some extent supported by various external economic studies and publicly available information.

> [T]here was a certain amount of publicly available information from the OECD and so on which could also be used, because it was a worldwide industry after all. And there were American economists at the FTC who had looked at particular aspects, even if they hadn't looked at all the aspects … it made it easier, obviously, if somebody else has done the work already. (Commission official)

But other non-economic factors were also influential in the decision to initiate these investigations. In particular, the Commission had a longstanding concern about the protection such conferences received from the application of competition law. Broader political considerations have also been suggested in relation to some matters, for example in *Cewal*:

> It was not really a significant market or trade route – between Zaire and Northern Europe – not when compared to other conferences. I think that they were really after those involved in corruption in West African governments … the Commission was keeping a close eye on West Africa. (Lawyer)

As with merger cases, the data and information collected and assessed in the preliminary stage of an investigation includes both economic and non-economic information, including information provided by complainants and public information. However, in relation to Article 82 investigations, the existence of documentary evidence showing coordination is generally perceived as necessary, with economic data playing only a secondary role. For example, in *Cewal*, the existence of an agreement between the undertakings was seen to relieve the Commission of the burden of collecting and analysing economic data to support its decision to initiate an investigation.

---

[71] Compare Weaver (n 40) 46 in US context.

Summary

The Commission has conducted only a limited number of formal investigations of abuse of a collective dominant position under Article 82. These investigations have typically followed the receipt of a complaint, and the Commission has not looked to its own economists to identify cases for investigation. The main involvement of economists in the preliminary stages of an investigation is as appointees of a complainant or an accused party. The limited number of investigations under Article 82 can, in part, be attributed to uncertainty on the part of both Commission officials and external economists as to how the legal notion of abuse of collective dominance relates to the economic theory of tacit collusion. Nevertheless, distilled economic understandings do help to inform the initial suspicions and 'gut feeling' of the case team, as well as their assessment of the strength of the complainant's arguments. No particular economic techniques are systematically employed at this preliminary stage. A range of non-economic factors tend to feature prominently in the decision to initiate an investigation, the most important being the existence of agreements between the parties.

5.3.3 Economics in Case Construction

Involvement of economists

As with merger cases, the composition of a case team assembled to investigate a suspected abuse of a collective dominant position under Article 82 has not necessarily included an economist. Where Commission economists are involved, the general approach, as with merger cases, is to be reactive rather than proactive in undertaking analysis, typically by responding and critiquing any economic analysis submitted by the accused and the complainants.

> The consultancies do much better economics than we can, partly because of resources and time constraints … we encourage them to do the economic studies and we just review them. It's better for us to be in review position than model yourself. It's easy to pick apart an economic model, so we encourage the firms to do this. (Commission official)

Again, the ability of a Commission case team (which may not include an economist), to understand and adequately critique analysis presented by the parties is questioned by some practitioners. However, in some Article 82 investigations, the Commission has appointed academic economists to undertake economic analysis on its behalf and to respond to the economic analysis presented by the parties (e.g. *TACA*).

Economists are not necessarily engaged by the accused or complainants in Article 82 investigations. In *Cewal*, for example, the heavy focus on legal evidence – in the form of documents – negated the need for any detailed economic input by the parties or the complainants. In addition, in less complex cases, lawyers may 'do the economics'.

Where economists are used by the parties under investigation (or a complainant) they are typically appointed, and managed by the lawyers. Their involvement in the development of the case typically occurs at a greater distance than in merger cases, and it is less common for economists to work alongside the lawyers throughout the process. A typical scenario is for the economist to be a given a specific remit, or to be asked to respond to specific issues, and for them to be sent a file. As one lawyer describes it: 'we give them only what they need to know'.

As with mergers, there is a perception that revealing the fact that economists are working for a party can raise the suspicions of the Commission and escalate the nature of the proceedings.

> Sometimes, for tactical reasons, you don't necessarily want to escalate the economic arguments at a stage where you might have a battle of the experts – but you make sure that you've got expert economic input so that when you talk about issues in either a brief to the Commission or a brief to the Court you get it sounding in a way that an economist on the other side will say: they obviously had some proper input. (Lawyer)

Nevertheless, in some Article 82 cases, the input of economists can form the central argument of the case. In *TACA*, for example, economic input in relation to how competition worked in the particular market played a crucial role in the substantive arguments presented by the parties under investigation.

Use of economic theory

In general, economic theory has a limited and secondary role in the construction of Article 82 cases.

> Economics is too rich in the area of oligopolies to prosecute a case. There are too many models. It provides you with the first order conditions only. ... How many real life situations are there where costs structures are known to competitors, and competitors know each other's residual demand curves as well? Not many, I would say none, in practice. (Commission official)

This reluctance of the Commission to rely principally on economic theory in these cases also follows from lessons learned in an early concerted practice decision known as *Woodpulp*.[72] That case demonstrated that the development

---

[72] Joined cases C-89/85, C-104/85, C-114/85, C-116/85, C-117/85 and C-125/85 to C-129/85 *A. Ahlström Osakeyhtiö and others v Commission of the European Communities.* [1993] ECR I-01307.

of elaborate hypotheses purporting to explain real-world behaviour is highly vulnerable to attack and will generally be insufficient to satisfy the required burden of proof.

> What the Commission tried to do in that case … was to say that there are certain circumstances in which parallel conduct could be explained only by the existence of collusion and it wasn't necessary for the Commission to demonstrate the collusion. And they lost on that – the Court said that there is a burden of proof here. (Lawyer)

The acceptance by the Courts of particular uses, and interpretations, of economic theory also influences how theory is used by both the Commission and the parties in constructing their respective cases. This is different to merger investigations where parties appear to be less influenced by interpretations of the Court. This may be a function of a more formal legal approach to collective dominance under Article 82, and the traditionally more legalistic approach to Article 82 investigations generally.

Use of economic approach

As noted above, there is a general scepticism by economists both at the Commission and who act for the parties under investigation as to the notion of collective dominance as it may apply in Article 82 investigations, and as to the practical ability to employ economics to enforce this provision. Accordingly, the Commission's approach in Article 82 cases is primarily legal, with economics playing a supporting role. In general, the Commission has looked closely at the nature and scope of any agreements between the parties, such as shipping agreements or other contractual relationships (the working presumption of the Commission being that agreement between undertakings allows for an inference that the undertakings are collectively dominant).

The Commission's predominantly legal approach in Article 82 cases has possibly had the effect of making the parties more averse to employing economic arguments, as ultimately any legal analysis presented will take precedence over such economic analysis.

On occasion, however, lawyers working for the parties under investigation do adopt an economic approach in constructing their case. In *TACA*, for example, there was a heavy focus on highlighting the differences between the shipping lines in the conference and argued that these differences provided the stimuli for internal competition to occur within the shipping conference.

Use of economic techniques

As with merger investigations, it is relatively rare for the Commission or the parties subject to investigation to undertake any 'high-tech' quantitative modelling or detailed econometric work in cases relating to alleged abuses of a collective dominant position under Article 82. The principal reason for this is the absence of an accepted applied methodology, or model of oligopoly, that could be used in these cases.

It follows that where economic techniques are employed they are almost entirely low-level quantitative or descriptive. These include the calculation of concentration ratios, or the conducting and interpreting of surveys of customers and competitors.

> Only simple economic techniques can be used in these cases. For example, to gauge transparency we can talk to customers as well as competitors – this helps to reveal whether or not there is tacit collusion. Surveys can also be important to see if detection in the industry is possible. (Commission official)

As with merger investigations, one technique commonly employed by the Commission involves the presentation of a theory of competitive harm, with varying degrees of evidence offered as support. For example, in *TACA*, the Commission presented the hypothesis that internal and external competition was weak, and inferred on that basis that the parties had abused a collective dominant position.

Economists working for the parties subject to investigation also typically use descriptive and low-level quantitative analysis in the construction of their case. This is perceived to be most useful and persuasive on the basis that sophisticated techniques, such as complex models of oligopolistic interaction, will be viewed with suspicion, and ignored, by the Commission, or be vulnerable to attack.

> At the end of the day, the econometric study got us nowhere, absolutely nowhere. It was quite a difficult piece of work. And my impression is that the Commission will automatically reject those studies on the basis that they don't fully understand what they do and they are slightly inconvenient, and that there are all sorts of ways of attacking them. Some poor guy having to make a judgement on the Durbin Watson statistic or something will look around and say: 'is there anything else I can base my judgement on?' (Lawyer)

As with mergers, empirical techniques developed by academic economists to test for collective dominance – such as critical discount factor analysis – were seen as both too vague and too impractical to be employed. In particular, problems have been identified in how to make a choice as to an appropriate discount rate to use.

It is worth noting that sophisticated empirical models of oligopolistic interaction have been employed in some national jurisdictions; however such models have rarely been influential in outcomes.[73] For example, economic

---

73 For example, such models have been used in the investigation of the petrol retailing markets in France, Austria and the Netherlands.

models of petrol retailing showing no ability to tacitly collude were presented in a French case but were contradicted by other evidence and ultimately ignored by the decision-maker.[74] Similarly, a model of petrol retailing presented to the Netherlands Competition Authority in an inquiry into national retail petrol markets was viewed by that authority as implausible; an inaccurate reflection of reality.[75]

Use of economic data

As with merger cases, the Commission has a formal right to request a broad range of data, including economic data, from the parties. However, because of the focus in Article 82 investigations on the nature and scope of any agreements or contacts between the parties, the Commission has principally sought to rely on non-economic information, such as letters and internal statements in the construction of its case. The views and opinions of customers and competitors regarding the alleged abuse of a collective dominant position are also collected.

Documents which refer to the intention of the undertakings – for example, boardroom statements or internal memorandums which relate to, or show an intention to, engage in coordinated behaviour – form a central part of the construction of Article 82 cases. In *TACA*, for example, the Commission's central argument concerned whether certain documents could be interpreted to reveal an intention to entice new members to join the shipping conference. Similarly, in *Cewal*, the existence of documentary evidence of intention was seen to largely negate the need for economic data.

Summary

The case team assembled at the Commission to investigate a case under Article 82 may not include an economist, and an economist is not always appointed by the parties in these cases. Where appointed, economists are typically given a specific remit or asked to produce an expert report. Economic theory is seen as important insofar as it provides 'the theory' in a general sense, however, it is perceived to have limitations in its application to specific cases. The overall approach to the investigation of potential infringements of

---

[74] As an enforcement official recalls of that case: 'We heard evidence from the parties that they exchange prices everyday on the phone through contacting head office with prices of local competitors, but the economists produced models which showed no price elasticity and therefore no ability to raise price and collude. I said: I don't care what the model says because I have these statements from the gas station owners saying that they engage in this practice. There was no adjustment by the economists between the facts of the case and their models'.

[75] RBB Economics 'Fine in theory' (RBB Brief, 9 June 2003) 1.

Article 82, particularly by the Commission, is primarily legal with economics playing a supporting role if required. Any economic techniques that are employed are almost entirely descriptive or low-level quantitative, as these are perceived to be more persuasive and likely to be understood by decision-makers. While some economic data is typically collected, a greater focus is on the nature and scope of any agreements or contacts between the parties.

5.3.4 Economics in Decision and Remedies

Involvement of economists in the formal decision and remedies processes

Following an investigation, the Commission – as represented by the College of Commissioners – takes a final decision in relation to the alleged infringement. Where an infringement of Article 82 is found to have occurred the Commission may issue a 'cease and desist order' or impose fines on the undertakings.

There is no formal requirement for an economist to be involved, or to be consulted, prior to a decision being taken by the Commission. However, as noted above, following recent changes in Commission practice, it is now likely that an internal panel will be assembled, which would include an economist, to review the draft decision of the Commission prior to submission to the College of Commissioners.

The involvement of economists in the design of potential remedies is very limited in cases of abuse of collective dominance brought under Article 82. In part, this reflects the inability of economists to present and propose suitable and practical remedies to stop coordinated behaviour between undertakings.

> What is the remedy with tacit collusion? You cannot fine them – how would you determine the fine, how do you know if the fine is high enough to stop them colluding, and what will it do to the competitive structure of the industry? And with divestment, which part do you divest to stop collusion? (Commission official)

The limited role for economists in remedy design also reflects a more limited involvement generally of the parties in this process.

> As far as remedies are concerned in these types of cases, as opposed to merger cases, it is not at all certain that you will get any feedback from the Commission as to what they are going to do. That's partly a legal issue because, let's suppose they decide that certain practices are unlawful, then those practices are prohibited – that's the remedy. The Commission just says the practices, concerted agreement, or practice by a collectively dominant or dominant undertaking is prohibited full stop. A cease and desist order. (Lawyer)

In some cases, however, the Commission does 'informally' consult with complainants to 'test' the proposed remedy prior to implementation.

> Sometimes complainants are brought into this process at the remedies stage. The Commission will contact them to ask their opinion of what effect A or B would have on the market – bear in mind that they brought the case to the attention of the authorities. This is not a formal process and doesn't necessarily happen in every case. (Lawyer)

One area where economists who act for the parties under investigation are seeking to have a greater involvement is in the calculation of fines for infringements of Article 82. The calculation of fines for abuses of a collective dominant position is an area where economists historically have not featured prominently, and where the Commission retains a broad discretion. This is despite the fact that the fines in *TACA* and *Cewal* under Article 82 were among the largest fines ever levied under European competition law. The breadth of the Commission's discretion in this respect has been criticised.

> At the moment the European Antitrust authority's position is that economics does not provide the appropriate mechanism. This leaves the Commission with broad discretion and is inconsistent with sanctions in other parts of law – such as tax evasion. (Consultant economist)

However, senior Commission Officials have expressed scepticism about bringing economists formally into the process of fine calculation because of a fear that such economists, backed by the substantial resources of the parties, will use econometric studies and other analysis to substantially and unduly lower fines.

Use of economics in final decision

In general, economic evidence features less frequently, and is less influential, in the Commission's determinations relating to collective dominance under Article 82 than in merger cases.

The most persuasive influence in establishing an abuse of a collective dominant position is the existence of documentary evidence. Consequently, in cases where economic analysis has featured, it is perceived to have played only a secondary role in the Commission's decision. For example in *TACA*, there is a perception that despite the 'mass of economic evidence' assembled, and economic discussion, the Commission decided the issue on other grounds.[76]

---

[76] By way of contrast, in some other jurisdictions, economic evidence has been influential in suspected coordination cases in the absence of documentary evidence. Compare OECD Directorate for Financial, Fiscal and Enterprise Affairs Committee on Competition Law and Policy 'Oligopoly' (Unclassified Document DAFFE/CLP(99) 25 October 1999) 149. Compare also the experience in the United States in G.J. Werden 'Economic evidence on the existence of collusion: reconciling antitrust law with oligopoly theory' (2004) 71 Antitrust Law Journal 719.

Influence of economics in developing remedies

As noted above, the parties have very limited involvement in the development of remedies in Article 82 cases. Consequently, when remedies are proposed, any analysis of the potential effects of the remedy is undertaken in-house by the case team at the Commission. The analysis undertaken by the Commission typically does not involve much economic analysis of the potential effects of the remedy.

In some cases, the Commission does not prescribe specific remedies but rather shifts the burden on to the parties to introduce sufficient remedies to alleviate the concerns raised by the Commission during proceedings. In *TACA*, for example, the burden was placed on the parties to introduce 'measures' such that the Commission would be satisfied with the level of internal competition within the shipping conference. In that case, the Commission adopted what can be considered a regulatory approach. It has since maintained an interest in how the various remedial measures are being implemented, to the extent that even small changes in the conference structure can raise their suspicions.

Where fines have been levied for an Article 82 infringement the extent of analysis used to support the calculation and amount of the fine is typically limited to examining the profits, and size, of the relevant undertakings. While European law requires the fine levied to be sufficient to 'wipe out' any illegal profits, this calculation is difficult to make in practice, and measures such as relative size and turnover are often employed as proxy indicators.

The use of proxy indicators to measure competitive harm rather than undertaking more detailed economic analysis has created a perception among some that there is arbitrariness in the Commission's calculation of fines.

> Sanctions should be a function of actual damage. In the EU, quantification of damage is done by the authorities through the use of proxies such as turnover, and the duration and the nature of the illicit agreement. The current deterrent mechanism is not working, the fines in Europe are arbitrary and are not having the desired effect. (Economist)

Summary

There is no formal requirement for an economist to be involved, or consulted, prior to a decision being taken by the Commission in relation to an alleged abuse of collective dominance under Article 82, however it is now likely that an internal panel will be assembled, which would include an economist, to review the draft decision of the Commission prior to submission to the College of Commissioners. Documentary evidence, rather than economic evidence, is the most persuasive influence in final decisions. Economic analysis and evidence, where it has featured, is perceived to have played only a secondary role in the final decision.

Both the parties, and their economists, play a limited role in the design of remedies under Article 82. The Commission is limited in the remedies it can implement to issuing a 'cease and desist' order, or imposing a fine on the undertakings. However, in some cases, rather than imposing formal remedies, the Commission has taken what can be considered to be a regulatory approach, by requiring undertakings to implement measures that address the Commission's concerns which it then monitors on an on-going basis. Economics does not play a significant role in assessing the potential effects of a proposed remedy, or in the calculation of fines for any abuses of collective dominance under Article 82.

5.4 ECONOMICS IN THE COURTS

5.4.1 Introduction

The task of the European Courts, in hearing appeals of both ECMR and Article 82 decisions where collective dominance features, is to review and assess the validity of the Commission's decision at the time at which the decision was taken.[77] This involves reviewing the primary material that was before the Commission at the time the decision was made, including any economic analysis, statements and reports. The judicial review of these cases occurs principally through written pleadings submitted to the Court, however, there is also an oral hearing at which the parties may ask questions or raise issues.

In general, the review of the contested decision is not intended to focus on how the Commission has exercised its discretion, nor to review the merits of any economic assessment made by the Commission, or to substitute its view for that of the Commission.[78] Rather it involves the applying of a 'margin of appreciation' to the contested parts of the Commission's decision, while allowing for the various constraints – in terms of available material and time – under which the Commission was operating.[79]

> The role of the Court is to put itself in the position of the Commission as an economically literate administrative organisation. Then it asks: 'Have they reached the proper conclusion, or put another way, have they reached a conclusion from a

---

[77] Article 230 of the EC Treaty provides that the ECJ may review the legality of acts taken by the Commission.

[78] Case C-12/03 P *Commission of the European Communities v Tetra Laval BV* Opinion of Mr Advocate General Tizzano delivered on 25 May 2004 [2005] ECR I-0 para [89].

[79] Compare B. Vesterdorf 'Standard of proof in merger cases: reflections in the light of recent case law of the Community courts' (paper presented at the BIICL third annual merger control conference, 6 December 2004) 5–6.

range of permissible conclusions that they could have reached?' and 'have they examined sufficient material to make this conclusion?' (Judge)

However, at a higher level, the Court is also required to ensure that the *process* of competition law enforcement is compliant with Article 6 of the European Convention on Human Rights, insofar as the fundamental rights of the parties are observed and the Commission (which has both investigative and decision-making functions) is subject to *effective* judicial review.[80]

It is well established in cases involving fines, such as may be imposed under Article 82, that the Court has 'unlimited jurisdiction' in undertaking its review and will interfere in any perceived error of the Commission.[81] However, in ECMR cases, the scope of the review a Court is prepared to undertake to satisfy itself that general principles regarding fundamental rights have been complied with has, at times, been less clear.[82] In recent decisions, however, and perhaps in response to concerns regarding how the wide discretion left to the Commission in complex economic assessments interacts with the protection of fundamental rights,[83] the CFI has been prepared to undertake

---

[80] Article 6(1) of the ECHR reads: 'In the determination of his civil rights and obligations or of any criminal charge against him…everyone is entitled to a fair and public hearing…by an independent and impartial tribunal'. The Commission itself is not considered to be a 'tribunal' for these purposes; Joined cases T-25/95 *Cimenteries CBR and Others v Commission of the European Communities* [2000] ECR II-700 para [717] (*Cimenteries case*). Although the Courts have no jurisdiction to apply the European Convention on Human Rights when reviewing an investigation under competition law, inasmuch as the Convention as such is not part of Community law, it is settled case-law that such fundamental rights form an integral part of Community law whose observance is ensured by the Community judicature: Case T-112/98 *Mannesmannröhren-Werke AG v Commission of the European Communities* [2001] ECR II-00729 para [59]–[60]; Case C-299/95 *Friedrich Kremzow v Republik Österreich* [1997] ECR I-02629 para [14].

[81] Case T-348/94 *Enso Espanola v Commission* [1998] ECR II-1875 paras [62]–[64]; Article 17 of Council Regulation (EEC) 17/62 First regulation implementing Articles 85 and 86 [now Articles 81 and 82] of the Treaty [1962] OJ Spec Ed 87 as amended [1999] OJ C148/5.

[82] Compare Schwarze who argues that the Court has, in the past, allowed the Commission a 'wide margin of appreciation' in cases involving complex economic assessments, which has effectively lowered the overall scope of judicial review': J. Schwarze 'Judicial review of European administrative procedure' (2004) 68 Law and Contemporary Problems 99.

[83] Compare Schwarze (n 82) 95–96 who notes that the Courts leave the evaluation of substance in complicated technical matters to the administration only if the discretion is exercised in strict observance of procedural guarantees, including those that protect fundamental rights; Also D. Geradin and N. Petit 'Judicial remedies under EC competition law: complex issues arising from the "modernisation"' Global Competition Law Centre working paper (2005) 29.

an exhaustive review of the substantive economic facts, and the Commission's appraisal of those facts.[84] Indeed, in one recent decision, the CFI drew no distinction, in the context of the rights of the parties under Article 6 of the European Convention on Human Rights, between Article 82 and ECMR proceedings.[85]

5.4.2 Involvement of Economists

In cases heard on appeal, economists are often appointed on behalf of the Commission and the parties contesting the decision. It is not uncommon for appeals to become what one lawyer described as a 'battle of experts', where economists for both sides 'try to explain to the Court what is going on'. However, in no case yet where collective dominance has featured have the Courts appointed an expert economist to assist the judges in hearing the appeal.

The Commission Legal Service is responsible for the conduct of actions before the European Courts. In constructing the case for appeal, the Legal Service will work with the team assembled by the Commission for the investigation and will rely in large part on any economic work they have already undertaken as part of that investigation. Typically, the Legal Service will have met with the Commission team previously in relation to the matter – often at the end of Phase I and a couple of times in Phase II.

Where economists are engaged by the parties for the appeal, they are most likely to have been retained from their involvement in the Commission investigation. However, the interaction between the counsel for the applicants, typically a barrister, and the economist, differs from that of the interaction between the solicitors and the economist in the initial proceedings. The interaction between the economist and counsel is more indirect and conducted at 'arm's-length' for a number of practical and strategic reasons.

---

[84] These recent CFI decisions under the ECMR may have been influenced by the proximate decision in *Cimenteries* where the obligations of the Courts in the context of the ECHR were considered. Although *Cimenteries* involved infringements of Article 85(1), the Court elaborated an obligation 'to undertake an exhaustive review of both the Commission's substantive findings of fact and its legal appraisal of those facts' *Cimenteries case* (n 80) para [719]; Compare W.P.J. Wils 'The combination of the investigative and prosecutorial function and the adjudicative function in EC Antitrust enforcement: a legal and economic analysis' (2004) 27 World Competition 209.

[85] Case T-210/01 *General Electric Co v Commission of the European Communities* [2005] ECR II 00000 para [631].

> I don't typically deal with economists directly for two reasons: temporal and geographic. Also it feels more natural if I deal with them remotely, the experts feel more comfortable, it doesn't help if they feel like a puppet. For these reasons I adopt a hands-off attitude, as long as their statement is relevant and well presented. (Barrister)

However, economists will not be appointed by the parties in every appeal. Some lawyers, in particular, take the view that an experienced lawyer will be able to construct and present the economic arguments to the Court without the detailed input of an economist.

> Collective dominance arguments can be put forward in an easily understood way, this is one area where an experienced lawyer could prepare the arguments. Those lawyers who deal with a lot of these cases could present a reasoned and understandable argument about the economics. The problem is with more technical areas, such as theories relating to conglomerates. (Lawyer)

Where appointed, the principal task of economists in the appeals process is to produce a new opinion or statement that directly addresses and attacks the issues raised, or any flaws, in the reasoning of the pleadings and the contested decision. As one lawyer explains his brief to economists:

> I say to the economists to take the contested decision and tell me what is wrong with it – only what is within their expertise – I don't want their opinion on issues of fact or procedure, there is a tendency for this to happen. I want them to take the decision as a benchmark, use the Commission as benchmark and tell me what within their expertise is wrong with it. I tell them to focus on the reasoning of the Commission. I don't want them to just re-run the same points as already submitted to the Commission previously. You need a new expert paper not the same as previously submitted.

5.4.3 Use of Economics in Court

Economic theory and approach

The submissions made to the Court by the Commission and the parties will typically include an interpretation of any underlying economic theory used in the contested decision. In the case of the parties, the interpretation of the theory used by the Commission will often be critically examined and an alternative interpretation presented.

The Court's understanding of the underlying economic theory of a case is based entirely on the pleadings presented before the Court, and as such the Court is dependent on the exposition of theory in the pleadings received. In general, there is a perception that the more broadly supported and well established the economic theory used in a case is, the more likely that the Court will be willing to accept the Commission's application of that theory.[86] For example, the economic theory relating to an increase in concentration and the potential for tacit coordination is not considered in itself a 'solid' enough theory upon which the Commission can base an assessment of collective dominance.

> The Court will exercise a tight control on the use of theory, and will scrutinise any theories or application of theories that it considers controversial. The more 'predictive' the Commission asks the Court to be, the more solid the theory has to be. The theory has to be uncontroversial in these very predictive cases. In *Airtours*, the Commission was in an unusual position of saying that there was no collective dominance before the merger and yet this shift from 4 to 3 would create the conditions that would lead to collective dominance. This was not considered solid theory. The Commission had to at least present some sign or indication of why it is that they thought that the conditions will change so significantly to bring about collective dominance post-merger. (Former Judge)

Some practitioners argue that the aversion of the Court to accept less established or complex applications of theory in cases of collective dominance amounts to a high burden of proof.[87]

Following the Courts' decisions in a number of recent controversial cases there has been much discussion about the Courts' approach to reviewing the Commission's exercise of its administrative discretion in interpreting and weighting economic evidence.[88] In part, that discussion has revolved around the scope and nature of the Commission's discretion to assess future competitive harm, and how the Commission uses economic analysis and evidence to

---

[86] Compare Vesterdorf (n 79) 22.

[87] In particular, some practitioners point to the decision in *Airtours v Commission* as an example of where the Court was seen to impose a higher standard of proof in relation to the Commission's assessment of a complex and difficult application of theory.

[88] Two decisions were single dominance cases: Case T-342/99 *Airtours plc v Commission of the European Communities* [2002] ECR II-02585; Case T-80/02 *Tetra Laval BV v Commission of the European Communities* [2002] ECR II-04519 and C-13/03P *Commission of the European Communities v Tetra Laval BV.* [2005] ECR I-01113; Case T-77/02 *Schneider Electric SA v Commission of the European Communities* [2002] ECR II-04201; Case T-464/04 *Independent Music Publishers and Labels Association (Impala, International Association) v Commission of the European Communities* [2006] ECR II-02289 para [289] (*Impala v Commission*); Case C-413/06P *Bertelsmann AG and Sony Corporation of America v Independent Music Publishers and Labels Association (Impala)* [2008] ECR-00000 *(Bertelsmann and Sony Corp. v Impala).* Compare Commission press release of 20 December 2002 'Commission clears acquisition of Sidel by Tetra Laval Group' IP/02/1952; Vesterdorf (n 79) 1; D.J. Gerber 'Courts as economic experts in European merger law' in B. Hawk (ed) *International Antitrust Law & Policy: Fordham Corporate Law 2004* (Juris Publishing, New York, 2004) 475.

support its conclusions. However, it has also focused on the more economic approach of the Courts in these cases. In the view of some, the Court has, in recent decisions, moved beyond its normal fact-finding role, and taken on the role of economic expert by:

> [A]ssuming that it has sufficient skill and knowledge in economic analysis to reject the Commission's conclusions on the basis of its own skill as an economic analyst. In those situations, it looks at the same data on which the Commission based its decision, but it draws different economic conclusions from the data, relying on its own analytical capacity to make those determinations.[89]

In particular, there is a perception among some that the Courts have responded to the increasingly sophisticated economic approach of the Commission by setting the standard of proof higher in their review of the economic evidence upon which the Commission has based its assessment.[90]

> We have seen a revolution in the CFI controlling the decisions of the Commission. The CFI has been invited by more professionally put arguments to look more closely at these decisions. In the past, it relied on the force of circumstances and the force of arguments put to them … A judge at the ECJ said to me recently that the CFI has overstepped the mark and put the standard too high for mergers, they need to take into account what is possible in the time – not search for an abstract answer in a perfect world. (Commission official)

> The danger with sophisticated economics in competition policy is one that we have to face anyway. The parties are getting more sophisticated advice, and Courts are listening more and more to this advice, and raising the standard of proof. It's about time Courts, including the ECJ, sat down and thought about what is the appropriate standard, as it can be raised much too high. (Former Judge)

To the extent that this perception of a shift in approach is accurate, it may, as discussed earlier in this chapter, reflect concerns of the Court to be ECHR compliant in cases involving complex economic assessments. Indeed, those outside the Commission argue that the Courts are not challenging the Commission's approach of using sophisticated economic arguments, but only the failure of the Commission to substantiate its arguments and conclusions with sufficient economic analysis and evidence. As two recent opinions of Advocate Generals of the ECJ have noted in relation to this issue:

---

[89] Gerber (n 88) 480–482.

[90] Compare A. Nikpay and F. Houwen 'Tour de force or a little local turbulence? A heretical view on the Airtours judgment' (2003) 24 European Competition Law Review 193; Gerber (n 88) 485, 489.

> [T]he fact that the Commission enjoys broad discretion … does certainly not mean that it does not have in any case to base its conviction on solid elements gathered in the course of a thorough and painstaking investigation or that it is not required to give a full statement of reasons for its decision, disclosing the various passages of logical argument supporting the decision.[91]

> If, in its assessment of the effect on competition of a concentration, the Commission attaches particular importance to certain factors which are relevant to the market, it must not only identify these factors in its decision but must also describe, sufficiently precisely, their effects on the functioning of the markets in question. … As the Court of First Instance correctly emphasises, what is instead necessary is for the Commission to substantiate the effects of this factor in its decision with specific details; it cannot simply rely on the surmise, hesitantly expressed, that 'this factor could reduce transparency in the market and may make tacit collusion more difficult', and just as little on the mere conjecture that 'it appears that campaign discounts are less transparent than file discounts'. In all, the Court of First Instance therefore rightly held that the Commission ought not to have restricted itself to 'vague assertions' as regards the factors which were decisive for its decision, which were 'unsubstantiated', 'rather limited' and in addition internally contradictory.[92]

On this view, the CFI's decisions in *Airtours v. Commission* and *Impala v Commission* are seen not so much as a rejection of the Commission's more economic approach but rather a rejection of the Commission's general fact-finding processes and the extent to which it substantiates any theory and analysis with evidence.[93]

> The Commission is prepared to prohibit a merger on the basis of economic theory alone, while the CFI is not prepared to do so … the burden of proof is higher at the Court. …. *Airtours* was subject to a Court in which close analysis was made on every point – it was difficult to substantiate the economic analysis, and economic theory alone won't hold up with this standard and close scrutiny. This is the difference between theoretical speculation and concrete evidence. (Lawyer)

> The Court doesn't criticise the economics in *Airtours*, only the Commission's internal consistency and the credibility of the evidence and analysis presented. It would be happy to follow the economic judgement of the Commission if it was consistent and credible. (Commission official)

---

91 Case C-12/03 P *Commission of the European Communities v Tetra Laval BV* Opinion of Mr Advocate General Tizzano delivered on 25 May 2004 [2005] ECR I-0 para [87].

92 Case C-413/06P *Bertelsmann AG and Sony Corporation of America v Independent Music Publishers and Labels Association (Impala)* Opinion of Advocate General Kokott delivered on 13 December 2007 [2008] ECR-00000 paras [128]–[130].

93 Compare Vesterdorf (n 79) 13–14.

Indeed, where the Court becomes 'suspicious' of the Commission's fact-finding procedures then it will examine a decision in close detail.

> When the Commission gets wrong a primary fact regarding the characteristics of the market, where this is apparent, then the Court is more willing to exercise a tighter control on any other analysis that follows. This was the case in *Airtours* and the 'one page report', and also the omitting of certain sentences and the use of others. In these circumstances then this makes the Court suspicious and it will exercise a tighter control on other elements of the decision. (Former Judge)

There has also been judicial discussion about the Commission's responsibility in cases where evidence or analysis is wholly or principally provided by the parties (a practice that, as discussed throughout this chapter, is commonplace). For example, in rejecting the Commission's assessment of collective dominance in *Impala v. Commission*, the CFI stated:

> It must be observed at the outset ... that the findings relating to campaign discounts are not only based solely on the data relating to the parties to the concentration but that, in addition, the tables setting out those data were prepared by those parties (or their economic advisers) according to a methodology and on the basis of data selected by the parties themselves, while there is no indication that the Commission ascertained whether they were accurate, relevant or objective and representative.
>
> Although, as the Commission stated at the hearing, the procedure for the control of concentrations does indeed rely to a large extent on trust, as the Commission cannot be required to ascertain on its own, in the slightest detail, the reliability and accuracy of all the information submitted to it, it cannot, on the other hand, go so far as to delegate, without supervision, responsibility for conducting certain parts of the investigation to the parties to the concentration, in particular where, as in the present case, those aspects constitute the crucial element on which the decision is based and where the data and assessments submitted by the parties to the concentration are diametrically opposite to the information gathered by the Commission during its investigation and also to the conclusions which it drew from that information.[94]

Nevertheless, on appeal, the ECJ rejected the CFI's view that the Commission's failure to conduct additional market investigations amounted to an unlawful 'delegation' of the investigation to the merger parties.[95] While the ECJ confirmed that the Commission is required to examine carefully the arguments of the merger parties as regards their exactitude, completeness and cogency, the ECJ also held that the CFI erred in law by applying more demanding requirements as regards the probative character of the evidence and arguments put forward by the notifying parties than are applied to competitors, customers and other third parties.

---

94 *Impala v Commission* (n 88) para [415].
95 *Bertelsmann and Sony Corp. v Impala* (n 88) para [95].

Economic techniques and data

The principal economic technique employed by economists in Court proceedings is the presentation of intuitive descriptive economic arguments, sometimes supported by simple quantitative analysis. This is the result of a perceived need to be persuasive and accessible.

Sophisticated analytical techniques or models feature rarely in pleadings. In part this reflects the empirical difficulty in demonstrating collective dominance on the facts of specific cases to a sufficiently high standard of proof.[96] However, it also reflects an aversion to the use of sophisticated techniques and models as evidence because they are too 'abstract and presumptive',[97] and might prove confusing to the judges, and be disregarded. In the words of a member of the Commission Legal Service: 'Courts don't like mathematical models'.

The focus on accessible economic arguments and techniques is consistent with a Court's aim in reviewing the Commission's exercise of its discretion, which is not to review the thoroughness of the Commission's economic analysis but rather to satisfy itself that the analysis is properly conducted. Economic analysis presented in pleadings will principally be used by the court to assess the reasonableness of the theory and analysis being presented and whether an economically literate organisation could have come to this conclusion.

The data and information that the Court considers in conducting its review of the contested decision is primarily the material that was before the Commission at the time when the decision was made. This includes any economic reports or submissions that were made to the Commission during its investigation. The principal usefulness of economic submissions of this kind for the Courts is in providing background information and highlighting areas of controversy. Where an economist has prepared an expert statement for the Court proceedings then they may be called upon to provide an oral presentation to the Court. In addition, the Court can also ask questions of economists at the oral hearing.

5.4.4 Economics in Decision

The overall importance of economic evidence in the decision of the Court is difficult to assess, and practitioners' opinions vary on this issue. For some, economics is important because it can create the right 'smell' for judges. In the view of one economist 'judges and decision makers rely on instinct' and

96 Compare J. Vickers 'Merger policy in Europe: retrospect and prospect' (paper presented at the Charles River Associates conference, Washington, DC, 11 February 2004) 8.

97 Compare Jenny (n 47) 195–6.

'economics can help in this regard'. In particular, for the party that must satisfy the burden of proof and convince a judge, economic analysis can help show how plausible an outcome is.[98]

Other practitioners suggest, however, that the influence of economic evidence depends greatly upon the specific judge's interest, and the economic sophistication of the Court.[99] Some judges are perceived by practitioners as being reluctant to tackle economic evidence while others are seen to have an especial interest in the area. Other practitioners suggest that the recent focus of the Court on economic arguments, such as in *Airtours v Commission* and *Impala v Commission*, is less an indication of the Court intending to engage more fully with economic evidence than part of a broader programme involving the Courts' review of the Commission's exercise of its administrative discretion.

> [J]udges very much see their role as reviewing a decision of the Commission as an administrative body. Now occasionally, as in the cases recently on the merger side, the Court gets the impression that things are slipping a little bit and the Commission just needs reminding that public confidence needs to be upheld and therefore it goes in a bit hard. Probably the effect of that will be that there are a number of judgments that go the other way towards the Commission. I think that you've got a pendulum that moves in these things. (Lawyer)

5.5 CONCLUSION

The examination of the role of economists, and the use of economics, in the entire enforcement process in collective dominance cases shows that the influence of economics is more pervasive than the text of the reported decisions considered alone would suggest. However, differences can be seen in how economics is applied in the different stages of the enforcement process, between merger and Article 82 investigations, and as between the Commission and the Courts. Tables 5.1 to 5.4 summarise these aspects.

Although economists do not feature in every investigation, they are increasingly involved in collective dominance cases, particularly merger cases. The

---

98 The Advocate General in *Bertelsmann and Sony Corp. v Impala* noted that 'plausibility' is the standard which must be satisfied before the Courts: 'Judicial review of such an assessment of probability is not so much about whether the Commission's prognosis on a concentration's positive or negative effects on competition is *capable of being proved* but rather about its *plausibility*.' Case C-413/06P *Bertelsmann AG and Sony Corporation of America v Independent Music Publishers and Labels Association (Impala)* Opinion of Advocate General Kokott delivered on 13 December 2007 [2008] ECR-00000 para [26].

99 Compare Gerber (n 88) 489, 493.

Table 5.1 Economics in case selection

	ECMR	Article 82
Involvement of economists	Commission case team may not include an economist. Appointment by parties varies depending upon the complexity of the case.	Limited use of Commission economists to identify cases. Complainants and accused parties may appoint economists to assist with their complaint/defence.
Theory	Until recently a checklist derived from theory was used to identify cases. Now a non-systematic approach is used.	Limited role of theory in the identification and selection of cases.
Approach	Commission's approach is non-systematic but economic focused. Distilled economic understandings can form the basis of hunches as to what is important. Commission encourages the parties to undertake and submit preliminary economic analysis.	Approach based on consideration of a variety of matters, such as the existence of any agreement; the strength of the complainant's arguments; and the complexity of the case. Distilled economic understandings can form the basis of hunches or 'gut' instincts.
Techniques	No systematic economic techniques employed. 'Low-tech' quantitative analysis of the number of competitors and calculation of market shares do typically feature. 'High-tech' analysis features rarely.	No systematic economic techniques employed. In some cases external economic studies have been relevant.
Data	Both economic and non-economic data collected from parties, customers and competitors.	Both economic and non-economic data collected from parties, complainants, customers and competitors. Heavy focus on whether any agreements exist between firms.

Commission's general approach is to be reactive rather than proactive in relation to any economic analysis that may be relevant to an investigation, and to encourage the parties to undertake such analysis. Where appointed, economists for the parties are typically employed and managed by lawyers. Their

Table 5.2 Economics in case construction

	ECMR	Article 82
Involvement of economists	If not a member of the case team, an economist will typically provide input into the Commission's case development at this stage. Economists will typically be involved at this stage for the parties.	An economist may not necessarily form part of the case team assembled at the Commission. Economists typically, but not necessarily, appointed by the parties.
Theory	Theory important to frame the investigation. In some cases, specific predictions are used as the basis of prognostications.	Theory useful in a general sense, but seen to have limited application in specific cases.
Approach	Broadly economic approach in terms of 'thinking' and indicators and evidence examined, based on economic understandings.	Approach has a legal focus with economic expertise playing a supporting role. Some cases where an economic approach has been adopted.
Techniques	Limited use of 'high-tech' economic techniques. More commonly use of descriptive, or low level quantitative, economic techniques.	Economic techniques employed are typically descriptive or low-level quantitative. Some examples of 'high-tech' economic analysis.
Data	Economic data is collected, but non-economic data also features. Limited use of external data sources.	Some economic data is collected, however, a heavy reliance on 'non-economic' data such as documents relating to the intention of the parties.

involvement in the development of a case varies from providing detailed economic substance to the legal arguments, to simply producing a report for the lawyers that highlights any specific issues. Economics plays a role in the selection, or non-selection, of cases for further investigation through the application of 'rules of thumb' and distilled economic understandings. In addition, in constructing a case, both the Commission and the parties sometimes put

Table 5.3 Economics in final decision and remedies

	ECMR	Article 82
Decision		
Involvement of economists	Formal decision made by the College of Commissioners, prior to which an economist may be involved as part of an internal review panel.	Formal decision made by the College of Commissioners. An economist may be involved as part of an internal review panel.
Influence of economic evidence	Perceptions vary as to importance of economic evidence in final decision. Typically insufficient on its own to be determinative.	Most persuasive influence is the existence of documentary evidence. Economic evidence perceived to play a supporting role.
Remedies		
Involvement of economists	At the Commission, depends on composition of case team. Typically, economists for the parties have limited involvement.	Depends on composition of case team at Commission. Currently limited involvement of parties' economists in this process.
Influence of economics	Beyond market testing, very limited economic assessment of potential effects of remedies.	Limited role for economic assessment of potential remedies, including any proposed 'regulatory' measures and the calculation of fines.

considerable effort into the development of economically persuasive and credible arguments. Where Commission decisions are appealed to the Courts, the Courts have on occasion scrutinised the robustness of economic analysis and evidence used by the Commission and the parties to support their conclusions.

A number of other observations emerge from this chapter. First, although economics has been shown to feature in investigations, numerous other factors have a significant influence on the course, and outcome, of an investigation. Specifically: documentary evidence, procedural matters, historical context, the impact of individual personalities, the objectives of enforcement officials, and a variety of broader political influences. It is difficult to assess the relative influence of each of these factors on the course of an investigation and the final decision. The probative weight of economic evidence relative to other

Table 5.4 Economics in the Courts

Involvement of economists	Commission Legal Service typically works with existing case team from initial investigation, but may appoint external economists. Similarly, the parties will typically retain the economists from the initial investigation. The Courts are yet to appoint an economist to assist judges in hearing appeals under the ECMR or Article 82.
Theory	The Courts' understanding of theory determined by submissions received. Generally, the more broadly supported the theory, the more likely the Court will accept its interpretation.
Approach	Perception by some that the Court has adopted an increasingly economic approach, particularly in relation to mergers, by re-examining the Commission's economic assessment.
Techniques	The choice of economic technique presented in pleadings is heavily influenced by the ability to be intuitive and persuasive. Pleadings typically do not feature 'high-tech' or sophisticated economic techniques or analysis.
Data	Typically limited to data before the Commission when making its assessment. Court may call for an expert statement by an economist.

evidence is also difficult to determine. In general, particularly in Article 82 investigations, economic evidence alone has been seen to be insufficient to be determinative in the absence of corroborative documentary evidence. Finally, it emerges from this review that both in the course of an investigation, and in the final determination, the Commission, in considering economic evidence, relies heavily on the analysis of data provided by lawyers and economists acting for the parties subject to investigation. This is despite the fact that the access to data of economists for those parties is typically less comprehensive than for the Commission.

The nature of economics used in the various stages of the enforcement process is essentially the same as we saw in Chapter 4, although in this chapter a greater insight is sometimes provided into the specific reasons for this use. In Chapter 4 it was concluded that some variation exists in respect of which 'factors' feature in assessments and the frequency, and standard, by which individual factors are assessed. Such a result is consistent with the views of practitioners expressed in this chapter that the practical utility of economic theory is located at the general level of framing an investigation, not in the precise application of the predictions of theory in specific cases. As a result, there is a focus on the pragmatic and adaptive use of theory to support specific lines of argument, which is not heavily constrained by the need to conform to the stringencies of theoretical economics. We also saw in Chapter

4 that the Commission's assessment of any particular economic factor can involve the consideration of different economic indicators in different decisions. This arguably follows from the tendency identified in this chapter of those involved in the enforcement process to rely on 'economic intuition' and 'distilled economic understandings' in determining the relevance of indicators. Such intuition and understandings will necessarily vary from case to case. The limited use of 'high tech' economic techniques identified in Chapter 4 was explained in part, in this chapter, by the practical difficulties of applying such techniques, particularly within the time constraints of the investigation. However, those involved in the enforcement process also expressed the view that low-level quantitative and descriptive techniques are more intuitive and persuasive, and can create the right 'gut feeling' in the decision-maker.

This chapter also provides insights into broader questions regarding the application of knowledge in practice. Specifically, it demonstrates the perspectives and interests of the various actors who use economic knowledge in the enforcement process, and how differences in such perspectives and interests affect the knowledge's application. As we have seen, the application of economic knowledge in merger and Article 82 investigations is not solely the domain of economists. Lawyers and administrators also 'do the economics'. In using economic knowledge, perceptions as to the appropriate use of such knowledge vary. This is well illustrated by the comment of one lawyer that the economist least useful in a case is one who doesn't realise he is acting as an advocate, and who is too keen to focus on what he *believes*. Differences in perspectives as to the use of economics were also revealed between academic and consultant economists, between Commission administrators and Commission lawyers, between the representatives of the Commission and the judiciary. Some of the purposive interests affecting the use of economic knowledge by these actors can be identified. For example, there is evidence that the judiciary's review of the Commission's use of economic knowledge in fulfilling its regulatory functions is informed, in part, by a need to maintain public confidence in these functions. Similarly, Commission officials acknowledged that their use of economic knowledge in specific cases has reflected concerns beyond the facts of that case, including their ability to regulate a broader range of behaviour or affect the structure of particular industries. Lawyers and consultant economists also reveal, at various points, their perspectives and interests in how economic expertise is used in the enforcement process.

Finally, this chapter suggests that where knowledge has a number of different audiences this can significantly impact how that knowledge is applied. For example, the audiences for economic knowledge in the enforcement process – Commission administrators, judges, lawyers – have different degrees of economic sophistication. This presents a potential explanation for the variation in the application of economics observed. We saw, for example, that judges are more willing to accept uncontroversial applications of economic theory and demonstrate an aversion to highly technical, non-intuitive economic reasoning and evidence. Similarly, the acceptance of economic knowledge by lawyers is informed by their role as advocates whose role is to structure persuasive arguments.

6. The contribution of economics to enforcement

> As I'm sure you all know, I am an economist by training. Now I am an antitrust enforcer by profession! As an economist, I want an economically sound framework. But as an enforcer, I need a workable and operational tool for making enforcement decisions.[1]
>
> Neelie Kroes, Member of the European Commission in charge of Competition Policy

6.1 INTRODUCTION

A general conclusion that emerges from the discussion so far is that while the economics of tacit collusion is a well established area of research activity in economics, the ability to apply this research – including its methodologies and conclusions – to individual collective dominance cases is, as demonstrated by the case study, not straightforward.

In particular, it is evident that while the overall predictions of theoretical models are used to provide the basis for a general enforcement approach, the application of such models to the factual settings of these cases has not typically, or systematically, been associated with the application of the appropriate techniques or the collection or analyses of relevant data. In this respect, the case study evidences a focus in the enforcement process on the pragmatic and adaptive use of theory to support specific lines of argument, which is not heavily constrained by the need to conform to the stringencies of theoretical economics. Accordingly, we see that factors derived from economic theory are employed variably across decisions; aspects of economic reasoning and data are emphasised over others; and descriptive techniques are employed far more frequently than quantitative techniques.

This result is not necessarily indicative of a flawed enforcement process. Rather it seems to reflect a number of issues identified previously including:

1 N. Kroes 'Preliminary thoughts on policy review of Article 82' (Speech at the Fordham Corporate Law Institute, New York, 23 September 2005).

the multiplicity of models that comprise the economics of tacit collusion, some of which present conflicting implications; the nature of economic models and analytical techniques, including their high levels of abstraction and underlying assumptions (and limitations); and the multiple actors that are involved in the process of enforcement of the relevant laws, each of whom have their own perspectives and interests in the use of economics in this process. Moreover, it is a result that studies on the transformation of areas of knowledge in practical settings suggest that we should anticipate; these studies predict that knowledge, generated in one area, will inevitably undergo a selective (and frequently substantial) transformation when applied in another area with different purposes and audiences.

The results show that, at the case level, the influence of economics in this area of enforcement is not principally derived from its technical or evidentiary potential. However, the case study also highlights the necessity of looking beyond the use of economic evidence in specific cases to how economics informs the enforcement process more broadly. In this respect, the case study demonstrates the influence of economics on the discourse of enforcement, the programme of reasoning employed in decision-making, and the perception of decision-makers as to the parameters of their discretion. At this level the empirical study evidences three crucial contributions of economics to the enforcement of the laws relating to collective dominance.

First, economic theory provides an analytical 'frame' for an investigation, indicating to practitioners *what* to look at in the investigation, by presenting specific predictions of when we might expect to observe coordinated behaviour. It also provides a set of concepts and a terminology that allows for the identification and collection of economic facts. Second, economics presents a method, or an approach, upon which an investigation can be structured – it gives practitioners a programme for *how* to analyse information relevant to an investigation. That is, it brings conceptual and descriptive tools to the enforcement process. Third, economics provides a descriptive technique that allows theory, metaphor and fact to be blended into intuitive and persuasive hypothetical 'stories' of existing or future behaviour.

6.2 ECONOMIC THEORY AS FRAME

While economic theory has been seen to have uneven and sometimes problematic application in specific cases, such theory does fulfil a general framing function in the enforcement of the collective dominant laws. It does so in three ways. First, it provides a 'vision' of oligopolistic interaction that provides parameters for the interpretation of relevant provisions of the EC Treaty and the ECMR, and allows for the development of legal norms in an otherwise highly political and morally ambiguous area. Second, it provides a set of concepts which allows for the identification of factors relevant to an investigation and for the collection of economic facts. Finally, it legitimises the enforcement of the law on the basis of the principled reasoning and conclusions of an established social science.

6.2.1 A 'Foundation' for Law

As we saw in Chapter 3, the EC Treaty and the ECMR do not specifically employ the term 'collective dominance'. Consequently, the substantive development of the notion of collective dominance under both Article 82 and the ECMR has been the result of interpretation by the Commission and Courts.

Economic theory has assisted this development in two ways. First, economic theory has addressed the generality of the ECMR and Article 82 by providing a 'vision', or a high-level framework, for interpreting the provisions in relation to oligopolies.[2] In particular, the economic theory relating to oligopolies has provided a system of meaning for the wording of the relevant laws.[3] Commission officials and private practitioners acknowledge the importance for European competition law to 'relate' or 'connect' to a body of knowledge like economics. This importance arises, in the views of these practitioners, because the rules are provided in two or three lines and have to be applied in all situations, and because the law needs to be approached in a rational way and economic theory provides this rational structure. As a Commission economist explains it: 'Without economics you have no idea what you are doing in competition law… oligopoly theory is crucial to frame the law, legal theory has nothing to say, no way to tackle it.'

Economic theory also 'operationalises' the collective dominance provisions, allowing for enforcement action to be taken. That is, it identifies the mischief that the law is addressing, while also providing a mechanism for translating the mischief so that practitioners can understand, illustrate and

---

[2] Compare: G. Niels 'Collective dominance: more than just oligopolistic interdependence' (2001) 22 European Competition Law Review 168; B. Etter 'The assessment of mergers in the EC under the concept of collective dominance: an analysis of the recent decisions and judgments – by an economic approach' (2000) 23 Journal of World Competition 125. In the US, the 'power of economics' in Antitrust has been described as its ability to provide 'visions of the world' through its theories: T.J. Muris 'Economics and antitrust' (1997) 5 George Mason Law Review 303.

[3] Compare Yeung who describes the role of economic theory in elucidating, and providing meaning to, concepts embodied in statute in Australian competition law: K. Yeung 'The court-room economist in Australian antitrust litigation: an underutilised resource?' (1992) 20 Australian Business Law Review 470–472.

recognise the relevant issues in an investigation.[4] As one lawyer explains it: 'Economics helps to inform whether there is a mischief – that is, what happens if you apply the law one way as opposed to another'. In this way, economic theory provides continuity between the two stages of legal planning and enforcement. Economic theory has been seen as important, for example, in the development of merger guidelines in Europe. As the former Chairman of the UK competition authority has noted, 'Guidelines provide the talk' of merger policy, 'and the language is economics.'[5]

Finally, economic theory provides a referential basis for the identification, and classification, of behaviour as either legal or illegal.[6] In classifying firms' conduct as either potentially competitive, or anti-competitive, economic theory gives a foundation and substance to the development of legal norms in relation to oligopolies.[7] For example, the CFI's decision in *Airtours v Commission*, is widely regarded as having brought the concept of collective dominance 'into line with the findings of non-cooperative game theory'.[8] Similarly, the Commission's Green Paper on the review of the Merger Regulation specifically discusses how economic theory has been used by both the Courts and the Commission to define the legal standard for collective dominance.[9]

4 In this respect, economic theory can be seen to be satisfying the need identified by Luhmann for congruence between the law and the expectations of those subject to it, or who have to enforce it, by introducing a conceptual framework that allows expectations to be formed and more accurately defined: Niklas Luhmann *A Sociological Theory of Law* (Routledge & Kegan Paul, London, 1985) 69.

5 J. Vickers 'Merger policy in Europe: retrospect and prospect' (paper presented at the Charles River Associates conference, Washington, DC, 11 February 2004) 14.

6 In the US, this function of economics in antitrust law has been termed 'economic authority': J.E. Lopatka and W.H. Page 'Economic authority and the limits of expertise in antitrust cases' (2005) 90 Cornell Law Review 619, 632.

7 Compare D. Neven, R. Nuttall and P. Seabright *Mergers in Daylight: The Economics and Politics of European Merger Control* (Centre for Economic Policy Research, London, 1993) 61; International Competition Network 'Coordinated effects analysis under International merger regimes' (working paper, International Competition Network Annual Conference, April 2004) 2; OECD Directorate for Financial, Fiscal and Enterprise Affairs Committee on Competition Law and Policy 'Oligopoly' (Unclassified Document DAFFE/CLP(99) 25 October 1999) 206.

8 V. Rabassa 'Joint ventures as a mechanism that may favour co-ordination: an analysis of the aluminum and music mergers' (2004) 24 European Competition Law Review 779; Compare H. Haupt 'Collective dominance under Article 82 E.C and E.C merger control in the light of the Airtours judgment' (2002) 23 European Competition Law Review 434; A. Nikpay and F. Houwen 'Tour de force or a little local turbulence? A heretical view on the Airtours Judgment' (2003) 24 European Competition Law Review 197.

9 Commission Green Paper on the Review of Council Regulation (EEC) No 4064/89 [2001] COM (2001) 745/6 paras [163]–[164].

6.2.2 Economic Concepts

A second high-level function fulfilled by economic theory in the enforcement process is the introduction of economic concepts and terminology.[10] The introduction into collective dominance investigations of economic concepts, such as 'asymmetry', 'retaliation' or 'homogeneity', which have a particular technical meaning in economic theory, introduces a common language of reference and meaning. The use of these concepts formats the parameters of an investigation and allows for the identification, collection and expression of 'economic facts'.

The introduction of economic concepts is particularly useful in enforcing laws under an 'effects-based', or rule of reason, approach to competition law enforcement – such as is used in collective dominance investigations – as this approach requires the collection and expression of economic facts.[11] For example, to assess product homogeneity some measure of the degree of similarity (and potential substitutability) between two products being sold is required. In contrast, in areas of law where a basic prohibition exists, such as a prohibition against horizontal agreements, this more readily allows for the collection of 'legal facts', such as the existence and nature of any agreement between firms.

The use of concepts derived from economic theory has an indirect procedural effect insofar as it delineates the nature, and type, of facts considered relevant to an investigation, and disciplines the arguments that can legitimately be employed in the discussion of a case. For example, notions of 'retaliation', 'multi-market contact' and 'buyer power' only have a technical meaning in economics and are now common, and, in some cases necessary, criteria for assessments in merger investigations.

The economic concepts that may be employed in the enforcement of the collective dominance laws are, by their nature, conceptually elastic. This allows them to be applied to different contexts, and for different 'economic facts' to be collected. For example, as we saw in Chapter 4, while an

---

[10] Compare F. Jenny 'Competition law enforcement: is economic expertise necessary?' in B. Hawk (ed.) *International Antitrust Law & Policy: Fordham Corporate Law 1998* (Juris Publishing, New York, 1998) 186; M. Brunt 'Antitrust in the courts: the role of economics and economists' in B. Hawk (ed.) *International Antitrust Law & Policy: Fordham Corporate Law 1998* (Juris Publishing, New York, 1998) 363.

[11] Compare Economic Advisory Group on Competition Policy Report 'An economic approach to Article 82' (paper prepared for the chief economist of the European Commission, July 2005) 5–7. More broadly: F.S. McChesney 'The role of economists in modern antitrust: an overview and summary' (1996) 17 Managerial and Decision Economics 120–121.

appropriate characterisation of the degree of buyer power in one case might be the size and strength of the largest customers, in other cases the appropriate characterisation of the concept of buyer power might refer to the spread of customers.

6.2.3 Source of Legitimacy

In addition to providing a foundation upon which to base the development of legal norms and a set of concepts that allows for the collection of 'economic facts', economic theory fulfils a third function in the enforcement of the collective dominance laws. Specifically, such theory offers a source of legitimacy to the enforcement process by presenting a credible, and 'scientific', basis for the reasoning and decisions of the Commission and the Courts.[12]

The need for law to 'connect' with a set of credible principles and reasoning has been advanced in a stream of research that has proposed that purposive, or policy oriented, law needs to open itself up, or connect, to the social sciences in order to be perceived to be legitimate.[13] This need is arguably significant in competition law because of its political nature, and the wide range of analytical criteria that can potentially be considered as relevant for the reasoning in such proceedings. The failure of competition law in some jurisdictions to systematically apply a common basis for its analytical approach and decisions, has, at times, led to claims that the competition laws are essentially state industrial law and that the enforcement actions instigated are arbitrary, political and ad hoc. For example, a former judge, in praising the greater use of economics in competition law proceedings, recalls that the reasoning adopted in one case in the days before economics was widely used was: 'we can't allow that merger, he's an entrepreneur'.

In using economic theory as the basis for reasoning and decisions, the process of enforcement of the collective dominance laws, and of competition laws more generally, is legitimised by its connection to an apparently apolitical framework and an established scientific body of knowledge.[14] In the

---

[12] Compare more generally C.A.G. Jones *Expert Witnesses* (Clarendon Press, Oxford, 1994) 222.

[13] G. Teubner 'Juridification: concepts, aspects, limits, solutions' in R. Baldwin, C. Scott and C. Hood (eds) *A Reader on Regulation* (Oxford University Press, Oxford, 1998) 404; Jones (n 12) 100, 113 more generally.

[14] The question of what constitutes expert advice and established science for legal purposes has not to date been highly controversial in the European context, but has been the subject of significant scrutiny in the United States following the Supreme Court's 1993 decision in *Daubert v Merrell Dow Pharmaceutical Inc* 509 U.S. 579, 113 S. Ct. 2786 (1993) (*Daubert*); Compare G. Edmond and D. Mercer 'The invisible branch: the authority of science studies in expert evidence jurisprudence' in G. Edmond

European Community context, where some enforcement powers remain with Member States, the introduction of such a common, apolitical framework is seen as particularly important in allowing for the perception of the uniform enforcement of the laws.

6.3 THE ECONOMIC APPROACH

In addition to providing a theoretical framework, economics presents an 'approach' for conceptualising how to enforce the collective dominance laws. Specifically, the 'economic way of thinking' can play a role in conceptualising oligopolistic interaction. In addition, the metaphor of the 'game', and the manner in which it is used, can permit a re-characterisation of oligopolistic interaction in strategic terms.

6.3.1 Economic 'Thinking'

An important element of the economic approach is the 'economic way of thinking'.[15] By adopting an economic way of thinking, lawyers and enforcement officials are presented with a methodology for structuring a collective dominance investigation, from which a set of questions become relevant, as do the indicators and evidence that should be assessed.[16] A Commission official describes the economic way of thinking in collective dominance cases:

(ed.) *Expertise in Regulation and Law* (Ashgate, Aldershot, 2004) 199. The potential admissibility of economic evidence of coordinated behaviour using the *Daubert* criteria is considered in B.H. Kobayashi 'Game theory and antitrust: a post-mortem' (1997) George Mason Law Review 418; A.I. Gavil 'After *Daubert*: discerning the increasingly fine line between the admissibility and sufficiency of expert testimony in antitrust litigation' (1997) 65 Antitrust Law Journal 667; G.J. Werden 'Economic evidence on the existence of collusion: reconciling antitrust law with oligopoly theory' (2004) 71 Antitrust Law Journal 787; Lopatka and Page (n 6) 617, and R.D. Blair and J.B. Herndon 'The implications of *Daubert* for economic evidence in antitrust cases' (2000) 57 Washington and Lee Law Review 817–828.

15 John Maynard Keynes famously pronounced that 'the theory of economics does not furnish a body of settled conclusions immediately applicable to policy. It is method rather than a doctrine, an apparatus of the mind, a technique of thinking' J.M. Keynes 'Introduction to the series' in E.A.G. Robinson *The Structure of Competitive Industry* (Nisbet & Co, London, 1931) *v.* Similarly, Coase noted that the 'main advantage which an economist brings to the other social sciences is simply a way of looking at the world' R.H. Coase *Essays on Economics and Economists* (University of Chicago Press, Chicago, 1994) 45.

16 Compare R.J. van den Bergh and P.D. Camesasca *European Competition Law and Economics: A Comparative Perspective* (Intersentia, Antwerp, 2001) 353; U. Böge

> It involves applying the basic thinking about industrial economics in a bidding market, for example, to the conclusion that there can't be an absence of competition since the facts are like this. It allows you to look at the oligopoly and say that statement doesn't make sense in this context because …

Thought experiments

One approach underlying the 'economic way of thinking', and used frequently by the Commission and the parties in the construction of their respective cases in collective dominance investigations, is the use of conceptual or 'thought experiments' to reveal different scenarios, and allow for the presentation of facts in different ways.[17] As in other areas of science, conceptual experiments, or *Gedankenexperimenten*, involve formulating a problem in such a way so as to present a solution through the distortion of the facts, which allows for the presentation of an intuitive and persuasive story while still capturing the essential features of complex problems.[18]

The use of thought experiments in competition law enforcement allows the economist to derive a 'deeper' meaning from a given set of indicators.[19] As one commentator notes: 'Things that seem innocuous to the business executive, or of no probative importance to the lawyer, may speak volumes to the economist'.[20] As another commentator expresses it: 'an economic expert can explain how superficially benign conduct actually could be very harmful'.[21] The ability to present intuitive 'thought experiments' and derive richer insights from a set of facts and indicators is, unsurprisingly a skill promoted by the

---

'Modernisation of Art. 82 EC' (paper presented at the UK Competition Commission guest lecture series, London, 19 April 2005) 2. More generally on the 'economic way of thinking' compare C. Shapiro 'Theories of oligopoly behavior' in R. Schmalensee and R.D. Willig (eds) *Handbook of Industrial Organization, Volume 1* (Elsevier Science Publishers, Amsterdam, 1989) 331; A.K. Klevorick 'Law and economic theory: an economist's view' in A.I. Ogus and C.G. Veljanovski (eds) *Readings in the Economics of Law and Regulation* (Clarendon Press, Oxford, 1984) 238.

[17] Compare J.E. Cairnes *The Character and Logical Method of Political Economy* (Macmillan and Co, London, 1888) 92–93.

[18] Compare R.W. Clower 'The ideas of economists' in A. Klamer, D.N. McCloskey and R.M. Solow (eds) *The Consequences of Economic Rhetoric* (Cambridge University Press, Cambridge, 1988) 91. The term '*Gedankenexperimenten*' features prominently in physics and philosophy and involves the consideration of certain questions and situations on the basis of 'instinctive knowledge' picked up from experience.

[19] More generally, compare Jones (n 12) 90.

[20] McChesney (n 11) 122; E. Gellhorn 'The practical uses of economic analysis: hope vs. reality' (1987) 56 Antitrust Law Journal 934.

[21] S.E. Nagin 'Selection, use and pay of an economist in an antitrust case' (1981) 35 University of Miami Law Review 258.

economic consulting firms who advertise their ability to apply economics to move beyond 'first sight' conclusions in competition law cases.[22]

Evidentiary value of thought experiments

It is important to note that while the 'economic way of thinking' about collective dominance presents a method for asking relevant questions, the answers to such questions will not always be sufficiently persuasive, or factual, to be used as legal evidence. Many lawyers consider the 'economic way of thinking' to be useful for conceptualising the issues, and presenting hypothetical thought experiments, but point out that this does not always translate into the type of legal evidence needed when arguing a case.[23] As one lawyer explains it:

> You have a set of economic facts and you say to the economist 'give me the benefit of your view on this', and 'what do you think this shows?' That's one thing. Saying we need to use this as evidence that this or that happened or didn't happen, is quite a different thing.

Enforcement officials have also expressed the view that such conceptual experiments have limited evidentiary potential and are most useful only insofar as they tell you what indicators to look at, or as an initial screen. These views highlight the dichotomy identified in Chapter 5 between the usefulness of economics as a method for structuring an investigation, and its usefulness at the specific level of providing evidence in cases.

6.3.2 The 'Game' Metaphor

An important element of the economic approach to the enforcement of the collective dominance laws is the use of the methodology and conclusions of game-theoretic oligopoly theory. As noted in Chapter 3, this body of theory involves the use of the 'game' metaphor to explain and predict the strategic behaviour of firms under different assumptions and in different environments. The use of game theory to explain and predict behaviour provides academic economists with a 'box of tools' that allows them to 'identify the main strategic aspects present in that industry', [24] as well as presenting a methodology for

[22] NERA 'Twelfth St. Gallen International Competition Law Forum' Press Release advertising NERA Events 1.

[23] Compare Yeung (n 3) 489 in relation to Australian competition law; and R.A. Milne and J.E. Pace III 'The scope of expert testimony on the subject of conspiracy in a Sherman Act case' (2003) 17 Antitrust 42 in the US context.

[24] Shapiro (n 16) 408.

framing the issues and a language for analysing specific dynamic competitive interactions.[25] The economic approach to the enforcement of the collective dominance laws therefore involves the law co-opting the 'game' metaphor as a conceptual aid.

Metaphors and science

Metaphors are widely used in science, not just for ornamental effect, but as a mechanism to allow for the creation of new ways of understanding a phenomenon, or different ways of seeing the world.[26] Metaphors also feature prominently in law.[27] Metaphors allow for two separate domains, a primary and a secondary domain, to interact and to be brought into a cognitive relation through the use of understandings, commonplaces and language 'directly appropriate to the one, as a lens for seeing the other'.[28] Bicchieri notes that *interactive* metaphors of this type, which rely on literal meanings as a basis of comparison between two domains, have historically played a major part in the development of economic thought.[29] However, she and others argue that in modern economics, as in other areas of science, *constitutive* metaphors, which derive meaning from within a developing body of theory, are more commonly employed.[30] Such 'metaphors are constitutive of the theories they express, rather than merely exegetical' and as such invite exploration of the similarities

---

25 D.M. Kreps *Game Theory and Economic Modelling* (Clarendon Press, Oxford, 1990) 87.

26 Compare A. Ortony 'Metaphor, language, and thought' in A. Ortony (ed.) *Metaphor and Thought* (2nd edn, Cambridge University Press, Cambridge, 1993) 5; D. Gentner and M. Jeziorski 'The shift from metaphor to analogy in Western science' in A. Ortony (ed.) *Metaphor and Thought* (2nd edn, Cambridge University Press, Cambridge, 1993) 448; T. Kuhn 'Metaphor in science' in A. Ortony (ed.) *Metaphor and Thought* (2nd edn, Cambridge University Press, Cambridge, 1993) 534.

27 M.S. Ball *Lying Down Together: Law, Metaphor and Theology* (University of Wisconsin Press, Madison, 1985) 23; T. Ross 'Metaphor and paradox' (1989) 23 Georgia Law Review 1053.

28 M. Black *Models and Metaphors: Studies in Language and Philosophy* (Cornell University Press, Ithaca, NY, 1962) 236.

29 For example, in the characterisations of the different parts of an economy by Adam Smith and the physiocrats as parts of the human body: C. Bicchieri 'Should a scientist abstain from metaphor?' in A. Klamer, D.N. McCloskey and R.M. Solow (eds) *The Consequences of Economic Rhetoric* (Cambridge University Press, Cambridge, 1988) 104.

30 Bicchieri (n 29) 104; An example is the use of terminology from computer science by psychologists as a basis of explaining and exploring the functioning of the human brain: R. Boyd 'Metaphor and theory change: what is "metaphor" a metaphor for?' in A. Ortony (ed.) *Metaphor and Thought* (2nd edn, Cambridge University Press, Cambridge, 1993) 486.

and analogies between the primary and secondary domains, and can be employed by many without their interactive quality being lost.[31] This process involves a 'metaphorical redescription' of phenomena in terms which: create new similarities; introduce a new dictionary and consequently allow for new predictions.[32]

The non-cooperative game metaphor

The use of the 'non-cooperative game' metaphor in oligopoly theory, and also in the approach to the enforcement of the laws of collective dominance, introduces all of the elements of a constitutive metaphor. First, a similarity is drawn between the choices faced by players in a 'non-cooperative game' and those choices faced by firms in an oligopolistic industry. This similarity is created through the introduction of an economic vocabulary to describe the behaviour of firms, including terms such as equilibrium and retaliation.[33] This new vocabulary allows new predictions about firm behaviour to be generated, such as statements in the reported decisions like: 'any equilibrium between the producers is disturbed by the arrival of additional capacity',[34] or 'a strict retaliation mechanism ... is a necessary condition for collective dominance'.[35] The overall effect of using the game metaphor to explain and predict oligopoly behaviour is that the primary subject (firms' expected behaviour) is re-described through the predicates drawn from a secondary subject (strategic interaction in a game).[36]

Law enforcement based on game theory

The approach to the enforcement of the collective dominance laws has been widely influenced by the game metaphor. This is reflected in official documents and studies,[37] by practitioners in the area, [38] in Commission decisions,[39] and decisions of the Court.[40]

---

31 Boyd (n 30) 487; Kuhn (n 26) 538.

32 Bicchieri (n 29) 106; Ross (n 27) 1072, 1076 concludes similarly that the use of metaphors in law presents a 'new reality'.

33 As Shubik describes it: 'The contribution of game theory to the law comes in the form of a new language to aid in the understanding of conflict, competition, collusion and cooperation': M. Shubik 'Game theory, law, and the concept of competition' (1992) 60 University of Cincinnati Law Review 300.

34 *Outokumpu/Avesta Sheffield* (Case No IV/ECSC 1342) [2001] OJ C083 14 para [34].

35 *Airtours/FirstChoice* (Case IV/M.1524) [2000] OJ L093 1 para [55].

36 Compare Bicchieri (n 29) 107.

37 Commission guidelines on the assessment of horizontal mergers under the Council Regulation on the control of concentrations between undertakings [2004] OJ C31/5; Institut d'Économie Industrielle (IDEI) Toulouse 'The economics of tacit collu-

> Game theory has been immensely useful in this field. Its description of how competitors might strategically react to each other has changed the way we think about competition. It has helped in examining what will happen in the future. (Judge)

> Game theory has helped to identify and recognise a set of criteria for a dominant oligopoly which can affect the market behaviour of companies. (Commission official)

> Game theory is the 'appropriate framework' to analyse coordinated behaviour because it 'provides us with useful insights on how firms interact, on the importance of specific factors and on the nature of certain market outcomes'.[41]

In a study prepared for the Commission in 1995, it was pointed out that 'game theory is the predominant instrument for evaluating collective dominance'.[42]

Nevertheless, the use of the game metaphor and other devices derived from economic theory require considered use in enforcement settings for a range of reasons. First, unlike the use of metaphors in science, which are constrained to some extent by empirical observation, the use of metaphors in law can become too literal; they can become a rhetorical device.[43] Specifically, in this context, the law can come to naturally treat firms as playing a non-cooperative game.[44]

---

sion' (2003) Final report prepared for DG Competition European Commission, March 2003.

38 J. Vickers 'Competition economics and policy' (paper presented at the occasion of the launch of the new social sciences building at Oxford University, 3 October 2002) 10.

39 *Exxon/Mobil* (Case No IV/M.1383) [2004] OJ L103 1 paras [452]–[552]–[640]; *UPM-Kymmene/Haindl* (Case No COMP/M.2498) [2002] OJ L233 38 para [129].

40 Case T-342/99 *Airtours plc v Commission of the European Communities* [2002] ECR II-02585 para [191].

41 K. Mehta and S. Santamato 'On the concepts of collusion and joint dominance' (2002) Butterworths Merger Review 2.

42 E. Katzenbach, E. Kottman, and R. Krueger 'New industrial economics and experiences from European merger control – new lessons about collective dominance?' (1995) Study prepared for the European Commission, Luxembourg, 20.

43 The use of metaphors derived from economics in other areas of law have, in some cases, led to the metaphor itself becoming the new orthodoxy. For example, Joo concludes that the use of the economic metaphor of the 'firm' to describe the 'corporation' for the purposes of corporations law has led to the law viewing 'corporations as firms' rather than using the metaphor to generate hypothesis on the basis that views corporations 'as-if' they are firms: T.W. Joo 'Contract, property and the role of metaphor in corporations law' (2001) 35 UC Davis Law Review 802.

44 T. Ross 'Metaphor and paradox' (1989) 23 Georgia Law Review 1053; 1083–1084.

Second, the appropriateness of relying on a metaphor depends on the degree of commonality of relational structures between two domains.[45] In the context of oligopolistic interaction this translates as to whether the 'non-cooperative' game shares a sufficient common relational structure to the behaviour of oligopolistic firms for it to serve as a useful referential basis for law enforcement. In considering this question it is important to recall that although the use of the metaphor of the game may be a useful tool to generate hypotheses it cannot by its very nature prove that firms will behave in a particular way.[46] Accordingly, and consistent with the findings of the case study in this book, the game metaphor has been seen to have limited usefulness in providing implementable tests that can be used as evidence in specific cases.[47]

Finally, in the specific context of collective dominance investigations, it can be seen that the law uses the game theory metaphor in a fundamentally different way to economics. Specifically, while the law looks to game theory to explain *how* or *when* coordination will, occur – that is the *process* of coordination – economists use the game theory metaphor to primarily examine the *effects* of coordinated behaviour, that is, the equilibrium that will result from coordinated interaction.[48] In short, economists use the game theory metaphor to focus on characterising equilibria, while the law uses the game theory metaphor to discuss *changes* in equilibria.[49]

6.4 DESCRIPTIVE ECONOMIC TECHNIQUES

The third way in which economic expertise features in the enforcement of the collective dominance laws is through the descriptive economic technique of positing hypothetical stories. As described in Chapters 4 and 5, this technique

---

45 Compare D. Gentner and M. Jeziorski (n 26) 456.

46 Compare Joo (n 43) 802.

47 Compare Kobayashi (n 14) 419; J. Kattan and W.R .Vigdor 'Game theory and the analysis of collusion in conspiracy and merger cases' (1997) 5 George Mason Law Review 442.

48 Stigler notes, for example, that the mechanism of coordinated behaviour, and even the announced or apparent purpose of coordinated behaviour, is interesting to the economist only to the degree that the mechanism and purpose influence actual behaviour: G.J. Stigler 'What does an economist know?' (1983) 33 Journal of Legal Education 312. Compare D.A. Yao and S.S. DeSanti 'Game theory and the legal analysis of tacit collusion' (Spring 1993) Antitrust Bulletin 125; J.B. Baker 'Two Sherman Act section 1 dilemmas: parallel pricing, the oligopoly problem, and contemporary economic theory' (1993) 38 Antitrust Bulletin 195; Office of Fair Trading 'Predicting cartels' (Economic discussion paper 19, prepared by P.A. Grout and S. Sonderegger, March, 2005) 35.

49 Compare Yao and DeSanti (n 48) 140.

is frequently employed in assessments, and involves the presentation of a hypothesis, with varying levels of supporting evidence, about how a particular market characteristic may or may not facilitate coordination.

6.4.1 Economic Stories

Economic stories combine facts, low level generalisations, high level theory and value judgements to present an account of potential behaviour or an observed event.[50] It should be stressed at the outset that economic stories are not unscientific – the theory of evolution is itself a story – but represent an alternative expository technique to those economic techniques which employ pure logic, axiomatic demonstration, or econometric or statistical tests to 'reveal' an argument.[51]

The use of economic stories, combining theory, facts and values, is an expository technique which features in many areas of economic enquiry.[52] A practical example is stories developed on the basis of the 'concentration-profits' hypothesis which, as we saw in Chapter 3, proceed on the basis of a combination of theoretical premise, empirical evidence from particular industries and, in some cases, values as to the appropriate levels of intervention into the operation of markets.

Stories as a form of exposition are particularly suited to areas of economic enquiry that are at the frontier of economic argument, insofar as they help to simplify a complex reality. In this sense, the use of stories is not a primitive method, but rather a response to a primitive environment, that is, an environment where 'a large number of variables are relevant and in which there is an inherent paucity of data'.[53] Robert Solow, a Nobel prize winning economist, argues that among the functions of analytical economics is the telling of 'plau-

---

[50] Blaug notes that the method is similar to what historians call 'colligation': M. Blaug *The Methodology of Economics* (2nd edn, Cambridge University Press, Cambridge, 1992) 110: Compare B. Ward *What's Wrong with Economics?* (Macmillan, London, 1972) 180.

[51] The theory of oligopoly has often been compared to the theory of evolution, insofar as it can provide a general account of outcomes (i.e. living species adapt to their environment to survive) but cannot provide particular explanations or predictions about which species are more likely to survive: Shapiro (n 16) 126.

[52] McCloskey notes that: 'Plainly and routinely, 90 per cent of what economists do is storytelling': D.N. McCloskey *If You're so Smart: The Narrative of Economic Expertise* (University of Chicago Press, Chicago, 1990) 16. Compare Ward (n 50) 185.

[53] Ward (n 50) 181; Compare A. Klamer and D.N. McCloskey 'Economics in the human conversation' in A. Klamer, D.N. McCloskey and R.M. Solow (eds) *The Consequences of Economic Rhetoric* (Cambridge University Press, Cambridge, 1988) 18.

sible – sometimes even convincing – causal stories with the help of a few central principles'.[54]

Economic stories as a technique of exposition are prevalent in the area of economic enquiry most relevant to competition law, namely industrial organisation economics. According to one industrial organisation economist, there is a long 'oral tradition' in industrial organisation, and, in applied oligopoly work, and that 'the important characteristic of much of this applied work is the use of informal models, "stories" '.[55] Other economists reflect on the body of oligopoly theory in similar terms:

> At present, oligopoly theory consists of a large number of stories, each one an anecdote describing what might happen in some particular situation. Such stories can be very interesting indeed. Elie Wiesel has said that "God made man because He loves stories" and economists (not merely game theorists) are plainly made in the divine image in this respect.[56]

When oligopoly theory is presented in these terms, it seems unsurprising that economists involved in collective dominance cases principally employ economic stories as an expository technique in applying this body of theory to real world contexts.

6.4.2 Collective Dominance Stories

It is the ability of applied economists to present plausible and intuitive hypothetical stories of what may or may not happen, based on game-theoretic oligopoly theory, that may be considered their main technical contribution to collective dominance investigations. The function of economist as storyteller in competition law proceedings more generally is well recognised by economists themselves.

> Economists often play the role of story-teller in a merger and acquisition review. A successful economist can marry empirical analysis, firm financial and economic incentives with market behaviour, and documentary evidence into a consistent presentation that effectively addresses the relevant issues in a case.[57] (Consultant economist)

[54] R.M. Solow 'Economic history and economics' (1985) 75 American Economic Review 329.

[55] P.L. Joskow 'Firm decision-making processes and oligopoly theory' (1975) 65 American Economic Review 270.

[56] F.M. Fisher 'Games economists play: a noncooperative view' (1989) 20 RAND Journal of Economics 118.

[57] N. von Hinten-Reed, S.H. Manning and J.C. Miller III 'The use of economics in merger control analysis' in *Global Counsel Competition Law Handbook 2002/03* (Practicallaw 2003) 42.

The question for 'enforcement agencies is 'can we make a fact consistent story'. That's perhaps a low way of describing it you could say – perhaps plausibility is better … clearly the more fanciful, remote, strained the story becomes, the less plausible. (Enforcement official)

Economics thus presents a narrative technique that connects economic theory to the facts of a specific case, and presents an explanation, or provides a basis, upon which inferences can be made. Economic stories can take a number of forms and include the use of anecdotes, counterfactual speculation or even physical metaphors and models to support the underlying narrative.[58] As noted above, these forms of explanation are familiar to economists trained in industrial organisation who, in examining oligopolies, are, according to one economist, taught to come: 'armed with a whole smorgasbord of formal models, ad hoc models, case study information, stories, and vague notions concerning the impact of business psychology and sociology'.[59]

It is in merger inquiries, which require enforcement agencies to 'extrapolate the counterfactual' into the post-merger world, that the technique of developing economic stories seems particularly well suited.[60] Consultant economists note that economists do more than collect facts in merger investigations, they impose a narrative structure on the facts and use this as the basis for 'extrapolating the hypothetical'.[61] The telling of 'complete and coherent' stories, and not just presenting facts, which provide explanations for firms' conduct, as collusive or competitive, is seen as the 'essence' of the economist's contribution in other jurisdictions such as the US and Australia.[62] For example, 1992, the year of the revision of the US merger guidelines – to reflect the predictions of game theory and introduce the concept of 'coordinated interac-

---

[58] Newberg examines some of the narrative techniques employed in the US investigation of Microsoft: J.A. Newberg 'The narrative construction of antitrust' (2003) 12 Southern California Interdisciplinary Law Journal 193–209.

[59] Joskow (n 55) 270.

[60] In assessing the competitive effects of a merger, the Commission compares the competitive conditions that would follow the merger with the conditions that would prevail absent the merger: Commission Notice on the appraisal of horizontal mergers under the Council regulation on the control of concentrations between undertakings [2002] COM (2002) 11 December 2002 para [10].

[61] M.E. Williams and A.J. Padilla 'Hypotheticals and counterfactuals: the economics of competition policy' in *The European Antitrust Review 2004* (Global Competition Review London 2004) 17. Compare Brunt (n 10) 362.

[62] Compare Yeung (n 3) 496 in relation to Australian competition law. In the US context compare: P.A. Klein 'How should economists do economics? A pragmatic perspective' in S.G. Medema and W.J. Samuels (eds) *Foundations of Research in Economics: How Do Economists Do Economics?* (Edward Elgar, Cheltenham, UK, and Brookfield, US, 1996) 434; Lopatka and Page (n 6) 639–640;

tion' – has been described as the 'year in which the antitrust storyteller moved back out of the shadows into the sunlight'.[63] Those involved in drafting the revised guidelines indicated that they were designed to encourage 'both government enforcers and the merging firms to tell a story about why a merger will or will not have adverse effects'.[64]

The presentation of economic stories of collective dominance may be perceived as 'soft economics', as compared to the 'hard economics' of complicated quantitative modelling and econometric analysis.[65] In Chapter 5, it was expressly noted by economists, both for the parties and the Commission, that this 'soft' approach is the only technique that economists have to work with in relation to collective dominance because of the impracticability of applying game-theoretic models to specific fact situations, and the inability to 'quantify' collective dominance using more traditional quantitative economic techniques.

However, the use of economic stories as an expository technique is a trend in economics more generally. This trend has been attributed to a failure of the formalist, axiomatic tradition of economic inquiry to generate expository methods capable of being applied to the real world.[66] This is particularly seen to be the case in the context of applying industrial organisation economic theory. An enforcement official outlines in some detail the practical problems encountered in applying game-theoretic oligopoly theory in enforcement actions:

> Theory in this area is persuasive and has created a general feeling, but it has also created a theory of the unobservable. This creates a problem for applied economics which is: How do you spot it? How do you take all this wonderful theory and make a decision? First answer is to go to a good IO textbook, like Scherer, and examine the list of factors that might suggest collusion. Then you go down the list and go check, check, check … but then you go down to the bottom of the list and say 'oh shit'. The problem is that you get some checks and some non-checks. Some even go the other way. How do you then add them up, what do you do?

Nevertheless for some game-theorists, this limited ability of 'hard' or quantitative techniques presented in game-theoretic oligopoly theory to be applied to real-world contexts is not a failing of game-theory, but rather a misunderstanding of

---

63 T.E. Kauper 'Antitrust in 1992: the year of the storyteller' (1993) 61 Antitrust Law Journal 350.

64 D. Paul 'An insider's look at the new horizontal merger guidelines' (1992) 6 Antitrust 6.

65 Compare Ward (n 50) 179.

66 Compare Ward (n 50) 179; F. Hahn 'The next hundred years' (1991) 101 Economic Journal 48.

how the theory might be used in an investigation. The use of a 'conversational' form of game theory, which can 'provide good analogies, and often illustrate or present paradoxes and open problems' has been identified by some as the most appropriate application for game theory in applied contexts.[67]

6.4.3 Economic Stories and the 'Effects-based' Approach

The use of economic stories as a technique of exposition in collective dominance investigations to provide an account that connects a set of principles, or a theory, to specific facts is compatible with the lawyer's traditional emphasis on the story in legal proceedings.[68] One former Commission official highlighted the similarity between the use of economic stories and the techniques employed by lawyers, noting that:

> But that's after all, to some extent what a lawyer does. A lawyer who is faced with a case that nobody has ever had before makes up, on the basis of general principles, whatever arguments he thinks makes sense in the context.

The telling of economic stories in collective dominance investigations is facilitated by the adoption of the 'effects-based' approach.[69] The use of per se rules

---

[67] Shubik (n 33) 300.

[68] Compare Newberg (n 58) 181–182, 216; W.K. Tom 'Game theory in the everyday life of the antitrust practitioner' (1997) 5 George Mason Law Review 457; More generally W.L. Bennett and M.S. Feldman *Reconstructing Reality in the Courtroom* (Tavistock Publications, London, 1981) 41; K.L. Scheppele 'Telling stories' in *Legal Storytelling: Special Issue* (1989) 87 Michigan Law Review 2073; J. Boyd White 'Law as rhetoric, rhetoric as law: the arts of cultural and communal life' (1985) 52 University of Chicago Law Review 691–2; J. Boyd White *Heracles' Bow: Essays on the Rhetoric and Poetics of the Law* (University of Wisconsin Press, Madison, 1985) 36,174; Jones (n 12) 197; P. Ewick and S.S. Sibley ' Subversive stories and hegemonic tales: toward a sociology of narrative' (1995) 29 Law and Society Review 206–7,217.

[69] According to the former Chief Competition Economist at the European Commission 'An effects-based approach requires a careful examination of how competition works in each particular market. By focussing on the effects of company actions rather than on the form that these actions may take. … It takes into account that many business practices may have different effects in different circumstances, distorting competition in some cases and promoting efficiencies and innovation in others. As the assessment is not based on the form of a particular practice but on the anticompetitive effect, the competition authority needs to identify a theory of harm and assess the extent to which such a negative effect on consumers is potentially outweighed by efficiency gains': L.H. Röller and O. Stehmann 'The year 2005 at DG Competition: the trend towards a more effects-based approach' (2006) 29 Review of Industrial Organization 282. This approach is conceptually similar to the 'rule of reason' approach adopted in other jurisdictions such as the United States.

or formal checklists would bind the legal approach, and as such would frustrate, and potentially limit the role for, the 'would-be' economic storyteller. Only under an 'effects-based' or rule of reason approach, which allows for a full open-ended inquiry, can economic stories be developed and made relevant in the legal process. It is not surprising, therefore, that economists both for the parties and in enforcement agencies are in favour of an effects-based approach to competition law generally.[70]

In relation to the enforcement of laws relating to coordinated behaviour, economists, in particular, tend to be averse to the development of specific rules, or even formal guidelines, that would bind the approach to be adopted in the enforcement of the law.[71] Nevertheless, as discussed in the next chapter, the substantial flexibility that is afforded to economic stories under effects-based approaches raises the potential that economics can be used in a manner inimical to the process of enforcement and to the law more generally. However, as discussed below, such potential in the area of collective dominance depends greatly on the nature of the stories that are presented to predict future behaviour or explain past behaviour, and critically, how closely the stories developed are constrained by facts.

6.4.4 Changes in the 'Art' of Economic Storytelling

That economists involved in collective dominance investigations and competition law matters more generally use 'stories' as a method of exposition is consistent with what J.N. Keynes termed the 'art' of economics, which he viewed as the most appropriate methodology for all areas of applied economics.[72] In this sense, the 'art' of economics involves the 'application of economics to real world situations and policies',[73] based on consideration of facts and factors derived from politics, psychology and sociology as well as economics. Nevertheless, the increasing dominance of the image of the economist as 'scientist', and of the positivist methodological approach in modern

---

70 Compare Economic Advisory Group on Competition Policy Report 'An economic approach to Article 82' (paper prepared for the chief economist of the European Commission, July 2005) 7; D. Ridyard 'An economic perspective on the EC merger regulation' (1990) 11 European Competition Law Review 251; L.H. Röller and O. Stehmann (n 69).

71 Compare D.W. Carlton, R.H. Gertner and A.M. Rosenfield 'Communication among competitiors: game theory and antitrust' (1997) 5 George Mason Law Review 424; Contrast a lawyer's perspective in Kobayashi (n 14) 416.

72 J.N. Keynes *The Scope and Method of Political Economy* (Macmillan, London, 1930) 55–60.

73 D. Colander 'The microeconomic myth' in D. Colander and R. Brenner (eds) *Educating Economists* (University of Michigan Press, Madison, 1992) 115.

economics, can be argued to have changed the nature of the 'art' of economics as applied economists now attempt to mimic the methods and precise conclusions of the pure economist.[74] One effect of this change is that the content, or narrative, of the stories told by applied economists tend to eschew observation or facts in preference for narratives based on hypothetical deduction from pure theory and 'stylised facts'. In short, while applied economists are still telling stories, the nature of the stories being told has changed.

The trend of telling economic stories based on hypothetical deduction from pure theory and on stylised facts is reflective of a more general trend in applied economics: a shift in emphasis from building pictures of events, and their causes, based on historical documents and observation, to solving hypothetical 'puzzles'.[75] Mayer describes the effect of this change in emphasis: economists now focus on the strongest link in their stories, the formal proof, which allows them to pretend that the whole argument is strong because of this one link. In this way, the telling of the story becomes a 'ceremonial activity of strengthening what is already a persuasive link' with only occasional allusions to real-world phenomena.

Consistent with this trend, the strongest link in the economic stories in collective dominance investigations is typically the logic and conclusions of game theoretic oligopoly theory and, accordingly, these tend to be emphasised over the facts or history of a particular industry.

There is some evidence that the trend has reached its natural limits within enforcement settings, and may be being reversed. For example, the courts have taken issue on a number of occasions – most notably in *Airtours v Commisssion* and *Impala v Commission* – with the Commission's failure to present adequate facts to support its theory of competitive harm.[76] More recently, a report by a group of academic economists commissioned by the Commission, confirms the importance of the Commission basing its economic arguments on facts. It states:

> The account should be both based on sound economic analysis and grounded on facts. In particular, since many practices can have pro- as well as anticompetitive effects,

---

[74] T. Mayer *Truth Versus Precision in Economics* (Edward Elgar, Aldershot, UK and Brookfield, US, 1993) 49–52.

[75] Compare Ward (n 50) 41, 18.

[76] Compare B. Vesterdorf 'Standard of proof in merger cases: reflections in the light of recent case law of the community courts' (paper presented at the BIICL third annual merger control conference, 6 December 2004) 22–23; D.J. Gerber 'Courts as economic experts in European merger law' in B. Hawk (ed.) *International Antitrust Law & Policy: Fordham Corporate Law 2004* (Juris Publishing, New York, 2004) 483.

> merely alluding to the possibility of a story is not sufficient. The required ingredients of the story must therefore be properly spelled out and shown to be present.[77]

The burden will not only affect the Commission. The parties to investigations will also be required to adapt their stories to take into account the factual context in which they are being applied.

In the United States, a number of court decisions have also emphasised the distinction between expert economists providing testimony based on theoretical speculation and those presenting empirical facts. In one case, a Nobel-prize winning economist's testimony was determined inadmissible because he made 'no effort to investigate the market', and 'his opinions were offered without any scientific basis or having been the subject of economic methodological testing'.[78] In another case, the economic expert's testimony was disallowed on the basis that he 'knew nothing about the baby food industry'.[79] In a third case, the Court described the expert's approach as 'an ostrich approach to knowledge'.[80]

To the extent that the economic stories being told in European enforcement actions are required to be grounded in market facts and evidence, some institutional changes will arguably be required. Case study work is time-intensive and the economic consulting profession is typically not geared to this type of work. Moreover, as we saw in Chapter 3, applied industrial economics is, in general, no longer focused on conducting detailed case studies, or on systematic attempts to collect or analyse empirical data. However, as discussed in the next chapter, there are signs that this issue is being recognised and addressed at a variety of levels, including by Member State competition authorities who are looking to undertake, or support, applied economic research targeted to the specific matters that arise in competition law proceedings, and through the increasing interest in the academic and practitioner community in 'forensic economics' which aims to develop applied skills and techniques for the use of economics in enforcement settings.

---

[77] Economic Advisory Group on Competition Policy Report 'An economic approach to Article 82' (paper prepared for the Chief Economist of the European Commission, July 2005) 13.

[78] *In re Brand Name Prescription Drugs Antitrust Litigation* (1999) No. 94 C 897, MDL 997, WL 33889 paras [11]–[12].

[79] *In re Baby Food Antitrust Litigation* 166 F.3d 112 (3rd Cir. 1999) para [16].

[80] *Brand Name Prescription Drugs* (n 78) para [12].

6.5 CONCLUSION

Economics makes three broad contributions to the enforcement of the laws relating to collective dominance.

First, economic theory provides an analytical frame for the enforcement of the laws. It does so by: providing a high-level framework for legislative interpretation and for the development of legal norms; bringing a set of concepts for the identification of relevant factors and the collection of 'economic facts'; and legitimising the enforcement of the law on the basis of the reasoning and conclusions of an established social science.

Second, economics presents an approach to the enforcement of the collective dominance laws which involves the adoption of an 'economic way of thinking', and the conceptual aid of the metaphor of the 'game'. The 'economic way of thinking' provides a methodological approach that allows for the 'right' questions to be asked, and for relevant indicators to be examined. In addition, the economic way of thinking involves the use of thought experiments that allow the problem of collective dominance to be formulated in such a way so as to present a solution through the distortion of the available facts and indicators. The co-opting by the law of the game metaphor reconceptualises firms' behaviour in terms of a strategic game and provides a methodology for framing and analysing specific dynamic competitive interactions.

Third, economics presents a descriptive expository technique that is open-ended, flexible and well suited to the enforcement of the collective dominance laws. The use of economic stories that combine theory, fact and values to present an intuitive story or picture is recognised by economists as an important, and at times the only feasible, technique that they can provide in a collective dominance investigation. Economic stories of collective dominance impose a narrative structure on a set of facts and can take a number of forms including anecdotes, counterfactual stories and descriptive models. This use of economic stories as an expository technique is well suited to the legal approach adopted in enforcing the collective dominance laws which is effects-based and focuses on assessing the effects, or potential effects, of different fact scenarios.

Nevertheless, the very characteristics of economics described in this chapter, which enable it to fulfil these functions, also arguably permit, in the absence of constraints, a use of economics in a manner that can be inimical to the purposes of the enforcement process. Accordingly the success with which economics fulfils the functions described depends on an identification of areas of tension in the enforcement process, and on the introduction of the appropriate institutional and procedural checks and balances. These issues are discussed more fully in the next chapter.

7. Towards a more economic approach

> The discussion on the 'more economic approach' at least sometimes bears some resemblance to lawyers and economists sitting in the car of competition law enforcement fiercely fighting over the steering wheel. It is quite obvious that this is not a promising scenario. Neither for keeping the car of competition law enforcement on the right track nor for avoiding dangerous hazards to other traffic participants – be it consumers or the business community.[1]
>
> Dr. Bernhard Heitzer, Präsident des Bundeskartellamtes, 3 December 2008

The purpose of this book was to place in perspective the growing use of economics in European competition law enforcement by providing empirical content to a number of questions regarding how economics is applied in one area of enforcement activity (coordinated behaviour in oligopolistic markets). Specifically, the case study sought to identify the nature of the expertise that economics provides in the *entire* enforcement process as revealed both by the reported decisions of the Commission and the Courts and by those involved in the enforcement process.

This chapter draws together the key conclusions of the book, and considers the potential implications of these conclusions in light of calls for 'more economics' in European competition law.

A central motivation for this research was the view that a precise and grounded understanding of the actual use of economics in the enforcement of competition law, and a realistic view of its potential for use, is necessary to underlie discussions as to 'more economics' in competition law enforcement. It has been emphasised throughout this book that the influence of economics in this area cannot be assessed in the abstract, on the basis of normative prescriptions, or selectively – in response to specific Court or Commission decisions. Moreover, it has been argued that it is only by recognising the nature of the economics being applied, and the complexities of the enforcement setting, that areas of tension can be identified, and the application of economics be improved to better meet the requirements of the law.

1 B. Heitzer 'Economic assessment in competition enforcement: developments in France and Germany' (Presentation to CRA International, Annual Conference 'Economic Developments in European Competition Policy' 3 December 2008) 3.

Although centred on the use of economics in the enforcement of one area of European competition law, the more general empirical insights derived from the case study have relevance to other areas of competition law enforcement where economics is used. This is because the process of investigation under the ECMR and Article 82 described in Chapter 5 is similar to other areas of competition law enforcement (i.e. unilateral effects investigations under the ECMR and single dominance abuse cases). Moreover, although collective dominance investigations are a difficult area of enforcement activity, they are not a peculiar area of competition enforcement. Complex economic assessments are frequently made in respect of unilateral effects as well as coordinated effects in merger investigations. Indeed, the assessment of the competitive impacts of mergers in other areas – such as mergers involving conglomerate effects, non-coordinated effects or diagonal effects – are arguably equally, if not more, complex than those involving collective dominance and require the application of economics to even more difficult factual settings.[2] Finally, most of the 'shipping cases' that have been brought under Article 82 have comprised joint actions where economic assessments were also made under Article 81, and in these cases, the same economic arguments and issues frequently featured under both assessments.

7.1 THE INFLUENCE OF ECONOMICS IN COMPETITION LAW ENFORCEMENT

The principal conclusion to emerge from this research is that the primary influence of economics in the enforcement process is located at a general level: it provides a broad theoretical framework, a conceptual approach and a descriptive expository technique.

Although this influence may not meet the standards of those who adopt a normative approach to the use of economics in competition law enforcement, this influence is not characterised in this work as necessarily inadequate or inappropriate. Rather such influence appears to reflect the nature of the

[2] More generally, it is difficult to conceive of a merger in a modern industrial economy which does not raise complex issues relating to the competitive dynamics, in particular, given that by nature the firms merging are typically large global firms and interact with a range of horizontal and vertical competitors in a number of markets. In this sense, all modern merger cases are 'hard' in that evidence of competitive dynamics is difficult to capture and assess. Moreover, in practical terms, those mergers which are more straightforward, and likely to be subject to prohibition, will either be deterred from proceeding to notification in the first instance, or alternatively will be submitted for approval with commitments.

economic knowledge being applied, its use by different actors and institutions, and the enforcement setting in which it is employed.

In reviewing the potential role of economics in the enforcement of the collective dominance laws, this book has emphasised a number of points: first, the multiplicity of models that comprise the economics of tacit collusion, some of which present conflicting implications; second, the nature of economic models and analytical technique; their underlying assumptions and limitations; third, the multiple actors that are involved in the process of enforcement of the relevant laws, along with the particular points, and contexts, at which they engage with economics; fourth, the need to look beyond the use of economic evidence in specific cases to how economics informs the enforcement process more broadly, including how it influences the discourse of enforcement, the programme of reasoning employed in decision-making, and the perception of decision-makers as to the parameters of their discretion; finally, the need to recognise theoretical perspectives on the transformative effects on formal knowledge of its application in practical settings.

The research demonstrates that economics can play an important role in framing an investigation. A view expressed by many involved in the enforcement process is that, without economic theory, there would be no way to give substance to competition laws, including those related to coordinated behaviour in oligopolistic markets. In addition, the economic approach or 'economic way of thinking' is seen to provide a methodological approach or programme for investigations; for determining relevant questions to ask and indicators to examine. The tendency identified to use descriptive economic methods was seen to reflect, in part, the impracticability of employing 'high-tech' economic methods within the context and constraints of investigations. However, it was also recognised that the use of economic stories – which combine theory, fact and values – is an intuitive and persuasive economic tool well suited to presentation before a decision-maker, and to the legal process in that it provides a flexible and adaptive mechanism which complements an effects-based criterion for the assessment of collective dominance.

While a constructive role for economics is evident in this respect, the research also reveals some tensions and difficulties associated with the uses of economics identified, and indicates some areas where there may be opportunities for procedural or institutional changes which may provide for its better use in the enforcement process.

It is argued in this chapter that a fuller acknowledgement of the areas where economics is, and can be, influential, and the corresponding areas of tension and difficulty, will make any discussion about the use of economics in European competition law enforcement more productive, and will allow for a more relevant discussion of opportunities to improve its use within these parameters.

7.2 THE IMPORTANCE OF CONTEXT IN THE APPLICATION OF ECONOMICS

The research has demonstrated the importance of the enforcement context when considering how economics is, and can be, applied. In this respect the work provides insights relevant to broader questions regarding the application of expert knowledge in practical settings. In the enforcement setting under review, we observed that the different parts of economic expertise – theory, approach, technique and data – become, at times, separated from one another resulting in a partial form of the knowledge coming to represent 'the economics' of the setting. For example, we saw that while the overall predictions of particular theoretical models were used to provide the basis for arguments in particular cases, the application of such models to the factual settings of those cases was not typically, or systematically, associated with the application of the appropriate techniques or the collection or analysis of relevant data. In addition, there was variability of use within each part of the expertise. For example, in Chapters 4 and 5 we saw that descriptive techniques were employed far more frequently than quantitative techniques; factors derived from economic theory were employed variably across decisions; and aspects of economic reasoning and data were emphasised over others. This result is consistent with other studies that have found a transformation of knowledge in its application in practical settings.[3] However, in the context of this study, two particular factors seem to have been significant in the transformation.

First, as we have seen, the knowledge was used by different actors, all of whom demonstrated different perspectives on economic knowledge and different interests in using it. The notion of 'perspectives and interests' in this context does not capture merely a tendency to use the knowledge instrumentally, but also encompasses the more deep-rooted and subconscious perspectives and interests of the actors – a function of a variety of things including their different forms of reasoning, different standards of proof, and different audiences.

While it is not possible to precisely identify and attribute to the various actors that engage with economics in the enforcement process their underlying perspectives and interests, the research does suggest insights at various points into these perspectives. Lawyers, for example, are seen to view the expert knowledge as a form of argumentation; something to give substance to

---

[3] E. Friedson *Professional Powers: A Study of the Institutionalization of Formal Knowledge* (University of Chicago Press, Chicago, 1986); A. Abbott *The System of the Professions: An Essay on the Division of Expert Labor* (University of Chicago Press, Chicago, 1988).

their arguments. Commission officials are also seen to use expert knowledge as a form of legal argumentation, but do so within a wider matrix of concerns including the scope of their discretionary powers, and their desire to achieve specific remedial outcomes. Judges, on the other hand, have at times used expert knowledge, especially theoretical knowledge, to help define the scope of the relevant legislative provisions and to delineate the Commission's discretion in applying such provisions. Most stark perhaps are the different perspectives on economic knowledge of the academic and consultant economic communities. The research indicates that the perspective of academic economists, such as game theoreticians, in developing theoretical economic knowledge is frequently removed from any concern for its practical application, and informed more by the challenge of the 'intellectual puzzle'. However, in applying the expert knowledge developed by the academic economists to factual situations, the perspective of economic consultants is not one of puzzle-solving but rather of providing substantively credible, intuitive and persuasive arguments. Their perspective is that the theoretical knowledge can be a practical tool which can be used to predict behaviour in real-world contexts.

A second factor that seems to have been influential in the observed transformation is that the economic knowledge, which had been generated in one arena, was being applied in another with substantially different purposes and audiences.[4] We saw in the current study that the academic process through which expert theoretical knowledge is generated places a heavy emphasis on the logic and rigour of expert *technique*, and less emphasis on the potential applicability of the conclusions generated to real-world contexts. By comparison, in enforcing the relevant legal provisions, there was a reduced emphasis on the rigour of a particular theoretical model and a detailed concern with what the model *predicts*. In addition, as noted in Chapter 5, all those involved in the enforcement process placed a strong emphasis on simplifying (making less complicated), and making intuitive, economic knowledge. This contrasts with the high levels of logic and abstraction that typically characterise academic models. In short, the academic process emphasises technique, and the logical elements of the knowledge, while the enforcement process focuses on that part of the knowledge that predicts outcomes and effects. In these circumstances,

[4] Compare Lopatka and Page who note that 'even economically sophisticated judges must make their choices under institutional circumstances very different from those of professional economists. Judicial recognition of a theory has far broader consequences of the same theory by a scholar; thus a judge may reject a theory as a basis for resolving a legal issue in a certain way, even if the judge accepted the theory as a matter of abstract economics': J.E. Lopatka and W.H. Page 'Economic authority and the limits of expertise in antitrust cases' (2005) 90 Cornell Law Review 637, 703.

it is not surprising that those who seek to apply economics in the context of an enforcement process work only with the predictions of theory and do not engage to any substantial degree with the rigour of the underlying logic and techniques of proof.

Accordingly, a general implication of the empirical research is that those who advocate for the greater use of economics in competition law enforcement need to take account of the perspectives and interests of the different actors who use economic knowledge, and the very different processes in which such knowledge is generated and applied. Existing studies on the use of expertise in law and regulatory settings already tell us that we need to modulate our expectations about the use of knowledge in these settings to take account of the different perspectives of those who use the knowledge and the environment in which it is applied.[5] This view is borne out in this study to the extent that these expectations encompass a view that economic knowledge can be applied in practical legal and regulatory settings in a wholly scientific and impartial manner.

7.3 WHAT DOES THIS MEAN FOR A 'MORE ECONOMICS' APPROACH?

The conclusions of this research give rise to a number of implications for the use of economics in the enforcement of European competition law, and in relation to calls for 'more economics' to feature in this enforcement process.

An overarching implication of this research is that expectations as to the role of economics in European competition law enforcement – particularly at the policy level – need to be modulated to incorporate a realistic view of the extent of its *potential* for use, and the relevant contributions and limitations associated with its use. Although at first sight this may appear trite, it is nevertheless a substantive suggestion supported by a body of research which has examined the inter- and intra-professional transformation of academic or formal knowledge in a range of practical settings. This research suggests that the type of issues we see in the application of economics in the enforcement setting under examination are not unique, and that similar difficulties and tensions arise in the practical application of a range of formal areas of knowledge from medicine to law.

---

5 G. Edmond 'Expertise in regulation and law' in G. Edmond (ed.) *Expertise in Regulation and Law* (Ashgate, Aldershot, 2004) 2; G. Edmond 'Judicial representations of scientific evidence' (2000) 63 Modern Law Review 217; S. Jasanoff 'Beyond epistemology: relativism and engagement in the politics of science' (1996) 26 Social Studies of Science 411–412; S. Jasanoff *Science at the Bar: Law, Science, and Technology in America* (Harvard University Press, Cambridge, MA, 1995) 53.

In this context it is suggested that the discourse as to the appropriate role for economics in the enforcement of European competition law may have, in recent years, failed to recognise these general conclusions about the transformation of knowledge in practical settings, and in particular, the critical distinction between academic or abstract economic knowledge and applied economics. As a result, there has been a tendency for the 'talk' of the 'more economics approach' to enforcement to pull way ahead of the 'walk' of day-to-day enforcement.

This is not to suggest that academic or formal economic knowledge has no utility in European competition law enforcement. Rather it is to suggest that it is unrealistic to hold expectations that this body of knowledge can be seamlessly translated from the pages of academic journals to the decisions of the Commissions and Courts.

Accordingly, an important task is to get a much closer alignment between the expectations for economics that are created at the policy level and the ability to satisfy these expectations at the level of day-to-day enforcement. In this respect, the research offers a number of relevant implications.

First, the research suggests that for economics to be most useful as a practical enforcement tool, a realistic and empirically grounded notion of 'economics' needs to be adopted in policy discourse, which takes account of the parts of economic knowledge and expertise that are most capable of being usefully applied in enforcement settings, and those parts which are not. Second, the research suggests that economics, as transformed by its application in specific enforcement settings, can exhibit a flexibility that can be inimical to the purposes of the enforcement process, and the law more generally, unless there are appropriate institutional checks and balances. Finally, based on the research, it is argued that one of the most effective constraints on such flexibility is the collection and considered weighing of economic facts, and, accordingly, this should play a central role in the enforcement process if 'more economics' is to be introduced into this process.

7.3.1 Identifying those Parts of Economics That are Most Useful in Enforcement

There are important differences between the environments in which 'pure' economic theory is constructed and the environment in which enforcement occurs. The methodology underlying the oligopoly theories used in collective dominance investigations is, as described in Chapter 2, generally abstract and highly mathematical. This differs significantly from the environment in which these theories are sought to be applied in enforcement processes. Put bluntly, when used to support the development of legal arguments, economic theory has to be made relevant to specific factual contexts and there are substantial questions about the ability to translate such abstract theory to real-world enforcement settings.[6] A Commission lawyer sees this methodological tension as irreconcilable:

> The real issue for lawyers is to simplify to a rule. This differs from economists who work in a world of perfect information which simplifies the issues. The problem comes when you have to apply the economic models to the real world, then the conclusions of the models cannot apply.

It is important that such a tension is acknowledged and that, moreover, the differences between the authorial and narrative audiences of economics are explicitly recognised. In general, the authorial audience – academic economists and pure theorists – readily accept the limitations of the use of abstract economic theory in real world contexts. The narrative audience – lawyers, consultant economists and decision-makers – on the other hand, may be less aware, or more unwilling to accept, the speculative nature of pure theory.[7]

In respect of the theory relevant to collective dominance investigations, academic economists, the authorial audience of game-theoretic oligopoly theory, generally recognise that such theory in its current state is only capable of generating testable empirical propositions in experimental settings.[8] In addition, some of these economists would argue that such laboratory experiments have limited potential relevance to the real world, having not resulted in even one universally accepted and definitive empirically based prediction about market behaviour.[9]

---

[6] Gavil notes that there is a need for a healthy appreciation of strengths and weaknesses of antitrust decision-making processes, and accordingly, that a flexible approach to embracing economic analysis be adopted which recognises the continued value of presumptions, filters and other legal devices for abbreviating antitrust inquiries. A. Gavil 'Competition policy, economics, and economists: are we expecting too much?' in B. Hawk (ed.) *International Antitrust Law & Policy: Fordham Corporate Law 2005* (Juris Publishing, New York, 2006) 590.

[7] This might reflect the law's tendency to co-opt a 'caricature' of science and scientific expertise more generally: C.A.G. Jones *Expert Witnesses* (Clarendon Press, Oxford, 1994) 5, 46, 72, 99; G. Edmond (n 5) 216.

[8] Compare A. Rubinstein 'A theorist's view of experiments' (2001) 45 European Economic Review 619; M. Bianchi and H. Moulin 'Strategic interactions in economics: the game theoretic alternative' in N. De Marchi and M. Blaug (eds) *Appraising Economic Theories* (Edward Elgar, Aldershot UK and Brookfield, US, 1991) 196.

[9] Compare Rubinstein (n 8) 617; J.A. List and S.D. Levitt 'What do laboratory experiments tell us about the real world?' (NBER Working Paper, 20 September 2005). Contrast A. Roth 'Laboratory vs. field experiments: what can we learn? Comments on Levitt–List paper' (presentation at the ASSA meetings Boston, 8 January 2006). More generally, compare: M. Blaug *The Methodology of Economics* (2nd edn, Cambridge

In this respect, the enforcement process might usefully institutionalize a greater appreciation of the different types of economic theory, and a working presumption that the most useful forms of economic theory for enforcement settings are likely to be those which can be empirically adapted to the context in which they need to be applied, and which, critically, allow for the collection and analysis of economic facts. The recent focus on 'forensic economics' in European competition policy discourse is a promising development in this respect and supports the view that the significant differences between pure and applied economic theory require that a specific sets of skills – a specific form of 'economics' – be employed in competition law investigations with a close linkage between facts and theory.[10]

It follows from the above that the introduction of 'more economics' in competition law enforcement should not be equated with the use of more sophisticated or high-tech economics or abstract econometric modelling. As we have seen, while usually conceptually elegant, the probative value of sophisticated economics as evidence is typically low. This is not to suggest that more sophisticated analysis might not have a role in some instances, but to emphasise again that the most useful economic analysis is tied closely to economic facts and evidence and presents a convincing (rather than simply plausible) account of the behaviour being investigated.

Having said this, it is recognised that economic facts do have a distinct nature; they are in many cases the result of intellectual construction rather than empirical observation.[11] This, in itself, impacts on the relevant standard of proof in investigations. As we saw in the case study, there has been an uneasy relationship between two standards of proof – mere plausibility versus convincing evidence – in collective dominance investigations over time.[12]

University Press, Cambridge, 1992) 240; S. Peltzman 'The Handbook of Industrial Organization' (1991) 99 Journal of Political Economy 206.

[10] M.P. Schinkel 'Forensic economics in competition law enforcement' (Amsterdam Center for Law and Economics Working Paper, no. 2007-05) 3–4. J.M. Connor 'Forensic economics: an introduction with special emphasis on price fixing' (2007) 4 Journal of Competition Law and Economics 31.

[11] A judge of the European court has noted that: 'Analysis in economics starts at a very primary level, to the point that there is no such thing as pure economic facts, any quantification being the result, and the origin, of intellectual construction'. H. Legal 'Standards of proof and standards of judicial review in EU competition law' in B. Hawk (ed.) *International Antitrust Law & Policy: Fordham Corporate Law 2005* (Juris Publishing, New York, 2005) 114.

[12] Compare Neven, who observes that the different standards of proof and standards of review may explain why economic evidence has sometimes been considered to have been mishandled by the Commission; it may have been satisfied with an unduly low standard of proof: D. Neven 'Competition economics and antitrust in Europe' (2006) 21 Economic Policy 23.

Precisely where this balance should lie will need to be given greater consideration if economics is to play a greater role in enforcement proceedings.

7.3.2 Allowing for Flexibility within a Constrained Framework

In areas of economic regulation there is a need for the law to be flexible, adaptable and responsive to complexity and variability in circumstances. In most circumstances, this requires a relatively loose framework of guiding standards rather than direct prohibitions of particular forms of conduct (i.e. bright-line rules).[13] The research demonstrates that economics provides just such a high level framework of standards to guide the enforcement of the competition laws, however, it also suggests that, in the absence of sufficient constraints, its inherent flexibility can allow it to be used in a manner inimical to the purposes of the enforcement of the relevant laws.[14]

In collective dominance investigations, the flexibility is a consequence of a variety of factors identified including: the inconclusiveness of the theory, the openness of the game-theoretic method – where multiple conclusions can be

---

[13] The balance between flexibility and predictability in competition law enforcement is often discussed in the context of the relative occurrence, and potential magnitude, of what are known as Type I and Type II errors. Type I errors, or false positives, arise where a pro-competitive practice is prohibited in a particular case, and Type II errors, or false negatives, arise when, for example, a dominant firm is able to engage in particular anti-competitive conduct because it is not prohibited. In this context, direct prohibitions of particular conduct (i.e. bright-line rules) are typically seen to minimise the potential for Type II errors insofar as they capture a wide range of conduct. While such an approach is seen to provide a high degree of legal certainty and accountability, it may inhibit a range of potentially pro-competitive behaviour. On the other hand, a more flexible approach which allows for the measurement of effects of particular conduct, and in which economics can feature prominently, is seen to minimise the potential for Type I errors in allowing for contextual nuance: the same conduct in different market contexts can be pro-competitive or anti-competitive.

[14] A related point is the effect that such unconstrained flexibility, and the potential uncertainty it can create, has on those subject to the regulation. This goes beyond the question of the efficacy of the use of the expertise in producing 'good' law, to the efficacy of the use of the expertise in producing the behaviour that the law aims to promote and prevent. It is well recognised that regulatory uncertainty can impact the incentives of businesses, making them more risk averse and less willing to combine their activities through merger, or to engage in specific practices which may be beneficial, which can have the perverse effect of making industries less competitive and efficient. Compare L. McGregor 'The future for the control of oligopolies following *Compagnie Maritime Belge*' (2001) 22 European Competition Law Review 436; K.U. Kühn 'Closing Pandora's Box? Joint dominance after the "Airtours" judgment' (Research Paper No. 02-013 Michigan Law and Economics 2002) 12.

generated within a given framework[15] – and the tendency to rely on the open-ended descriptive technique of story-telling. Compounding these factors is the historical tendency identified in investigations to not systematically collect and analyse empirical economic facts. While flexibility is undoubtedly one of the principal contributions of economics in this area (permitting an application of the law in a variety of different settings), unconstrained flexibility can have undesirable outcomes on enforcement processes, and the law more generally.

In the United States, where economics has played a substantially larger role in the enforcement process, under-enforcement of competition laws has been seen by some to have resulted from the combination of a flexible economic approach and an enforcement setting that has permitted un-proven economic arguments to be readily accepted by courts and enforcement agencies.[16] Indeed, the perceived ability of lawyers and economists to use economics to contextualise arguments to any market conditions has led some judges in the United States to characterise the introduction of a more nuanced rule of reason economic approach in relation to some areas of antitrust (notably vertical agreements) as a shift from per se *illegality* to per se legality.

That this potential risk is not limited to jurisdictions outside Europe can be evidenced by a comment of the former Chief Competition Economist of the Commission, who, in 2005, while trumpeting the success of a 'more effects-based' economic approach to enforcement in terms of its focus on more thorough fact investigations, observed at the same time that this had resulted in no merger prohibitions.[17]

The risk is not just of under-enforcement but also for over-enforcement. This is because economic arguments based on the hypothetical and the

---

[15] As we saw in Chapter 6, the use of game-theory as a method for examining indicators and generating facts is highly sensitive to the modeller's assumptions and specification of what will happen. Game theorists themselves recognise the tractable nature of the methodology. As one economist says: 'Crudely put, anything that one might imagine as sensible can turn out to be the answer' F.M. Fisher 'Games economists play: a noncooperative view' (1989) 20 RAND Journal of Economics 116. A game theoretician makes a similar point: 'Game theorists are very clever individuals, and given almost any form of behaviour, they can build models that explain the behaviour as a result of an equilibrium in a sufficiently complex elaboration of the game originally written down' (compare D.M. Kreps *Game Theory and Economic Modelling* (Clarendon Press, Oxford, 1990) 104).

[16] J. Baker and C. Shapiro 'Reinvigorating horizontal merger enforcement' (paper presented at the Kirkpatrick, Conference Georgetown University, October 2007) 43.

[17] L.H. Röller and O. Stehmann 'The year 2005 at DG Competition: the trend towards a more effects-based approach' (2006) 29 Review of Industrial Organization 282.

counterfactual can, given sufficient imagination, always identify some plausible relaxation of competitive constraints, some plausible lessening of competition.[18]

The effect of such enforcement errors can be significant. A number of recent studies have shown that where the enforcement of competition law is imperfect (either too lax or over-zealous) and the incidence of enforcement errors is large, this may be counterproductive to economic welfare in so far as it stimulates forms of behaviour that competition law is intended to deter (such as encouraging firms to collude as a precautionary measure).[19]

For all these reasons, economics, as applied in enforcement settings, needs to be subject to appropriate constraints. Accordingly, there is a need for discussion about possible institutional and procedural reforms. There are many possibilities in this respect, some of which have been mooted in the European context, others in relation to other jurisdictions. It is beyond the scope of this work to analyse each of these in detail, however it is worth surveying some of these suggestions briefly.

First, for the reasons noted above it is often argued that if there is to be 'more economics' at the policy level, there might sensibly be 'more economists' at the Commission level. At minimum, this would help address the substantial asymmetry in resources between the Commission competition directorate and private parties. Recent estimates show that the turnover of the four largest economic consulting firms in Europe increased by around 25–30 per cent per annum in the decade from 1994 to 2004, with revenue increasing from £2.4 million in 1994 to £24 million in 2004, and that during that time the number of professional industrial economists grew to around 150.[20] By comparison, in 2005 the Commission employed about 10 economists with a PhD in industrial economics.

Second, an increased focus on economics in Court proceedings, or an increasingly active role by the judiciary in reviewing the economic evidence underlying Commission assessments, and the Commission's appraisal of such evidence, might warrant additional training for judges on the underlying

---

[18] S. Bishop and D. Ridyard 'Prometheus unbound: increasing the scope for intervention in EC merger control' (2003) 24 European Competition Law Review 359; Also D.J. Neven ' "Collusion" under Art 81 and the merger regulation' (paper presented at the 3rd Nordic Competition Policy Conference, Stockholm, 11 September 2000) 6.

[19] On this basis it has sometimes been argued that it may be desirable to have a more permissive competition regime, or in the extreme, no competition law whatsoever. M. Schinkel and J. Tuinstra 'Imperfect competition law enforcement' 24 International Journal of Industrial Organization (2006) 1288. A. Mattoo 'Can no competition policy be better than some competition policy?' International Journal of Industrial Organization 19 (2001) 55.

[20] Neven (n 12) 3.

methodologies and mechanics of economics, or the more ready use of court appointed economists to assist it in making judgments involving complex economic evidence.

There are a range of changes that might be considered in relation to the rules regarding access to, and disclosure of, economic evidence. Among the suggestions that have been advanced: the introduction of U.S. 'Daubert-style' rules, which determine the form and type of economic testimony and evidence that can be admissible in enforcement proceedings;[21] a requirement for opposing economic experts to produce a common document which highlights areas of agreement and disagreement for submission to decision-makers;[22] and the reform of access rights in relation to economic evidence to allow all parties to access, and interact with, the specific models underlying the arguments being presented.

More radical, far reaching, changes have also been proposed. Some have suggested – among these, the current Chief Competition Economist at the Commission – that competition law enforcement in Europe might become more adversarial and less inquisitorial in nature, which would open economic arguments up to more detailed scrutiny,[23] and address an incentive in inquisitorial systems toward suppressing economic evidence and toward failing to consider alternative interpretations of economic evidence.[24]

A further suggestion (and one that has also been made in the United States context) is the (re)introduction of formalised rebuttable presumptions, including in relation to coordinated effects. Under such an approach, an enforcement agency would, for example, assume that a merger in a very concentrated market, will create economic harm, and the burden will lie with the merging firms to rebut such a presumption.[25] This structuralist approach to competition law enforcement would mean that important presumptions derived from economic theory are used as presumptions for *prima facie* concerns, which then must be rebutted by the parties with economic evidence disproving such a presumption. Under such an approach, the burden of (dis)proof is shifted on to the parties under investigation. Such a change might address some of the

---

[21] G.J. Werden 'Making economics mores useful in competition cases: procedural rules governing expert opinions' in B. Hawk (ed.) *International Antitrust Law & Policy: Fordham Corporate Law 2005* (Juris Publishing, New York, 2005) 601.

[22] For example, a similar process is currently undertaken in Australia: Werden (n 21) 612–613.

[23] Neven notes for example that: 'Evidence which is not subject to rigorous scrutiny can be easily abused: key assumptions in theoretical reasoning can be disguised as innocuous and empirical results that are not robust can be disguised as such' Neven (n 12) 31.

[24] Neven (n 12) 5–6, 30.

[25] Baker and Shapiro (n 16) 35–40.

resource asymmetry issues discussed above, however such a change would not, in itself, alter the manner in which economics is used in proceedings, or address standard of proof issues, and so would not, in the absence of other changes, necessarily improve decision-making.

For this reason, and as discussed below, it is argued here that the most useful possible institutional development, irrespective of where the burden of proof is allocated, is a more central role for economic facts in the enforcement process, and in particular more substantiated reasoning which connects the economic facts to the story being presented.

7.3.3 The Centrality of 'Economic Facts' in Enforcement: Toward a More 'Fact-based' Economic Approach

The ability to collect and analyse facts on the operation of real-market contexts is arguably the expertise that economists should bring to the enforcement process in applied competition work, but the research suggests that, in recent years in particular, there has been a tendency in enforcement proceedings not to focus on the collection and analysis of empirical economic facts.

To the extent that the enforcement process permits economists and lawyers to structure their analysis around theoretically consistent anecdotal evidence and propositions, around the 'hypothetical' or the 'counterfactual', the significance of the actual observed history and idiosyncrasies of a specific industry will continue to be ignored. Under such an approach, economics legitimises the enforcement actions and reasoning employed in investigations but the actual reasoning and analysis are a non-systematic combination of legal reasoning, non-fact based hypothetical prognostications and other evidence.[26] Such an approach also relies heavily on 'facts' derived from documents. Economic conclusions drawn solely from documents are exercises in economic logic or terminology, not valid economic analyses of the workings of real markets.[27] Accordingly, it is analysis in respect of which the economist has no special skill.

---

[26] A similar observation has been made in relation to US antitrust. The Senior Economic Counsel at the US Department of Justice has noted for example that: 'Economists, however, may frustrate the accomplishment of their own objectives in the way they provide analysis in particular cases. All too often, economic experts offer strong conclusions supported by minimal explanation. This makes it impossible to determine exactly how any conclusion was reached. … Moreover, the minimal explanation may be concealing the absence of a sound basis, in economics or fact, for the strong conclusions offered': Werden (n 21) 601.

[27] G.J. Stigler 'What does an economist know?' (1983) 33 Journal of Legal Education 312.

The tendency not to focus on the collection and analysis of economic facts in enforcement proceedings to date is amplified when the economic stories being presented are themselves not required to be tightly constrained by facts. In these circumstances, the role of the decision-maker in the enforcement process is not to assess the facts presented, which in many cases are hypothetical and unobserved, but rather to assess the likelihood of the different stories presented becoming reality.[28]

One potential consequence of this is that the focus moves from concerns about the accuracy of the economic facts or the robustness of any economic analysis undertaken, to the narration provided in respect of the economic facts and analysis.[29] In this respect account needs to be taken of the fact that the stories are being developed in a context where the various narrators have purposive interests in how the economic facts or evidence are presented.[30] There are two potentially detrimental outcomes of an undue emphasis on narrative within competition law enforcement. First, it shifts the focus of an investigation away from the collection of evidence and data relevant to an examination of the undertakings' actions, and more importantly the competitive effects of those actions, toward a focus on evidence which relates to the motives and character of the actors.[31] Second, it can encourage the greater use of highly 'reductive and simplistic' accounts of economic behaviour to ensure a persuasive narrative that assumes away the complexities of the competitive environment.[32]

More generally, under such an approach, economics can be employed to support a range of theories or stories of competitive harm at an abstract or hypothetical level, without a corresponding focus on the need to collect and

---

28 Compare E. Gellhorn 'The practical uses of economic analysis: hope vs. reality' (1987) 56 Antitrust Law Journal 945.

29 More generally, Jones highlights at various points the conclusion that *persuasive* scientific evidence is not the same as *correct* scientific evidence: Jones (n 7) 149.

30 As we saw in Chapter 5, the Commission has historically relied on parties for the development of facts. The CFI decision in *Impala v Commission* has indicated a need for a new procedural approach in such circumstances: Case T-464/04 *Independent Music Publishers and Labels Association (Impala, International Association) v Commission of the European Communities* [2006] ECR II-02289 paras [415]; [422] – [425].

31 Compare Newberg who describes, in the context of the US Microsoft investigation, how the Government successfully employed a narrative account which focused heavily on the characterisation of Microsoft as dishonest and criminal, and which allowed the Court's attention to be directed away from a consideration of market dynamics and other relevant economic facts. J.A. Newberg 'The narrative construction of antitrust' (2003) 12 Southern California Interdisciplinary Law Journal 212–213, 215.

32 Newberg (n 31) 214–215

assess facts and evidence to support the stories being presented.[33] The Nobel Laureate Ronald Coase identified the potential negative effects associated with the involvement of economists in US Antitrust generally, noting that it has:

> encouraged men to become economic statesmen – men, that is, who provide answers even when there are no answers. This tendency has discouraged a critical questioning of the data and the worth of the analysis, leading the many able scholars in this field to tolerate standards of evidence and analysis which, I believe, they would otherwise have rejected.[34]

Nevertheless, it is recognised that the resolution of this 'fact collection' issue is not a simple one. Case study work is time-intensive and the economic consulting profession is typically not geared to this type of work. Moreover, as we saw in Chapter 3, applied industrial economics is, in general, no longer focused on conducting detailed case studies, or on systematic attempts to collect or analyse empirical data.

However, there are signs that this issue is being recognised and addressed at a variety of levels. First, the European Courts have, in recent decisions, increasingly required that economic evidence submitted be 'relevant, reliable and credible'.[35] More important, in *Tetra Laval v Commission*, the Court established the need for a clear link between the economic argument being presented and the facts or evidence upon which that argument is based:

> Not only must the Community Courts, *inter alia*, establish whether the evidence relied on is factually accurate, reliable and consistent but also whether that evidence contains all the information which must be taken into account in order to assess a complex situation and whether it is capable of substantiating the conclusions drawn from it.[36]

Second, competition authorities in some Member States have stated that they are looking to undertake, or support, applied economic research which is targeted to the specific matters that arise in competition law proceedings.

---

33 Again compare theories of autopoiesis which posit that hybrid creatures such as 'legal economics' are the result of the legal process borrowing *authority* from social sciences, and that what happens to these constructs once they enter the legal process is no longer in the hands of the social sciences: G. Teubner 'How the law thinks: toward a constructivist epistemology of law' (1989) 23 Law & Society Review 750.

34 R.H. Coase *The Firm, the Market, and the Law* (University of Chicago Press, Chicago, 1988) 66.

35 T 168/01 *GlaxoSmithKline Services v Commission* [2006] ECR II-02969 para [263].

36 C-12/03P *Commission v Tetra Laval* [2005] ECR I-00987 para [39].

Finally, as discussed earlier, there is a small, but growing, interest in the academic community in Europe in forensic industrial organisation economics, which aims to develop applied skills and techniques for the use of economics in applied settings.[37]

Whatever the outcome of these specific developments, economics is likely to retain its prominent position in European competition policy discourse. It has been among the purposes of this book to place economics on a more secure footing in this discourse by identifying the specific contribution of economics to the enforcement process, highlighting areas of tension, and suggesting ways in which these tensions might be addressed. It has also been a purpose of this book to emphasise that the consideration of the appropriate role for economics in the enforcement process cannot be done in the abstract, or on the basis of normative prescriptions, or selectively – in response to specific Court or Commission decisions. Rather, such consideration demands a grounded examination of actual practice, which accounts both for the complexities of economics, the purposive interests and perspectives of those who engage with it and the enforcement setting in which it is applied.

[37] In this context, forensic 'IO' economics has been defined as 'the application of theoretical and empirical industrial organization economics in one or more of the various stages of the legal process of competition law enforcement' Schinkel (n 10) 4.

Appendix The economics of tacit collusion

A.1.1 INTRODUCTION

The factors identified in Chapter 3 as relevant to a consideration of tacit collusion can be divided into three categories: factors relating to similarity conditions between firms, predictions relating to market structure, and predictions relating to conditions relevant for the mechanics of collusion. The discussion in respect of each factor below incorporates the conclusions of theoretical studies, and where available, empirical work.

Much of the empirical work in this area relates to studies of explicit collusion (or cartels). While the mechanics of explicit and tacit collusion obviously differ in important respects, a consideration of studies of explicit collusion is nevertheless relevant insofar as explicit and tacit collusion arguably share a common continuum, and as a result many of the conditions discussed below are arguably relevant for both.[1] Nevertheless, it is important to bear in mind that studies of explicit collusion suffer from two well-recognised biases. First, there is a 'selection effect' in that all the studies relate to cases that have previously been identified or prosecuted by enforcement authorities because they display a specific characteristic(s) (i.e. product homogeneity).[2] Second, some cases of explicit collusion were permitted under specific legal regimes which affected the scope of the arrangements and allowed different structures to develop.[3]

---

[1] It is argued, for example, that explicit collusion is more likely in markets where tacit collusion is too complex to sustain: Compare A.G. Fraas and D.F. Greer 'Market structure and price collusion: an empirical analysis' (1977) 26 Journal of Industrial Economics 36,42; T.W. Ross and A. Baziliauskas 'Lessening of competition in mergers under the Competition Act: unilateral and interdependence effects' (2000) 33 Canadian Business Law Journal 392–395.

[2] Compare M. Raith 'Product differentiation, uncertainty and the stability of collusion' (STICERD Economics of Industry Paper Number 16, London School of Economics, 1996) 4.

[3] Compare G. Symeonidis 'In which industries is collusion more likely? Evidence from the UK' (2003) 51 Journal of Industrial Economics 45–6; A. Jacquemin, T. Nambu and I. Dewez 'A dynamic analysis of export cartels: the Japanese case'

A.1.2 SIMILARITY CONDITIONS

A number of factors relate to similarities between firms. The general hypothesis here is that similar firms have similar incentives to tacitly collude and that such similarity also supports the stability of collusion. In this subsection the effects on collusion of a number of similarity factors are discussed.

Similar Costs

An important prediction of economic theory is that differences in firms' cost structures hinder tacit collusion.[4] This is the case for two reasons. First, asymmetrical cost structures make it difficult for firms to introduce a workable collusive arrangement because of the difficulties associated with finding agreement on common elements, such as price or output levels and the mechanisms for distributing the collusive profits.[5] Second, the presence of asymmetric cost structures will impact the stability of the collusive agreement insofar as it increases the incentive for low-cost firms to deviate from collusive behaviour.[6]

(1981) 91 Economic Journal 17; V.Y. Suslow 'Cartel contract duration: empirical evidence from international cartels' (Working Paper No. E-88–7, Hoover Institution, October 2001); A.R. Dick 'Identifying contracts, combinations and conspiracies in restraint of trade' (1996) 17 Managerial and Decision Economics 204–205.

4 C.F. Mason, O.R. Phillips and C. Nowell 'Duopoly behaviour in asymmetric markets: an experimental evaluation' (1992) 74 Review of Economics and Statistics 663. Contrast a recent study which concludes that if side payments are feasible then cost asymmetry can facilitate collusion: J. Miklos-Thal 'Optimal collusion under cost asymmetry' (June 2008) Working Paper MRPA no.11044 4.

5 J.S. Bain 'Output quotas in imperfect cartels' (1948) 62 Quarterly Journal of Economics 620; However, where firms only have private information they may have an incentive to misrepresent their position; K. Roberts 'Cartel behaviour and adverse selection' (1985) 33 Journal of Industrial Economics 411.

6 R. Rothschild 'Cartel stability when costs are heterogeneous' (1999) 17 International Journal of Industrial Organization 729; Institut d'Economie Industrielle (IDEI) Toulouse 'The economics of tacit collusion' (2003) Final report prepared for DG Competition European Commission, March 2003 37 *(IDEI Toulouse)*. One study concluded that cheating is more likely to occur when costs are low: M.E. Slade 'Cheating on collusive agreements' (1990) 8 International Journal of Industrial Organization 538. Another study concluded that the impact of the merger will depend critically on how a merger increases the distribution of asset holdings and associated costs between firms: H. Vasconcelos 'Tacit collusion, cost asymmetries and mergers' (2005) 36 RAND Journal of Economics 40. Also compare a recent study on the impact of persistent cost shocks on collusion in the presence of differences in the cost types of firms: S. Athey and K. Bagwell 'Collusion with persistent cost shocks' (2008) 76 Econometrica 493.

While some empirical studies of explicit collusion confirm that collusion is more difficult in markets with asymmetric costs,[7] other studies suggest that cost asymmetries do not represent an important barrier to collusive arrangements.[8] On balance, however, for the purposes of the analysis in Chapter 4, it has been assumed that symmetrical costs are more likely to facilitate tacit collusion.

Similar Capacity Constraints

The theoretical studies predict two potentially conflicting effects of capacity constraints on the stability of tacit collusion.[9] First, the presence of capacity constraints in the short term may reduce the potential gain for any individual firm from deviation, implying a *more* stable collusive arrangement. Second, the existence of capacity constraints may reduce the potential ability of firms to credibly retaliate in the event of deviation, implying that collusion would be *less* stable.[10] Recent studies conclude that which of these two effects dominates depends on the symmetry of capacity constraints among firms; total aggregate capacity; market demand; and the relative distribution of capacities among firms.[11] The ambiguous effect of capacity constraints on collusion is consistent with a recent empirical study examining past examples of collusion in Europe, where similar capacity constraints both stabilised and destabilised collusion in different industries.[12]

---

[7] P.L. Eckbo *The Future of World Oil* (Ballinger Publishing Company, Cambridge, MA, 1976) 43.

[8] A.G. Fraas and D.F. Greer 'Market structure and price collusion: an empirical analysis' (1977) 26 Journal of Industrial Economics 39.

[9] J. Tirole *The Theory of Industrial Organization* (MIT Press, Cambridge, MA, 1988) 242; O. Compte, F. Jenny and P. Rey 'Capacity constraints, mergers and collusion' (2002) 46 European Economic Review 2.

[10] One study concludes that where all firms face exogenous symmetric capacity constraints this effect depends upon how close aggregate capacity is to the monopoly capacity level, which is impacted by the number of firms in the industry: W.A. Brock and J.A. Scheinkman 'Price setting supergames with capacity constraints' (1985) 52 Review of Economic Studies 372.

[11] For example, if aggregate capacity is less than market demand this increases the incentive for firms with relatively large production capacity to deviate. Asymmetrical capacity constraints might help stabilise collusion when aggregate capacity is larger than market size as it increases the ability of smaller firms to retaliate: Compte, Jenny and Rey (n 9) 17; IDEI Toulouse (n 6) 44–45. See Vasconcelos (n 6) 39.

[12] Office of Fair Trading 'Predicting cartels' (Economic discussion paper 19 prepared by P.A. Grout and S. Sonderegger, March 2005) 24.

Excess Capacity

The reciprocal of the above discussion of capacity constraints is where firms hold excess production capacity. Once again, the predictions as to whether excess capacity facilitates collusion are mixed. Early studies concluded that excess capacity stabilised collusion as it increased the ability of firms to retaliate in the event of deviation, as well as improving a firm's relative bargaining position by allowing it to make more potent threats.[13] This prediction was often based on two-stage models, where firms choose capacity first and then set prices, and where capacity is 'cheaper'[14] and relatively 'inflexible'.[15] However, as noted above, recent studies conclude that the impact on collusion of one firm holding excess capacity depends *significantly* on the relative distribution of capacity between firms, and the relationship of aggregate capacity to market demand. This implies that excess capacity can under certain circumstances hinder tacit collusion.[16] Empirical studies of explicit collusion have not generally included an examination of the role that excess capacity plays in these arrangements.[17]

Similar Size and Strength

There is no clear prediction from economic theory as to whether firms who are of a similar size and financial capacity are more or less likely to tacitly collude.[18] Some studies have concluded that collusion is more likely in industries where a group of firms have similar asset structures and profiles.[19] However, there is little theoretical support for this proposition, with a number of studies concluding that collusive understandings can potentially be reached among heterogeneous firms.[20]

---

[13] Some studies go so far as to suggest that excess capacity is necessary for tacit collusion: J.P. Benoit and V. Krishna 'Dynamic duopoly: prices and quantities' (1987) 54 Review of Economic Studies 30; M.J. Osborne and C. Pitchik 'Cartels, profits and excess capacity' (1987) 28 International Economic Review 415.

[14] C. Davidson and R. Deneckere 'Excess capacity and collusion' (1990) 31 International Economic Review 524.

[15] Benoit and Krishna (n 13) 31.

[16] Compte, Rey and Jenny (n 9) 12.

[17] Contrast Office of Fair Trading 'Predicting cartels' (n 12) 16; M. Fusillo 'Excess capacity and entry deterrence: the case of ocean liner shipping markets' (2003) 5 Maritime Economics and Logistics 100.

[18] Compare: International Competition Network 'Coordinated effects analysis under International Merger Regimes' (Working Paper presented at the International Competition Network Annual Conference, April 2004) 23–24.

[19] K.U. Kühn 'Closing Pandora's Box? Joint dominance after the "Airtours" judgment' (Research Paper No. 02-013, Michigan Law and Economics, 2002) 16.

[20] F. Verboven 'Collusive behavior with heterogeneous firms' (1997) 33 Journal of Economic Behavior and Organization 122.

The empirical studies of explicit collusion suggest that similarly sized firms are more likely to sustain collusion,[21] and that larger (i.e. financially stronger) firms in particular are associated with collusion.[22] The evidence of recent cases involving international cartels also tends to support the finding that large multinational corporations are able to engage in explicit collusion on a world-wide basis.[23]

While there is some anecdotal evidence that size and financial strength were characteristics of the firms involved in explicit collusion, it is assumed for the analysis in Chapter 3 that similarity in the size and financial strength of firms has an ambiguous effect on tacit collusion, a position consistent with that adopted in the surveys.

Similar Levels of Vertical Integration

It is often posited that firms with similar levels of vertical integration are more likely to tacitly collude.[24] In recent studies, for example, it is predicted that under certain circumstances vertical integration can facilitate collusion, on the basis that a vertically integrated firm has a greater potential to punish deviations by either foreclosing a related market or by more effectively reacting to deviations.[25] However, the majority of theoretical work in this area has focused on examining how vertical relationships increase individual market power and not necessarily focused on how vertical integration relates to collusion.[26]

---

[21] M.C. Levenstein and V.Y. Suslow 'What determines cartel success?' (Working Paper No. 02-001, University of Michigan Business School, 31 January 2002) 7.

[22] P. Asch and J.J. Seneca 'Characteristics of collusive firms' (1975) 23 Journal of Industrial Economics 230.

[23] J.M. Griffin 'An inside look at a cartel at work: common characteristics of international cartels' (Presentation at American Bar Association 48th Annual Spring Meeting, April 6 2000) 2.

[24] Europe Economics 'Assessment criteria for distinguishing between competitive and dominant oligopolies in merger control' (Enterprise Papers No 6-2001 prepared for DG Enterprise European Commission, 2001) 41.

[25] V. Nocke and L. White 'Do vertical mergers facilitate collusion?' (Discussion Paper No 4186, Centre for Economic Policy Research, 2004) 33. See also V. Nocke and L. White 'Do vertical mergers facilitate upstream collusion' (2007) 97 American Economic Review 1321; and H.T. Normann 'Vertical integration, raising rivals' costs and upstream collusion' (Max Planck Institute for Research on Collective Goods Working Paper 2008/30, August 2008) 3.

[26] In one study, for example, the model examines the case of an upstream duopoly, in which one firm is vertically integrated, and examines the potential responses (in terms of pricing and output to customers) of the independent upstream rival firm in these circumstances: J.A. Ordover, G. Saloner and S.C. Salop 'Equilibrium vertical foreclosure' (1990) 80 American Economic Review 129.

Similar Incentives to Remove 'Maverick' Competitor

A further prediction from economic theory is that firms might have similar incentives to remove a non-similar, or 'maverick', firm in order to facilitate tacit collusion.[27] According to some studies a maverick firm is one which might have a 'drastically' different profile to other firms in the industry, for example cost structure or production capacity,[28] or place a different valuation on short-term versus long-term profits and constantly undercut its rivals and destabilise any collusive arrangement.[29]

Homogenous Products

The impact that more similar, or homogenous, products have on the stability of tacit collusion is unclear in the theory. While it is generally recognised that the more homogenous the products offered by different firms the easier it is to identify a focal point upon which to tacitly collude, it is less clear how product homogeneity relates to the stability of collusion.[30] In particular, where products are differentiated from one another through differences in quality, but are based on similar costs, then it is predicted that collusion will be *less* stable. This is because the firm selling the higher quality product has a stronger incentive to deviate.[31] However, where products are sold at a common price but differentiated by other characteristics,[32] which limits customer switching, this has an ambiguous effect on the prospects for collusion.[33] On the one hand, differences in products *stabilise* collusion by decreasing the payoff from deviation (as it is more difficult to attract customers). Conversely, differences in products can also potentially *destabilise* collusion by limiting the severity of retaliation.[34] Various theoretical studies have concluded that collusion is both

---

27 G.A. Hay and D. Kelley 'An empirical survey of price fixing conspiracies' (1974) 17 Journal of Law and Economics 16.

28 IDEI Toulouse (n 6) 55.

29 J.E. Harrington Jr 'Collusion among asymmetric firms: the case of differentiated discount factors' (1989) 7 International Journal of Industrial Organization 292.

30 Raith (n 2) 2; Asch and Seneca (n 22) 224.

31 This is known as 'vertical' differentiation: J. Häckner 'Collusive pricing in markets for vertically differentiated products' (1994) 12 International Journal of Industrial Organization 157.

32 Examples might include products such as soft drinks, soap and toothpaste: J. Häckner 'Optimal symmetric punishments in a Bertrand differentiated products duopoly' (1996) 14 International Journal of Industrial Organization 612.

33 This is known as 'horizontal differentiation' which means that different consumers rank equally priced products differently.

34 IDEI Toulouse (n 6) 47; Contrast B. Wernerfelt 'Tacit collusion in differentiated Cournot games' (1989) 29 Economics Letters 305 who concludes the opposite,

more, or less, likely with increasing 'horizontal' product differentiation, depending upon assumptions made about: whether collusion occurs on prices or quantities;[35] the shape of the demand function; [36] differences in consumer preferences;[37] the degree of concentration;[38] whether firms produce more than one product of a type;[39] the observability of any defection;[40] and the relative gains from deviation given the magnitude of the punishment that follows defection.[41]

The majority of empirical studies of explicit collusion suggest that collusion is more likely to be sustainable in markets with 'high product homogeneity',[42] and where fewer variations on a product were accounted for in the collusive agreement.[43] However, the recent investigations into the global vitamins, citric acid, graphic electrodes and lysine markets show that a number of product variations were successfully incorporated into collusive agreements.[44]

Similar Market Shares

The predictions as to how similarity of market shares relates to the potential for tacit collusion in the economic theory is ambiguous. A commonly held view is that it is possible to infer from the degree of symmetry in market shares the underlying incentives and market strategies of competitors.[45] However, some studies emphasise the endogeneity of market shares and that they are only a reflection of the underlying similarities or differences between firms'

---

that is, that product differentiation increases both the gains from deviation and also the potential penalty from deviation.

35 R. Deneckere 'Duopoly supergames with product differentiation' (1983) 11 Economics Letters (1983) 42; S. Albæk and L. Lambertini 'Collusion in differentiated duopolies revisited' (1998) 59 Economics Letters 305.

36 R.K. Tyagi 'On the relationship between product substitutability and tacit collusion' (1999) 20 Managerial and Decision Economics 294.

37 M.H. Chang 'The effects of product differentiation on collusive pricing' (1991) 9 International Journal of Industrial Organization 455.

38 Wernerfelt (n 34) 306; L.P. Østerdal 'A note on the stability of collusion in differentiated oligopolies' (2003) 57 Research in Economics 59.

39 G. Symeonidis 'Cartel stability with multiproduct firms' (2002) 20 International Journal of Industrial Organization 340.

40 Raith (n 2) 17.

41 Häckner (n 32) 613; T.W. Ross 'Cartel stability and product differentiation' (1992) 10 International Journal of Industrial Organization 10–11.

42 Hay and Kelley (n 27) 24; Levenstein and Suslow (n 21) 11; Jacquemin, Nambu and Dewez (n 3) 692; Symeonidis (n 3) 68; Dick (n 3) 204.

43 Suslow (n 3) 22.

44 Griffin (n 23) 14.

45 Europe Economics (n 24) 74.

costs and products, and that it is *these* factors that are relevant for tacit collusion.[46] In this respect, it is acknowledged that market share symmetry can potentially be used as an indicator of the degree of similarity of firms.[47] In a recent empirical study it was concluded that explicit collusion was sustained in some European markets despite considerable heterogeneity in the market shares of the colluding firms.[48]

A.1.3 STRUCTURAL CONDITIONS

In this subsection a set of structural factors which might support or frustrate collusion are discussed.

Market Concentration

It is a common presumption that tacit collusion is more likely to occur in concentrated markets because of the increased interdependence of firms.[49] This is because tacit collusion is commonly presumed to be more profitable for individual firms in more concentrated markets, as each individual firm gets a higher share of any collusive profit. In addition, it is argued that the incentive to cheat is greater in *less* concentrated markets as a cheating firm can potentially capture a larger share of the market by undercutting the other firms. Finally, there is also an argument that it is easier to communicate and monitor collusive arrangements in more concentrated markets.[50]

There is, however, some theoretical and empirical work that challenges this widely held presumption.[51] One stream of theoretical work challenges the concentration-collusion presumption on the basis that 'two bitter and combative

---

46 IDEI Toulouse (n 6) 16.

47 Tirole (n 9) 223.

48 Office of Fair Trading 'Predicting cartels' (n 12) 13.

49 On this basis, the merger laws of some countries feature market share thresholds which trigger an automatic investigation for potential coordinated effects of a merger, these include Germany, Canada and Australia: OECD Directorate for Financial, Fiscal and Enterprise Affairs Committee on Competition Law and Policy 'Oligopoly' (Unclassified Document DAFFE/CLP(99), 25 October 1999) 21–31.

50 Europe Economics (n 24) 21.

51 Compare Hay and Kelley (n 27) 15; J.S. Bain 'Relation of profit rate to industry concentration: American manufacturing, 1936–1940' (1951) 65 Quarterly Journal of Economics 294, 323; J.S. Bain 'Workable competition in oligopoly: theoretical considerations and some empirical evidence' (1950) 40 American Economic Review 44.

rivals can hold down prices more effectively than a dozen companies'.[52] Other studies have focused on how increased concentration can result in cost reductions that may dominate any collusive effect,[53] and on how increased concentration might reduce the potential for tacit collusion on the basis that, as the market becomes more concentrated, the *payoff* from deviation may actually increase.[54]

Empirical studies present mixed conclusions as to how market concentration relates to collusion. Some studies conclude that explicit collusion is more likely to occur, and be sustained for longer, in highly concentrated markets.[55] Other studies conclude that explicit collusion has also featured in less concentrated markets.[56]

On balance, while the broader literature raises some uncertainty regarding the relationship between collusion and high market concentration, as a general position – particularly because of issues such as focal points and market transparency – it is accepted for the purposes of the analysis in Chapter 4 that concentrated markets are more likely to facilitate collusion, a position that is consistent with the majority of the surveys.

Number of Firms

Another common presumption in the surveys is that tacit collusion is more likely the smaller the number of firms in an industry. This is consistent with some studies in the broader literature which conclude that tacit collusion is more likely to occur in industries with a smaller number of firms because of reduced problems associated with coordination,[57] potentially higher payoffs from participation,[58] and a greater ability to detect deviations.[59]

---

52 W.J. Baumol 'Horizontal collusion and innovation' (1992) 102 Economic Journal 131. Similarly, a recent study concludes that increased concentration in an industry 'has little explanatory power in the assessment of collective dominance and coordinated effects': M. Ganslandt and P.J. Norbäck 'Do mergers result in collusion?' (Working Paper No 621 Research Institute of Industrial Economics, Stockholm, 14 June 2004) 31.

53 S. Peltzman 'The gains and losses from industrial concentration' (1977) 20 Journal of Law and Economics 254.

54 Compare C. Davidson and R. Deneckere 'Horizontal mergers and collusive behavior' (1984) 2 International Journal of Industrial Organization 117–8.

55 Hay and Kelley (n 27) 23; Fraas and Greer (n 8) 42; Office of Fair Trading 'Predicting cartels' (n 12) 15; See also G.J. Stigler 'A theory of oligopoly' (1964) 72 Journal of Political Economy 59.

56 Symeonidis (n 3) 67; Jacquemin, Nambu and Dewez (n 3) 692; Dick (n 3) 213; R.A. Posner 'A statistical study of antitrust enforcement' (1970) 13 Journal of Law and Economics 410.

57 Europe Economics (n 24) 21.

58 IDEI Toulouse (n 6) 12.

59 Ross and Baziliauskas (n 1) 396; Hay and Kelley (n 27) 14.

However, some theoretical and empirical work raises questions as to the number of firms capable of sustaining collusive arrangements. For example, one theoretical model has shown that under certain reasonable assumptions 'tacit collusion works perfectly so long as there are no more than 400 firms'.[60] This conclusion is supported to some extent by a recent empirical study of the NASDAQ trading system where it was implied that up to 60 traders tacitly colluded.[61]

The empirical evidence on the relationship between the number of firms and explicit collusion is mixed. Some studies have found that some collusive arrangements have had a large number of firms participating in the agreement,[62] including relatively stable collusive agreements.[63] Others have concluded that collusion is more likely to be sustainable where there are a relatively small number of participants,[64] a conclusion supported by experimental studies of collusion.[65]

For similar reasons to those discussed above under concentration levels it is considered that, on balance, it is reasonable to accept for the purposes of the analysis in Chapter 4 that as a general proposition, tacit collusion is more easily facilitated among a smaller number of competitors in an industry.

Market Share Volatility

Although only a limited number of surveys and studies have examined how

---

60 C Shapiro 'Theories of oligopoly behavior' in R. Schmalensee and R.D. Willig (eds) *Handbook of Industrial Organization, Volume 1* (Elsevier Science Publishers, Amsterdam, 1989) 366.

61 W.G. Christie and P.H. Schultz 'Why do NASDAQ market makers avoid odd-eighth quotes?' (1994) XLIX Journal of Finance 1839; In a follow-up study, the same authors report that tacit collusion between some traders subsequently collapsed and bidding became more random: W.G. Christie, J. Harris and P.H. Schultz 'Why did NASDAQ market makers stop avoiding odd-eighth quotes?' (1994) XLIX Journal of Finance 1858.

62 The number of participating firms can vary from two to several hundred: Levenstein and Suslow (n 21) 16, 44; Dick (n 3) 204.

63 A.R. Dick 'When are cartels stable contracts?' (1996) 39 Journal of Law and Economics 267.

64 Fraas and Greer (n 8) 43 suggest less than 12 members; Hay and Kelley (n 27) 20 found 79 per cent of explicit collusion cases had less than ten members; Suslow (n 3) 16 found that 34 of 41 cartels examined had less than ten members; Posner (n 56) 399 found 64 per cent had less than ten members; Office of Fair Trading 'Predicting cartels' (n 12) 13.

65 A survey of these studies suggests that tacit collusion is rare in markets with more than two or three firms. S. Huck, H. Normann and J. Oechssler 'Two are few and four are many: number effects in experimental oligopolies' (2004) 53 Journal of Economic Behaviour and Organization 440.

market share volatility relates to tacit collusion, a general presumption is that tacit collusion is less likely in markets with volatile market shares. This presumption is based on the conclusion that market share volatility makes tacit collusion unstable because of the difficulty for firms in differentiating between market share changes that reflect deviations, and those changes that are the result of exogenous changes in the environment.[66] One recent theoretical study, however, qualifies this presumption and suggests that market share volatility may be consistent with tacit collusion insofar as it represents a way of allocating shares over time between firms to account for relative cost differences.[67] The empirical evidence for this prediction is less clear, with one early study implying that market share volatility made collusion *more* difficult to sustain.[68] On balance, however, for the purposes of the analysis in Chapter 4, it is assumed that market share volatility can potentially act to destabilise tacit collusion.

Demand Stability

Taken as a whole, economic theory suggests that tacit collusion is less likely to occur in markets characterised by unstable, or volatile, demand. This is because it is presumed to be more difficult to sustain tacit collusion in markets where demand levels fluctuate because of the difficultly in differentiating between a secret price cut and changes in demand which creates an 'inference problem'.[69] Specific studies have predicted that collusion can be expected to break down in periods of unexpected low demand,[70] unexpected high demand,[71] high demand

---

[66] More generally, information problems associated in policing these agreements is seen to be one of the principal obstacles to maintaining tacit collusion: Stigler (n 55) 44.

[67] S. Athey and K. Bagwell 'Optimal collusion with private information' (2001) 32 RAND Journal of Economics 431. See also P. Buccirossi 'Does parallel behavior provide some evidence of collusion?' (2006) 2 Review of Law and Economics 86.

[68] R.E. Caves and M.E. Porter 'Market structure, oligopoly and stability of market shares' (1978) 26 Journal of Industrial Economics 310.

[69] R.H. Porter 'A note on tacit collusion under demand uncertainty' (1986) 19 Canadian Journal of Economics 556.

[70] R.W. Staiger and F.A. Wolak 'Collusive pricing with capacity constraints in the presence of demand uncertainty' (1992) 23 RAND Journal of Economics 203; F.M. Scherer and D. Ross *Industrial Market Structure and Economic Performance* (3rd edn, Houghton Mifflin, Boston, 1990) 286–292; Suslow (n 3) 24–26.

[71] Compare: J.J. Rotemberg and G. Saloner 'A supergame-theoretic model of price wars during booms' (1986) 76 American Economic Review 390; T.F. Bresnahan 'Competition and collusion in the American automobile industry: the 1955 price war' (1987) 35 Journal of Industrial Economics 478–479; R.H. Porter 'A study of cartel stability: the Joint Executive Committee, 1880–1886' (1983b) 15 Bell Journal of

variability,[72] or in the mere presence of demand uncertainty.[73] Other studies have predicted that high *within period* demand volatility lowers the collusive price and may, but does not necessarily, lead to a breakdown of collusion.[74]

An important implication of one set of theoretical studies is that periods of unexpected low demand, and low prices, may still be consistent with tacit collusion – that is, demand volatility does not necessarily preclude tacit collusion.[75] For example, one set of studies has predicted that tacit collusion is still possible in markets with demand volatility through the use of 'trigger strategies'.[76] Similarly, other studies have suggested that the periodic breakdown in tacit collusion through a changed environment is seen as 'part of a bargaining process in which one of the producers demands a re-negotiation of the collusive agreement'.[77]

Economics 301; Contrast G. Ellison 'Theories of cartel stability and the Joint Executive Committee' (1994) 25 RAND Journal of Economics 37.

72 Dick (n 63) 266; IDEI Toulouse (n 6) 32.

73 A.J. Robson and J. McMillan 'Dynamic duopoly under demand uncertainty' (1984) 17 Canadian Journal of Economics 698.

74 K. Bagwell and R.W. Staiger 'Collusion over the business cycle' (1997) 28 RAND Journal of Economics 97. Other studies conclude that demand volatility will not necessarily facilitate collusion where cartels operate in relatively stable markets: K.P. Wong 'Does market demand volatility facilitate collusion?' (2008) 25 Economic Modelling 696.

75 E.J. Green and R.H. Porter 'Noncooperative collusion under imperfect price information' (1984) 52 Econometrica 90. Compare a recent study which concluded that in the presence of capacity constraints, collusion can be easier to sustain in recessions rather than booms for firms with sufficiently small capacities: N. Fabra 'Collusion with capacity constraints over the business cycle' (2006) 24 International Journal of Industrial Organization 70.

76 A number of studies show that once a trigger price is reached, regardless of whether the fall in price is caused by a secret price cut or a reduction in demand, the response of the firms is to automatically revert to individual profit maximising behavior 'for some fixed period of time before resuming monopolistic competition': R.H. Porter 'A study of cartel stability: the Joint Executive Committee, 1880–1886' (1983b) 15 Bell Journal of Economics 303; R.H. Porter 'Optimal cartel trigger price strategies' (1983b) 29 Journal of Economic Theory 314. In other studies this is shown to result in the development of two 'regimes' where only two quantities are ever produced corresponding to the best and worst equilibria: Green and Porter (n 75) 89; D. Abreu, D. Pearce and E. Stacchetti 'Optimal cartel equilibria with imperfect monitoring' (1986) 39 Journal of Economic Theory 253. Contrast this 'trigger price' equilibria with the 'wait and see' approach: J. Hörner and J. Jamison 'Collusion with (almost) no information' (2007) 38 RAND Journal of Economics 806.

77 C. Fershtman and A. Pakes 'A dynamic oligopoly with collusion and price wars' (2000) 31 RAND Journal of Economics 234. Some studies conclude that following a demand shock, firms' engage in a price war but gradually and continuously use price as a learning device to bring them back toward a new collusive equilibrium: M.E. Slade 'Price wars in price-setting supergames' (1989) 56 Economica 300.

The possibility of demand volatility not being inconsistent with collusion has some empirical support in relation to studies of explicit collusion,[78] and also an empirical study of the Vancouver gasoline market that implied some tacit collusion was occurring.[79]

While some of the broader theoretical and empirical work suggests that tacit collusion can also be accommodated under certain conditions in markets characterised by some degree of demand volatility, for the purposes of the analysis that follows it appears reasonable to accept that, as a general position, tacit collusion is more likely to be facilitated and sustainable in markets characterised by stable (i.e. non-volatile) demand.

Market Growth

The predictions of economic theory as to how market growth relates to tacit collusion are unclear. One set of studies predicts that in markets where demand is growing, strong incentives exist for new competitors to enter the market which makes collusive behaviour more difficult.[80] Other studies predict that even in markets where there are a fixed number of competitors, when the market is growing, the incentives for these firms to compete to gain a large market share in order to secure potentially large future profits are *greater* than the incentives to collude.[81] However, another stream of studies predict that high growth markets, with a fixed number of participants, can facilitate tacit collusion because firms face the prospect of earning greater joint profits in the future.[82]

In declining markets it is generally accepted that tacit collusion is more difficult to sustain as firms have a greater incentive to deviate and reap the higher profits of the current period.[83]

---

78 R.H. Porter 'On the incidence and duration of price wars' (1985) 33 Journal of Industrial Economics 415; Ellison (n 71) 38; Levenstein and Suslow (n 21) 18; M.C. Levenstein 'Price wars and the stability of collusion: a study of the pre-World War I bromine industry' (1997) 45 Journal of Industrial Economics 135; Contrast Office of Fair Trading 'Predicting cartels' (n 12) 27.

79 M.E. Slade 'Interfirm rivalry in a repeated game: an empirical test of tacit collusion' (1987) 35 Journal of Industrial Economics 515; M.E. Slade 'Cheating on collusive agreements' (1990) 8 International Journal of Industrial Organization 533.

80 E. Katzenbach, E. Kottman and R. Krüger *New Industrial Economics and Experiences from European Merger Control – New Lessons about Collective Dominance?*, HWWA Institut für Wirtschaftsforschung Hamburg (Study prepared for the European Commission DG Competition, 1995) 71.

81 Europe Economics (n 24) 34.

82 IDEI Toulouse (n 6) 27.

83 IDEI Toulouse (n 6) 27.

The empirical studies of explicit collusion present mixed support for these predictions. A number of these studies show that explicit collusion is *less* likely to occur in growing markets.[84] Other studies have concluded that explicit collusion is more likely to dissolve in periods of decline,[85] or that explicit collusion is more likely under moderate growth.[86]

Demand Elasticity

A common presumption is that tacit collusion is more likely to occur in markets with low demand elasticity as the loss to any individual firm from deviation, in terms of profits forgone, will be greater.[87] However, when taken as a whole there is no clear prediction from economic theory as to how the price elasticity of demand can affect the stability of tacit collusion. Some theoretical studies note demand elasticity is irrelevant to an assessment of tacit collusion as it only reflects consumer demand characteristics, and as such does not directly feature in the assessment by firms as to the relative gains from short-term versus long-term competition.[88] However, these studies recognise that demand elasticity can make collusion more or less profitable by changing the collusive price.[89] The presumption that markets with high demand elasticity present little prospect for successful collusion is supported by some studies of explicit collusion.[90]

Links

As a general proposition economic theory suggests that tacit collusion is more likely to occur when links exist between firms in a market. However, this general conclusion is to some extent mediated by the nature, scope and types of links that exist. One set of studies, for example, has presented mixed conclusions on the effect of cross-ownership links on collusion.[91] In an empirical

---

[84] Jacquemin, Nambu and Dewez (n 3) 692; J. Palmer 'Some economic conditions conducive to collusion' (1978) 6 Journal of Economic Inquiry 31.

[85] Dick (n 63) 271.

[86] Symeonidis (n 3) 46; Dick (n 3) 213.

[87] Europe Economics (n 24) 24.

[88] Shapiro (n 60) 364; IDEI Toulouse (n 6) 51.

[89] IDEI Toulouse (n 6) 50.

[90] R.S. Pindyck 'The cartelization of world commodity markets' (1979) 69 American Economic Review 155; Levenstein and Suslow (n 21) 47.

[91] R.J. Reynolds and B.R. Snapp 'The competitive effects of partial equity interests and joint ventures' (1986) 4 International Journal of Industrial Organization 142; J. Farrell and C. Shapiro 'Asset ownership and market structure in oligopoly' (1990) 21 RAND Journal of Economics 287; D. Gilo, Y. Moshe and Y. Spiegel 'Partial cross

study of the US telephone industry it was concluded that cross-ownership of licences increased the potential for collusion.[92] Other studies have concluded that research and development links, such as participation in a joint venture, can facilitate tacit collusion insofar as the threat of withdrawal from the R&D venture represents an additional punishment mechanism.[93] Finally, tacit collusion can be facilitated where firms are linked by a common marketing agency, such as a broker or travel agent, and have similar compensation schemes with the agent.[94]

Entry and Expansion

Economic theory predicts that tacit collusion is more likely, and more stable, in markets with high entry barriers or high expansion costs.[95] Some studies have focused on cost, entry and capacity conditions and have predicted that tacit collusion is impacted by factors such as: entry costs;[96] relative cost effi-

ownership and tacit collusion' (2006) 37 RAND Journal of Economics 81. Contrast D.A. Malueg 'Collusive behavior and partial ownership of rivals' (1992) 10 International Journal of Industrial Organization 30.

92 P.M. Parker and L.H. Röller 'Collusive conduct in duopolies: multimarket contact and cross-ownership in the mobile telephone industry' (1997) 28 RAND Journal of Economics 320.

93 S. Martin 'R&D joint ventures and tacit product market collusion' (1995) 11 European Journal of Political Economy 734; V. Rabassa 'Joint ventures as a mechanism that may favour coordination: an analysis of the aluminium and music mergers' (2004) 24 European Competition Law Review 779. This conclusion is supported by experimental evidence: S. Suetens 'Does R&D cooperation facilitate price collusion? An experiment' (2008) 66 Journal of Economic Behavior and Organization 822. However, under different assumptions, relating to the degree of contractualisation and observability of R&D arrangements, it has been predicted that R&D links might frustrate collusion insofar as firms have a greater incentive to deviate with higher co-ordinated prices: L.M.B. Cabral 'R&D cooperation and product market competition' (2000) 18 International Journal of Industrial Organization 1040.

94 B.D. Bernheim and M.D. Whinston 'Common marketing agency as a device for facilitating collusion' (1985) 16 RAND Journal of Economics 270.

95 IDEI Toulouse (n 6) 19; Contrast with other studies which conclude that new entry, can, under certain assumptions regarding efficiency, promote coordinated behaviour insofar as it creates a situation where the existing competitors find it too costly to compete : J. Boone 'Balance of power' (paper presented at Wissenschaftszentrum Berlin Conference on Collusion and Cartels, 23 October 2004) 27.

96 P.C. Cramton and T.R. Palfrey 'Cartel enforcement with uncertainty about costs' (1990) 31 International Economic Review 35; W.J. Baumol 'Contestable markets: an uprising in the theory of industrial structure' (1982) 72 American Economic Review 14; M. Schwartz and R. Reynolds 'Contestable markets: an uprising in the theory of industrial structure: comment' (1983) 73 American Economic Review 488.

ciency;[97] and the costs of installing additional capacity.[98] Other studies have sought to identify an optimal number of firms for tacit collusion to remain stable and show how new entry beyond this point destabilises collusion.[99]

A number of empirical studies have concluded that explicit collusion has occurred more frequently in industries with high barriers to entry.[100] Conversely, one study of explicit collusion concluded that firms operating in industries with low entry barriers were more likely to collude.[101]

Innovation

An important prediction of economic theory is that tacit collusion is less likely to occur in innovative markets. This is because innovation creates greater incentives for firms to deviate and reap the immediate short-term benefits of the innovation, or in the case where an external firm introduces the innovation, because tacit collusion is no longer sustainable.[102] This prediction is confirmed by empirical studies of explicit collusion which imply that techno-

---

97 M.P. Donsimoni, N.S. Economides and H.M. Polemarchakis 'Stable cartels' (1986) 27 International Economic Review 325.

98 L. Sørgard 'Judo economics reconsidered: capacity limitation, entry and collusion' (1995) 15 International Journal of Industrial Organization 364.

99 J.W. Friedman and J.F. Thisse 'Sustainable collusion in oligopoly with free entry' (1994) 38 European Economic Review 281–282; Cramton and Palfrey (n 96) 19; C. d'Aspremont, A. Jacquemin, J.J. Gabszewicz and J.A. Weymark 'On the stability of collusive price leadership' (1983) 16 Canadian Journal of Economics 18; Office of Fair Trading 'Predicting cartels' (n 12) 11. The relationship between entry and competition more generally is examined in: T.F. Bresnahan and P.C. Reiss 'Entry and competition in concentrated markets' (1991) 99 Journal of Political Economy 1006.

100 Dick (n 3) 204; Eckbo (n 7) 43.

101 Asch and Seneca (n 22) 233.

102 However, if patents are granted for innovations, there can be incentives for firms to collude in respect of the granting of rights of existing or future patent rights through the use of a 'patent pool' (where an entire set of licences are granted in a package). In particular, where a patent pool exists for *substitute or rival* patents (as compared to *complementary* patents) firms effectively agree not to patent their existing licences independently, and share the royalties from the patent pool. This form of coordination is seen to be particularly harmful to the incentives for innovation where the 'pool' is prospective: C. Shapiro 'Navigating the patent thicket: cross licences, patent pools and standard setting' in A. Jaffe, J. Lerner and S. Stern (eds) *Innovation Policy and the Economy, Volume 1* (MIT Press, Cambridg, MA, 2001); R. Gilbert, C. Shapiro, L. Kaplow and R. Gertner 'Antitrust issues in the issuing of intellectual property: the nine no-no's meet the nineties' (1987) Brookings Papers on Economic Activity. Microeconomics 326. Contrast: V. Denicoló 'Sequential innovation and the patent–antitrust conflict' (2002) 54 Oxford Economic Papers 649.

logical change is a factor leading to the breakdown of collusion,[103] and that collusion is less likely to occur in research and development intensive industries.[104]

Buyer Power

Early theoretical papers recognised the power of consumers to destabilise tacit collusion, and predicted that tacit collusion is more likely to be stable where there are many common small buyers who report prices.[105] Subsequent theoretical studies have supported this conclusion, predicting that collusion is *less* stable where buyers are powerful or large,[106] or have an ability to accumulate demand backlogs and create artificial 'booms'.[107] However, other studies have noted that large buyers will only have the ability to destabilise collusion if they have a better ability than small buyers, in aggregate, to identify and impact the suppliers' behaviour, for example through sponsoring a new entrant or vertical integration.[108]

The empirical studies of explicit collusion that have tested whether collusion occurred more frequently in markets with small and atomistically distributed buyers, or, with large buyers, have presented mixed results.[109] Some empirical studies have looked at buyer concentration and have concluded that it may not be a good proxy for buyer power,[110] or have implied that high buyer concentration may actually stabilise collusion.[111] On balance, however, for the

---

[103] Levenstein and Suslow (n 21) 10.

[104] Symeonidis (n 3) 46.

[105] Stigler (n 55) 47–48; T. Scitovsky 'Ignorance as a source of oligopoly power' (1950) 40 American Economic Review 52.

[106] IDEI Toulouse (n 6) 53.

[107] C.M. Synder 'A dynamic theory of countervailing power' (1996) 27 RAND Journal of Economics 764.

[108] Ross and Baziliauskas (n 1) 397; compare J.E. Harrington Jr 'Cartel pricing dynamics with cost variability and endogenous buyer detection' (paper presented at Wissenschaftszentrum Berlin Conference on Collusion and Cartels, 22 October 2004) 6–8.

[109] Compare Dick (n 3) 204 who finds that buyers were dispersed and small, with Dick (n 63) 261 who finds support for claim that collusion is less stable with large buyers; Levenstein and Suslow (n 21) 23, 49; N. Mazzarotto 'Retail mergers and buyer power' (Working Paper CCR 04-3 Centre for Competition and Regulation CCR 2004) 2.

[110] P.R. Cowley 'Business margins and buyer/seller power' (1986) 68 Review of Economics and Statistics 336.

[111] For example, if customers are sufficiently concentrated and can pass on costs to consumers they would have limited incentives to disturb upstream collusion: Levenstein and Suslow (n 21) 24.

purposes of the analysis in Chapter 4 it is concluded that buyer power acts to hinder tacit collusion.

Tendering and Bidding Procedures

According to economic theory, the structure of bidding and tendering procedures can, in repeated settings, affect the potential for tacit collusion. Some studies have concluded that tacit collusion is easier where: public bids are held;[112] there are open auctions where bidders' identities are not concealed;[113] a small number of bidders participate repeatedly;[114] advance price announcements of posted prices are made;[115] many contracts are offered for sale;[116] no private communication occurs but prices can be publicly observed;[117] where no reserve prices in procurement processes are imposed;[118] transfers or side payments and 'knockout auctions' are made prior to official bidding;[119] or successful bids can be rotated among various participants.[120] Other studies have concluded that the ability of parties to tacitly collude is severely restricted where all forms of communication between the parties is absent (i.e. names of winners are not even known), [121] or where, in a repeated auction, the amount of information available to participants is limited.[122]

A number of empirical studies have examined the mechanics of actual bidding markets and auctions where tacit collusion has been suspected. These

---

112 Stigler (n 55) 48.

113 J. McMillan 'Selling spectrum rights' (1994) 8 Journal of Economic Perspectives 153.

114 IDEI Toulouse (n 6) 62.

115 A. Raskovich 'Competition or collusion? Negotiating discounts off posted prices' (2007) 25 International Journal of Industrial Organization 341.

116 M. Pesendorfer 'A study of collusion in first-price auctions' (2000) 67 Review of Economic Studies 406.

117 Athey and Bagwell (n 67) 430–432.

118 C.J. Thomas 'Using reserve prices to deter collusion in procurement competition' (2005) 3 Journal of Industrial Economics 301.

119 R.P. McAfee and J. McMillan 'Bidding rings' (1992) 82 American Economic Review 586. Compare the interesting empirical study of the imperfect nature of the bidding ring in the collectable postage stamp cartel in the United States: J. Asker 'A study of the internal organisation of a bidding cartel' (July 2008) Working Paper Stern School of Business New York University.

120 W.S. Comanor and M.A. Schankerman 'Identical bids and cartel behavior' (1976) 7 Bell Journal of Economics 286. Compare R.C. Marshall and L.M. Marx 'Bidder collusion' (2007) 133 Journal of Economic Theory 374.

121 A. Blume and P. Heidhues 'Modeling tacit collusion in auctions' (Working Paper, Wissenschaftszentrum Berlin, September 2002) 39.

122 A. Skrzypacz and H. Hopenhayn 'Tacit collusion in repeated auctions' (2004) 114 Journal of Economic Theory 168.

studies have concluded that: the choice of which auctions to participate in, and the distance of suppliers from the contracts, can form strategic variables in collusive bidding decisions;[123] that the use of ascending auctions and the sequencing of auctions can impact the likelihood of collusion;[124] single uniform clearing price auctions with capacity constrained firms in repeated auctions can facilitate collusion;[125] the relative ranking of bids submitted in various auctions might show a pattern of 'phantom bids' used to allocate the contracts;[126] and that various signalling and retaliatory bidding strategies have been adopted in auctions in the past.[127]

Frequency of Interaction

Economic theory predicts that the more frequently firms interact with one another the more likely tacit collusion is going to be sustainable.[128] This is because less frequent interaction makes the future more distant and less relevant and can provide incentives, particularly where a market is characterised by large and infrequent orders, for cheating.[129] In addition, more frequent interaction reduces the potential for detection lags to occur and can allow for more rapid retaliation.[130] Empirical studies of explicit collusion support the view that collusion is more likely to occur in settings where firms meet frequently.[131]

---

[123] R.H. Porter and J.D. Zona 'Ohio school milk markets: an analysis of bidding' (1999) 30 RAND Journal of Economics 287.

[124] P. Klemperer 'How (not) to run auctions: The European 3G telecom auctions' (2002) 46 European Economic Review 831.

[125] E. Dechenaux and D. Kovenock 'Tacit collusion and capacity withholding in repeated uniform price auctions' (2007) 38 RAND Journal of Economics 1044.

[126] R.H. Porter and J.D. Zona 'Detection of bid rigging in procurement auctions' (1993) 101 Journal of Political Economy 537.

[127] P. Cramton and J.A. Schwartz 'Collusive bidding in the FCC spectrum auctions' (2002) 1 Contributions to Economic Analysis and Policy 1.

[128] However, in one study which distinguishes between the frequency of interaction and the frequency with which information about defections is received, it is concluded that less frequent interaction can under certain circumstances reduce the potential for defection and make collusion more effective: D. Abreu, P .Milgrom and D. Pearce 'Information and timing in repeated partnership' (Discussion Paper No 875, Cowles Foundation for Research in Economics at Yale University, May 1988) 33.

[129] Tirole (n 9) 241; Shapiro (n 60) 378.

[130] Stigler (n 55) 46.

[131] Pesendorfer (n 116) 381; Hay and Kelley (n 27) 25–26.

Profitability and Prices

A common, and at times controversial, presumption in economic theory is that markets which feature high profits, or high and stable prices, are possibly being monopolised by a group of tacitly colluding firms. Early studies supported this presumption and concluded that there was a positive relationship between high concentration and high profitability implying that collusion might be occurring in concentrated industries.[132] However, subsequent studies have been critical of this 'structural presumption' noting that it ignores cost and efficiency improvements,[133] and the impact of business cycle effects.[134] These studies have concluded either that no relationship between concentration and profitability exists,[135] or that high profits in concentrated industries do not necessarily come from anti-competitive behaviour.[136] Some studies have found a positive relationship between concentration and profitability, but have also found evidence of cost and price decreases in concentrated markets,[137] or have shown that this relationship is principally affected by the level of capacity utilisation.[138]

The price–concentration studies are subject to many of the limitations of the profitability–concentration studies noted above in their inability to account for other potential factors which might be the cause of high prices, other than collusion.[139]

The empirical studies of explicit collusion are equally mixed as to whether collusion is more or less likely to occur in profitable industries,[140] and the extent to which collusion is associated with price increases.[141] For example,

---

132 J.S. Bain 'Relation of profit rate to industry concentration: American manufacturing, 1936–1940' (1951) 65 Quarterly Journal of Economics 323.

133 Peltzman (n 53) 229–230.

134 I. Domowitz, R.G. Hubbard and B.C. Petersen 'Business cycles and the relationship between concentration and price–cost margins' (1986) 17 RAND Journal of Economics 2.

135 R. Clarke 'Profit margins and market concentration in UK manufacturing industry: 1970–6' (1984) 16 Applied Economics 66.

136 H. Demsetz 'Industry structure, market rivalry, and public policy' (1973) 16 Journal of Law and Economics 5.

137 Peltzman (n 53) 257; M. Salinger 'The concentration–margins relationship reconsidered' (1990) 22 Brookings Papers in Microeconomics 291.

138 Cowley (n 110) 336.

139 C.M. Newmark 'Price–concentration studies: there you go again' (paper presented at the DOJ/FTC Merger Workshop Concentration and Market Shares Panel, 14 February 2004) 9.

140 Asch and Seneca (n 22) 235.

141 Levenstein and Suslow (n 21) 42. One study of the lysine cartel concludes that the mark-up of prices over marginal costs during collusive phases were lower than

increases in concentration have been related to price increases in the banking,[142] airline,[143] liner shipping[144] and cement industries.[145] Conversely, increases in concentration have been related to price decreases over time in industries such as beer,[146] bread and bakeries[147] and grocery retailing.[148]

On balance, while some studies in the broader literature raise questions about the relationship between prices and profitability and collusion, for the purposes of the analysis in chapter 4 it is accepted that markets characterised by high prices and profits may be more likely to be tacitly collusive.[149]

---

expected: N. de Roos 'Examining models of collusion: the market for lysine' (2006) 24 International Journal of Industrial Organization 1084.

142 D. Neumark and S.A. Sharpe 'Market structure and the nature of price rigidity: evidence from the market for consumer deposits' (1992) 107 Quarterly Journal of Economics 660.

143 S. Borenstein 'Hubs and high fares: dominance and market power in the US airline industry' (1989) 20 RAND Journal of Economics 362; S.A. Morrison and C. Winston 'The dynamics of airline pricing and competition' (1999) 80 American Economic Review 392.

144 P.S. Clyde and J.D. Reitzes 'The effectiveness of collusion under antitrust immunity: the case of liner shipping conferences' (Bureau of Economics Staff Report, Federal Trade Commission, December 1995) 32; contrast Sjostrom who concludes that rate movements in liner shipping are better explained by empty core theory than collusive theory: W. Sjostrom 'Collusion in ocean shipping: a test of monopoly and empty core models' (1989) 97 Journal of Political Economy 1160.

145 D.I. Rosenbaum 'Efficiency v collusion: evidence cast in cement' (1994) 9 Review of Industrial Organization 379.

146 W.J. Lynk 'Interpreting rising concentration: the case of beer' (1984) 57 Journal of Business 54.

147 T. Dunne and M.J. Roberts 'Costs, demand and imperfect competition as determinants of plant-level output prices' (Discussion Paper CS 92-5, Center for Economic Studies, U.S. Bureau of the Census, June 1992) 16.

148 K.B. Anderson *A Review of Structure-Performance Studies in Grocery Retailing* (Federal Trade Commission, Government Printing Office, Washington, DC, 1990).

149 This is consistent with the position repeatedly adopted by the UK Competition Commission. In justifying this position the former Chairman of the Commission has noted that an examination of profitability *can* assist in determining potential coordination in cases where the profit levels are significantly above cost-of-capital levels with no indication of substantial cost efficiency: D. Morris 'Dominant firm behaviour under UK Competition law' (paper presented to the Fordham Corporate Law Institute Thirtieth Annual Conference on International Antitrust Law and Policy, 23–24 October 2003) 17; Competition Commission 'Market investigation references: Competition Commission Guidelines' (June 2003) 32.

A.1.4 CONDITIONS RELEVANT FOR THE MECHANICS OF COLLUSION

In this sub-section the focus is on the mechanics of tacit collusion and, in particular, what conditions are considered necessary for firms to be able to successfully engage in tacit collusion.

Transparency

Economic theory predicts that high levels of market transparency facilitate tacit collusion as it allows for greater monitoring of a tacit arrangement and the detection of cheating.[150] These theoretical studies present three general predictions about market transparency and tacit collusion. First, long time lags in the detection of deviations affect the speed with which retaliation can occur, and make collusion *less* likely.[151] Second, the less accurate and specific the information observed, the more difficult it is to sustain collusion.[152] Finally, where markets are subject to demand or other exogenous shocks, which impact the observability of deviations, collusion is more difficult.[153]

Nevertheless, some studies have shown that collusion is still feasible in markets with less than perfect transparency through the use of a range of public and private indicators to identify deviations.[154] These include the use of 'publicly' available indicators such as market price movements,[155] customer switching,[156] or announcements of the results of public bids.[157] Where public

---

150 Stigler (n 55) 44; contrast with a recent study which postulates that high levels of transparency can potentially destabilise collusion by promoting consumer switching which can increase the short-term incentive for firms to deviate: P. Møllgaard and P.B. Overgaard 'Market transparency: a mixed blessing?' (Discussion Paper 1999–15, University of Copenhagen, Institute of Economics, Centre for Industrial Economics CIE, 2000) 5.

151 Tirole (n 9) 241.

152 M. Kandori 'The use of information in repeated games with imperfect monitoring' (1992) 59 Review of Economic Studies 581; K.U. Kühn 'Fighting collusion' (2001) 16 Economic Policy 196.

153 Contrast Green and Porter (n 75) 89.

154 M. Kandori 'Introduction to repeated games with private monitoring' (2002) 102 Journal of Economic Theory 5. In addition, a recent study concluded that full collusion can be sustained under minimal information provided firms are sufficiently patient and 'wait and see' to distinguish between changes in costs and cheating: J. Hörner and J. Jamison 'Collusion with (almost) no information' (2007) 38 RAND Journal of Economics 804.

155 Green and Porter (n 75) 91; Abreu, Pearce and Stacchetti (n 76) 253.

156 Stigler (n 55) 46.

157 Comanor and Schankerman (n 120) 282.

information is not available, deviations may still be able to be detected by using private information such as movements in market share,[158] or movements in sales and demand levels.[159]

A different set of theoretical studies have focused on how high market transparency can allow firms to identify a suitable focal point upon which to base, or adjust, collusive arrangements.[160] However, it has been suggested that this *ex ante* coordination outcome is only relevant in situations where the level of transparency is also sufficient to allow for a collusive agreement to be enforced *ex post*.[161]

The empirical studies of collusion suggest that high levels of transparency can facilitate both explicit and tacit collusion.[162] In a study of the NASDAQ system, for example, it is implied that tacit collusion between up to 60 dealers was sustained by the high levels of market transparency.[163] Two other studies, one in relation to the Danish concrete market,[164] the other in relation to US railroads,[165] have also found that statutory requirements to publish firm-specific prices or rates may have facilitated tacit collusion. These studies are supported by observations on bidding behaviour in auctions for spectrum licences in various countries, where the more observable the bid, the more likely collusion.[166]

Retaliation

An important prediction of economic theory is that, for collusion to be sustainable, there must exist credible retaliation mechanisms through which firms

---

158 Stigler (n 55) 46; Ellison (n 71) 43.

159 In some models private information is subsequently communicated through some mechanism: M. Kandori and H. Matsushima 'Private observation, communication and collusion' (1998) 66 Econometrica 628; O. Compte 'Communication in repeated games with imperfect private monitoring' (1998) 66 Econometrica 598.

160 For example, one study looks at coordination in the context of entry into a monopoly industry: J. Farrell 'Cheap talk, coordination and entry' (1987) 18 RAND Journal of Economics 39.

161 IDEI Toulouse (n 6) 26.

162 However, one study concluded that many EC and US cartels operated in markets that were not fully transparent: Office of Fair Trading 'Predicting cartels' (n 12) 12.

163 Christie and Schultz (n 61) 1834.

164 S. Albæk, P. Møllgaard and P.B. Overgaard 'Government-assisted oligopoly coordination? A *Concrete* case' (1997) 45 Journal of Industrial Economics 430.

165 J. Schmitz and S.W. Fuller 'Effect of contract disclosure on railroad grain rates: an analysis of corn belt corridors' (1995) 31 Logistics and Transportation Review 121.

166 Klemperer (n 124) 830–831; Cramton and Schwartz (n 127) 14; McMillan (n 113) 152.

that deviate can be punished. The ability of firms to credibly 'retaliate' to deviations thus underpins the mechanics of collusion, and theoretical studies have focused on two different aspects of retaliation.[167]

The first set of studies has focused on the severity of punishment necessary to sustain tacit collusion and prevent future deviations.[168] In early models of tacit collusion the collusive behaviour was enforced by the threat of a 'grim' retaliation strategy to any deviation, which involved all firms reverting to non-cooperative behaviour *forever*.[169] In subsequent studies, this grim punishment rule was refined and equilibrium points were identified where: finite punishments are used in which all firms participate;[170] players are 'rewarded' for participating in the punishment of a deviator;[171] and 'optimal' penal codes are developed which allow for swifter and more severe punishments.[172]

A second set of studies has examined how the possibility of renegotiation might impact upon the mechanics of tacit collusion. A general prediction of these studies is that if renegotiation is possible, and deviating firms are 'forgiven', then collusion will be more difficult, if not impossible.[173] That is, if renegotiation is very difficult then collusion is shown to be more likely to occur as deviating firms are aware that they will not be forgiven and are forced

---

167 Stigler (n 55) 46 noted that 'no conspiracy can neglect the problem of enforcement'; Selten identified the need for threats of punishment to be 'credible' to be effective: R. Selten 'A simple model of imperfect competition where four are few and six are many' (1973) 2 International Journal of Game Theory 141.

168 A weakness of these studies is that they are based on the assumption of perfect information – which implies perfect detection of any deviation – and as a result no firm ever deviates in equilibrium.

169 J.W. Friedman 'A non-cooperative equilibrium for supergames' (1971) 38 Review of Economics and Statistics 5.

170 R.J. Aumann and L.S. Shapley 'Long-term competition – a game theoretic analysis' (Economics Working Papers No 676, UCLA, 23 September 1992) 14.

171 D. Fudenberg and E. Maskin 'The folk theorem in repeated games with discounting or with incomplete information' (1986) 54 Econometrica 544.

172 This optimal punishment strategy has been characterised in some studies as a 'stick-and-carrot' punishment path: D. Abreu 'Extremal equilibria of oligopolistic supergames' (1986) 39 Journal of Economic Theory 220; D. Abreu 'On the theory of infinitely repeated games with discounting' (1988) 56 Econometrica 385.

173 D.G. Pearce 'Renegotiation-proof equilibria: collective rationality and intertemporal cooperation' (Discussion Paper No 855, Cowles Foundation for Research in Economics at Yale University, 1987) 2; B. McCutcheon 'Do meetings in smoke-filled rooms facilitate collusion?' (1997) 105 Journal of Political Economy 337. Contrast with another study based on an examination of explicit collusion in the sugar industry which concluded that renegotiation was not a serious impediment to collusion: D. Genesove and W.P. Mullin 'Rules, communication and collusion: narrative evidence from the Sugar Institute case' (2001) 91 American Economic Review 396.

to remain committed to the initial tacit understanding.[174] The prospect, and costs, of renegotiation thus directly impacts on the credibility of any threat of retaliation.[175] In response, some theoretical studies have sought to identify 'renegotiation proof' equilibria by imposing certain conditions on the re-negotiation process and environment.[176] Other studies have focused on the punishment strategy employed and concluded that the use of a 'tit-for-tat' punishment strategy might allow for renegotiation to occur.[177]

The empirical studies of explicit collusion show that retaliation can take many forms, can be of differing levels of severity, and, in some instances of 'occasional' cheating, may not even occur.[178] The forms which retaliation has taken in these studies include: outright termination of a collusive agreement following 'cheating',[179] temporary price wars,[180] or other measures designed to financially harm a deviating firm.[181]

Multimarket Contacts

A further prediction is that tacit collusion is more likely to be sustainable where the same firms meet each other in a number of markets, for example, where they are multi-product firms, or operate in a number of different geographical markets.[182] The intuition behind this proposition is that multi-

---

174 It has been noted that because cartels are per se illegal this has the perverse effect of serving as a 'commitment device for firms' to the original agreement (i.e. it is more difficult and costly for firms to continually meet to renegotiate so they are forced to remain committed to the original agreement): McCutcheon (n 173) 331; Shapiro (n 60) 380.

175 In particular if the equilibrium after a deviation harms both the 'deviator' and 'punishers' then these equilibria are particularly vulnerable to re-negotiation: J.P. Benoit and V. Krishna 'Renegotiation in finitely repeated games' (1993) 61 Econometrica 304.

176 D.G. Pearce (n 173) 29; J. Farrell and E. Maskin 'Renegotiation in repeated games' (1989) 1 Games and Economic Behavior 348–352; B.D. Bernheim and D. Ray 'Collective dynamic consistency in repeated games' (1989) 1 Games and Economic Behavior 314–321; J. Bergin and W.B. McLeod 'Efficiency and renegotiation in repeated games' (1993) 61 Journal of Economic Theory 49–56; P. Aghion, M. Dewatripont and P. Rey 'Renegotiation design with unverifiable information' (1994) 62 Econometrica 262; Benoit and Krishna (n 175) 318.

177 E. van Damme 'Renegotiation-proof equilibria in repeated Prisoners' Dilemma' (1989) 47 Journal of Economic Theory 208.

178 Levenstein (n 78) 134; Genesove and Mullin (n 173) 381.

179 Suslow (n 3) 38; Levenstein and Suslow (n 21) 41; Dick (n 3) 249.

180 R.H. Porter (n 71) 312.

181 Griffin (n 23) 12.

182 However, one study concludes that multimarket contact does not support collusion where markets and firms are identical *and* technology is constant: B.D.

market contact creates a situation of extended interdependence between the firms,[183] allowing firms to 'pool' and 'transfer' their retaliation and enforcement powers across a number of potential markets.[184]

A number of empirical studies support the prediction that tacit collusion is more sustainable where firms have multimarket interactions, including studies of the: US airline industry,[185] US mobile telephony industry,[186] the commercial banking sector,[187] and the US cement industry.[188] Other empirical studies have concluded that multi-market interaction increases the scope for price signalling and coordination between firms,[189] and allows firms to transfer retaliatory power from less competitive to more competitive markets.[190]

Bernheim and M.D. Whinston 'Multimarket contact and collusive behavior' (1990) 21 RAND Journal of Economics 4. Similarly, another study notes that multimarket contact may not facilitate collusion in the presence of substantial information asymmetries about rivals' actions across markets: C.J. Thomas and R.D. Willig 'The risk of contagion from multimarket contact' (2006) 24 International Journal of Industrial Organization 1158. Conversely, other studies conclude that multimarket contact *always* facilitates collusion when specific assumptions are made regarding the profit functions of firms which allows for firms to recognise the interdependence of actions in different markets: G. Spagnolo 'On interdependent supergames: multimarket contact, concavity and collusion' (1999) 89 Journal of Economic Theory 128. Compare T. Sorenson 'Credible collusion in multimarket oligopoly' (2007) 28 Managerial and Decision Economics 115.

183 P. Areeda and D. Turner 'Conglomerate mergers: extended interdependence and effects on interindustry competition as grounds for condemnation' (1978) 127 University of Pennsylvania Law Review 1084; L.G. Telser 'A theory of self-enforcing agreements' (1980) 53 Journal of Business 41.

184 Bernheim and Whinston (n 94) 2. Similarly, it has been concluded that the bundling or tying of complementary products in different markets can facilitate collusion: D. Spector 'Bundling, tying and collusion' (2007) 25 International Journal of Industrial Organization 576.

185 W.N. Evans and I.N. Kessides 'Living by the "Golden Rule": multimarket contact in the US airline industry' (1994) Quarterly Journal of Economics 343.

186 Parker and Röller (n 92) 320.

187 A.A. Heggestad and S.A. Rhoades 'Multi-market interdependence and local market competition in banking' (1978) 60 Review of Economics and Statistics 532.

188 I. Jans and D.I. Rosenbaum 'Multimarket contact and pricing: evidence from the U.S. cement industry' (1996) 15 International Journal of Industrial Organization 407.

189 M.R. Busse 'Multimarket contact and price coordination in the cellular telephone industry' (2000) 9 Journal of Economics and Management Strategy 296.

190 N. Fernández and P.L. Marín ' Market power and multimarket contact: some evidence from the Spanish hotel industry' (1998) 46 Journal of Industrial Economics 303.

Other Dimensions of Tacit Collusion

Finally, economic theory suggests that tacitly collusive understandings between firms need not be limited to pricing and quantity decisions. Some studies have focused on the potential for tacit collusion to develop in relation to firms' decisions in regard to capacity expansion and investment,[191] and research and development.[192]

Studies as to the feasibility of tacit collusion in respect of decisions relating to capacity expansion present mixed conclusions, but imply that tacit collusion of this type depends on whether: capacity is short or long-lived; investment occurs relatively frequently or infrequently (i.e. is lumpy), and the irreversibility of investment decisions.[193] Empirical studies present some support that tacit collusion on capacity decisions has occurred in the US newsprint industry,[194] and that some coordination of investment decisions by larger firms had occurred in the US chemical industry.[195]

A.1.5 SUMMARY: FACTORS THAT FACILITATE OR FRUSTRATE TACIT COLLUSION

Although there is no single economic theory relating to oligopoly, there are a number of broad methodological approaches to modelling oligopolistic interaction. A general prediction of 'dynamic' approaches to modelling oligopoly is that tacit collusion may be a not uncommon occurrence in oligopolistic markets, and that it may be sustained independent of the number of competitors or the demand conditions in the market. In recent times, the game-

---

[191] A theoretical exposition of this type of 'two-stage' game where decisions about capacity are set in the first stage, and competition occurs subject to capacity constraints in the second stage is presented in: D.M. Kreps and J.A. Scheinkman 'Quantity precommitment and Bertrand competition yield Cournot outcomes' 14 (1983) Bell Journal of Economics 327; C. Davidson and R. Deneckere (n 14) 521. See also C. Hogendorn 'Tacit collusion in capacity investment: the role of capacity exchanges' (2007) 1 B.E. Journal of Theoretical Economics 1.

[192] Cabral (n 93) 1033.

[193] IDEI Toulouse (n 6) 60.

[194] D.L. Booth, V. Kanetkar, I. Vertinsky and D. Whistler 'An empirical model of capacity expansion and pricing in an oligopoly with barometric price leadership: a case of the newsprint industry in North America' (1991) 39 Journal of Industrial Economics 273.

[195] M. Lieberman 'Postentry investment and market structure in the chemical processing industry' (1987) 18 RAND Journal of Economics 548; R.J. Gilbert and M. Lieberman 'Investment and coordination in oligopolistic industries' (1987) 18 Rand Journal of Economics 30.

theoretic approach to modelling the dynamic interaction between firms in an oligopoly has come to dominate oligopoly theory. Studies using these game-theoretic models suggest a range of specific predictions as to which factors make tacit collusion more or less likely. In relation to these predictions, there is a substantial degree of consensus as to the effect of a core set of factors on tacit collusion. However, in respect of some factors the predictions are more ambiguous.

Taken as a whole these studies predict that tacit collusion is more likely to be observed when firms: meet frequently and in multiple markets; are in a highly concentrated industry with a small number of competitors which has high entry barriers, high levels of prices and profits, and high levels of market transparency; have a mechanism, and the means, to retaliate in the event of 'cheating'; are linked in some fashion or display similar levels of vertical integration; and have similar incentives to remove a 'maverick' competitor. These studies predict that tacit collusion is less likely to be supported where firms: have asymmetrical cost structures; operate in markets with low entry barriers or where customers have significant countervailing power; and in industries characterised by business cycle effects, rapid technological change and demand volatility or where market shares are volatile. The results of these studies are unclear in relation to the impact of the following conditions on tacit collusion: symmetrical capacity constraints; excess capacity; product homogeneity and market growth.

Table A1.1 Surveys of factors that facilitate or hinder collusion (academic/consultant studies)

Factor	IDEI Toulouse (DG Competition)[a]	HWWA Institut für Wirtschaftsforschung (DG Competition)[b]	Europe Economics (DG Enterprise)[c]
Frequent interaction	Facilitates	Facilitates	Facilitates
Market share symmetry	No clear prediction	Facilitates	Not considered
Stable demand	Facilitates	Facilitates	Facilitates
Small no. of competitors	Facilitates	Not considered	Facilitates
Market growth	Facilitates	Hinders	Hinders
Product homogeneity	No clear prediction	No clear prediction	No clear prediction
Demand elasticity	No clear prediction	Facilitates	Facilitates
Removal of 'maverick'	Facilitates	Not considered	Facilitates
Business cycle effects	Hinders	Not considered	Hinders
High market concentration	Facilitates	Not considered	Facilitates
Symmetrical costs	Facilitates	Facilitates	Facilitates
Multimarket contacts	Facilitates	Facilitates	Facilitates
Prices and margins	Not considered	Not considered	Not considered
Entry barriers	Facilitates	Facilitates	Facilitates
Market transparency	Facilitates	Facilitates	Facilitates
Technology/innovation	Hinders	Hinders	Hinders
Symmetrical capacity constraints	No clear prediction	No clear prediction	Not considered
Excess capacity	No clear prediction	Not considered	No clear prediction
Bidding procedures	No clear prediction	Not considered	Not considered
Buyer power	Hinders	Hinders	Hinders

Structural links	Facilitates	Facilitates	Facilitates
Club and network effects	Hinders	Not considered	Not considered
Ability to retaliate	Facilitates	Facilitates	Facilitates
Post-capacity expansion & R&D	No clear prediction	No clear prediction	Not considered
Volatility of market shares	Not considered	Not considered	Not considered
Size and financial strength	Not considered	Facilitates	Facilitates
Vertical integration	Not considered	Facilitates	Facilitates

Notes:

a. M Ivaldi, B. Jullien, P. Rey, P. Seabright and J. Tirole 'The economics of tacit collusion', Institut d'Économie Industrielle (IDEI) Toulouse (Final report prepared for DG Competition European Commission, March 2003).

b. E. Katzenbach, E. Kottman and R. Krüger *New Industrial Economics and Experiences from European Merger Control – New Lessons about Collective Dominance?*, HWWA Institut für Wirtschaftsforschung Hamburg (Study prepared for the European Commission DG Competition, 1995).

c. Europe Economics 'Assessment criteria for distinguishing between competitive and dominant oligopolies in merger control' (Enterprise Papers No 6-2001 prepared for DG Enterprise European Commission, 2001).

Table A1.2 Surveys of factors that facilitate or hinder collusion (Member State guidelines)

Factor	NERA (UK OFT)[a]	UK Office of Fair Trading[b]	UK Comp. Commission[c]	Bundeskartellamt[d]
Frequent interaction	Not considered	Not considered	Facilitates	Not considered
Market share symmetry	Not considered	Facilitates	Facilitates	Facilitates
Stable demand	Facilitates	Facilitates	Facilitates	Not considered
Small no. of competitors	Facilitates	Not considered	Facilitates	Facilitates
Market growth	Hinders	Not considered	Not considered	Facilitates
Product homogeneity	Facilitates	Facilitates	Facilitates	No clear prediction
Demand elasticity	Not considered	Not considered	Not considered	Not considered
Removal of 'maverick'	Not considered	Not considered	Not considered	Not considered
Business cycle effects	Not considered	Not considered	Not considered	Not considered
High market concentration	Facilitates	Not considered	Facilitates	Facilitates
Symmetrical costs	Facilitates	Facilitates	Facilitates	Facilitates
Multimarket contacts	Not considered	Facilitates	Not considered	Not considered
Prices and margins	Not considered	Not considered	Facilitates	Not considered
Entry barriers	Facilitates	Facilitates	Facilitates	Facilitates
Market transparency	Facilitates	Facilitates	Facilitates	Facilitates
Technology/innovation	Hinders	Not considered	Not considered	Hinders
Symmetrical capacity constraints	Not considered	Not considered	Not considered	Facilitates
Excess capacity	Facilitates	Facilitates	Facilitates	Not considered
Bidding procedures	Not considered	Not considered	Not considered	No clear prediction
Buyer power	Hinders	Hinders	Hinders	Hinders
Structural links	Not considered	Not considered	Not considered	Facilitates

Club and network effects	Not considered	Not considered	Not considered	Not considered
Ability to retaliate	Facilitates	Not considered	Not considered	Facilitates
Post capacity expansion & R&D	Not considered	Not considered	Not considered	Not considered
Volatility of market shares	Not considered	Not considered	Not considered	Hinders
Size and financial strength	Facilitates	Not considered	Facilitates	Facilitates
Vertical integration	Facilitates	Not considered	Not considered	Facilitates

Notes:

a. Office of Fair Trading 'Merger appraisal in oligopolistic markets' (Research paper 19, prepared by NERA, November 1999) 33–57.

b. Office of Fair Trading 'Market investigation references: a consultation paper' (OFT 501 July 2002) 21–25.

c. Competition Commission 'Market investigation references: Competition Commission guidelines' (consultation document, September 2002) 40–50.

d. Bundeskartellamt 'Principles of interpretation of market dominance in merger cases' (General policy division E/G 4 October 2000) 39–53.

Table A1.3 Surveys of factors that facilitate or hinder collusion (international bodies)

Factor	U.S. DOJ Guidelines[a]	OECD roundtable on oligopoly[b]	International Competition Network[c]
Frequent interaction	Facilitates	Facilitates	Facilitates
Market share symmetry	Not considered	Not considered	Facilitates
Stable demand	Facilitates	Facilitates	Facilitates
Small no. of competitors	Not considered	Facilitates	Facilitates
Market growth	Not considered	Hinders	Not considered
Product homogeneity	Facilitates	No clear prediction	Facilitates
Demand elasticity	Not considered	Facilitates	Facilitates
Removal of 'maverick'	Facilitates	Facilitates	Facilitates
Business cycle effects	Hinders	Not considered	Not considered
High market concentration	Facilitates	Facilitates	Facilitates
Symmetrical costs	Facilitates	Facilitates	Facilitates
Multimarket contacts	Facilitates	Facilitates	Not considered
Prices and margins	Not considered	Not considered	Not considered
Entry barriers	Facilitates	Facilitates	Facilitates
Market transparency	Facilitates	Facilitates	Facilitates
Technology/innovation	Not considered	Hinders	Not considered
Symmetrical capacity constraints	Not considered	Not considered	Facilitates
Excess capacity	Not considered	No clear prediction	No clear prediction
Bidding procedures	Not considered	Not considered	No clear prediction
Buyer power	Hinders	Hinders	Not considered
Structural links	Not considered	Facilitates	Facilitates

Club and network effects	Not considered	Not considered	Not considered
Ability to retaliate	Facilitates	Facilitates	Facilitates
Post-capacity expansion & R&D	Not considered	Not considered	Not considered
Volatility of market shares	Not considered	Not considered	Not considered
Size and financial strength	Facilitates	Facilitates	No clear prediction
Vertical integration	Facilitates	Facilitates	Facilitates

Notes:
a. U.S. Department of Justice and the Federal Trade Commission *Horizontal Merger Guidelines* (1992) 57 Fed. Reg. 41552.
b. OECD Directorate for Financial, Fiscal and Enterprise Affairs Committee on Competition Law and Policy 'Oligopoly' (Unclassified Document DAFFE/CLP(99) 25 October 1999) 21–31.
c. International Competition Network 'Coordinated effects analysis under international merger regimes' (Working Paper presented at the International Competition Network Annual Conference, April 2004) 10–25.

Table A1.4 Surveys of factors that facilitate or hinder collusion (European academic papers and texts)

Factor	Klemperer[a]	Motta[b]	Tirole[c]
Frequent interaction	Facilitates	Facilitates	Facilitates
Market share symmetry	Not considered	Not considered	Not considered
Stable demand	Facilitates	Facilitates	Facilitates
Small no. of competitors	Facilitates	Facilitates	Facilitates
Market growth	Not considered	Facilitates	Not considered
Product homogeneity	Facilitates	No clear prediction	Not considered
Demand elasticity	Not considered	No clear prediction	Not considered
Removal of 'maverick'	Not considered	Not considered	Not considered
Business cycle effects	Not considered	Not considered	Not considered
High market concentration	Not considered	Facilitates	Facilitates
Symmetrical costs	Facilitates	Facilitates	Facilitates
Multimarket contacts	Not considered	Facilitates	Facilitates
Prices and margins	Not considered	Not considered	Not considered
Entry barriers	Facilitates	Facilitates	Not considered
Market transparency	Facilitates	Facilitates	Facilitates
Technology/innovation	Hinders	Hinders	Not considered
Symmetrical capacity constraints	Not considered	Facilitates	Not considered
Excess capacity	Not considered	No clear prediction	Not considered
Bidding procedures	No clear prediction	No clear prediction	Not considered
Buyer power	Not considered	Hinders	Hinders
Structural links	Not considered	Facilitates	Not considered
Club and network effects	Not considered	Not considered	Not considered

Ability to retaliate	Not considered	Facilitates	Facilitates
Post-capacity expansion & R&D	Not considered	Not considered	Not considered
Volatility of market shares	Not considered	Not considered	Not considered
Size and financial strength	Not considered	Facilitates	Not considered
Vertical integration	Not considered	Not considered	Not considered

Notes:

a. P. Klemperer 'Bidding markets' Occasional Paper No.1 UK Competition Commission (2005) 11–12.
b. M. Motta *Competition Policy: Theory and Practice* (Cambridge University Press, Cambridge, 2004) 142–202.
c. J. Tirole *The Theory of Industrial Organization* (MIT Press, Cambridge, MA, 1988) 240–262.

Table A1.5 Surveys of factors that facilitate or hinder collusion (other academic texts)

Factor	Scherer and Ross[a]	Carlton and Perloff[b]	Jacquemin and Slade[c]
Frequent interaction	Facilitates	Facilitates	Facilitates
Market share symmetry	Facilitates	Not considered	Not considered
Stable demand	Not considered	Facilitates	Not considered
Small no. of competitors	Facilitates	Facilitates	Facilitates
Market growth	Not considered	Not considered	Not considered
Product homogeneity	No clear prediction	Facilitates	Facilitates
Demand elasticity	Not considered	Facilitates	Not considered
Removal of 'maverick'	Facilitates	Not considered	Not considered
Business cycle effects	Hinders	Not considered	Not considered
High market concentration	Facilitates	Facilitates	Not considered
Symmetrical costs	Facilitates	Not considered	Facilitates
Multimarket contacts	Facilitates	Not considered	Not considered
Prices and margins	Not considered	Not considered	Not considered
Entry barriers	Facilitates	Facilitates	Facilitates
Market transparency	Facilitates	Facilitates	Facilitates
Technology/innovation	Hinders	Not considered	Hinders
Symmetrical capacity constraints	Facilitates	Not considered	Not considered
Excess capacity	Facilitates	Not considered	Not considered
Bidding procedures	Not considered	Not considered	Not considered
Buyer power	Hinders	Hinders	Hinders
Structural links	Not considered	Not considered	Not considered
Club and network effects	Not considered	Not considered	Not considered

Ability to retaliate	Facilitates	Facilitates	Facilitates
Post-capacity expansion & R&D	Not considered	Not considered	Not considered
Volatility of market shares	Not considered	Not considered	Not considered
Size and financial strength	Not considered	Not considered	Not considered
Vertical integration	Facilitates	Facilitates	Not considered

Notes:

a. F.M. Scherer and D. Ross *Industrial Market Structure and Economic Performance* (3rd edn, Houghton Mifflin, Boston, 1990) 235–317; 519–535.

b. D.W. Carlton and J.M. Perloff *Modern Industrial Organization* (3rd edn, Addison Wesley Longman, Reading, MA. 2000) 126–148; 361–68.

c. A. Jacquemin and M.E. Slade 'Cartels, collusion and horizontal merger' in R. Schmalensee and R.D. Willig (eds) *Handbook of Industrial Organization, Volume 1* (Elsevier Science Publishers, Amsterdam, 1989) 417–441.

Bibliography

Abbott, A. *The System of the Professions: An Essay on the Division of Expert Labor* (University of Chicago Press, Chicago, 1988).

Abbott, A. *Chaos of Disciplines* (University of Chicago Press, London, 2001).

Abraham, J. 'Scientific expertise and regulatory decision-making' in G. Edmond (ed.) *Expertise in Regulation and Law* (Ashgate, Aldershot, 2004) 51.

Abreu, D. 'Extremal equilibria of oligopolistic supergames' (1986) 39 Journal of Economic Theory 191.

Abreu, D. 'On the theory of infinitely repeated games with discounting' (1988) 56 Econometrica 383.

Abreu, D., D. Pearce and E. Stacchetti 'Optimal cartel equilibria with imperfect monitoring' (1986) 39 Journal of Economic Theory 251.

Abreu, D., P. Milgrom and D. Pearce 'Information and timing in repeated partnership' (Discussion Paper No 875, Cowles Foundation for Research in Economics at Yale University, May 1988).

Abreu, D., D. Pearce and E. Stacchetti 'Toward a theory of discounted repeated games with imperfect monitoring' (1990) 58 Econometrica 1041.

Abreu, D., P.K. Dutta and L. Smith 'The folk theorem for repeated games: a NEU condition' (1994) 62 Econometrica 939.

Aghion, P., M. Dewatripont and P. Rey 'Renegotiation design with unverifiable information' (1994) 62 Econometrica 257.

Aigner, G., O. Budzinski and A. Christiansen 'The analysis of coordinated effects in EU merger control: Where do we stand after *Sony/BMG* and *Impala*?' (Working Paper, Philipps-University of Marburg, 28 September 2006).

Albæk, S. and L. Lambertini 'Collusion in differentiated duopolies revisited' (1998) 59 Economics Letters 305.

Albæk, S. and L. Lambertini 'Price vs quantity in duopoly supergames with close substitutes' (2004) 38 Annals of Regional Science 567.

Albæk, S., P. Møllgaard and P.B. Overgaard 'Government-assisted oligopoly coordination? A *Concrete* Case' (1997) 45 Journal of Industrial Economics 429.

Alfter, M. and J. Young 'Economic analysis of cartels – theory and practice' (2005) 26 European Competition Law Review 546.

Allais, M. 'My conception of economic science' (1990) 2 Methodus 5.

Anderson, K.B. *A Review of Structure-Performance Studies in Grocery Retailing* (Federal Trade Commission, Government Printing Office, Washington DC, 1990).

Andersson, O. and E. Wengström 'Do antitrust laws facilitate collusion? Experimental evidence on costly communication in duopolies' (2007) 109 Scandinavian Journal of Economics 321.

Areeda, P. and D. Turner 'Conglomerate mergers: extended interdependence and effects on interindustry competition as grounds for condemnation' (1978) 127 University of Pennsylvania Law Review 1082.

Asch, P. 'The determinants and effects of antitrust activity' (1975a) 18 Journal of Law and Economics 575.

Asch, P., A. Phillips and J.W. McKie 'Discussion' (1970) 60 American Economic Review 105.

Asch, P. and J.J. Seneca 'Characteristics of collusive firms' (1975) 23 Journal of Industrial Economics 223.

Asker, J. 'A study of the internal organization of a bidding cartel' (Stern School of Business working paper, 17 July 2008).

Athey, S. and K. Bagwell 'Optimal collusion with private information' (2001) 32 RAND Journal of Economics 428.

Athey, S. and K. Bagwell 'Collusion with persistent cost shocks' (2008) 76 Econometrica 493.

Aumann, R.J. and L.S. Shapley 'Long-term competition – a game theoretic analysis' (Economics Working Papers No 676, UCLA, 23 September 1992) <http://www.econ.ucla.edu/workingpapers/wp676.pdf> (26 May 2005).

Azevedo, J.P. and M. Walker 'Dominance: meaning and measurement' (2002) 23 European Competition Law Review 363.

Bagwell, K. and R.W. Staiger 'Collusion over the business cycle' (1997) 28 RAND Journal of Economics 82.

Bain, J.S. 'Output quotas in imperfect cartels' (1948) 62 Quarterly Journal of Economics 617.

Bain, J.S. 'Workable competition in oligopoly: theoretical considerations and some empirical evidence' (1950) 40 American Economic Review 35.

Bain, J.S. 'Relation of profit rate to industry concentration: American Manufacturing, 1936–1940' (1951) 65 Quarterly Journal of Economics 293.

Bain, J.S. 'Economies of scale, concentration, and the condition of entry in twenty manufacturing industries' (1954) 44 American Economic Review 15.

Bain, J. *Barriers to New Competition* (Harvard University Press, Cambridge, MA, 1956).

Baker, J.B. 'Two Sherman Act section 1 dilemmas: parallel pricing, the oligopoly problem, and contemporary economic theory' (1993a) 38 Antitrust Bulletin 143.

Baker, J.B. 'Introduction to symposium on tacit collusion' (1993b) 38 Antitrust Bulletin 1.

Baker, J.B. 'Maverick firms and coordinated competitive effects in merger analysis' (paper presented at the Charles River Associates conference Current Topics in Merger and Antitrust Enforcement, 11 December 2002) <http://www.crai.com/Agenda/Baker.ppt> (21 July 2005).

Baker, J.B. and T.F. Bresnahan 'The gains from merger or collusion in product-differentiated industries' (1985) 33 Journal of Industrial Economics 427.

Baker, J. and C. Shapiro 'Reinvigorating horizontal merger enforcement' (paper presented at the Kirkpatrick Conference Georgetown University, October 2007)

Ball, M.S. *Lying Down Together: Law, Metaphor and Theology* (University of Wisconsin Press, WI, 1985).

Barla, P. 'Firm size inequality and market power' (2000) 18 International Journal of Industrial Organization 693.

Baumol, W.J. 'Contestable markets: an uprising in the theory of industrial structure' (1982) 72 American Economic Review 1.

Baumol, W.J. 'Horizontal collusion and innovation' (1992) 102 Economic Journal 129.

Baumol, W.J. and J.A. Ordover 'Use of antitrust to subvert competition' (1985) 28 Journal of Law and Economics 247.

Baxter, W. 'Substantive review under merger regulation' in B. Hawk (ed.) *International Antitrust Law & Policy: Fordham Corporate Law 1990* (Juris Publishing, New York, 1990) 564.

Bennett, W.L. and M.S. Feldman *Reconstructing Reality in the Courtroom* (Tavistock Publications, London, 1981).

Benoit, J.P. and V. Krishna 'Dynamic duopoly: prices and quantities' (1987) 54 Review of Economic Studies 23.

Benoit, J.P. and V. Krishna 'Renegotiation in finitely repeated games' (1993) 61 Econometrica 303.

Berger, P.L. and T. Luckmann *The Social Construction of Reality: A Treatise on the Sociology of Knowledge* (Allen Lane, London, 1966).

Bergin, J. and W.B. MacLeod 'Efficiency and renegotiation in repeated games' (1993) 61 Journal of Economic Theory 42.

Bergman, M. 'What kind of economics does a medium-sized competition authority really use?' (presentation at the Charles River Associates conference on the Role of Economics in Competition Law, Brussels 26 May 2004) <http://www.crai.com/.%5CAgenda%5CBergman.ppt> (2 June 2005).

Bergman, M.A., M. Jakobsson and C. Razo 'An econometric analysis of the European Commission's merger decisions' (Working Paper 6, Department of Economics, Uppsala University 2003) <http://www.nek.uu.se/Pdf/wp2003_6.pdf> (25 May 2005).

Bergmann, B.R. 'The current state of economics needs lots of work' (2005) 600 ANNALS of the American Academy of Political and Social Science 52.

Bernheim, B.D. and D. Ray 'Collective dynamic consistency in repeated games' (1989) 1 Games and Economic Behavior 295.

Bernheim, B.D. and M.D. Whinston 'Common marketing agency as a device for facilitating collusion' (1985) 16 RAND Journal of Economics 269.

Bernheim, B.D. and M.D. Whinston 'Multimarket contact and collusive behavior' (1990) 21 RAND Journal of Economics 1.

Bernini, G. 'Administrative/prosecutorial discretion of antitrust authorities' in B. Hawk (ed.) *International Antitrust Law & Policy: Fordham Corporate Law 1999* (Juris Publishing, New York, 1999) 573.

Bertrand, J. 'Théorie mathématique de la richesse sociale' (1883) 67 Journal des Savants 499.

Besanko, D. and D.F. Spulber 'Antitrust enforcement under asymmetric information' (1989) 99 Economic Journal 409.

Bianchi, M. and H. Moulin 'Strategic interactions in economics: the game theoretic alternative' in N. De Marchi and M. Blaug (eds) *Appraising Economic Theories* (Edward Elgar, Aldershot, UK and Brookfield, US, 1991) 181.

Bicchieri, C. 'Rationality and predictability in economics' (1987) 38 British Journal for the Philosophy of Science 501.

Bicchieri, C. 'Should a scientist abstain from metaphor?' in A. Klamer, D.N. McCloskey and R.M. Solow (eds) *The Consequences of Economic Rhetoric* (Cambridge University Press, Cambridge, 1988).

Bicchieri, C. 'Norms of cooperation' (1990) 100 Ethics 838.

Bicchieri, C. *Rationality and Coordination* (Cambridge University Press, Cambridge, 1993).

Bishop, S. and D. Ridyard 'Prometheus unbound: increasing the scope for intervention in EC merger control' (2003) 24 European Competition Law Review 357.

Black, M. *Models and Metaphors: Studies in Language and Philosophy* (Cornell University Press, Ithaca, 1962).

Black, O. 'Collusion and co-ordination in EC merger control' (2003) 24 European Competition Law Review 408.

Blair, J.M. 'Lawyers and economists in antitrust: a marriage of necessity, if not convenience' (1962) 20 ABA Antitrust Section 29.

Blair, R.D. and J.B. Herndon 'The implications of *Daubert* for economic evidence in antitrust cases' (2000) 57 Washington and Lee Law Review 801.

Blaug, M. *The Methodology of Economics* (2nd edn, Cambridge University Press, Cambridge, 1992).

Blume, A. 'Private monitoring in auctions' (paper presented at Wissenschaftszentrum Berlin Conference on Collusion and Cartels, 23 October 2004).

Blume, A. and P. Heidhues 'Modeling tacit collusion in auctions' (Working Paper, Wissenschaftszentrum, Berlin, September 2002) <http://www.wz-berlin.de/~heidhues/papers/tacit16.PDF> (3 June 2005).

Bó, P.D. 'Tacit collusion under interest rate fluctuations' (2007) 38 RAND Journal of Economics 533.

Board of Editors 'Competition law and the turn of the century' (2001) 28 Legal Issues of Economic Integration 135.

Böge, U. 'The role of economics in German competition policy' (presentation at the Charles River Associates conference on the Role of Economics in Competition Law Brussels, 26 May 2004) <http://www.crai.com/.%5CAgenda%5CBoge.pdf> (2 June 2005).

Böge, U. 'Modernisation of Art.82 EC' (paper presented at the UK Competition Commission guest lecture series, London, 19 April 2005) <http://www.competition-commission.org.uk/our_role/cc_lectures/abuse_of_market_190405_boge.pdf>. (5 June 2005).

Böge, U. and E. Muller 'From the market dominance test to the SLC test: are there any reasons for a change' (2002) 23 European Competition Law Review 495.

Bonanno, G. and J. Vickers 'Vertical separation' (1988) 36 Journal of Industrial Economics 257.

Boone, J. 'Balance of power' (paper presented at Wissenschaftszentrum Berlin Conference on Collusion and Cartels, 23 October 2004).

Booth, D.L., V. Kanetkar, I. Vertinsky and D. Whistler 'An empirical model of capacity expansion and pricing in an oligopoly with barometric price leadership: a case of the newsprint industry in North America' (1991) 39 Journal of Industrial Economics 255.

Borenstein, S. 'Hubs and high fares: dominance and market power in the U.S. airline industry' (1989) 20 RAND Journal of Economics 344.

Borenstein, S. 'Airline mergers, airport dominance, and market power' (1990) 80 American Economic Review 400.

Bork, R.H. *The Antitrust Paradox: A Policy at War with Itself* (Free Press, New York, 1993).

Botteman, Y. 'Mergers, standard of proof and expert economic evidence' (2006) 2 Journal of Competition Law and Economics 71.

Boulding, K.E. *Economic Analysis* (4th edn, Harper & Row, New York, 1941).

Boulding, K.E. 'The economics of knowledge and the knowledge of economics' (1966) 56 American Economic Review 1.

Boyd, R. 'Metaphor and theory change: what is "metaphor" a metaphor for?' in A Ortony (ed.) *Metaphor and Thought* (2nd edn, Cambridge University Press, Cambridge, 1993).

Boyd White, J. *Heracles' Bow: Essays on the Rhetoric and Poetics of the Law* (University of Wisconsin Press, WI, 1985a).

Boyd White, J. 'Law as rhetoric, rhetoric as law: the arts of cultural and communal life' (1985b) 52 University of Chicago Law Review 684.

Brenner, R. 'Making sense out of nonsense: economics in context' in D. Colander and R. Brenner (eds) *Educating Economists* (University of Michigan Press, Ann Arbor, 1992).

Brent, R. 'The certain pursuit of oligopoly: a reply' (1996) 17 European Competition Law Review 163.

Bresnahan, T.F. 'Competition and collusion in the American automobile industry: the 1955 price war' (1987) 35 Journal of Industrial Economics 457.

Bresnahan, T.F. and P.C. Reiss 'Entry and competition in concentrated markets' (1991) 99 Journal of Political Economy 977.

Bresnahan, T.F. and R. Schmalensee 'The empirical renaissance in industrial economics: an overview' (1987) 35 Journal of Industrial Economics 371.

Bresnahan, T.F. and V.Y. Suslow 'Short-run supply with capacity constraints' (1989) 32 Journal of Law and Economics S11.

Briones, J. 'Oligopolistic dominance: is there a common approach in different jurisdictions? A review of decisions adopted by the Commission under the Merger Regulation' (1995) 16 European Competition Law Review 334.

Briones, J. and A.J. Padilla 'The complex landscape of oligopolies under EU competition policy' (2001) 24 World Competition 307.

Brock, W.A. and J.A. Scheinkman 'Price setting supergames with capacity constraints' (1985) 52 Review of Economic Studies 371.

Brunt, M. 'Antitrust in the courts: the role of economics and economists' in B. Hawk (ed.) *International Antitrust Law & Policy: Fordham Corporate Law 1998* (Juris Publishing, New York, 1998) 359.

Buccirossi, P. 'Does parallel behavior provide some evidence of collusion?' (2006) 2 Review of Law and Economics 85.

Buchanan, J.M. 'Economics as a public science' in S.G. Medema and W.J. Samuels (eds) *Foundations of Research in Economics: How Do Economists Do Economics?* (Edward Elgar, Cheltenham, UK and Brookfield, USA, 1996).

Budzinski, O. and I. Ruhmer 'Merger simulation in competition policy: a survey' (Joint Discussion Paper Series in Economics Philipps-University Marburg, 29 May 2008) <http://ssrn.com/abstract=1138682> (9 September 2008).

Budzinski, O. and K. Wacker 'The prohibition of the proposed Springer-Prosiebensat.1 merger: how much economics in German merger control?' (2007) 3 Journal of Competition Law and Economics 281.

Bulow, J.I., J.D. Geanakoplos and P. Klemperer 'Multimarket oligopoly: strategic substitutes and complements' (1985) 93 Journal of Political Economy 488.

Bundeskartellamt 'Principles of interpretation of market dominance in merger cases' (General policy division E/G 4 October 2000) <http://www.bundeskartellamt.de/wDeutsch/download/pdf/Merkblaetter/Merkblaetter_englisch/02_Checkliste_e.pdf> (15 October 2005).

Busse, M.R. 'Multimarket contact and price coordination in the cellular telephone industry' (2000) 9 Journal of Economics and Management Strategy 287.

Cabral, L.M.B. 'R&D cooperation and product market competition' (2000) 18 International Journal of Industrial Organization 1033.

Cabral, L.M.B. 'Collusion theory: where to go next?' (2005) 5 Journal of Industry, Competition and Trade 199.

Cairnes, J.E. *The Character and Logical Method of Political Economy* (Macmillan and Co London 1888).

Calkins, R.D. 'The production and use of economic knowledge' (1966) 56 American Economic Review 530.

Capuano, C. 'Demand growth, entry and collusion sustainability' (FEEM Working Paper No. 62.2002, University of Naples Federico II, September 2002) <http://www.feem.it/NR/rdonlyres/8635DEBB-82B7-4A23-BA59-64263BE9FB2C/351/6202.pdf> (25 May 2005).

Carlton, D.W. and J.M. Perloff *Modern Industrial Organization* (3rd edn, Addison Wesley Longman, Reading, MA, 2000).

Carlton, D.W., R.H. Gertner and A.M. Rosenfield 'Communication among competitiors: game theory and antitrust' (1997) 5 George Mason Law Review 423.

Caves, R.E. and M.E. Porter 'Market structure, oligopoly and stability of market shares' (1978) 26 Journal of Industrial Economics 289.

Caves, R.E. and B.S. Yamey 'Risk and corporate rates of return: comment' (1971) 85 Quarterly Journal of Economics 513.

Chamberlain, E.H. 'Duopoly: value where sellers are few' (1929) 43 Quarterly Journal of Economics 63.

Chamberlain, E.H. *The Theory of Monopolistic Competition: A Re-orientation of the Theory of Value* (7th edn, Harvard University Press, Cambridge, MA, 1956).

Chang, M.H. 'The effects of product differentiation on collusive pricing' (1991) 9 International Journal of Industrial Organization 453.

Chen, Y. 'On vertical mergers and their competitive effects' (2001) 32 RAND Journal of Economics 667.

Christensen, L.R. and R.E. Caves 'Cheap talk and investment rivalry in the pulp and paper industry' (1997) 45 Journal of Industrial Economics 47.

Christensen, P. and P. Owen 'Comment on the judgement of the Court of First Instance of 25 March 1999 in the merger case IV/M.619 – Gencor/Lonrho' (1999) Competition Directorate-General of the European Commission Competition Policy Newsletter, June page 19.

Christensen, P. and V. Rabassa 'The Airtours decision: is there a new Commission approach to collective dominance?' (2001) 22 European Competition Law Review 227.

Christie, W.G. and P.H. Schultz 'Why do NASDAQ market makers avoid odd-eighth quotes?' (1994) XLIX Journal of Finance 1813.

Christie, W.G., J. Harris and P.H. Schultz 'Why did NASDAQ market makers stop avoiding odd-eighth quotes?' (1994) XLIX Journal of Finance 1841.

Clark, J.M. 'Toward a concept of workable competition' (1940) 30 American Economic Review 241.

Clarke, R. 'Profit margins and market concentration in UK manufacturing industry: 1970–6' (1984) 16 Applied Economics 57.

Clower, R.W. 'The ideas of economists' in A. Klamer, D.N. McCloskey and R.M. Solow (eds) *The Consequences of Economic Rhetoric* (Cambridge University Press Cambridge 1988).

Clyde, P.S. and J.D. Reitzes 'The effectiveness of collusion under antitrust immunity: The case of liner shipping conferences' (Bureau of Economics Staff Report, Federal Trade Commission, December 1995) <http://www.ftc.gov/reports/shipping.pdf> (25 May 2005).

Coase, R.H. 'Economics and contiguous disciplines' (1978) 7 Journal of Legal Studies 201.

Coase, R.H. *The Firm, the Market, and the Law* (University of Chicago Press, Chicago, 1988).

Coase, R.H. *Essays on Economics and Economists* (University of Chicago Press, Chicago, 1994).

Coate, M.B. 'Alive and kicking: collusion theories in merger analysis at the Federal Trade Commission' (Working Paper Federal Trade Commission, January 2008).

Coate, M.B. and F.S. McChesney 'Empirical evidence on FTC enforcement of the merger guidelines' (1992) 30 Economic Inquiry 277.

Colander, D. 'The microeconomic myth' in D. Colander and R. Brenner (eds) *Educating Economists* (University of Michigan Press, Ann Arbor, 1992).

Colander, D. and A. Klamer 'The making of an economist' (1987) 1 Journal of Economic Perspectives 95.

Coleman, M.T. 'Empirical analyses of potential coordinated effects from a merger' (paper presented at a conference at George Mason University, January 2003) <http://www.ftc.gov/be/seminardocs/gmucoleman.pdf> (4 February 2003).

Collins, S.M. 'The use of social research in the courts' in W.M. Evans (ed.) *The Sociology of Law: A Social-Structural Perspective* (Free Press, New York, 1980) 563.

Comanor, W.S. and M.A. Schankerman 'Identical bids and cartel behavior' (1976) 7 Bell Journal of Economics 281.

Commission of the European Communities *XVIth Report on Competition Policy* (Luxembourg Office for Official Publications of the European Communities, 1987).

Commission of the European Communities *Commission Adopts Comprehensive Reform of EU Merger Control*, press release IP/02/1856 (11 December 2002a) 1 <http://europa.eu.int/rapid/pressReleasesAction.do? reference=IP/02/1856&format=HTML&aged=0&language=EN&guiLanguage=en> (17 October 2005).

Commission of the European Communities *Commission Appeals CFI ruling on Tetra Laval/Sidel to the European Court of Justice,* press release IP/02/1952 (20 December 2002) 1 <http://europa.eu.int/rapid/pressReleasesAction.do?reference=IP/02/1952&format=HTML&aged=0&language=EN&guiLanguage=en> (17 October 2005) .

Commission of the European Communities *Commission Energy Sector Inquiry Confirms Serious Competition Problems*, press release IP/07/26 (10 January 2007).

Commission of the European Communities Competition Directorate-General 'Merger review and horizontal merger guidelines: the economic framework for assessing mergers' (unpublished paper presented at the MTF House meeting on horizontal merger guidelines, 15 January 2003).

Commission of the European Communities Competition Directorate-General 'Merger control: merger review package in a nutshell' <http://europa.eu.int/comm/competition/publications/special/3_merger.pdf> (25 May 2005).

Competition Commission 'Market investigation references: Competition Commission guidelines' (consultation document, September 2002).

Competition Commission 'Market Investigation References: Competition Commission Guidelines' (June 2003) http://www.competition-commission.org.uk/rep_pub/rules_and_guide/pdf/ 15073compcommguidance3final.pdf (21 July 2005)

Competition Commission 'Merger References: Competition Commission Guidelines June 2003' <http://www.competition-commission.org.uk/rep_pub/rules_and_guide/pdf/ 15073 compcommguidance2final.pdf> (21 July 2005b).

Compte, O. 'Communication in repeated games with imperfect private monitoring' (1998) 66 Econometrica 597.

Compte, O., F. Jenny and P. Rey 'Capacity constraints, mergers and collusion' (2002) 46 European Economic Review 1.

Connor, J.M. 'Collusion and price dispersion' (2005) 12 Applied Economics 335.

Connor, J.M. 'Forensic economics: an introduction with special emphasis on price fixing' (2007) 4 Journal of Competition Law and Economics 31.

Cournot, A.A. *Researches into the Mathematical Principles of the Theory of Wealth* translated by N.T. Bacon (Macmillan, New York, 1897).

Cowley, P.R. 'Business margins and buyer/seller power' (1986) 68 Review of Economics and Statistics 333.

Cowling, K. and D.C. Mueller 'The social costs of monopoly power' (1978) 88 Economic Journal 727.

Cramton, P.C. and T.R. Palfrey 'Cartel enforcement with uncertainty about costs' (1990) 31 International Economic Review 17.

Cramton, P. and J.A. Schwartz 'Collusive bidding in the FCC spectrum auctions' (2002) 1 Contributions to Economic Analysis and Policy 1.

d'Aspremont, C., A. Jacquemin, J.J. Gabszewicz and J.A. Weymark 'On the stability of collusive price leadership' (1983) 16 Canadian Journal of Economics 17.

Davidson, C. and R. Deneckere 'Horizontal mergers and collusive behavior' (1984) 2 International Journal of Industrial Organization 117.

Davidson, C. and R. Deneckere 'Long-run competition in capacity, short-run competition in price, and the Cournot model' (1986) 17 RAND Journal of Economics 404.

Davidson, D. and R. Deneckere 'Excess capacity and collusion' (1990) 31 International Economic Review 521.

Davies, S. and M. Olczak 'Tacit versus overt collusion firm asymmetries and numbers: what's the evidence?' (University of East Anglia Working Paper 08-32 October 2008).

Davis, P. 'Coordinated effects merger simulation with linear demands' (Competition Commission Working Paper, April 2006).

de la Mano, M. 'Coordinated effects' (Presentation at Fordham Competition Law Institute, New York, July 2006) < http://ec.europa.eu/dgs/competition/economist/delamano2.pdf>

de la Mano, M. 'A theory on the use of economic evidence in competition policy cases' (Presentation at Association of Competition Economists conference, Budapest, November 2008). <http://www.competitioneconomics.org/dyn/files/basic_items/139-file/RoundTable_DeLaMano.pdf>

de Roos, N. 'A model of collusion timing' (2004) 22 International Journal of Industrial Organization 351.

de Roos, N. 'Examining models of collusion: the market for lysine' (2006) 24 International Journal of Industrial Organization 1083.

Dechenaux, E. and D. Kovenock 'Tacit collusion and capacity withholding in repeated uniform price auctions' (2007) 38 RAND Journal of Economics 1044.

Demsetz, H. 'Industry structure, market rivalry, and public policy' (1973) 16 Journal of Law and Economics 1.

Deneckere, R. 'Duopoly supergames with product differentiation' (1983) 11 Economics Letters 37.

Deneckere, R. and C. Davidson 'Incentives to form coalitions with Bertrand competition' (1985) 16 RAND Journal of Economics 473.

Denicoló, V. 'Sequential innovation and the patent–antitrust conflict' (2002) 54 Oxford Economic Papers 649.

Desai, K.S. 'Limitations on the use of economic analysis in EC competition law proceedings – Part 1' (2002) 23 European Competition law Review 524.

Dewey, D. 'The economic theory of antitrust: science or religion?' (1964) 50 Virginia Law Review 413.

Dewey, D. 'Information, entry and welfare: the case for collusion' (1979) 69 American Economic Review 587.

Dibble, V.K. 'Occupations and ideologies' in J.E. Curtis and J.W. Petras (eds) *The Sociology of Knowledge: A Reader* (Gerald Duckworth & Co, London, 1970) 434.

Dick, A.R. 'Identifying contracts, combinations and conspiracies in restraint of trade' (1996a) 17 Managerial and Decision Economics 203.

Dick, A.R. 'When are cartels stable contracts?' (1996b) 39 Journal of Law and Economics 241.

Dick, A.R. 'Coordinated interaction: pre-merger constraints and post-merger effects' (paper presented at the Charles River Associates conference Current Topics in Merger and Antitrust Enforcement, 11 December 2002) <http://www.crai.com/Agenda/Dick.pdf> (21 July 2005).

Dixit, A. 'Recent developments in oligopoly theory' (1982) 72 American Economic Review 12.

Domowitz, I., R.G. Hubbard and B.C. Petersen 'Business cycles and the relationship between concentration and price–cost margins' (1986) 17 RAND Journal of Economics 1.

Donsimoni, M.P. 'Stable heterogeneous cartels' (1985) 3 International Journal of Industrial Organization 451.

Donsimoni, M.P., N.S. Economides and H.M. Polemarchakis 'Stable cartels' (1986) 27 International Economic Review 317.

Dore, M., S. Chakravarty and R. Goodwin *John von Neumann and Modern Economics* (Clarendon Press, Oxford, 1989).

Doyle, M.P. and C.M. Synder 'Information sharing and competition in the motor vehicle industry' (1999) 107 Journal of Political Economy 1326.

Dunne, T. and M.J. Roberts 'Costs, demand and imperfect competition as determinants of plant-level output prices' (Discussion Paper CS 92-5 Center for Economic Studies, U.S. Bureau of the Census, June 1992).

Durkheim, E. *Elementary Forms of Religious Life* (Macmillan, New York, 1915).

Easterbrook, F.H. 'The Limits of Antitrust' (1984) 63 Texas Law Review 1.

Eckard Jr, E.W. 'Advertising, competition and market share instability' (1987) 60 Journal of Business 539.

Eckbo, P.L. *The Future of World Oil* (Ballinger Publishing Company, Cambridge, MA, 1976).

Economic Advisory Group on Competition Policy Report 'An economic approach to Article 82' (paper prepared for the Chief Economist of the European Commission, July 2005) <http://europa.eu.int/comm/competition/publications/studies/eagcp_july_21_05.pdf> (21 August 2005).

Edgeworth, F. 'The pure theory of monopoly' in F. Edgeworth (ed.) *Papers Relating to Political Economy* (Macmillan, London, 1925) 111.

Edmond, G. 'Judicial representations of scientific evidence' (2000) 63 Modern Law Review 216.

Edmond, G. 'Expertise in regulation and law' in G. Edmond (ed.) *Expertise in Regulation and Law* (Ashgate, Aldershot, 2004) 1.

Edmond, G. 'Judging facts: managing expert knowledge in legal decision-making' in G. Edmond (ed.) *Expertise in Regulation and Law* (Ashgate, Aldershot, 2004) 136.

Edmond, G. and D. Mercer 'The invisible branch: the authority of science studies in expert evidence jurisprudence' in G. Edmond (ed.) *Expertise in Regulation and Law* (Ashgate, Aldershot, 2004) 199.

Edwards, C.D. 'Use and abuse of economics in antitrust litigation' (1962) (1962) 20 ABA Antitrust Section 38.

Eisner, M. 'Protecting the environment at the margin' in G. Edmond (ed.) *Expertise in Regulation and Law* (Ashgate, Aldershot, 2004) 67.

Eisner, M.A. *Antitrust and the Triumph of Economics* (University of North Carolina Press, Chapel Hill, 1991).

Elhauge, E. and D. Geradin *Global Competition Law and Economics* (Hart Publishing, Oxford, 2007).

Ellison, G. 'Theories of cartel stability and the Joint Executive Committee' (1994) 25 RAND Journal of Economics 37.

Engel, C. 'How much collusion? A meta-analysis of oligopoly experiments' (2007) 3 Journal of Competition Law and Economics 491.

Esposito, F.F. and L. Esposito 'Excess capacity and market structure' (1974) 56 Review of Economics and Statistics 188.

Esposito, F.F. and L. Esposito 'Excess capacity and market structure: another look at the evidence' (1979) 61 Review of Economics and Statistics 159.

Etter, B. 'The assessment of mergers in the EC under the concept of collective dominance: an analysis of the recent decisions and judgments – by an economic approach' (2000) 23 Journal of World Competition 103.

Europe Economics 'Assessment criteria for distinguishing between competitive and dominant oligopolies in merger control' (Enterprise Papers No 6-2001 prepared for DG Enterprise European Commission, 2001).

Europe Economics 'One's a monopoly, two's collectively dominant, three's alright?' (Discussion paper, Europe Economics, August 2002).

European Commission 'Guidance on the Commission's enforcement priorities in applying Article 82 EC Treaty to abusive exclusionary conduct by dominant undertakings ((COM) 2008, 3 December 2008).

Evans, W.N. and I.N. Kessides 'Living by the "Golden Rule": multimarket contact in the US airline industry' (1994) Quarterly Journal of Economics 341.

Evans, W.N., L. Froeb and G.J. Werden 'Endogeneity in the concentration–price relationship: causes, consequences and cures' (1993) 41 Journal of Industrial Economics 431.

Ewick, P. and S.S. Sibley 'Subversive stories and hegemonic tales: toward a sociology of narrative' (1995) 29 Law & Society Review 197.

Fabra, N. 'Collusion with capacity constraints over the business cycle' (2006) 24 International Journal of Industrial Organization 69.

Farrell, J. 'Cheap talk, coordination and entry' (1987) 18 RAND Journal of Economics 34.

Farrell, J. and E. Maskin 'Renegotiation in repeated games' (1989) 1 Games and Economic Behavior 327.

Farrell, J. and M. Rabin 'Cheap talk' (1996) 10 Journal of Economic Perspectives 103.

Farrell, J. and C. Shapiro 'Asset ownership and market structure in oligopoly' (1990) 21 RAND Journal of Economics 275.

Febbrajo, A. and G. Teubner 'Autonomy and regulation in the autopoietic perspective: an introduction' in G. Teubner and A. Febbrajo (eds) *State, Law, and Economy as Autopoietic Systems: Regulation and Autonomy in a New Perspective* (Dott. A. Giuffre, Milan, 1992) 3.

Federal Court of Australia *Guidelines for Expert Witnesses in Proceedings in the Federal Court of Australia* (version 3) 19 March 2004 <http://www.fedcourt.gov.au/how/prac_direction.html> (20 March 2005)

Federal Judicial Center 'Expert testimony in federal civil trials: a preliminary analysis', Report by the Federal Judicial Center (2000) <http://www.fjc.gov/public/pdf.nsf/lookup/ExpTesti.pdf/$file/ExpTesti.pdf> (31 May 2005).

Federal Judicial Center *Reference Manual on Scientific Evidence* (2000) <http://air.fjc.gov/public/f jcweb.nsf/pages/16> (31 May 2005).

Federal Trade Commission 'Empirical industrial organization roundtable' (transcript of meeting held at Federal Trade Commission, 11 September 2001) <http://www.ftc.gov/be/empiricalioroundtabletranscript.pdf> (15 November 2002).

Federal Trade Commission 'Cruise investigation: empirical economic & financial analyses' November 2002 <http://www.ftc.gov/be/hilites/ftcbeababrownbag.pdf> (4 February 2003).

Fellner, W. 'Collusion and its limits under oligopoly' (1950) 40 American Economic Review 54.

Fernández, N. and P.L. Marín 'Market power and multimarket contact: some evidence from the Spanish hotel industry' (1998) 46 Journal of Industrial Economics 301.

Fershtman, C. and A. Pakes 'A dynamic oligopoly with collusion and price wars' (2000) 31 RAND Journal of Economics 207.

Fershtman, C. and A. Pakes 'A dynamic oligopoly model with asymmetric information' (paper presented at a seminar at the Association for the Development of Research in Economics and Statistics, Paris, 2 December 2002) <http://www.adres.polytechnique.fr/SEMINAIRE/ARCHIVES/ROY/0203/021202.pdf> (25 May 2005).

Feuerstein, S. 'Collusion in industrial economics – a survey' (2005) 5 Journal of Industry, Competition and Trade 163.

Fishburn, P.C. 'Decision theory: the next 100 years?' (1991) 101 Economic Journal 27.

Fisher, F.M. 'Games economists play: a noncooperative view' (1989) 20 RAND Journal of Economics 113.

Fisher, F.M. 'Economic analysis and "bright-line" test' (2007) 4 Journal of Competition Law and Economics 129.

Fonseca, M.A. and H.T. Normann 'Mergers, asymmetries and collusion: experimental evidence' (2008) 118 Economic Journal 387.

Foucault, M. *The Archaeology of Knowledge* (Routledge, London, 1972).

Fraas, A.G. and D.F. Greer 'Market structure and price collusion: an empirical analysis' (1977) 26 Journal of Industrial Economics 21.

Franzosi, M. 'Oligopoly and the Prisoner's Dilemma: concerted practices and "as-if" behaviour' (1988) 9 European Competition Law Review 385.

Fraysse, J. and M. Moreaux 'Collusive equilibria in oligopolies with finite lives' (1985) 27 European Economic Review 45.

Freshfields Bruckhaus Deringer 'New EC merger regime: a director's overview' (client briefing April 2004) 1. <http://www.freshfields.com/practice/comptrade/publications/pdf/8289.pdf> (25 May 2005).

Friedman, J.W. 'A non-cooperative equilibrium for supergames' (1971) 38 Review of Economics and Statistics 1.

Friedman, J.W. and J.F. Thisse 'Sustainable collusion in oligopoly with free entry' (1994) 38 European Economic Review 27.

Friedman, M. *Essays in Positive Economics* (University of Chicago Press, Chicago, 1953).

Friedson, E. *Professional Powers: A study of the Institutionalization of Formal Knowledge* (University of Chicago Press, Chicago, 1986).

Froeb, L.M. 'Economic methodologies for antitrust' (paper presented at the Charles River Associates Merger conference, 10 February 2004).

Froeb, L.M. 'The use of economics in merger analysis' (paper presented at the IBC conference, Brussels, 27 January 2005) <http://www.ftc.gov/speeches/froeb/050127ibcbrussels1.pdf> (25 May 2005).

Fudenberg, D. and D.K. Levine 'The Nash threats folk theorem with communication and approximate common knowledge in two player games' (Levine's Working Paper Archive Number 618897000000000030 UCLA Department of Economics June 17 2004) <http://www.dklevine.com/papers/private_rpd.pdf> (25 May 2005).

Fudenberg, D. and E. Maskin 'The folk theorem in repeated games with discounting or with incomplete information' (1986) 54 Econometrica 533.

Fudenberg, D. and J. Tirole 'Understanding rent dissipation: on the use of game theory in industrial organization' (1987) 77 American Economic Review 176.

Fudenberg, D. and J. Tirole 'Noncooperative game theory for industrial organization: an introduction and overview' in R. Schmalensee and R.D. Willig (eds) *Handbook of Industrial Organization, Volume 1* (Elsevier Science Publishers, Amsterdam, 1989).

Fudenberg, D., D.K. Levine and E. Maskin 'The folk theorem with imperfect public information' (1994) 62 Econometrica 997.

Fusillo, M. 'Excess capacity and entry deterrence: the case of ocean liner shipping markets' (2003) 5 Maritime Economics and Logistics 100.

Ganslandt, M. and P.J. Norbäck 'Do mergers result in collusion?' (Working Paper No 621, Research Institute of Industrial Economics, Stockholm, 14 June 2004).

Gavil, A.I. 'After *Daubert*: discerning the increasingly fine line between the admissibility and sufficiency of expert testimony in antitrust litigation' (1997) 65 Antitrust Law Journal 663.

Gavil, A.I. 'Competition policy, economics, and economists: are we expecting too much?' in B. Hawk (ed.) *International Antitrust Law & Policy: Fordham Corporate Law 2005* (Juris Publishing, New York, 2006) 575.

Gavil, A.I. 'The challenges of economic proof in a decentralized and privatized European competition policy system: lessons from the American experience' (2007) 4 Journal of Competition Law and Economics 1.

Gellhorn, E. 'The practical uses of economic analysis: hope vs. reality' (1987) 56 Antitrust Law Journal 933.

Genesove, D. and W.P. Mullin 'Testing static oligopoly models: conduct and cost in the sugar industry, 1890–1914' (1998) 29 RAND Journal of Economics 355.

Genesove, D. and W.P. Mullin 'Rules, communication and collusion: narrative evidence from the Sugar Institute case' (2001) 91 American Economic Review 379.

Gentner, D. and M. Jeziorski 'The shift from metaphor to analogy in Western science' in A. Ortony (ed.) *Metaphor and Thought* (2nd edn, Cambridge University Press, Cambridge, 1993).

Geradin, D. and N. Petit 'Judicial remedies under EC competition law: complex issues arising from the "Modernisation"' Global Competition Law Centre working paper (2005) <http://professorgeradin.blogs.com/professor_geradins_weblog/files/judicial_remedies_under_ec_competition_law_geradinpetit.pdf> (21 January 2006).

Gerber, D.J. *Law and Competition in Twentieth Century Europe: Protecting Prometheus* (Oxford University Press, Oxford, 1998).

Gerber, D.J. 'Courts as economic experts in European merger law' in B. Hawk (ed.) *International Antitrust Law and Policy: Fordham Corporate Law 2004* (Juris Publishing, New York, 2004) 475.

Gerrard, B. 'On matters methodological in economics' (1990) 4 Journal of Economic Surveys 197.

Gilbert, G.N. and M. Mulkay *Opening Pandora's Box: A Sociological Analysis of Scientists' Discourse* (Cambridge University Press, Cambridge, 1984).

Gilbert, R., C. Shapiro, L. Kaplow and R. Gertner 'Antitrust issues in the issuing of intellectual property: the nine no-no's meet the nineties' (1987) Brookings Papers on Economic Activity: Microeconomics 283.

Gilbert, R.J. and M. Lieberman 'Investment and coordination in oligopolistic industries' (1987) 18 RAND Journal of Economics 17.

Gilo, D., Y. Moshe and Y. Spiegel 'Partial cross ownership and tacit collusion' (2006) 37 RAND Journal of Economics 81.

Goodwin, C.D. 'The heterogeneity of the economists' discourse: philosopher, priest, and hired gun' in A. Klamer, D.N. McCloskey and R.M. Solow (eds) *The Consequences of Economic Rhetoric* (Cambridge University Press, Cambridge, 1988).

Goyder, D.G. *EC Competition Law* (3rd edn, Oxford University Press, Oxford, 1998).

Grady, M.F. 'Toward a positive economic theory of antitrust' (1992) 30 Economic Inquiry 225.

Green, E.J. and R.H. Porter 'Noncooperative collusion under imperfect price information' (1984) 52 Econometrica 87.

Greenfield, J. 'The use of experts from the plaintiff's perspective' (1992) 60 Antitrust Law Journal 339.

Grether, E.T. 'Industrial organization: past history and future problems' (1970) 60 American Economic Review 83.

Griffin, J.M. 'An inside look at a cartel at work: common characteristics of international cartels' (Presentation at American Bar Association 48th Annual Spring Meeting, April 6 2000) < http://www.usdoj.gov/atr/public/speeches/4489.htm> (25 May 2005).

Grillo, M. 'Collusion and facilitating practices: a new perspective in antitrust analysis' (2002) 14 European Journal of Law and Economics 151.

Grossman, G.M. and C. Shapiro 'Research joint ventures: an antitrust analysis' (1986) 2 Journal of Law, Economics and Organization 315.

Habermas, J. 'The idea of the theory of knowledge as social theory' in J. Habermas (translated by J. Shapiro) *Knowledge and Human Interests* (2nd edn, Polity, Cambridge, 1987).

Häckner, J. 'Collusive pricing in markets for vertically differentiated products' (1994) 12 International Journal of Industrial Organization 155.

Häckner, J. 'Optimal symmetric punishments in a Bertrand differentiated products duopoly' (1996) 14 International Journal of Industrial Organization 611.

Hahn, F.H. 'Some adjustment problems' (1970) 38 Econometrica 1.

Hahn, F.H. 'The next hundred years' (1991) 101 Economic Journal 47.

Haltiwanger, J. and J.E. Harrington Jr 'The impact of cyclical demand movements on collusive behavior' (1991) 22 RAND Journal of Economics 89.

Harberger, A. 'Monopoly and resource allocation' (1954) 44 American Economic Review 77.

Harrington Jr, J.E. 'Collusion among asymmetric firms: the case of differentiated discount factors' (1989a) 7 International Journal of Industrial Organization 289.

Harrington Jr, J.E. 'Collusion and predation under (almost) free entry' (1989b) 7 International Journal of Industrial Organization 381.

Harrington Jr, J.E. 'Cartel pricing dynamics with cost variability and endogenous buyer detection' (paper presented at Wissenschaftszentrum Berlin Conference on Collusion and Cartels, 22 October 2004).

Harris, B.C. and C.G. Veljanovski 'Critical loss analysis: its growing use in competition law' (2003) 24 European Competition Law Review 213.

Haskel, J. and P. Scaramozzino 'Do other firms matter in oligopolies?' (1997) 45 Journal of Industrial Economics 27.

Haupt, H. 'Collective dominance under Article 82 E.C and E.C merger control in the light of the Airtours judgement' (2002) 23 European Competition Law Review 434.

Hausman, D.M. *The Inexact and Separate Science of Economics* (Cambridge University Press, Cambridge, 1992).

Hawk, B. and G.A. Motta 'Oligopolies and collective dominance: a solution in search of a problem' (Treviso Conference on Antitrust Between EC Law and National Law, Fordham Law Legal Studies Research Paper number (1301693) 2008) 59.

Hawkins, K. *Law as Last Resort: Prosecution Decision-Making in a Regulatory Agency* (Oxford University Press, Oxford, 2002).

Hay, D. 'The assessment: competition policy' (1993) 9 Oxford Review of Economic Policy 1.

Hay, G.A. and D. Kelley 'An empirical survey of price fixing conspiracies' (1974) 17 Journal of Law and Economics 13.

Heggestad, A.A. and S.A. Rhoades 'Multi-market interdependence and local market competition in banking' (1978) 60 Review of Economics and Statistics 523.

Heitzer, B. 'Economic assessment in competition enforcement: developments in France and Germany' (Presentation to CRA International, Annual Conference Economic Developments in European Competition Policy, 3 December 2008).

Henriques, I. 'Cooperative and noncooperative R&D in duopoly with spillovers: comment' (1990) 80 American Economic Review 638.

Hicks, J. 'Annual survey of economic theory: the theory of monopoly' (1935) 3 Econometrica 1.

Hogendorn, C. 'Tacit collusion in capacity investment: the role of capacity exchanges' (2007) 7 B.E Journal of Theoretical Economics 1.

Hopt, K.J. 'Restrictive trade practices and juridification: a comparative law study' in G. Teubner (ed.) *Juridification of Social Spheres: A Comparative Analysis in the Areas of Labor, Corporate, Antitrust and Social Welfare Law* (Walter de Gruyter, Berlin, 1987).

Hörner, J. and J. Jamison 'Collusion with (almost) no information' (2007) 38 RAND Journal of Economics 804.

Hovenkamp, H. 'Fact, value and theory in antitrust adjudication' (1987) 5 Duke Law Journal 897.

Huck, S., H. Normann and J. Oechssler 'Two are few and four are many: number effects in experimental oligopolies' (2004) 53 Journal of Economic Behaviour and Organization 440.

Hutter, M. 'How the economy talks the law into co-evolution: An exercise in autopoietic social theory' in G. Teubner and A. Febbrajo (eds) *State, Law, and Economy as Autopoietic Systems: Regulation and Autonomy in a New Perspective* (Dott. A. Giuffre, Milan, 1992) 265.

International Competition Network 'The role of economists and economic evidence in merger analysis' (working paper presented at the International Competition Network First Annual Conference, September 2002) <http://www.internationalcompetitionnetwork.org/Role%20of%20Economists.pdf > (2 July 2003).

International Competition Network 'Coordinated effects analysis under international merger regimes' (working paper presented at the International Competition Network Annual Conference, April 2004) <http://www.internationalcompetitionnetwork.org/seoul/amg_chap4_coordinated.pdf> (1 July 2004).

Ivaldi, M., B. Jullien, P. Rey, P. Seabright and J. Tirole 'The economics of tacit collusion', Institut d'Économie Industrielle (IDEI) Toulouse 'Final report

prepared for DG Competition European Commission, March 2003' <http://europa.eu.int/comm/competition/mergers/review/the_economics_of_tacit_collusion_en.pdf> (12 May 2004).
Jacquemin, A. and M.E. Slade 'Cartels, collusion and horizontal merger' in R. Schmalensee and R.D. Willig (eds) *Handbook of Industrial Organization, Volume 1* (Elsevier Science Publishers, Amsterdam, 1989).
Jacquemin, A., T. Nambu and I. Dewez 'A dynamic analysis of export cartels: the Japanese case' (1981) 91 Economic Journal 685.
James, C.A. 'Rediscovering coordinated effects' (paper presented at the American Bar Association Annual Meeting Section of Antitrust Law Washington, DC, 13 August 2002) <http://www.usdoj.gov/atr/public/speeches/200124.htm> (25 May 2005).
Jans, I. and D.I. Rosenbaum 'Multimarket contact and pricing: evidence from the U.S. cement industry' (1996) 15 International Journal of Industrial Organization 391.
Jasanoff, S. *Science at the Bar: Law, Science, and Technology in America* (Harvard University Press, Cambridge, MA, 1995).
Jasanoff, S. 'Beyond epistemology: relativism and engagement in the politics of science' (1996a) 26 Social Studies of Science 393.
Jasanoff, S. 'Research subpoenas and the sociology of knowledge' (1996b) 59 Law and Contemporary Problems 95.
Jenny, F. 'Competition law enforcement: is economic expertise necessary?' in B. Hawk (ed.) *International Antitrust Law and Policy: Fordham Corporate Law 1998* (Juris Publishing, New York, 1998) 185.
Jenny, F., A.I. Gavil, L.H. Röller and G.J. Werden 'Economics experts before authorities and courts roundtable' in B. Hawk (ed.) *International Antitrust Law & Policy: Fordham Corporate Law 2005* (Juris Publishing, New York, 2006) 615.
Jimenez-Martín, S. and P.L. Marín 'Multimarket contact in pharmaceutical markets' (Working Paper 215/2004, DIW Berlin, 12 March 2004) <http://www.diw.de/english/produkte/veranstaltungen/earie2004/papers/docs/2004-215-V01.pdf> (25 May 2005).
Jones, A. 'Woodpulp: concerted practice and/or conscious parallelism' (1993) 14 European Competition Law Review 273.
Jones, A. and B. Sufrin *EC Competition Law* (Oxford University Press, Oxford, 2001).
Jones, C.A.G. *Expert Witnesses* (Clarendon Press, Oxford, 1994).
Joo, T.W. 'Contract, property and the role of metaphor in corporations law' (2001) 35 UC Davis Law Review 779.
Jorde, T.M. and D.J. Teece 'Innovation and cooperation: implications for competition and antitrust' (1990) 4 Journal of Economic Perspectives 75.
Joskow, P.L. 'Firm decision-making processes and oligopoly theory' (1975) 65 American Economic Review 270.

Jullien, B. and P. Rey 'Resale price maintenance and collusion' (working paper, GREMAQ and IDEI Université des Sciences Sociales Toulouse 1, 9 May 2000) <http://www.cepr.org/pubs/dps/DP2553.asp> (25 May 2005).

Kamien, M.I., E. Muller and I. Zang 'Research joint venture and R&D cartels' (1992) 82 American Economic Review 1293.

Kandori, M. 'Correlated demand shocks and price wars during booms' (1991) 58 Review of Economic Studies 171.

Kandori, M. 'The use of information in repeated games with imperfect monitoring' (1992) 59 Review of Economic Studies 581.

Kandori, M. 'Introduction to repeated games with private monitoring' (2002) 102 Journal of Economic Theory 1.

Kandori, M. and H. Matsushima 'Private observation, communication and collusion' (1998) 66 Econometrica 627.

Kaneko, M. 'Some remarks on the folk-theorem in game theory' (1982) 3 Mathematical Social Sciences 281.

Kaplan, D.P. 'The nuts and bolts of antitrust analysis: some thoughts on how to develop the facts' (1996) 17 Managerial and Decision Economics 179.

Karlsson, J. 'Clearance of near-duopoly' (2006) 27 European Competition Law Review 514.

Karp, L.S. and J.M. Perloff 'Dynamic oligopoly in the rice export market' (1989) 71 Review of Economics and Statistics 462.

Karp, L.S. and J.M. Perloff 'A dynamic model of oligopoly in the coffee export market' (1993) 75 American Journal of Agricultural Economics 448.

Kattan, J. and W.R. Vigdor 'Game theory and the analysis of collusion in conspiracy and merger cases' (1997) 5 George Mason Law Review 441.

Katz, M.L. and J.A. Ordover 'R&D cooperation and competition' (1990) Brookings Papers on Microeconomics 137.

Katzenbach, E., E. Kottman and R. Krueger 'New industrial economics and experiences from European merger control – new lessons about collective dominance?' (Study prepared for the European Commission Office of Official Publications, Luxembourg, 1995).

Katzmann, R.A. *Regulatory Bureaucracy: The Federal Trade Commission and Antitrust Policy* (MIT Press, Cambridge, MA, 1980).

Kauper, T.E. 'Antitrust in 1992: the year of the storyteller' (1993) 61 Antitrust Law Journal 347.

Keynes, J.M. 'Introduction to the series' in E.A.G. Robinson *The Structure of Competitive Industry* (Nisbet & Co, London, 1931).

Keynes, J.N. *The Scope and Method of Political Economy* (Macmillan, London, 1930).

Klamer, A. 'Academic dogs' in D. Colander and R. Brenner (eds) *Educating Economists* (University of Michigan Press, Ann Arbor, 1992).

Klamer, A. and D.N. McCloskey 'Economics in the human conversation' in

A. Klamer, D.N. McCloskey and R.M. Solow (eds) *The Consequences of Economic Rhetoric* (Cambridge University Press, Cambridge, 1988).

Klein, P.A. 'How should economists do economics? A pragmatic perspective' in S.G. Medema and W.J. Samuels (eds) *Foundations of Research in Economics: How Do Economists Do Economics?* (Edward Elgar, Cheltenham, UK and Brookfield, USA, 1996).

Klemperer, P. 'How (not) to run auctions: the European 3G telecom auctions' (2002a) 46 European Economic Review 829.

Klemperer, P. 'Using and abusing economic theory: lessons from auction design' (Alfred Marshall Lecture to the European Economic Association, 14 October 2002b) <http://www.nuff.ox.ac.uk/users/klemperer/usingandabusing.pdf> (23 October 2002).

Klemperer, P. 'Bidding markets' Occasional Paper No.1, UK Competition Commission (2005) <http://www.nuff.ox.ac.uk/users/klemperer/biddingmarkets.pdf> (15 October 2005).

Klevorick, A.K. 'Law and economic theory: an economist's view' in A.I. Ogus and C.G. Veljanovski *Readings in the Economics of Law and Regulation* (Clarendon Press, Oxford, 1984).

Kloosterhuis, E. 'Joint dominance and the interaction between firms' (2001) 22 European Competition Law Review 79.

Kobayashi, B.H. 'Game theory and antitrust: a post-mortem' (1997) George Mason Law Review 411.

Kokkoris, I. 'The reform of the European Control Merger Regulation in the aftermath of the Airtours case – the eagerly expected debate: SLC v Dominance test' (2005) 26 European Competition Law Review 37.

Kokkoris, I. 'The development of the concept of collective dominance in the ECMR. From its inception to its current status' (2007) 30 World Competition 419.

Korah, V. 'The control of mergers under the EEC Competition Law' (1987) 8 European Competition Law Review 239.

Korah, V. 'Gencor v Commission: collective dominance' (1999) 20 European Competition Law Review 337.

Kovacic, W.E. 'The influence of economics on antitrust law' (1992) 30 Economic Inquiry 294.

Kovacic, W.E. 'The identification and proof of horizontal agreements under the antitrust laws' (Spring 1993) Antitrust Bulletin 5.

Kovacic, W.E. and C. Shapiro 'Antitrust policy: a century of economic and legal thinking' (2000) 14 Journal of Economic Perspectives 43.

Kovacic, W.E., R.C. Marshall, L.M. Marx and S.P. Schulenberg 'Coordinated effects in merger review: quantifying the payoffs from collusion' in B. Hawk (ed.) *International Antitrust Law & Policy: Fordham Corporate Law 2006* (Juris Publishing, New York, 2007).

Kreps, D.M. *Game Theory and Economic Modelling* (Clarendon Press, Oxford, 1990).

Kreps, D.M. and J.A. Scheinkman 'Quantity precommitment and Bertrand competition yield Cournot outcomes' 14 (1983) Bell Journal of Economics 326.

Kroes, N. 'Preliminary thoughts on policy review of Article 82' (Speech at the Fordham Corporate Law Institute, New York, 23 September 2005).

Kroes, N. 'Taking competition seriously – anti-trust reform in Europe' (paper presented at the International Bar Association/European Commission Conference 'Antitrust reform in Europe: a year in practice', 10 March 2005) <http://www.ibanet.org/images/downloads/Neelie_Kroes_Speech_2005_Mar10_Brussels_IBA_&_EC_Antitrust_Conference.pdf> (25 May 2005).

Krüger, R. and L. Papadias 'Collective dominance in recent competition cases and the Guidelines' (paper presented at DG Competition Conference on the Economics of Antitrust in the Telecommunications Sector, Brussels, 16 September 2002).

Kühn, K.U. 'An economists' guide through the joint dominance jungle' (Research Paper No. 02-014, Michigan Law and Economics, 2001a) <http://www.ssrn.com/abstract_id=349521> (25 May 2005).

Kühn, K.U. 'Fighting collusion' (2001b) 16 Economic Policy 167.

Kühn, K.U. 'Closing Pandora's box? Joint dominance after the "Airtours" judgment' (Research Paper No. 02-013, Michigan Law and Economics, 2002) <http://www.ssrn.com/abstract_id=349521> (16 March 2005).

Kühn, K.U. 'Collusion theory in search of robust themes: A comment on Switgard Feuerstein's survey' (2005) 5 Journal of Industry, Competition and Trade 207.

Kuhn, T. 'Metaphor in science' in A. Ortony (ed.) *Metaphor and Thought* (2nd edn, Cambridge University Press, Cambridge, 1993).

Laffont, J.J., P. Rey and J. Tirole 'Network competition I: overview and nondiscriminatory pricing' (1998) 29 RAND Journal of Economics 1.

Lambertini, L. 'Prisoners' Dilemma in duopoly (super) games' (1997) 77 Journal of Economic Theory 181.

Lambertini, L., S. Poddar and D. Sasaki 'Standardization and the stability of collusion' (1998) 58 Economic Letters 303.

Lambson, V.E. 'Optimal penal codes in price-setting supergames with capacity constraints' (1987) 54 Review of Economic Studies 385.

Lambson, V.E. 'Optimal penal codes in nearly symmetric Bertrand supergames with capacity constraints' (1995) 24 Journal of Mathematical Economics 1.

Leedy, M. 'The 1992 US Horizontal Merger Guidelines and some comparisons with EC enforcement policy' (1993) 14 European Competition Law Review 15.

Legal, H. 'Standards of proof and standards of judicial review in EU competition law' in B. Hawk (ed.) *International Antitrust Law & Policy: Fordham Corporate Law 2005* (Juris Publishing, New York, 2006) 107.

Leontief, W. 'Theoretical assumptions and nonobserved facts' (1971) 61 American Economic Review 1.

Leontief, W. 'Academic economics' (1982) 217 Science 104.

Levenstein, M.C. 'Price wars and the stability of collusion: a study of the pre-World War I bromine industry' (1997) 45 Journal of Industrial Economics 117.

Levenstein, M.C. and V.Y. Suslow 'What determines cartel success?' (working paper No. 02-001, University of Michigan Business School, 31 January 2002) <http://ssrn.com/abstract=299415> (25 May 2005).

Lever, J. 'UK economic regulation: use and abuse of the law' (1992) 13 European Competition Law Review 55.

Lever, J. and P. Lasok 'Mergers and joint ventures in the EEC' in *Yearbook of European Law* (Oxford University Press, Oxford, 1988) 121.

Lexecon 'Collective dominance and capacity coordination' Competition memo 31 January 2002 < http://www.lexecon.co.uk/assets/nskog_dominance.pdf > (20 August 2002).

Lexecon 'After the *Airtours* Appeal' Competition memo, June 2002 http://www.lexecon.co.uk/assets/Airtours_Appeal.pdf (16 September 2005).

Lieberman, M. 'Postentry investment and market structure in the chemical processing industry' (1987) 18 RAND Journal of Economics 533.

List, J.A. and S.D. Levitt 'What do laboratory experiments tell us about the real world?' (NBER Working Paper, 20 September 2005). <http://pricetheory.uchicago.edu/levitt/Papers/LevittList2005.pdf> (14 March 2006).

Lopatka, J.E. and W.H. Page 'Economic authority and the limits of expertise in antitrust cases' (2005) 90 Cornell Law Review 617.

Lowe, P. 'Review of the EC Merger Regulation – forging a way ahead' (paper presented at the European Merger Control Conference, Brussels, 8 November 2002).

Luhmann, N. *Rechtssystem und Rechtsdogmatik* (Kolhammer, Stuttgart, 1974).

Luhmann, N. *A Sociological Theory of Law* (Routledge & Kegan Paul, London, 1985).

Luhmann, N. 'The autopoeisis of social systems' in F. Geyer and J. Zouwen (eds) *Sociocybernetic Paradoxes* (Sage Publishers, London, 1986) 172.

Luhmann, N. 'Law as a social system' (1988) 83 Northwestern University Law Review 136.

Lynch, M. and S. Jasanoff 'Contested identities: science, law and forensic practice' (1998) 28 Social Studies of Science 681.

Lynk, W.J. 'Interpreting rising concentration: the case of beer' (1984) 57 Journal of Business 43.

Machlup, F. *Methodology of Economics and Other Social Sciences* (Academic Press, New York, 1978).

Malueg, D.A. 'Collusive behavior and partial ownership of rivals' (1992) 10 International Journal of Industrial Organization 27.

Mandel, M.J. 'Going for gold: economists as expert witnesses' (1999) 13 Journal of Economic Perspectives 113.

Mann, H.M., J.W. Meehan and G.A. Ramsay 'Market structure and excess capacity: a look at some evidence' (1979) 61 Review of Economics and Statistics 156.

Mannheim, K. *Ideology and Utopia: Collected Works, Volume One* (Routledge, London, 1936).

Markovits, R.S. 'Antitrust: alternative to delegalization' in G. Teubner (ed.) *Juridification of Social Spheres: A Comparative Analysis in the Areas of Labor, Corporate, Antitrust and Social Welfare Law* (Walter de Gruyter, Berlin, 1987).

Marshall, R. 'Bidder collusion' (paper presented at Wissenschaftszentrum Berlin Conference on Collusion and Cartels, 22 October 2004).

Marshall, R.C. and L.M. Marx 'Bidder collusion' (2007) 133 Journal of Economic Theory 374.

Martin, S. 'Endogenous firm efficiency in a Cournot principal–agent model' (1993) 59 Journal of Economic Theory 445.

Martin, S. 'R&D joint ventures and tacit product market collusion' (1995) 11 European Journal of Political Economy 733.

Martin, S. 'Competition policy, collusion, and tacit collusion' (2006) 24 International Journal of Industrial Organization 1299.

Martin, S.J. and P.L. Marin 'Multimarket contact in pharmaceutical markets' (paper presented at the DIW Berlin 31st conference of the European Association for Research in Industrial Economics (EARIE), 5 September 2004). <http://www.diw.de/english/produkte/veranstaltungen/earie2004/papers/docs/2004–215-V01.pdf> (15 March 2005).

Mason, C.F., O.R. Phillips and C. Nowell 'Duopoly behaviour in asymmetric markets: an experimental evaluation' (1992) 74 Review of Economics and Statistics 662.

Massey, P. and M. McDowell 'Joint dominance and tacit collusion: an analysis of the Irish Vodafone/O2 case and the implications for competition and regulatory policy' (UCD School of Economics Working Paper 2008) 1.

Masso, J. and R.W. Rosenthal 'More on the "anti-folk theorem"' (1989) 18 Journal of Mathematical Economics 281.

Mayer, T. *Truth Versus Precision in Economics* (Edward Elgar, Aldershot, UK and Brookfield, US, 1993).

Mayer, T. *Doing Economic Research* (Edward Elgar, Aldershot, UK and Brookfield, US, 1995).

Mazzarotto, N. 'Retail mergers and buyer power' (Working Paper CCR 04-3, Centre for Competition and Regulation CCR 2004) <http://www.ccp.uea.ac.uk/public_files/workingpapers/ccr04-3.pdf> (25 May 2005).

McAfee, R.P. and J. McMillan 'Bidding rings' (1992) 82 American Economic Review 579.

McChesney, F.S. *Economic Inputs, Legal Outputs* (John Wiley & Sons, Chichester, 1996a).

McChesney, F.S. 'The role of economists in modern antitrust: an overview and summary' (1996b) 17 Managerial and Decision Economics 119.

McChesney, F.S. and W.F. Shughart II *The Causes and Consequences of Antitrust: The Public Choice Perspective* (University of Chicago Press, Chicago, 1995).

McCloskey, D.N. *If You're So Smart: The Narrative of Economic Expertise* (University of Chicago Press, Chicago, 1990).

McCloskey, D.N. *Knowledge and Persuasion in Economics* (Cambridge University Press, Cambridge, 1994).

McCloskey, D.N. *The Rhetoric of Economics* (2nd edn, University of Wisconsin Press, Madison, 1998).

McCurdy, G. 'How does Brussels really work?: major procedural issues for complainants and respondents in Article 81 and 82 investigations' (Corporate Attorney Litigation and Competition Law Microsoft presentation to the Association of Counsel) <http://www.acca.com/chapters/program/gcca/brussels.pdf> (25 May 2005).

McCutcheon, B. 'Do meetings in smoke-filled rooms facilitate collusion?' (1997) 105 Journal of Political Economy 330.

McGregor, L. 'The future for the control of oligopolies following *Compagnie Maritime Belge*' (2001) 22 European Competition Law Review 434.

McMillan, J. 'Selling spectrum rights' (1994) 8 Journal of Economic Perspectives 145.

Medema, S.G. and W.J. Samuels *Foundations of Research in Economics: How Do Economists Do Economics?* (Edward Elgar, Cheltenham, UK and Brookfield, US, 1996).

Mehta, K. 'Comments on Switgard Feuerstein's "Collusion in Industrial Economics – A survey"' (2005) 5 Journal of Industry, Competition and Trade 217.

Mehta, K. and S. Santamato 'On the concepts of collusion and joint dominance' (2002) Butterworths Merger Review 1.

Merton, R.K. 'Paradigm for the sociology of knowledge' in J.E. Curtis and J.W. Petras (eds) *The Sociology of Knowledge: A Reader* (Gerald Duckworth & Co, London, 1970) 342.

Miklos-Thal, J. 'Optimal collusion under cost asymmetry' (MRPA Working Paper 11044 4, University of Munich, June 2008).

Mill, J.S. *Principles of Political Economy: with Some of their Applications to Social Philosophy* (7th edn, Longmans Green & Co, London, 1923).

Milne, R.A. and J.E. Pace III 'The scope of expert testimony on the subject of conspiracy in a Sherman Act case' (2003) 17 Antitrust 36.

Møllgaard, P. and P.B. Overgaard 'Market transparency: a mixed blessing?' (Discussion Paper 1999-15, University of Copenhagen Centre for Industrial Economics CIE, 2000) <http://www.econ.ku.dk/CIE/Discussion%20Papers/1999/Pdf%20files/9915.pdf> (25 May 2005).

Monti, G. 'The scope of collective dominance under Article 82 EC' (2001) 38 Common Market Law Review 131.

Monti, M. 'Analytical framework of merger review' (paper presented at the International Competition Network Inaugural Conference, 28 September 2002) <http://www.internationalcompetitionnetwork.org/speech_ mmonti.pdf > (25 May 2005).

Monti, M. 'European competition policy: quo vadis?' (paper presented at the XX International Forum on European Competition Policy, Brussels, 10 April 2003) <http://europa.eu.int/rapid/pressReleasesAction.do?reference=SPEECH/03/195&format=HTML&aged=1&language=EN&guiLanguage=en> (15 October 2005)

Monti, M. 'A reformed competition policy: achievements and challenges for the future' (Competition Policy Newsletter, Competition Directorate-General of the European Commission, 2004).

Morris, D. 'Dominant firm behaviour under UK Competition law' (paper presented to the Fordham Corporate Law Institute Thirtieth Annual Conference on International Antitrust Law and Policy, 23–24 October 2003).

Morris, P. 'The relationship between industrial sales prices and concentration of natural gas pipelines' (Bureau of Economics Working Paper No. 168, Federal Trade Commission, November 1988).

Morrison, S.A. and C. Winston 'The dynamics of airline pricing and competition' (1990) 80 American Economic Review 389.

Motta, M. 'E.C. merger policy and the Airtours case' (2000) 21 European Competition Law Review 199.

Motta, M. *Competition Policy: Theory and Practice* (Cambridge University Press, Cambridge, 2004).

Mulkay, M. 'Knowledge and utility: implications for the sociology of knowledge' (1979) 9 Social Studies of Science 69.

Muris, T.J 'Economics and antitrust' (1997) 5 George Mason Law Review 303.

Nagin, S.E. 'Selection, use and pay of an economist in an antitrust case' (1981) 35 University of Miami Law Review 255.

Nash, J.F. 'Non-cooperative games' (1951) 54 Annals of Mathematics 286.
NERA 'Fixing remedies in European merger control' Competition Policy Insights, July/August 2002.
NERA 'The increasing use of empirical methods in European merger enforcement: lessons from the past and a look ahead' Competition Policy Insights, Spring 2004 <http://www.nera.com/NewsletterIssue/Insights_Spring 20Edition202004.pdf> (25 May 2005).
NERA 'Twelfth St.Gallen International Competition Law Forum' Press Release advertising NERA Events <http://www.nera.com/event.asp?e_ID=2372> (25 May 2005).
Neumark, D. and S.A Sharpe. 'Market structure and the nature of price rigidity: evidence from the market for consumer deposits' (1992) 107 Quarterly Journal of Economics 657.
Neven, D. '"Collusion" under Art 81 and the merger regulation' (paper presented at the 3rd Nordic Competition Policy Conference, Stockholm, 11 September 2000).
Neven, D. 'Competition economics and antitrust in Europe' (2006) 21 Economic Policy 1.
Neven, D., R. Nuttall and P. Seabright *Mergers in Daylight: The Economics and Politics of European Merger Control* (Centre for Economic Policy Research, London, 1993).
Neven, D., P. Papandropoulos and P. Seabright *Trawling for Minnows: European Competition Policy and Agreements between Firms* (Centre for Economic Policy Research, London, 1998).
Newberg, J.A. 'The narrative construction of antitrust' (2003) 12 Southern California Interdisciplinary Law Journal 181.
Newmark, C.M. 'Price-concentration studies: there you go again' (paper presented at the DOJ/FTC Merger Workshop Concentration and Market Shares Panel, 14 February 2004) < http://www.ftc.gov/bc/mergerenforce/presentations/040217newmark.pdf> (3 June 2005).
Niels, G. 'Collective dominance: more than just oligopolistic interdependence' (2001) 22 European Competition Law Review 168.
Nikpay, A. and F. Houwen 'Tour de force or a little local turbulence? A heretical view on the Airtours judgment' (2003) 24 European Competition Law Review 193.
Nilssen, T. 'On the consistency of merger policy' (1997) 45 Journal of Industrial Economics 89.
Nocke, V. and L. White 'Do vertical mergers facilitate collusion?' (Discussion Paper No 4186, Centre for Economic Policy Research, 2004) <http:www.cepr.org/pubs/dps/DP4186.asp> (25 May 2005).
Nocke, V. and L. White 'Do vertical mergers facilitate collusion?' (2007) 97 American Economic Review 1321.

Normann, H.T. 'Vertical integration, raising rivals' costs and upstream collusion' (working paper, Max Planck Institute for Research on Collective Goods, 30 July 2008) <http://ssrn.com/abstract=1275303>.

OECD Directorate for Financial, Fiscal and Enterprise Affairs Committee on Competition Law and Policy 'Oligopoly' (unclassified document DAFFE/CLP(99), 25 October 1999) <http://www.oecd.org/dataoecd/35/34/1920526.pdf> (25 May 2005).

OECD Directorate for Financial, Fiscal and Enterprise Affairs Committee on Competition Law and Policy 'Substantive criteria used for the assessment of mergers' (DAFFE/COMP(2003), 11 February 2003) <http://www.oecd.org/dataoecd/54/3/2500227.pdf> (25 May 2005).

Office of Fair Trading 'Quantitative techniques in competition analysis' (Research paper 17, prepared by LECG October 1999) <http://www.oft.gov.uk/NR/rdonlyres/FAF287E3-511B-4055-81CE-9AD2042FA57F/0/oft266.pdf> (6 March 2002).

Office of Fair Trading 'Merger appraisal in oligopolostic markets' (Research paper 19, prepared by NERA, November 1999) <http://www.oft.gov.uk/NR/rdonlyres/ADBFFE6D-CB71-45D5-8280-857FC9A5F732/0/oft267.pdf> (16 January 2003).

Office of Fair Trading 'Market investigation references: A consultation paper' (OFT 501, July 2002).

Office of Fair Trading 'Assessing profitability in competition policy analysis' (Economic discussion paper 6, prepared by Oxera, July 2003) <http://www.oft.gov.uk/NR/rdonlyres/C410132C-F322-47CD-8AFA-38B13247A0AE /0/oft657.pdf> (25 May 2005).

Office of Fair Trading 'Predicting cartels' (Economic discussion paper 19, prepared by P.A. Grout and S. Sonderegger, March 2005) <http://www.oft.gov.uk/NR/rdonlyres/4E9FFDC4-31F4-4F7D-896E-FFE635A136F3/0/OFT773.pdf> (25 May 2005).

Ordover, J.A., G. Saloner and S.C. Salop 'Equilibrium vertical foreclosure' (1990) 80 American Economic Review 127.

Ortony, A. 'Metaphor, language, and thought' in A. Ortony (ed.) *Metaphor and Thought* (2nd edn, Cambridge University Press, Cambridge, 1993).

Osborne, M.J. and C. Pitchik 'Cartels, profits and excess capacity' (1987) 28 International Economic Review 413.

Østerdal, L.P. 'A note on the stability of collusion in differentiated oligopolies' (2003) 57 Research in Economics 53.

Overd, A. 'After the Airtours appeal' (2002) 23 European Competition Law Review 375.

Palmer. J. 'Some economic conditions conducive to collusion' (1978) 6 Journal of Economic Inquiry 29.

Parker, P.M. and L.H. Röller 'Collusive conduct in duopolies: multimarket contact and cross-ownership in the mobile telephone industry' (1997) 28 RAND Journal of Economics 304.

Parret, L. 'Sense and nonsense of rules of proof in cartel cases: how to reconcile a more economics-based approach to competition law with more attention for rules on proof?' (2008) 4 European Competition Journal 169.

Parsons, T. 'An approach to the sociology of knowledge' in J.E. Curtis and J.W. Petras (eds) *The Sociology of Knowledge: A Reader* (Gerald Duckworth & Co, London, 1970) 282.

Paul, D. 'An insider's look at the new horizontal merger guidelines' (1992) 6 Antitrust 6.

Pautler, P. 'Evidence on mergers and acquisitions' (Working Paper No. 243, Federal Trade Commission, September 2001). <http://www.ftc.gov/be/workpapers/wp243.pdf> (15 October 2005).

Pearce, D.G. 'Renegotiation-proof equilibria: collective rationality and intertemporal cooperation' (Discussion Paper No 855, Cowles Foundation for Research in Economics at Yale University, 1987).

Peeperkorn, L. 'Competition policy implications from game theory: an evaluation of the Commission's policy on information exchange' (paper presented at the CEPR/European University Institute Workshop on Recent Developments in the Design and Implementation of Competition Policy, 29 November 1996) < http://europa.eu.int/comm/competition/speeches/text/sp1996_057b_en.pdf> (25 May 2005).

Peltzman, S. 'The gains and losses from industrial concentration' (1977) 20 Journal of Law and Economics 229.

Peltzman, S. 'The Handbook of Industrial Organization' (1991) 99 Journal of Political Economy 201.

Pera, A. 'Changing views of competition, economic analysis and EC antitrust law' (2008) 4 European Competition Journal 127.

Perlman, M. 'Knowledge and ignorance in economics' (1978) 16 Journal of Economic Literature 582.

Perry, M.K. and R.H. Porter 'Oligopoly and the incentive for horizontal merger' (1985) 75 American Economic Review 219.

Pesendorfer, M. 'A study of collusion in first-price auctions' (2000) 67 Review of Economic Studies 381.

Phelps Brown, E.H. 'The underdevelopment of economics' (1972) 82 Economic Journal 1.

Pindyck, R.S. 'The cartelization of world commodity markets' (1979) 69 American Economic Review 154.

Pope, D. 'Some reflections on Italian Flat Glass' (1993) 14 European Competition Law Review 172.

Porter, R.H. 'Optimal cartel trigger price strategies' (1983) 29 Journal of Economic Theory 313.

Porter, R.H. 'A study of cartel stability: the Joint Executive Committee, 1880–1886' (1983b) 15 Bell Journal of Economics 301.

Porter, R.H. 'On the incidence and duration of price wars' (1985) 33 Journal of Industrial Economics 415.

Porter, R.H. 'A note on tacit collusion under demand uncertainty' (1986) 19 Canadian Journal of Economics 556.

Porter, R.H. 'Detecting collusion' (2005a) 25 Review of Industrial Organization 147.

Porter, R.H. 'Collusion in industrial economics: a comment' (2005b) 5 Journal of Industry, Competition and Trade 231.

Porter, R.H. and J.D. Zona 'Detection of bid rigging in procurement auctions' (1993) 101 Journal of Political Economy 518.

Porter, R.H. and J.D. Zona 'Ohio school milk markets: an analysis of bidding' (1999) 30 RAND Journal of Economics 263.

Posner, R.A. 'Oligopoly and the antitrust laws: a suggested approach' (1968–69) 21 Stan. L Rev 1562.

Posner, R.A. 'A statistical study of antitrust enforcement' (1970) 13 Journal of Law and Economics 365.

Posner, R.A. *Antitrust Law: An Economic Perspective* (University of Chicago, Chicago, 1976).

Posner, R.A. 'The law and economics of the expert witness' (1999) 13 Journal of Economic Perspectives 91.

Preece, S. 'Compagnie Maritime Belge: missing the boat' (2000) 21 European Competition Law Review 388.

Prokop, J. 'Process of dominant-cartel formation' (1999) 17 International Journal of Industrial Organization 241.

Rabassa, V. 'Joint ventures as a mechanism that may favour co-ordination: an analysis of the aluminum and music mergers' (2004) 24 European Competition Law Review 771.

Radner, R. 'Repeated partnership games with imperfect monitoring and no discounting' (1986) 53 Review of Economic Studies 43.

Raith, M. 'Product differentiation, uncertainty and the stability of collusion' (STICERD Economics of Industry Paper Number 16, London School of Economics, 1996) <http://sticerd.lse.ac.uk/dps/ei/ei16.pdf> (25 May 2005).

Rapp, R.T. 'The application of economic argument in anti-trust cases: recent American trends' (1988) 9 European Competition Law Review 207.

Raskovich, A. 'Competition or collusion? Negotiating discounts off posted prices' (2007) 25 International Journal of Industrial Organization 341.

RBB Economics 'Airtours/Firstchoice: CFI holds Commission to Account' (RBB Brief, 2 June 2002) < http://www.rbbecon.com/publications/downloads/rbb_brief02.pdf > (16 January 2003).

RBB Economics 'Fine in Theory' (RBB Brief, 9 June 2003) <http://www.rbbecon.com/publications/downloads/rbb_brief09.pdf> (25 May 2005).

RBB Economics 'The Emperor's new clothes? – the role of merger simulation models' (RBB Brief, 12 January 2004) <http://www.rbbecon.com/ publications/downloads/rbb_brief12.pdf> (25 May 2005).

Rees, R. 'Tacit collusion' (1993) 9 Oxford Review of Economic Policy 27.

Rey, P. 'Towards a theory of competition policy' (Working Paper No 121, Institut d'Economie Industrielle (IDEI), Toulouse IDEI 2001).

Rey, P. 'Collective dominance' (paper presented at DG Competition Conference on the Economics of Antitrust in the Telecommunications Sector, Brussels, 16 September 2002).

Reynolds, R.J. and B.R. Snapp 'The competitive effects of partial equity interests and joint ventures' (1986) 4 International Journal of Industrial Organization 141.

Richardson, R. and C. Gordon 'Collective dominance: the third way?' (2001) 22 European Competition Law Review 416.

Ridyard, D. 'An economic perspective on the EC merger regulation' (1990) 11 European Competition Law Review 247.

Ridyard, D. 'Joint dominance and the oligopoly blind spot under the EC merger regulation' (1992) 13 European Competition Law Review 161.

Ridyard, D. 'Economic analysis of single firm and oligopolistic dominance under the European merger regulation' (1994) 5 European Competition Law Review 255.

Ridyard, D. 'The Commission's new horizontal merger guidelines – an economic commentary' (paper presented at European Competition Law Workshops series organised by the Université libre de Bruxelles, 17 February 2004).

Riley, J.G. and W.F. Samuelson 'Optimal auctions' (1981) 71 American Economic Review 381.

Rill, J.F. and H. Rosenblatt 'Coordinated interaction and collective dominance: a remarkable journey towards convergence' in P. Lugard and L. Hancher (eds) *On the Merits: Current Issues in Competition Law and Policy* (Antwerp, Intersentia, 2005) 127–156.

Riordan, M.H. 'Anticompetitive vertical integration by a dominant firm' (1998) 88 American Economic Review 1232.

Robert, G. and C. Hudson 'Past coordination and the Commission notice on the appraisal of horizontal mergers' (2004) 25 European Competition Law Review 163.

Roberts, K. 'Cartel behaviour and adverse selection' (1985) 33 Journal of Industrial Economics 401.

Robinson, J. *The Economics of Imperfect Competition* (2nd edn, Macmillan, London, 1969).

Robson, A.J. and J. McMillan 'Dynamic duopoly under demand uncertainty' (1984) 17 Canadian Journal of Economics 695.

Rodger, B.J. 'Oligopolistic market failure: collective dominance versus complex monopoly' (1995) 16 European Competition Law Review 21.

Röller, L.H. 'Recent economic developments in EU competition policy' (presentation at the Charles River Associates conference on the Role of Economics in Competition Law, Brussels, 26 May 2004) <http://www.crai.com/.%5CAgenda%5CRoller.pdf> (2 June 2005).

Röller, L.H. 'Using economic analysis to strengthen competition policy enforcement in Europe' (presentation at the ECN conference on Modelling European Mergers: Theory, Competition Policy and Case Studies, 21 March 2005) <http://europa.eu.int/comm/competition/speeches/text/sp2005_011 _en.pdf> (26 August 2005).

Röller, L.H. and P.A. Buigues 'The Office of the Chief Competition Economist at the European Commission' (2005) Global Competition Review, June, 3.

Röller, L.H. and F. Steen 'On the workings of a cartel: evidence from the Norwegian cement industry' (Discussion Paper 25/03, Norwegian School of Economics and Business Administration, June 2003) <http://www.nhh.no/sam/res&publ/2003/25.pdf> (25 May 2005).

Röller, L.H. and O. Stehmann 'The year 2005 at DG Competition: the trend towards a more effects-based approach' (2006) 29 Review of Industrial Organization 281.

Rosenbaum, D.I. 'Efficiency v collusion: evidence cast in cement' (1994) 9 Review of Industrial Organization 379.

Rosenberg, A. *Economics: Mathematical Politics or Science of Diminishing Returns?* (University of Chicago Press, Chicago, 1992).

Ross, T. 'Metaphor and paradox' (1989) 23 Georgia Law Review 1053.

Ross, T.W. 'Cartel stability and product differentiation' (1992) 10 International Journal of Industrial Organization 1.

Ross, T.W. and A. Baziliauskas 'Lessening of competition in mergers under the Competition Act: unilateral and interdependence effects' (2000) 33 Canadian Business Law Journal 373.

Rotemberg, J.J. and G. Saloner 'A supergame-theoretic model of price wars during booms' (1986) 76 American Economic Review 390.

Rotemberg, J.J. and G. Saloner 'The cyclical behavior of strategic inventories' (1989) 104 Quarterly Journal of Economics 73.

Roth, A. 'Laboratory vs. field experiments: what can we learn?: comments on Levitt–List paper' (presentation at the ASSA meetings, Boston, 8 January 2006) <http://kuznets.fas.harvard.edu/~aroth/papers/LabVersusField.Roundtable.ASSA.Jan.2006.pdf> (13 March 2006).

Roth, A.E. 'Game theory as a part of empirical economics' (1991) 101 Economic Journal 107.

Rothschild, R. 'Cartel stability when costs are heterogeneous' (1999) 17 International Journal of Industrial Organization 717.

Rubinstein, A. 'Equilibrium in supergames with the overtaking criterion' (1979) 21 Journal of Economic Theory 1.

Rubinstein, A. 'Comments on the interpretation of game theory' (1991) 59 Econometrica 909.

Rubinstein, A. 'A theorist's view of experiments' (2001) 45 European Economic Review 615.

Rubli, I. 'The Advocate-General's opinion in Woodpulp: another setback for the Commission's competition policy' (1993) 14 European Competition Law Review 26.

Sabbatini, P. 'How to simulate the coordinated effect of a merger' Autorità Garante della Concorrenza e del Mercato, Temi e Problemi (2006).

Salinger, M.A. 'Vertical mergers and market foreclosure' (1988) Quarterly Journal of Economics 345.

Salinger, M. 'The concentration–margins relationship reconsidered' (1990) 22 Brookings Papers in Microeconomics 287.

Salop, S. and D.T. Scheffman 'Cost-raising strategies' (1987) 36 Journal of Industrial Economics 19.

Salvanes, K.G., F. Steen and L. Sorgard 'Collude, compete, or both? Deregulation in the Norwegian airline industry' (Discussion Papers 18/98, Norwegian School of Economics and Business Administration, 1998) <http://www.fagbokforlaget.no/konkurransestrategi/download/salvanes-steen-sorgard-collude-240203.pdf> (15 October 2005).

Scheffman, D.T. and M.T. Coleman 'Quantitative analyses of potential competitive effects from a merger' (presentation of 9 June 2003) <http://www.ftc.gov/bc/mergerenforce/presentations/040218scheffman02.pdf> (7 July 2003).

Scheffman, D.T. and M.T. Coleman 'FTC perspectives on the use of econometric analyses in antitrust cases' (FTC presentation of 2002) <http://www.ftc.gov/be/ftcperspectivesoneconometrics.pdf> (15 November 2002).

Scheler, M. 'Occupations and ideologies' in J.E. Curtis and J.W. Petras (eds) *The Sociology of Knowledge: A Reader* (Gerald Duckworth & Co, London, 1970) 170.

Scheffman, D.T. 'Hot topics in economics: using new economic arguments and evidence in antitrust investigations and litigation' (paper presented at the Conference Board 2003 Antitrust Conference, March 2003).

Scheppele, K.L. 'Telling stories' in *Legal Storytelling: Special Issue* (1989) 87 Michigan Law Review 2073.

Scherer, F.M. and D. Ross *Industrial Market Structure and Economic Performance* (3rd edn, Houghton Mifflin, Boston, 1990).

Schinkel, M.P. 'Forensic economics in competition law enforcement' (Amsterdam Center for Law and Economics, Working Paper no.2007–05)

Schinkel, M.P. and J. Tuinstra 'Imperfect competition law enforcement' (2006) 24 International Journal of Industrial Organization 1267.

Schmalensee, R. 'Antitrust and the new industrial economics' (1982) 72 American Economic Review 24.

Schmitz, J. and S.W. Fuller 'Effect of contract disclosure on railroad grain rates: an analysis of corn belt corridors' (1995) 31 Logistics and Transportation Review 97.

Schodermeier, M. 'Collective dominance revisited: an analysis of the EC Commission's new concepts of oligopoly control' (1990) 11 European Competition Law Review 28.

Schön, D.A. 'Generative metaphor: A perspective on problem-setting in social policy' in A. Ortony (ed.) *Metaphor and Thought* (2nd edn, Cambridge University Press, Cambridge, 1993).

Schotter, A. 'You're not making sense, you're just being logical' in S.G. Medema and W.J. Samuels (eds) *Foundations of Research in Economics: How Do Economists Do Economics?* (Edward Elgar, Cheltenham, UK and Brookfield, USA, 1996).

Schulte, M. 'The use of knowledge in the legal system: the relationship between scientific expertise and legal decisions' in N. Stehr (ed.) *The Governance of Knowledge* (Transaction Publishers, London, 2004) 211.

Schultz, C. 'Transparency on the consumer side and tacit collusion' (2005) 49 European Economic Review 279.

Schumpeter, J.A. *History of Economic Analysis* (Routledge, London, 1954).

Schwartz, M. and R. Reynolds 'Contestable markets: an uprising in the theory of industrial structure: comment' (1983) 73 American Economic Review 488.

Schwarze, J. 'Judicial review of European administrative procedure' (2004) 68 Law and Contemporary Problems 85.

Scitovsky, T. 'Ignorance as a source of oligopoly power' (1950) 40 American Economic Review 48.

Seabright, P. 'The ups and downs of the doctrine of collective dominance: using game theory for merger policy' (Presentation to Japan Fair Trade Commission, 20 March 2007).

Selten, R. 'A simple model of imperfect competition where four are few and six are many' (1973) 2 International Journal of Game Theory 141.

Shaffer, S. 'Stable cartels with a Cournot fringe' (Working Paper number 93-8, Federal Reserve Bank of Philadelphia, 1993).

Shaked, A. and J. Sutton 'Multiproduct firms and market structure' (1990) 21 RAND Journal of Economic 45.

Shapin, S. 'Here and everywhere: sociology of scientific knowledge' (1995) 21 Annual Review of Sociology 289.

Shapiro, C. 'Exchange of cost information in oligopoly' (1986) 53 Review of Economic Studies 433.

Shapiro, C. 'The theory of business strategy' (1989a) 20 RAND Journal of Economics 125.
Shapiro, C. 'Theories of oligopoly behavior' in R. Schmalensee and R.D. Willig (eds) *Handbook of Industrial Organization, Volume 1* (Elsevier Science Publishers, Amsterdam, 1989b).
Shapiro, C. 'Navigating the patent thicket: cross licences, patent pools and standard setting' in A. Jaffe, J. Lerner and S. Stern (eds) *Innovation Policy and the Economy, Volume 1* (MIT Press, Cambridge, MA, 2001).
Shubik, M. 'A game theorist looks at the antitrust laws and the automobile industry' (1956) 8 Stanford Law Review 594.
Shubik, M. 'A curmudgeon's guide to microeconomics' (1970) 8 Journal of Economic Literature 405.
Shubik, M. 'Game theory, law, and the concept of competition' (1992) 60 U Cincinnati Law Rev 285.
Sjostrom, W. 'Collusion in ocean shipping: a test of monopoly and empty core models' (1989) 97 Journal of Political Economy 1160.
Sjostrom, W. 'Price discrimination by shipping conferences' (1992) 28 Logistics and Transportation Review 207.
Skrzypacz, A. and H. Hopenhayn 'Tacit collusion in repeated auctions' (2004) 114 Journal of Economic Theory 153.
Slade, M.E. 'Interfirm rivalry in a repeated game: an empirical test of tacit collusion' (1987) 35 Journal of Industrial Economics 499.
Slade, M.E. 'Price wars in price-setting supergames' (1989) 56 Economica 295.
Slade, M.E. 'Cheating on collusive agreements' (1990a) 8 International Journal of Industrial Organization 519.
Slade, M.E. 'Strategic pricing models and interpretation of price-war data' (1990b) 34 European Economic Review 524.
Slade, M.E. 'Vancouver's gasoline-price wars: an empirical exercise in uncovering supergame strategies' (1992) 59 Review of Economic Studies 257.
Sleeuwagen, L. 'On the nature and significance of collusive price leadership' (1986) 4 International Journal of Industrial Organization 177.
Smith, A. *The Wealth of Nations* ed by W. Letwin (Everyman's Library, London, 1975).
Smith, R. and D. Round 'Competition assessment and strategic behaviour' (1998) 4 European Competition Law Review 225.
Soames, T. 'An analysis of the principles of concerted practice and collective dominance: a distinction without a difference' (1996) 17 European Competition Law Review 24.
Solow, R.M. 'Economic history and economics' (1985) 75 American Economic Review 328.
Solow, R.M. 'Comments from inside economics' in A. Klamer, D.N.

McCloskey and R.M. Solow (eds) *The Consequences of Economic Rhetoric* (Cambridge University Press, Cambridge, 1988).

Sorenson, T.L. 'Credible collusion in multimarket oligopoly' (2007) 28 Managerial and Decision Economics 115.

Sørgard, L. 'Judo economics reconsidered: capacity limitation, entry and collusion' (1995) 15 International Journal of Industrial Organization 349.

Spagnolo, G. 'On interdependent supergames: multimarket contact, concavity and collusion' (1999) 89 Journal of Economic Theory 127.

Spector, D. 'Bundling, tying and collusion' (2007) 25 International Journal of Industrial Organization 575.

Staiger, R.W. and F.A. Wolak 'Collusive pricing with capacity constraints in the presence of demand uncertainty' (1992) 23 RAND Journal of Economics 203.

Stark, W. *The Sociology of Knowledge: Toward a Deeper Understanding of the History of Ideas* (Transaction Publishers, London, 1991).

Stelzer, I.M. 'Experts – Use and abuse (Part I): the expert's view' (1992) 60 Antitrust Law Journal 355.

Stenborg, M. 'Forest for the trees: economics of joint dominance' (2004) 18 European Journal of Law and Economics 365.

Stephan, J., J.P. Murmann, W. Boeker and J. Goodstein 'Bringing managers into theories of multimarket competition: CEOs and the determinants of market entry' (2003) 14 Organization Science 403.

Stevens, D. 'Covert collusion and conscious parallelism in oligopolistic markets: a comparison of E.C. and U.S. competition law' in A. Barav and D.A. Wyatt (eds) *Yearbook of European Law Volume 15* (Oxford University Press, Oxford, 1995).

Stigler, G.J. 'Notes on the theory of duopoly' (1940) 48 Journal of Political Economy 521.

Stigler, G.J. 'The kinky oligopoly demand curve and rigid prices' (1947) 55 The Journal of Political Economy 432.

Stigler, G.J. 'Monopoly and oligopoly by merger' (1950) 40 American Economic Review 23.

Stigler, G.J. 'A theory of oligopoly' (1964) 72 Journal of Political Economy 44.

Stigler, G.J. 'The economists and the problem of monopoly' (1982a) 72 American Economic Review 1.

Stigler, G.J. *The Economist as Preacher* (University of Chicago Press, Chicago, 1982b).

Stigler, G.J. 'What does an economist know?' (1983) 33 Journal of Legal Education 311.

Stigler, G.J. and J.S. Bain 'Discussion' (1950) 40 American Economic Review 63.

Stroux, S. 'Is EC oligopoly control outgrowing its infancy?' (2000) 23 World Competition 3.

Suetens, S. 'Does R&D cooperation facilitate price collusion? An experiment' (2008) 66 Journal of Economic Behavior and Organization 822.

Suslow, V.Y. 'Estimating monopoly behavior with competitive recycling: an application to Alcoa' (1986) 17 RAND Journal of Economics 389.

Suslow, V.Y. 'Cartel contract duration: empirical evidence from international cartels' (Working Paper No. E-88-7, Hoover Institution, October 2001).

Sutton, J. 'Explaining everything, explaining nothing' (1990) 34 European Economic Review 505.

Sutton, J. 'Market structure: theory and evidence' in M. Armstrong and R.H. Porter (eds) *Handbook of Industrial Organization, Volume 3* (Elsevier Science Publishers, Amsterdam, 2007).

Suzumura, K. 'Cooperative and noncooperative R&D in an oligopoly with spillovers' (1992) 82 American Economic Review 1307.

Symeonidis, G. 'Cartel stability with multiproduct firms' (2002) 20 International Journal of Industrial Organization 339.

Symeonidis, G. 'In which industries is collusion more likely? Evidence from the UK' (2003) 51 Journal of Industrial Economics 45.

Synder, C.M. 'A dynamic theory of countervailing power' (1996) 27 RAND Journal of Economics 747.

Talley, E. 'Interdisciplinary gap filling: game theory and the law' (1997) 22 Law & Social Inquiry 1055.

Telser, L.G. 'A Theory of self-enforcing agreements' (1980) 53 Journal of Business 27.

Telser, L.G. 'Cooperation, competition and efficiency' (1985) 28 Journal of Law and Economics 271.

Temple Lang, J. 'Oligopolies and joint dominance in community antitrust law' in B. Hawk (ed.) *International Antitrust Law and Policy: Fordham Corporate Law 2001* (Juris Publishing, New York, 2001) 269.

Temple Lang, J. 'Fundamental issues concerning abuse under Article 82 EC' (paper presented to the Oxford Competition Conference, 12 July 2005) <http://www.rpieurope.org/2005%20Conference/Temple_Lang_Abuse_under_article_82EC.pdf> (30 September 2005).

Teubner, G. 'Substantive and reflexive elements in modern law' (1983) 17 Law and Society Review 239.

Teubner, G. 'How the law thinks: towards a constructive epistemology of law' (1989) 23 Law & Society Review 727.

Teubner. G. 'Juridification: concepts, aspects, limits, solutions' in R. Baldwin, C. Scott and C. Hood (eds) *A Reader on Regulation* (Oxford University Press, Oxford, 1998).

Thal, J. 'Optimal collusion under cost asymmetry' (paper presented at

Wissenschaftszentrum Berlin Conference on Collusion and Cartels, 23 October 2004).
Thomas, C.J. 'The effect of asymmetric entry costs on Bertrand competition' (2002) 20 International Journal of Industrial Organization 589.
Thomas, C.J. 'Using reserve prices to deter collusion in procurement competition' (2005) 3 Journal of Industrial Economics 301.
Thomas, C.J. and R.D. Willig 'The risk of contagion from multimarket contact' (2006) 24 International Journal of Industrial Organization 1157.
Tillotson, J. and A. MacCulloch 'EC competition rules, collective dominance and maritime transport' (1997) 21 World Competition 53.
Tirole, J. *The Theory of Industrial Organization* (MIT Press, Cambridge, MA, 1988).
Tom, W.K. 'Game theory in the everyday life of the antitrust practitioner' (1997) 5 George Mason Law Review 451.
Treacy, P. and T. Feaster 'Compagnie Maritime Belge Transports SA v Commission of European Communities: Case Comment' (1997) 18 European Competition Law Review 467.
Turner, D.F. 'The definition of agreement under the Sherman Act: conscious parallelism and refusals to deal' (1962) 75 Harvard Law Review 661–681.
Tyagi, R.K. 'On the relationship between product substitutability and tacit collusion' (1999) 20 Managerial and Decision Economics 293.
U.S. Department of Justice and the Federal Trade Commission *Horizontal Merger Guidelines* (1992) 57 Fed. Reg. 41552 < http://www.ftc.gov/bc/docs/horizmer.htm> (21 September 2005).
Van Damme, E. 'Renegotiation-proof equilibria in repeated prisoners' dilemma' (1989) 47 Journal of Economic Theory 206.
Van Damme, E. 'Rationality and coordination' (1995) 62 Economica 416.
Van den Bergh, R. 'Modern industrial organisation versus old-fashioned European competition law' (1996) 17 European Competition Law Review 75.
Van den Bergh, R.J. and P.D. Camesasca *European Competition Law and Economics: A Comparative Perspective* (Intersentia, Antwerp, 2001).
Van Rompuy, B. 'Implications for the standard of proof in EC merger proceedings: Bertelsmann and Sony Corporation of America v. Impala (C-413/06 P), ECJ' (2008) 29 European Competition Law Review 608.
Varian, H.R. 'What use is economic theory?' in S.G. Medema and W.J. Samuels (eds) *Foundations of Research in Economics: How Do Economists Do Economics?* (Edward Elgar, Cheltenham, UK and Brookfield, USA, 1996).
Vasconcelos, H. 'Tacit collusion, cost asymmetries and mergers' (2005) 36 RAND Journal of Economics 39.
Venit, J.S. 'Two steps forward and no steps back: economic analysis and

oligopolistic dominance after *Kali & Salz*' (1998) 35 Common Market Law Review 1101.

Verboven, F. 'Collusive behavior with heterogeneous firms' (1997) 33 Journal of Economic Behavior and Organization 121.

Vesterdorf, B. 'Standard of proof in merger cases: reflections in the light of recent case law of the community courts' (paper presented at the BIICL third annual merger control conference, 6 December 2004).

Vickers, J. 'Competition economics and policy' (paper presented at the occasion of the launch of the new social sciences building at Oxford University, 3 October 2002a) <http://www.oft.gov.uk/NR/rdonlyres/651EF7E9-77C0-4311-A22A-0F639ED329C0/0/spe0702.pdf> (25 May 2005).

Vickers, J. 'How to reform the EC Merger test?' (paper presented at the European Merger Control Conference Brussels, 8 November 2002b) <http://www.oft.gov.uk/NR/rdonlyres/80E5D0FE-7CF0-4606-A502-DD42FDD06AAF /0/spe0802.pdf> (25 May 2005).

Vickers, J. 'Merger policy in Europe: retrospect and prospect' (paper presented at the Charles River Associates conference Washington, DC, 11 February 2004a) <http://www.oft.gov.uk/NR/rdonlyres/C99B70E7-3BFF-410C-B786-D92B51628D7A /0/spe0104.pdf> (25 May 2005).

Vickers, J. 'Abuse of market power' (paper presented at the 31st conference of the European Association for Research in Industrial Economics, Berlin, 3 September 2004b) <http://www.oft.gov.uk/NR/rdonlyres/948B9FAF-B83C-49F5-B0FA-B25214DE6199 /0/spe0304.pdf> (25 May 2005).

Vickers, J. 'Law and economics: the case for bundling' (paper presented at the UK Competition Commission guest lecture series, London, 19 April 2005) <http://www.competition-commission.org.uk/our_role/cc_lectures/abuse_of_market_190405_vickers_slides.pdf> (5 June 2005).

Viscusi, W.K., J.M. Vernon and J.E. Harrington Jr *Economics of Regulation and Antitrust* (2nd edn, MIT Press, Cambridge, MA, 1995).

Voigt, S. and A. Schmidt *Making European Merger Policy More Predictable* (Springer, Dordrecht, 2005).

von Hayek, F.A. 'Economics and knowledge' (1937) 4 Economica 33.

von Hayek, F.A. 'Scientism and the study of society' (1942) 9 Economica 267.

von Hayek, F.A. 'Scientism and the study of society' (1943) 10 Economica 34.

von Hayek, F.A. 'The use of knowledge in society' (1945) 35 American Economic Review 518.

von Hinten-Reed, N., S.H. Manning and J.C. Miller III 'The use of economics in merger control analysis' in *Global Counsel Competiton Law Handbook 2002/03* (Practical Law, London, 2003).

von Neumann, J. and O. Morgenstern *Theory of Games and Economic Behavior* (Princeton University Press, Princeton, 1947).

von Stackelberg, H. *Marktform und Gleichgewicht* (Springer, Vienna, 1934).

Ward, B. *What's Wrong with Economics?* (Macmillan, London, 1972).
Weatherill, S. and P. Beaumont *EU Law* (3rd edn, Penguin, London, 1999)
Weaver, S. *Decision to Prosecute: Organization and Public Policy in the Antitrust Division (*MIT Press, Cambridge, MA, 1977).
Weir, C. 'Merger policy and competition: an analysis of the Monopolies and Mergers Commission's decisions' (1993) 25 Applied Economics 57.
Weiss, L. 'The concentration–profits relationship and antitrust' in H. Goldschmid, H.M. Mann and J.F. Weston (eds) *Industrial Concentration: The New Learning* (Little-Brown & Co, Boston, 1974).
Werden, G.J. 'Economic evidence on the existence of collusion: reconciling antitrust law with oligopoly theory' (2004) 71 Antitrust Law Journal 719.
Werden, G.J. 'Making economics more useful in competition cases: procedural rules governing expert opinions' in B. Hawk (ed.) *International Antitrust Law & Policy: Fordham Corporate Law 2005* (Juris Publishing, New York, 2006) 601.
Wernerfelt, B. 'Tacit collusion in differentiated Cournot games' (1989) 29 Economic Letters 303.
Whish, R. *Competition Law* (4th edn, Butterworths, London, 2001).
Whish, R. and B. Sufrin 'Oligopolistic markets and EC competition law' in A. Barav and D.A. Wyatt (eds) *Yearbook of European Law Volume 15* (Oxford University Press, Oxford, 1992) 59.
White, L.J. 'The growing influence of economics and economists on antitrust: an extended discussion' (working paper, Stern School of Business, 24 January 2008) 1.
Williams, M.E. and A.J. Padilla 'Hypotheticals and counterfactuals: the economics of competition policy' in *The European Antitrust Review 2004* (Global Competition Review, London, 2004).
Wils, W.P.J. 'The combination of the investigative and prosecutorial function and the adjudicative function in EC Antitrust enforcement: a legal and economic analysis' (2004) 27 World Competition 201.
Winckler, A. and M. Hansen 'Collective dominance under the EC merger control regulation' (1993) 30 Common Market Law Review 787.
Withers, C. and M. Jephcott 'Where to now for E.C. oligopoly control?' (2001) 8 European Competition Law Review 295.
Wong, K.P. 'Does market demand volatility facilitate collusion' (2008) 25 Economic Modelling 696.
Woo, H.K.H. *What's Wrong with Formalization in Economics?* (Victoria Press, Newark, CA, 1986).
Wright, K. 'Perfect symmetry? Impala v Commission and standard of proof in mergers' (2007) 32 European Law Review 408.
Yao, D.A. and S.S. DeSanti 'Game theory and the legal analysis of tacit collusion' (Spring 1993) Antitrust Bulletin 113.

Yarrow, G.K. 'Welfare losses in oligopoly and monopolistic competition' (1985) 33 Journal of Industrial Economics 515.
Yeung, K. 'The court-room economist in Australian antitrust litigation: an underutilised resource?' (1992) 20 Australian Business Law Review 461.
Yoerg, N. 'The use of an economist in a contested merger' (1987) 56 Antitrust Law Journal 789.
Ysewyn, J. and C. Caffara, 'Two's company, three's a crowd: the future of collective dominance after the *Kali & Salz* judgment' (1998) 19 European Competition Law Review 468.

Index